Birchbark Canoes

of the

Fur Trade

by Timothy J. Kent

Volume II

Silver Fox Enterprises
Ossineke, Michigan
1997

All drawings by the author.
All photographs by the author unless otherwise noted.
Printed by Offset Press, Oak Park, Illinois
Typesetting/Layout by Rita Frese, Chicagoland Canoe Base, Inc. 1997

Publishers Cataloging-in-Publication Data
Kent, Timothy J.
Birchbark Canoes of the Fur Trade.
686 pp. in two volumes, 8-1/2 x 11 inches.
Includes bibliographic references.
Contents:
  1. Canoes. 2. Watercraft. 3. Transportation.
  4. Fur Trade. 5. Commerce. 6. Exploration.
  7. Indians/Native Americans, U.S. and Canada.
  8. Missionaries of North America.
  9. North American History. 10. United States History.
  11. Canadian History.

Library of Congress Catalog Card Number 97-91670
International Standard Book Number 0-9657230-0-3

Front Cover: Human figure headboard in the Ojibwa Canoe of the Ohio
Historical Society.

Title Page: Frances Anne Hopkins (1838-1919)
(National Archives of Canada, C-2774).

Back Cover: The author studying the Royal Canoe in the Neptune
Gallery, National Maritime Museum, Greenwich, London, England.

For Doree, Kevin, and Ben, my family, whose understanding, patience, and wholehearted support made this work possible.

Table of Contents
<u>*Volume One*</u>

Preface

In the following descriptions and discussions of surviving fur trade canoes, no attempt has been made to fully present the procedures involved in the construction of birchbark canoes. Several other publications present excellent descriptions of these steps (see Appendix). The only discussions of procedures included here are those which are necessary to present a full description of the canoes. The order in which the various elements of each canoe are described often does not reflect the order in which these elements were installed on the canoe. The identical format is followed in describing each of the canoes, to facilitate comparisons between the various craft.

The four full size canoes are described first, followed by the four model canoes. The description of the full size Quebec canoe, although it represents the Type A-1 style, is presented after the Type B-1 and B-2 full size canoes. This is due to the somewhat incomplete nature of the Quebec canoe data (since the craft was destroyed before the author had access to it for a complete study). The models are presented in the order of Types A-1, B-1, and B-2.

The Royal Canoe

Contents

The Royal Canoe

Several features of the Royal canoe suggest that it is a Type B-1 style of voyaging canoe. These traits include the moderate height and breadth of the ends in relation to the height of the walls in the midsection, the moderate degree of undercut in the profile of the ends, and the form of the interior curvature of the stempieces. The canoe was built in the large, eight-place (nine-thwart) format, in the size category of a bastard canoe.

Overall Dimensions

Length: 28' 9-1/2".
Distance between the outboard sides of the tips of the outwales: 25' 9-1/2" (Fig. 3).
Distance between the inboard sides of the tips of the gunwale caps: 25' 6-1/4".
Distance between the inboard faces of the heads of the headboards: 25' 5".
Depth at the midpoint, from the top of the gunwale caps to the top of the ribs on the floor: 24-1/2".
Height above the baseline: at the midpoint 26," at the bow 47", at the stern 46-1/4".
Beam at the midpoint: 5' 6-3/4" (Fig. 4).
Interior beam, inside the gunwales: 5' 3-1/4".
Total girth around the hull, from gunwale top to gunwale top: 7' 9-1/2" .

In comparing the dimensions of the Royal canoe to the description in Adney and Chapelle of a typical four-fathom 29' 11" canoe of the late period of the fur trade, the following observations can be made.[1] The depth is typical in relation to the length. The height of the ends is about five or six inches lower than usual, when compared to the description. But the end height and the depth at the midpoint of the Royal canoe are virtually identical to those of the 29' 11" Cree-built version which Adney depicted in model form. In addition, the ends of the Royal canoe rise above the height at the midpoint by an increase of 45 percent, compared to the 41 percent rise of the Adney model of a classic 36-1/2 foot *canot du Maitre*.[2] The beam at the gunwales of the Royal canoe is about six

inches wider than usual (this is considered in the discussion of its body plan).

Hull Form
Profile of the Bottom and Ends

Along the keel line, the horizontal span of 19 feet 3-1/2 inches appears to lie exactly centered within the total length of the canoe (Fig. 3). A span of 41 inches of moderate rocker (measured on the horizontal baseline) gradually rises from each end of the horizontal area, extending to sharp, definite chins. Thus, the total bottom length between the chins is 26 feet 1-1/2 inches (on the baseline). At the chins, the rocker has risen above the baseline 2-1/4 inches at the bow and 2 inches at the stern. Each end extends 16 inches outboard from the chin (measured on the baseline) to the outermost point of the ends.

The cutwater edge at each end curves upward quite sharply from the chin. It extends upward and outward for 40 inches (measured on the curve) to the point of maximum length of the canoe, creating a moderately undercut profile. Then it curves upward and inboard over 14 inches to the highest point of the end, and finally downward and inboard over a span of 9-1/2 inches to meet the outwales. The total length of the cutwater edge, measured on the curve from chin to outwales, is 63-1/2 inches at each end of the canoe.

Body Plan

The bottom is narrow and moderately rounded (Fig. 4). The bilge is gradually rounded, while the upper walls are straight and flare outward moderately. The five cross sections in the end-view drawing illustrate the contours of the hull as it gradually tapers between the midpoint of the canoe and the headboards. The five sections correspond roughly to the five thwart positions between the midpoint and the headboards (Fig. 8).

The widest area of the bottom appears to lie directly at the midpoint of the length of the canoe. This width tapers gradually and symmetrically from the midpoint to each end of the canoe.

The Royal canoe was built in a style designed for fast paddling. Its features, including a narrow moder-

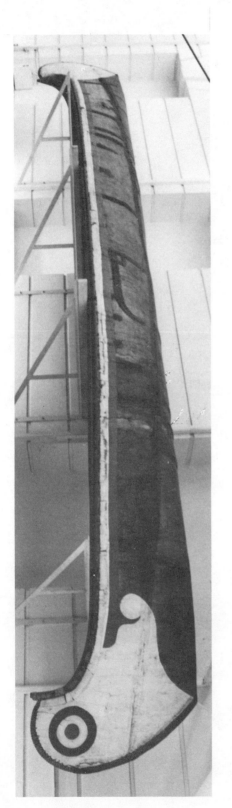

Fig. 1. Royal Canoe, with bow to left.

Fig. 2. Royal Canoe during 1971 restoration, after removal of pitched fabric strips from earlier restoration. Gunwale caps also removed (National Maritime Museum, Greenwich, Neg. B4126-3).

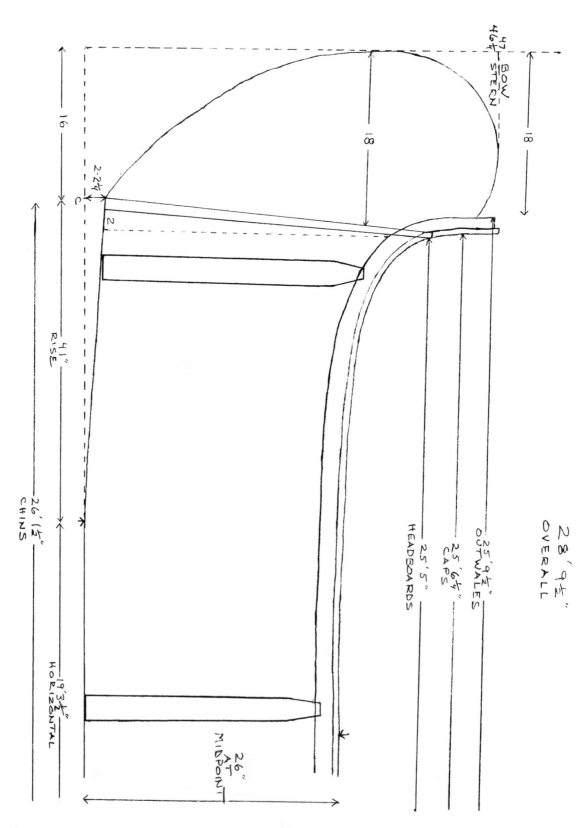

Fig. 3. Royal Canoe: Hull profile and dimensions.

—4—

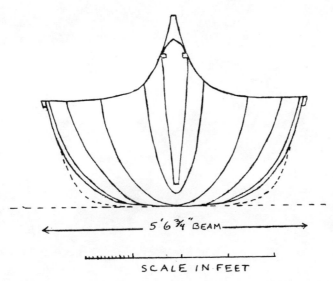

Fig. 4. Royal Canoe: Body plan (express canoe). Broken lines indicate contours of standard freight canoe.

Fig. 5. Royal Canoe: End view of bow.

Fig. 6 (left). Royal Canoe: End view of right wall of bow.
Fig. 7 (right). Royal Canoe: Bottom view from stern.

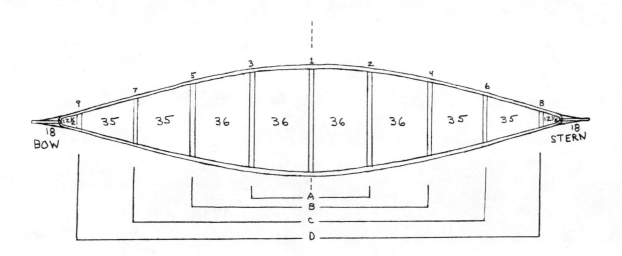

Fig. 8. Royal Canoe: Hull form and thwart positions.

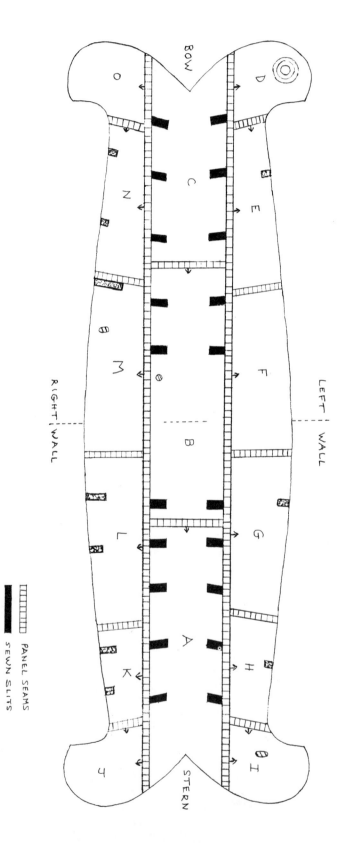

Fig. 9. Royal Canoe: Bark cover.

PANEL SEAMS

SEWN SLITS

SEWN DAMAGE

PITCH-SEALED DAMAGE

DIRECTION OF OVERLAPPING
EDGE ON EXTERIOR

BOW

STERN

RIGHT WALL

LEFT WALL

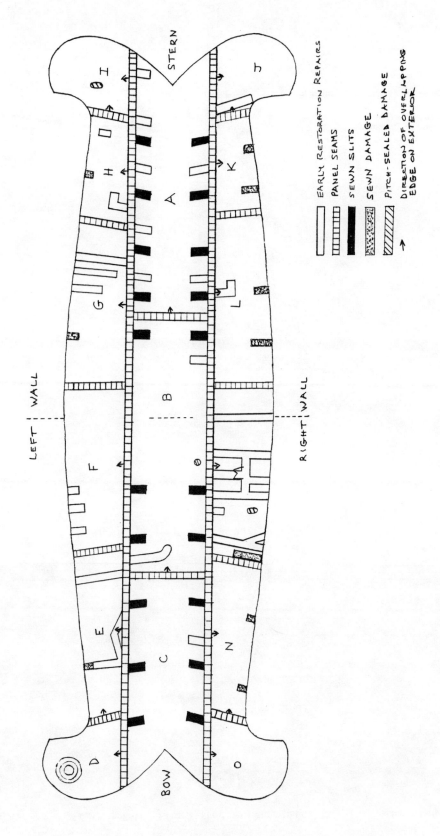

Fig. 10. Royal Canoe: Pitched fabric repairs applied during an early restoration.

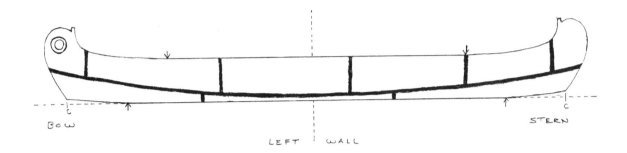

Fig. 11. Royal Canoe: Bark panels.

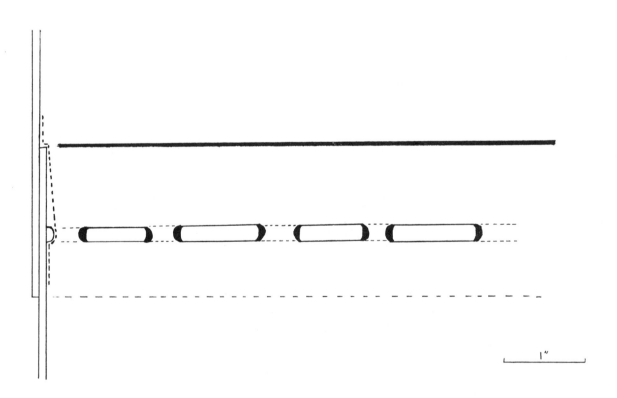

Fig. 12. Royal Canoe: In-and-out stitches of overlapping seams which join bottom panels together, as well as side panels to bottom panels.

– 10 –

ately rounded bottom and a gradually rounded bilge, a long slender taper to the ends, and a sharp V form inboard of the headboards, all contributed to its speed.[3] (See the description of the sharp V form of the endmost ribs in the ribs section.)

Yet its beam at the gunwales is unusually wide in relation to its length: the interior beam is equal to 18.30 percent of the overall length. This is the broadest beam, proportionately, of the eight canoes in this study. It is only one to three inches narrower than the width that was normally built into the largest 36 foot models.[4] This generous width increased the roominess, which otherwise would have been reduced by the narrow speed features that were built into the canoe. However, the spaciousness was added at the gunwale level, rather than in the floor and bilge area.

The moderately rounded bottom of the canoe is much narrower and the bilge area considerably more undercut (thus a faster craft) than the standard cargo canoes of the period as portrayed by Adney, with their slightly rounded or nearly flat bottoms and moderately curved bilges. In addition, it has an oversize beam at the gunwale level in proportion to its length and the typical degree of outward flare of the upper walls. This form would provide generous space for paddlers sitting on raised seats, but limited room on the floor for passengers and cargo. Its design suggests that this craft was built to serve as an express canoe, transporting fur trade, military, governmental, or clerical personnel and mail. Nearly all period photos and artistic depictions of fur trade canoes show the passengers sitting low, on the floor of the canoe. Possibly passengers in the Royal canoe sat on raised seats of some sort, to take advantage of the roominess in the upper areas of the hull. In contrast to the Royal canoe, some other express canoes of the same era were built relatively narrow at both the bottom and the gunwales.[5]

Bark Cover

The diagram of the bark cover (Fig. 9) portrays the canoe as if it had been placed upside down and flattened by unsewing the end seams. The drawing is not to exact scale or proportion, and the locations and dimensions of the seams and repairs are approximate. All seams and repairs have been widened for ease of identification.

Before discussing the features of the bark cover, a synopsis of the restoration history of the canoe is necessary. After many decades of storage in a repository of the Royal Family (possibly a dockside warehouse), time and apparently rough treatment had put the Royal canoe in poor condition. The root lashings of the gunwales and the ends needed replacement, and the bark cover had been seriously broken in numerous places.

Late in the nineteenth or early in the twentieth century, a major restoration project was undertaken on the canoe. The goal of this project was visual rather than functional restoration. The gunwale caps and guard strips were temporarily removed, and the gunwale lashings were replaced, using furniture cane strips. The caps and guard strips were then reinstalled, using round-headed wire nails; presumably these were driven into the nail holes previously made by the original machine-cut nails. The lashings at the ends of the canoe were likewise replaced with furniture cane strips.

It is assumed that the identical patterns and techniques of the original lashings were replicated in the replacements. Since London was the home of the Hudson's Bay Company, there is a very real possibility that the restorer of the Royal canoe may have been familiar with canoe repairs from having served in Canada.

The bark cover was also repaired in numerous places on the exterior of the walls and the bottom (Fig. 10). Narrow strips of fabric were glued to the broken areas of bark with blackened pitch; then the exterior side of the fabric and the bark around its perimeter was coated with more blackened pitch. (This procedure was identical to that which was done to seal the seams during the original construction of the canoe.) In four areas of major breakage, the edges of the cracks were sewed together with tan cord 3/32 inch in diameter before the pitched fabric strips were applied. These widely spaced stitches ran through small, tapered awl holes in the bark.

By 1971, the replacement cane lashings on the gunwales and the ends had become very dry and brittle. They were broken in many areas, and in some places were entirely missing. In addition, the bark cover had sustained further breakage, some of it major damage. Another restoration was in order.

Before the conservation staff of the National Maritime Museum began the restoration in 1971, they removed all of the pitched fabric strips that had been applied to the walls in the earlier restoration process; in addition, they removed the original gunwale caps. Detailed photos were then taken, to document the earlier restoration of the damaged bark walls as well as the replacement of the lashings of the gunwales and the ends (Fig. 2).

The staff apparently did not remove any of the pitched fabric strips which had been applied to cover damaged areas on the bottom of the canoe during the earlier restoration. No photos were taken which showed the full bottom view, to record features of the early restoration there.

In the N.M.M. restoration, the lashings of the gunwales and the ends were again replaced with furniture cane strips, copying exactly the styles and techniques of the lashings of the early restoration. Fabric strips were applied to replace those of the early restoration that had been removed in order to take the photographs. The pitch for these strips was replaced with tar. In addition, tar was used to replace any areas of missing pitch which dated from the original construction as well as from the early restoration repairs on the bottom. Fabric strips and tar were also applied to cover a number of new breaks in the bark cover which had been sustained since the early restoration.

Due to this series of restorations of the Royal canoe, careful scrutiny was required by the author to decipher the periods in which the myriad seams presently on the canoe had been placed there. Any seams which had only tar as a sealant dated from the 1971 N.M.M. restoration. (These are not shown in the diagrams.) Fabric-covered repair seams on the canoe walls which dated from the early restoration were clearly visible in the 1971 photos. Although they had been resealed with tar in 1971, they still showed traces of their pitch sealant in some areas around the perimeter. The photos also revealed which seams dated from the original construction, having been sewn with root stitches. These likewise had been touched up with tar in 1971, but still had some areas of original pitch which were not covered by the tar. Some of these original seams had been covered with pitched fabric during the original construction, while others had been covered only with pitch as a sealant.

No photos from 1971 show clear views of the entire bottom of the canoe. Therefore, it was less clear which of the short strips of pitched fabric extending inboard from the edges of the bottom panel were those cover-

ing the original gore slits, and which ones were added during the early restoration. Both of these sets of fabric strips had been applied with blackened pitch, which was later touched up with tar in 1971 (leaving some traces of original pitch visible).

The five opposing pairs of these fabric strips in the bow half of the bottom are clearly those that were applied during the original construction to seal gore slits. In the stern half, seven such opposing pairs of fabric strips occur. Five of these pairs are assumed to cover the original gore slits, corresponding to the five pairs in the bow half. This leaves two pairs of opposing fabric strips and four single strips in the stern half of the bottom. These are presumed to have been added during the early restoration. However, gore slits were not always installed in opposing pairs, and in equal numbers in both halves at a canoe. Thus, some of the pitched fabric strips which are presented in this study as early restoration repairs may have been installed during the original manufacture over gore slits.

The early restoration project can be placed within a general time frame by two factors. The round-headed wire nails which were used to reinstall the gunwale caps and bump strips did not become readily available until about 1879.[6] Thus, the restoration must postdate that year. Yet the replacement lashings of furniture cane had become very brittle and broken well before 1971. They must have been installed many decades before. Therefore, the evidence suggests a time frame of the late nineteenth century to the early twentieth century for the early restoration of the canoe.

Color and Thickness

The color of the bark varies from panel to panel on the exterior, ranging from golden tan to light brownish tan. After a century or more of color fading and grime accumulation, it is not possible to determine now whether some of the bark panels may have originally been reddish brown "winter bark." The thickness ranges from 1/8 to 3/16 inch. (The thickness profile is visible in several locations.)

Panels

On the diagram in Figure 9, the seams joining the fifteen panels of bark are marked with crosshatching. The arrows indicate the direction of the exposed overlapping edges on the exterior of the canoe.

Exact measurements of the individual panels cannot be taken, since the pitch covering the seams in many cases hides from view the exact positions of the edges of the panels. Only the portions of bark visible on the exterior of the canoe were measured, making no allowance for hidden overlaps. The measurement of the height of the side panels runs to the top of the outwales, where the bark was cut off flush with the top of the outwale and the inwale. Each side panel was measured at its widest point.

Bottom Panels
A. 129 inches long x 38 inches wide
B. 109" L x 38" W
C.   89" L x 38" W

Left Wall Panels (including the two high end panels)
D.   29" L x 30" W
E.   84" L x 25" W
F.   76" L x 28" W
G.   73" L x 28" W
H.   63" L x 24" W
I.   28" L x 30" W

Right Wall Panels (including the two high end panels)
J.   29" L x 30" W
K.   52" L x 24" W
L.   82" L x 28" W
M.   84" L x 28" W
N.   78" L x 25" W
O.   28" L x 30" W

If the bark cover were flattened, as in the diagram, the maximum width in the midsection would be 7 feet 9-1/2 inches (the total girth of the bark of the canoe). The width near the ends measures 4 inches more. The length would be 29 feet 5 inches at the level of the gunwales. This total length of the side and end panels of each wall of the canoe is 7-1/2 inches longer than the length of the assembled canoe, because the side panels follow the curvature of the broadening midsection of the canoe, rather than a straight line down the midline.

The bottom of the canoe was made with three long panels of bark, while each wall was formed by joining two high end panels and four side panels (Fig. 11). In the profile drawing, the panels and seams are positioned exactly as they lie on the canoe.

The canoe builders apparently had no concern about creating weak points in the hull by positioning vertical wall seams directly opposite each other across the hull of the canoe. The seams which attach the side of the two high end panels at each end (seams D-E and N-O, plus H-I and J-K) lie directly opposite each other. The seams between panels F-G and L-M likewise lie opposite each other. These latter two seams are the longest vertical side panel seams in each wall, about thirteen to fourteen inches sternward from the midpoint of the canoe.

The vertical seams between side panels E-F and M-N are offset from each other by seven or eight inches, while those between side panels G-H and K-L are offset by eight or nine inches from each other.

The builders positioned the seams in the walls well distant from the two seams in the bottom. No wall seams were placed closer than about twelve inches from a bottom seam. This may reflect the intention of the builders, to avoid creating weak points in the hull that could be caused by close proximity of wall seams to bottom seams.

Sewn Seams

The original lashing material still survives in all of the sewn seams and in the area of original damage repair. A minute sample of this original lashing root was analyzed microscopically. It has been identified as either spruce or eastern larch (tamarack). When analyzing only a sample of root material, without any accompanying trunkwood, it is impossible to differentiate between these two tree types.[7] If the roots were spruce, they would most likely be black spruce, which is the best and most common type of root for canoe construction.[8] There is no evidence that suggests that a batten strip of wood or root was incorporated into any of the seams for added strength, on either the exterior or the interior side of the bark cover.

Bottom Seams

The two seams connecting the three panels of the bottom to each other were the first seams that were sewn in building the canoe. They are overlapped so that the exposed edge on the exterior faces toward the stern. These seams are sewn with split roots in a simple in-and-out stitch, with a single stitch per hole in the bark (Fig. 12). The stitches are about 3/4 to 1 inch long, with a space between stitches of about 3/8 to 1/2 inch. The lashing roots are about 3/16 to 1/4 inch wide (about the same width as the diameter of the awl holes) and about 3/32 inch thick, with a half-round cross section (Fig. 12). The rounded side of the root, which was scraped a little flat before being used, is the side which faces toward the exterior.

No photo was taken of the interior side of these bottom seams in the interior of the canoe when some of the ribs and sheathing were removed during the 1971 restoration process. Thus, it is not possible to determine the amount of overlap of the bark panels over each other on the interior. However, it is highly likely that an overlap of four or five inches was made, since this is a feature of the seams which connect the side wall panels to these bottom panels. (An interior photo was taken of these side seams during the 1971 restoration: see Fig. 16 and the description on page 19.)

Gore Slits

After the three bottom panels were joined together, the long span of bottom bark was laid out on the building bed, and the building frame was placed upon it and weighted down. This frame determined the general outline of the bottom of the canoe, particularly the shape of the taper toward the ends. The building frame was about as long as the bottom of the canoe, from chin to chin. Each end of the long span of bark was raised slightly, to create the upward curve of the rocker. The bark was bent upward around the perimeter of the building frame, to create the walls of the canoe. The bark tended to buckle slightly, because of its raised ends, as well as the curved shape of the midsection of the frame around which the bark was bent. To prevent this buckling, a number of gore slits were sliced at intervals along the sides of the bottom panels. These slices ran from the edges of the bark inboard nearly to the building frame (Fig. 13). At each of these slits, a narrow triangular slice of bark was removed, to eliminate any overlapping of the edges of the gore slits. Then the slits were stitched closed.

All of the gore slits appear to be flush seams, with the bark edges butting against each other, rather than overlapping. They are sewn with split roots in a series of widely spaced spiral stitches, with one stitch per hole (Fig. 14). The portion of each stitch on the exterior side of the canoe is horizontal, while the connector portion running to the next stitch on the interior of the canoe is diagonal. The stitches run through pairs of opposing awl holes which lie about 1/4 to 3/8 inch from the edges of the slit. The visible horizontal portions are about 5/8 to one inch long, and are spaced about 3/4 to 1-1/2 inches apart.

The lashing roots are 3/16 to 1/4 inch wide (about the same as the diameter of the awl holes) and about 3/32 inch thick, with a half-round cross-section. The rounded side, which was scraped somewhat flat, is the side of the root lashing which faces the exterior of the canoe.

No photo was taken of the interior side of these gore slit seams during restoration, so it is not known whether a strip of birch bark was added for reinforcement on the interior side when each seam was sewn. But no such bark strip was added when the comparable repair seams in the gunwale areas of the wall panels were sewn during manufacture. (A photo was taken in 1971 of the interior side of one of these upper wall repair seams.)

The gore slits in the bottom panels are positioned at relatively regular intervals along most of the length of the canoe, except in a short span in the midsection (Figs. 9 and 15). They are located on the profile drawing exactly as they lie on the canoe. Each of the slits has a mate located nearly exactly opposite (having been cut on the opposite side of the building frame). Five such pairs of opposing slits are found in each half of the bottom. Whether intentionally or not, the builder installed the series of gore slits in the bow half so that they extend slightly closer to the midpoint and to the end of the canoe than the series in the stern half.

When the canoe is viewed in side profile, the gore slits extend downward from the longitudinal main seam, which runs the full length of each side of the canoe. In the central, widest area of the canoe, this seam curves down close to the horizontal baseline of the canoe. Here, the gore slits are barely visible in a profile view; they extend to the rounded bottom of the canoe in this area. Toward the ends of the canoe, where the main seam rises, the full length of each gore slit is visible, running down the curved bilge area of the lower walls.

The length of each gore slit cannot be measured

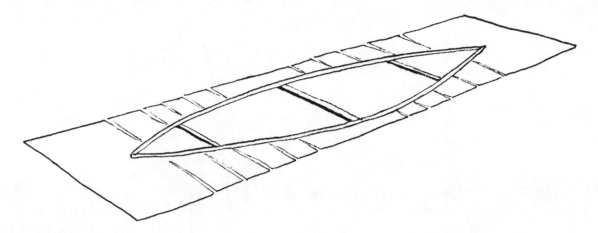

Fig. 13. Building frame and gore slits in the bark cover.

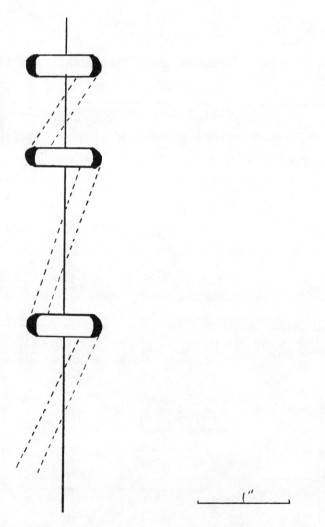

1"

Fig. 14. Royal Canoe: Spiral stitches of butted seams which join gore slits, side panels to side panels, gunwale area repairs, and the main wall panel repair.

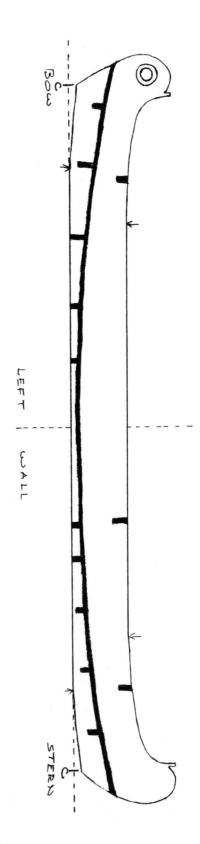

Fig. 15. Royal Canoe: Gore slits and gunwale area repairs.

Fig. 16. Royal Canoe: Interior view with sheathing and ribs removed during 1971 restoration. Original left gunwale cap temporarily restored to its original position after gunwale lashings replaced (National Maritime Museum, Greenwich, Neg. B5903-3).

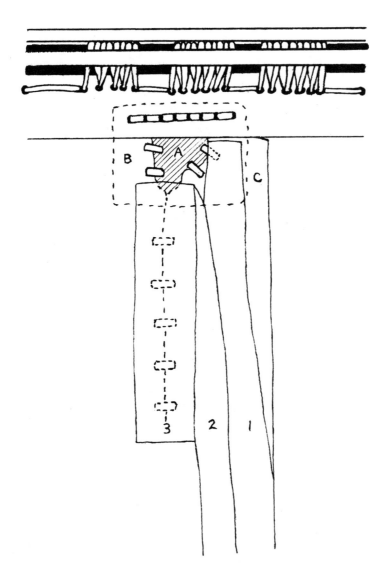

Fig. 17. Royal Canoe: Wall repair. A. puncture hole, B. bark patch on interior, C. fabric sealant strip on wall seam, 1-2-3. fabric sealant strips of repair, in the order in which they were applied.

exactly, since each is covered by a strip of pitch-coated fabric. This pitched sealant strip extends inboard toward the midline of the canoe beyond the end of each slit. Measurement can be made of the length of each pitched strip, which ought to imply the general length of the gore slit which it covers.

Bottom panel B contains the pair of opposing gore slits which lies closest to the midpoint of the canoe. The length of their pitched fabric strips is only about seven or eight inches, creating a span of 23 inches between the inboard tips of the two strips. In panel A, the first and second pairs of opposing gore slit strips at the stern end have spans between their tips which measure 12 and 11-1/2 inches, respectively.

Since the gore slits were sliced from opposite edges of the bottom bark panels inboard nearly to the building frame, the spans between the opposing pairs of slits across the bottom of the canoe ought to reflect the shape and dimensions of the building frame. As previously mentioned, the pitched fabric strip sealing each gore slit extends further inboard than the actual end of the gore slit itself. Thus, the span measured between the tips of a pair of opposing pitched slits is shorter than the actual span between the tips of the slits, and likewise shorter than the span across the building frame. Also, the pitch was not applied to the gore slits in a precise or regular fashion. Finally, during the various restorations, pitch, fabric strips, and tar were added to repair breaks in the original gore slits. This has further distorted the apparent lengths of the slits. Therefore, to avoid misrepresentation, all of the gore slits are presented in the Figure 9 diagram as being of roughly equal length.

However, some generalities may be deduced concerning the form of the building frame. It was presumably about 26 feet long, since the length of the bottom (the distance between the chins) is 26 feet 1-1/2 inches. The span between the pitched pair of fabric strips nearest to the midpoint of the canoe measures 23 inches. Thus, the point of maximum width of the building frame at its exact midpoint would have been somewhat greater than this measurement. In addition, some further width must be added to this span to account for the actual lengths of the gore slits, rather than their longer pitched fabric covering strips. The maximum width of the building frame that was used to construct slightly rounded and nearly flat-bottomed fur trade canoes was often two-thirds of the interior beam at the gunwales.[9] In the case of the Royal canoe, this ratio would produce a measurement of 42 inches. The span between the pitched pair of strips nearest to the stern end measures twelve inches. This represents in a general manner the degree of taper from the wide midpoint of the building frame to its pointed ends.

Side Panels to Bottom Panels

After the gore slits were cut and stitched along the side edges of the bottom panels, the side panels were attached to the bottom panels. The seam connecting the side and bottom panels to each other is the prominent longitudinal seam which arcs across the full length of the canoe on each wall.

This seam curves downward toward the middle of the canoe because there, at its widest beam, nearly the entire width of the bottom bark panels is used to form the bottom of the canoe. There is very little width remaining in the bottom panels to extend up the walls. Toward each end, as the canoe becomes gradually narrower, the bottom panels have gradually more and more excess bark beyond the width of the bottom to extend up the side walls.

When the side panels were attached to the bottom panels, a wider panel was installed at each end of both walls, to create the high upswept ends of the canoe.

The lower edges of the side panels are positioned inside the edges of the bottom bark panels (Fig. 16). Thus, the edges of the bottom panels are exposed on the exterior of the canoe, facing upward toward the gunwales. The side panels overlap about 4-1/2 to 5 inches on the interior side of the bottom panels

The description of the root sewing which joins the side panels to the bottom panels is identical to that which was used to connect the three bottom panels to each other, as presented on page 14 and Figure 12. The long horizontal row of simple in-and-out stitches lies about an inch below the exposed edge of the bark panel on the exterior. The pitch-covered strip of fabric which seals these seams on the interior (visible in the photo) is discussed on page 20.

Side Panels to Side Panels

The seams which join the side panels to each other all appear to be flush seams, with the edges butting against each other rather than overlapping each other.

The only exceptions to this are the seams that join the side of each of the four high end panels to the adjacent side panel. These seams are overlapped for three or four inches, for greater strength (Fig. 16). The exposed edge on the exterior faces toward the stern in each instance.

The description of the root sewing which connects the side panels is the same as the spiral stitches used to sew the gore slits in the bottom panels, as presented on page 14 and Figure 14. The only difference is that in the side panel seams the maximum distance between the horizontal stitches on the exterior is about 1-1/4 inches (instead of 1-1/2 inches, as in the gore slits).

In the Figure 16 photo (taken during the 1971 restoration when the ribs and sheathing were removed from the bow end), the interior side of the seam which joins the side panels together is visible in the upper left wall, below the thwart. The long diagonal connectors between the horizontal stitches can be seen beneath the strip of pitched fabric.

The photo shows several different types of seams: seams which sew side panels to bottom panels and side panels to side panels, as well as those which repair breaks in the walls in the gunwale areas. The photo illustrates the manner in which the beginning and end of the split roots were finished off in the stitching of the bark cover. Each end of a root is tucked back under the adjacent stitch. There it is left long, up to about three inches, rather than being cut off. This end treatment is particularly visible at the bottom of the vertical left wall seam, beneath the thwart. Here the long tucked end extends far sternward, well beyond the pitched fabric strip.

Seam Sealing

All of the seams in the canoe were sealed with a coating of charcoal-blackened melted pitch. The pitch or gum that was used in the manufacture and later repair of the canoe, resin from black or white spruce or pine trees,[10] was blackened by mixing in pulverized charcoal. In addition, animal fat was added to the mixture, to produce the proper consistency for flexibility without runniness. The remaining original pitch is now very brittle; it does not indent under thumb pressure.

A wide swath of gum was applied to all of the seams on the interior side of the canoe (Fig 16). This was done with the canoe in the upright position, as indi-

cated by the direction of the runs of melted gum, which extend downward toward the bottom.

Fabric of moderately fine weave, very light or white in color, was torn into strips about two inches wide with straight, even edges. The uniformly frayed condition of the edges indicates that the cloth was torn to size, rather than being cut.

A fabric strip was pressed firmly along each pitch-smeared seam. The pitch soaked through the cloth and glued it to the root stitches and the adjacent bark of the seam area. The pressing molded the pitched fabric around each stitch of root. The wide swath of melted pitch extends about 1/2 to 2 inches beyond the edges of the cloth strips on the surface of the bark. In addition to gumming the interior side of the seams, any small breaks or holes in the bark were also gummed at this time on the interior.

With the canoe turned upside down, all of the seams except the repairs in the upper walls below the gunwales were sealed on the exterior of the canoe, using the same procedures of pitch and fabric strips. The position of the canoe is indicated by the runs of melted pitch, which extend toward the gunwales. The strips of cloth are about 1-1/2 to 2 inches wide, with the swaths of melted gum extending about 1/2 to 1 inch out from the edges of the fabric. A final coat of gum was then applied over the exterior of the fabric strips, to ensure a complete seal. On some of the vertical side panel seams, the cloth strip ends one or two inches below the reinforcement bark strip which runs beneath the outwale. The gum alone continues up to the lower edge of the reinforcement bark strip.

Along the longitudinal main seam, the exposed edge of the bottom panel of bark faces upward; parallel to this edge, about an inch below, runs the horizontal row of root stitches (Fig. 12). When the pitched fabric was molded along this seam, it conformed to the exposed edge and the row of stitches, to produce an interesting effect. The result looks as if the cloth strip has covered a flat, straight-edged horizontal slat of wood, 1 to 1-1/4 inches wide and 1/8 inch thick, that runs down the midline of the seam and the cloth strip.

The sewn repairs in the gunwale areas were sealed on the exterior side with only a coating of pitch, which extends up to the reinforcement bark strip. No fabric was deemed necessary: these seams, usually well above the water line, were less likely to bend or be struck or scraped during usage, compared to the other seams in the canoe.

Applying a strip of fabric to the pitched seams offered several advantages over a coating of pitch alone. The fabric served to strengthen and solidify the seams. If a seam were struck or scraped, the stiff gummed fabric layer would tend to protect the underlying layer of sealant gum on the stitches as well as the root lashings themselves. Acting as a stiffener, it would also reduce the likelihood that the seams would bend and thus cause the pitch to crack or break loose. If the pitch did break loose, it would tend to remain adhered to the weave of the fabric, rather than falling off. Then it could be simply heated with a torch and reattached.

After the exterior side of each of the seams was sealed, any small breaks or holes found in the bark were also gummed on the exterior. Three small areas on the canoe are sealed with only pitch, without any root stitches or fabric strip (Fig. 9). It is not possible to determine whether these places were pitched during the construction of the canoe, or whether they represent damage incurred and repaired during usage.

The first of these areas is found in roughly the midpoint of panel I, the high end panel of the stern end of the left wall. Here was applied a narrow vertical strip of blackened pitch, roughly one inch wide and three inches tall.

Another such repair occurs in bottom panel B, a little forward of the midpoint of the canoe and about four inches inboard of the longitudinal main seam of the right wall. A generally round area about three inches in diameter is covered with gum.

In the forward half of panel M, in the right wall, is found a third area sealed with only pitch. Below the blue painted gunwale stripe, a narrow vertical strip of pitch was applied, similar to the one in panel I.

Exterior Hull Surface

Each of the seams on the Royal canoe produces a disruption in the smooth, even surface of the hull. Overlapping seams were installed to join the bottom panels together and to join the inboard side of each of the high end panels to the adjacent side panels. At these overlaps, there is a very obvious difference in level between the two layers of bark, up to 3/16 to 1/4 of an

inch. The edges of the panels were not thinned before they were overlapped and sewed together.

Also, the fabric and layers of pitch on each of the exterior seams, after repeated reapplications of pitch during usage, made all of the seams stand out up to 1/8 to 3/16 of an inch above the flat surface of the bark. This is the case even with the flush seams, which have butted rather than overlapping edges. All of these seams projecting above the flat surface of the bark hull would tend to impede the flow of the canoe through the water.

In addition, the edges of the overlapping seams would tend to catch on obstructions in the water. To encourage the smooth flow of the canoe through the water, and to decrease the likelihood of catching on obstructions, all of the overlapping seams were made so that the exposed exterior edges face sternward or upward. The canoe was given obvious interior and exterior markings indicating which end of the canoe was the bow, to show which direction the canoe should travel through the water to make the overlapping edges face sternward.

It must be borne in mind, however, that the design of the hull was much more critical to the efficient movement of the craft than overlapped and thickly gummed seams. In addition, the side seams of the end panels stood generally above the waterline.

Damage and Repairs

A number of vertical breaks occurred at irregular intervals in the upper walls, in the areas of the gunwales (Figs. 9 and 15). These were areas where the edges of the panels were accidently split during the removal of the bark from the tree or during the manufacture of the canoe. They are located on the profile drawing exactly as they lie on the canoe.

Three of the cracks are found in the left wall, and six in the right wall. They occur in three of the four long side panels of each wall, in all of the long panels except panels F and M. (Close scrutiny of the 1971 photos verifies that none of the early restoration seams in panels F and M were originally sewn gunwale breaks.)

The cracks extend straight downward from the top edge of the bark wall for about 6-3/4 to 8 inches, ending at or slightly below the lower edge of the blue painted stripe. They are straight, since they follow the grain of the bark. The topmost 1-3/8 inch span of each break is held firmly in place between the nailed and lashed inwale and outwale. The portion that lies behind the reinforcement bark strip below the outwale is not sewn. (One such portion of a slit is visible in an area where part of the bark strip has broken away).

Beneath the reinforcement strip, the lower 3-1/4 to 4 inches of the each crack was sewed with root stitches at the time the canoe was built. These spiral stitches, usually three in number, are the same in nearly all respects as those used to sew the gore slits in the bottom panels, as presented on page 14 and Figure 14. The only difference is the spacing between stitches: those in the bottom panel gore slits are 3/4 to 1-1/2 inches apart, while the stitches in the upper walls are 1 to 1-3/4 inches apart. The slightly closer stitches in the bottom may reflect the greater strength and firmness required there, compared to the stitches in the walls.

Of the nine gunwale area cracks, three are longer than the others. These three breaks are all adjacent to each other, in panels K and L. They extend from 2-1/2 to 4 inches lower on the wall than their shorter counterparts. These breaks usually have one more stitch than the shorter cracks.

Breaks in the upper edges of the wall panels are often observed in early photos of large voyaging canoes. The craft which appears in the 1907 photos appears to have four such gunwale area repairs in the one wall which is visible. In addition, a photo from about 1904 shows a fur trade canoe being portaged in northern Ontario, possibly on the Missinaibi River; this canoe also appears to have two or possibly three comparable gunwale breaks in the one wall that is visible.[11] Some of the repaired cracks seen in the early photos extend the full distance from the gunwales down to the longitudinal side seam. These appear to be cases in which the original short cracks from the period of manufacture grew much longer during the usage of the craft.

The bark cover shows ample evidence that the canoe saw considerable service in North America before it ultimately became the property of the Royal Family. There are innumerable deep scratches, scrapes, and gouges in the bark cover over the entire bottom and up nearly the full height of the walls. The majority of these marks run in a longitudinal direction (the usual direction of travel of the canoe), either horizontally or diagonally. Many of the scratches and gouges are major

ones, such as a deep one which extends down the midline area of the bottom in the midsection for about 39 inches, and another deep gouge which runs along the left wall in the midsection, down 15 to 16 inches below the gunwales, for a span of 46 inches.

In addition to the numerous scratches and scrapes, the canoe during its period of usage also sustained one area of major damage which required repair at the time. The damage occurred in the forward portion of the right wall, beside the vertical seam between panels M and N; this area is just below the rear edge of the third thwart from the bow (Fig. 9). Immediately below the lower edge of the reinforcement strip of bark which runs below the outwale, the bark cover was punctured. From the puncture hole, a crack extended downward for about ten inches (Fig. 17).

To repair the damage, the ribs and sheathing strips were shifted inside the canoe, to expose the interior side of the damaged area. Then a bark patch was sewed to the inside of the bark wall.

The root stitches which attach the patch enclose an irregular area roughly 4-1/4 inches long by 2-3/4 inches high. The bark patch is somewhat larger than these dimensions, with its margins extending beyond the stitched portion of the patch. The margins shown in the drawing are conjectural. It is not possible to determine whether the bark patch extends downward behind the crack which descends from the puncture hole.

The split roots used for the stitches are 3/16 to 1/4 inch wide (about the diameter of the awl holes), with a half-round cross section. The round outer side, which was scraped somewhat flat before use, faces the exterior of the canoe.

The top of the patch is sewn with a horizontal row of stitches 1-1/2 to 1-3/4 inches below the bottom edge of the outwale; the row lies a little below the midline of the reinforcement strip of bark beneath the outwale. The stitches, about 1/2 to 3/4 inch long, form a horizontal line made up of seven stitches in eight holes. They are sewn in a harness stitch pattern, with the two ends of a single root passing in opposite directions through the same hole (Fig. 18). This row of stitches firmly joins three layers of bark: the patch, the canoe wall, and the reinforcement strip.

Four other moderately-spaced stitches attach the bark patch to the two sides of the puncture hole in the wall panel. About 3/4 to 7/8 inch long, these spiral stitches are joined to each other by long diagonal connectors on the interior side of the patch.

The crack, which extends downward from the puncture hole, is sewed with the same size of split roots, in five spiral stitches. Spaced at intervals of 1 to 1-1/4 inches, these stitches are 3/4 to 7/8 inch long.

All of the ends of the sewing roots used to repair the damage were presumably tucked under adjacent stitches on the inside of the canoe. No ends are visible on the exterior.

After the sewing was completed, all of the damaged area except the patched puncture hole was sealed on the exterior with three successive layers of pitched fabric, in strips about two inches wide. The first of the strips partly overlaps the original fabric sealant strip covering the side panel seam. The second strip overlaps portions of both of the previous strips. The top layer of fabric extends from the base of the puncture hole to about an inch below the end of the crack; it overlaps only the adjacent fabric strip. This layering technique strengthened both the cracked area and the adjacent wall, firmly joining them to the strong wall panel seam.

Finally, the entire damaged area was covered on the exterior with a coat of pitch, including the bark-patched puncture hole. The coat of pitch extends downward from the lower edge of the reinforcement bark strip, and out about 1/2 inch beyond the perimeter of the fabric strips. Before the ribs and sheathing strips were returned to their original positions behind the damaged area, the interior side of the repair was probably also sealed with pitch or pitched cloth strips.

This is an excellent example of a repair carried out on a fur trade canoe during its usage. Travel journals of the era are replete with references to such repairs being done on a regular basis en route.

Gunwale Elements

The wood which was used to fashion the inwales and outwales of the Royal canoe has been microscopically identified from minute samples as spruce. It is not possible to determine which type of spruce without samples of bark or needles.[12] However, the builders probably used black spruce, as this was the common type of spruce used in canoe construction.[13]

The gunwale caps and guard strips were replaced during the 1971 restoration. Therefore, no samples from their original versions are available. It is presumed that these were also made of black spruce, as were the inwales and outwales.

All of the gunwale elements are angled moderately outward, at the same degree of outward flare as the topsides of the bark walls to which they are attached (Fig. 19).

Inwales

The total length of the inwale on the curve is projected to be about 28 feet 3 inches (nearly equal to the length of the outwale, which measures 28 feet 4-1/4 inches). This is based on the measurement of 26 feet 3-1/2 inches of its length which is visible plus the projected length of about 12 inches at each end that is hidden from view, outboard of the headboards (Fig. 28). In the midsection, the inwale strip is 3/4 inch wide across the top and 1-1/2 inches deep (Fig. 19). The bottom surface is only 1/2 inch across, since the lower outboard edge is planed off into a beveled surface about 3/4 inch wide; this produces a 3/4 inch high space into which the tips of the ribs fit. At each of the nine locations where a thwart is mortised into the inwale, this lower outboard edge has not been beveled off; in these areas, the original full square edge extends for a span a little greater than the 2 to 2-1/8 inch width of the thwart.

Beginning at the second thwart from each end of the canoe, the width and depth of the inwale taper very gradually over 48 inches to the headboards. There, the width has tapered down to 1/2 inch and the depth has reduced to 1 inch. All surfaces of the inwale are planed flat and smooth, and all edges are sharp.

The inwale runs nearly horizontally over much of the length of the canoe, and then rises very gradually toward the ends. About 13 inches inboard of each end thwart, it begins to curve up moderately to its ends. To facilitate the bending of the upward curve of the ends, three saw kerfs were cut in the ends, each 1/32 to 3/64 inch wide, to produce four lamination layers. The kerfs extend inboard from the tips of the inwale to a point 22 inches inboard of the headboard. From this point, the central kerf alone extends for another four inches inboard, dividing the inwale into two layers. The lashings which bind the inwale to the outwale cover the area where

Fig. 18. Royal Canoe: Top view cross section of harness stitches.

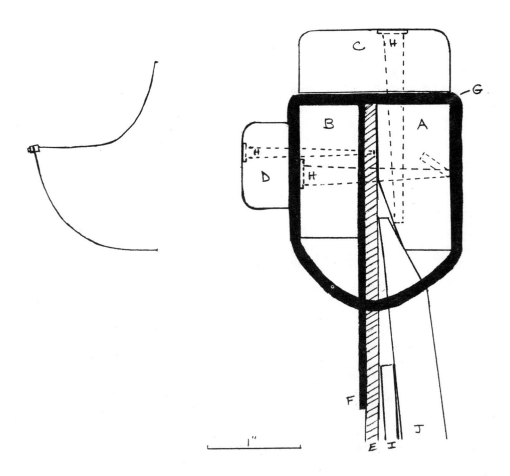

Fig. 19. Royal Canoe: Cross section of gunwales. A. inwale, B. outwale, C. gunwale cap, D. guard strip, E. bark wall, F. reinforcement bark strip, G. root lashings, H. nails, I. sheathing, J. rib.

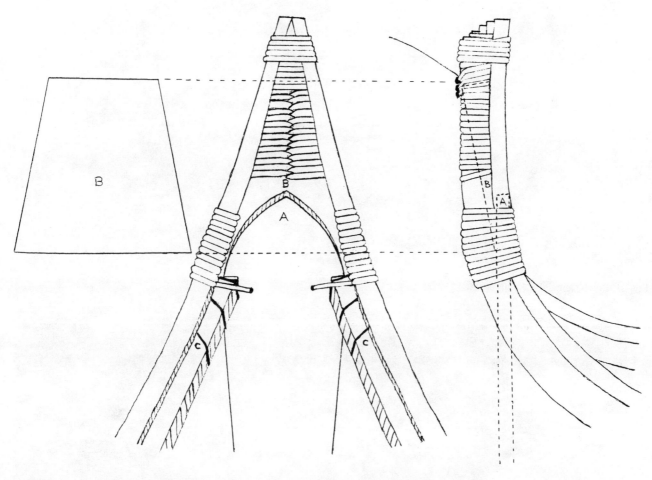

Fig. 20. Royal Canoe: Gunwale ends and bark deck piece. A. headboard, B. bark deck piece, C. string wrappings on inwale tips.

Fig. 21. Royal Canoe: Left wall of bow.

Fig. 22. Royal Canoe: Lashings of cutwater edge and gunwales, end of guard strip, serrated cut bark edges, and painted decorations.

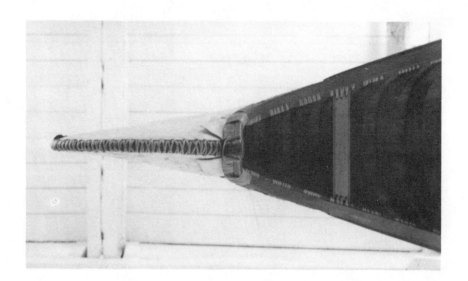

Fig. 23. Royal Canoe: Top view of stern end.

Fig. 24. Royal Canoe: Bow end view of original guard strip before replacement during 1971 restoration. Gunwale cap removed (National Maritime Museum, Greenwich, Neg. B4126-3).

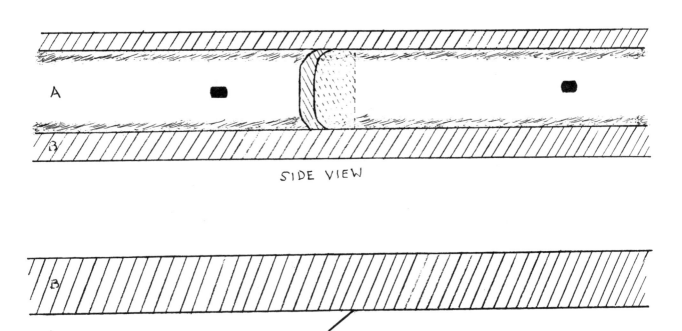

SIDE VIEW

TOP VIEW

1"

Fig. 25. Royal Canoe: Joint in the midsection of guard strip. A. guard strip, B. outwale.

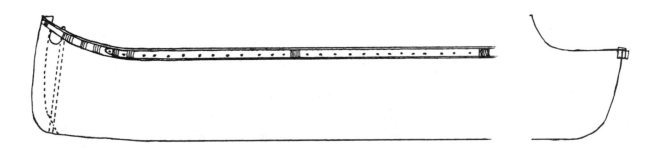

Fig. 26. Guard strip on Ojibwa 18-1/2 foot freight canoe. Redrawn after Adney and Chapelle.

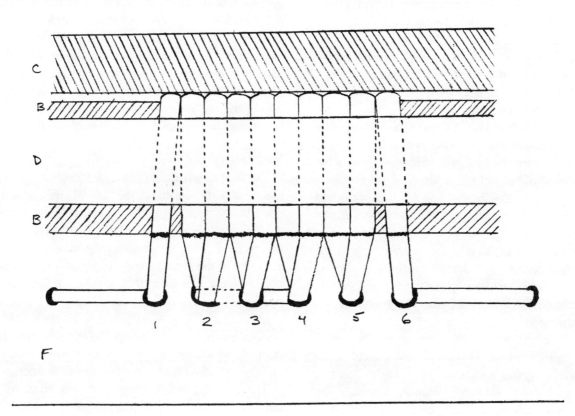

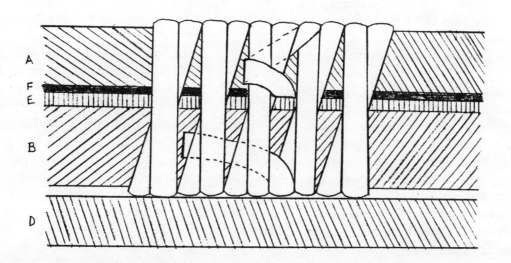

Fig. 27. Royal Canoe: Side view of gunwale lashings from exterior (upper) and top view minus gunwale cap, showing two ending techniques (lower). A. inwale, B. outwale, C. gunwale cap, D. guard strip, E. bark wall, F. reinforcement bark strip.

the outer two saw kerfs end, as well as where the single central kerf ends. These lashings prevent the kerfs from splitting further inboard. When the gunwale lashings were installed, they squeezed the saw kerfs together, thus reducing slightly the depth of the inwale. The procedure of extending the central kerf beyond the outer two kerfs would create a more gradual taper in the depth than if all three kerfs ended in the same area.

The inwale fits into a notch which is cut into the side of each headboard (Fig. 20). One or two turns of split root bind the inwale to the headboard at the notch. In the area outboard of each of the headboards, the inwale is hidden behind the headboards and the bark walls and deck. Since the ends are hidden, no observations can be made concerning their taper over the final 12 inches of length at each end. In this area, the upward sweep of the ends of the inwale is less than that of the outwale. The tip of the inwale is lashed to the top of the stempiece, slightly inboard and downward from the point of maximum height of the stempiece.

Before the installation of the inwale onto the canoe, its laminated ends were bent upward and spirally bound with widely spaced wrappings of a single strand of commercial string about 3/64 inch in diameter. The string is now dark tan in color; this may have been its original color, or it may have darkened with age from a light tan. Three of the spiral wrappings are visible beside and inboard of the headboard, positioned at intervals of about 1 to 1-1/4 inches. Comparable string wraps on the laminated ends of the inwales are also found on the Ojibwa and Catlin canoes.

The inwale is nailed to the outwale over the entire span in which the two strips run parallel, from headboard to headboard (including the area extending about 22 inches inboard from the headboards where they are each laminated). The two wooden strips have sandwiched between them the top edge of the bark wall and a strip of reinforcement bark (Fig. 19). The machine-cut nails extend horizontally from the exterior face of the outwale. The nails run generally down the midline of the two wooden elements, at intervals of 4-1/2 to 6 inches. The nail heads are 3/16 by 5/16 inch (see the nail information summary on page 53). The ends of the nail shanks protrude through the inboard face of the inwale up to 1/4 to 3/8 inch; they are clinched over horizontally.

Most of the nails lie beneath the groups of lashings

between the ribs; a few are exposed beside the tips of the ribs. The interval between the nails reduces to 3 to 4-1/2 inches as the ends of the parallel inwale and outwale begin to gradually rise. The series of nails continues in the laminated area of the moderately curved portion of the gunwales until reaching the headboards. There, the end most nail runs through the outwale and inwale and into the edge of the headboard, at the point where the inwale rests in its headboard notch.

Outwales

The total length of the outwale is 28 feet 4-1/4 inches, measured on the outside of the curve. In the midsection, it is 5/8 inch wide across the top and 1-3/8 inches deep; these dimensions are 1/8 inch less in both directions than the inwale (Fig. 19). Beginning at the second thwart from each end of the canoe, the depth tapers very gradually over 59 inches, to a depth of one inch at the tips. The width (thickness) of 5/8 inch across the top remains constant for the full length. All surfaces are planed flat and smooth, and all edges are sharp. The horizontal machine-cut nails which fasten the outwale to the inwale have already been discussed in the inwale information.

The outwale runs horizontally over much of the length of the canoe, and then rises very gradually toward the ends. About 13 inches inboard of each end thwart, it begins to curve moderately upward. The ends begin to diverge from the parallel curvature of the inwale 1-1/2 inches inboard of the headboards; they sweep upward in a strong curve to reach a virtually vertical position at the tips (Figs. 21 and 28).

The ends of the outwale sweep upward and slightly outboard for 11 inches on the curve beyond the headboards. The tips reach a point 2-1/2 inches above the edge of the adjoining stempiece, and 1/2 inch higher than the maximum height of the prow. The corners and edges of the tips are sharp.

To facilitate the bending of the upward curve and the extreme upsweep at the tips, the same lamination procedure was done as on the inwales: three saw kerfs were cut, 1/32 to 3/64 inch wide, to produce four lamination layers (Fig. 22). The kerfs extend from the tips inboard for a span of 32 to 34 inches, to a point 22 inches inboard of the headboards. (This is the same point at which the inwale kerfs also end.) Presumably, the central saw kerf alone extends for another four inches inboard, as it does on the inwale. However, it is not visible, since the midline portion of the outwale is hidden in this area behind the guard strip. The ends of the three saw kerfs are not covered by any of the gunwale lashings, but such a lashing is placed immediately inboard of the kerf ends, to prevent their splitting further inboard. The four lamination layers at the tip are arranged in a four-step pattern, with the layer on the inboard side extending up the highest, and the outboard one ending 7/8 inch lower (Fig. 20). The two middle layers end at two intermediate heights. This step formation is caused by the different curvatures followed by each of the four lamination layers as the end of the outwale sweeps sharply upward.

At the juncture of the tips of the two outwales, a 1/4 inch thick piece of bark, 2 inches vertically by 3/4 inch, is fitted vertically between the tips. This bark acts as a wedge that assists in making the root lashings tight. No nail or peg joins the outwale tips together. The split root lashings, beginning 1/2 inch below the ends, wrap around the two converged outwales for a span of 1-3/4 inches (Fig. 20). The lower four to six lashing wraps also run through two or three holes in the adjacent bark wall, passing through the stempiece inside the bark wall as well. The original split root lashing material was 3/16 to 1/4 inch wide, with a half-round cross section. Immediately below these wrapped lashings, the triangular area between the two converging outwales is filled for a vertical span of 3-3/4 inches with an over-and-under root lashing that wraps around the outwales in a figure-eight pattern. These lashings do not run through holes in the bark walls.

The remaining area between the converging gunwales extends from the lower edge of the figure-eight lashings inboard for five inches to the headboard. This area is covered by a bark deck. The rectangular piece of bark, measuring nine inches vertically, begins just outboard of the headboard. It covers the five inches of open area between the converging inwales, and runs underneath the entire span of figure-eight lashings. Its ends extend over the bark walls and beneath the outwales for only about 1/4 to 1 inch; they are not visible on the exterior of the canoe. It is an additional reinforcement strip of bark which is visible on the exterior beneath each outwale, rather than the ends of this bark deck.

The deck appears to be held in place by only the

pressure of the outwales and the figure-eight lashings, which squeeze the bark down against the top edges of the bark wall panels. No root stitches are visible that may have fastened the piece of bark.

Since the bark deck and figure-eight lashings completely fill the area outboard of the headboard, there is no possibility that a flagstaff or any other item could have ever been inserted outboard of the headboard, at either the bow or the stern.

Gunwale Caps

During the 1971 N.M.M. restoration project, the conservation staff installed replacements for the gunwale caps and the guard strips. The original ones were presumably much damaged, through removal and reinstallation during the two restoration projects. The 1971 photos clearly show the original caps and guard strips, and verify the closeness with which the N.M.M. conservators copied the originals.

The only variance from the original caps is that the machine-cut attachment nails were replaced with wood screws. The nails visible in the 1971 photo (Fig. 16) are the round-headed wire nails which were used to reattach the gunwale caps during the early restoration project. In the photo, the gunwale lashings have been already replaced, and the original left gunwale cap has been temporarily returned for the photo.

The total length of the gunwale cap is 27 feet 10-1/4 inches, measured on the inside of the curve. (This is six inches shorter than the outwale, which was measured on the opposite side of the curvature.) In the midsection, the cap is 1-5/8 inches wide by 5/8 inch thick (deep) (Fig. 19). Beginning about 13 inches inboard from the end thwarts, the width of the cap gradually tapers over a distance of 37 inches, to a width of 5/8 inch at the tips. This dimension matches the 5/8 inch thickness (depth) which the cap maintains for its full length. All surfaces are planed flat and smooth. The lower two edges are sharp, while the upper two are carved or planed moderately round.

The combined width of the inwale (3/4 inch) and the outwale (5/8 inch) is 1/4 inch less than the width of the gunwale cap. But the bark wall and the reinforcement bark strip sandwiched between the inwale and the outwale add as much as 1/4 to 3/8 inch of thickness to the combined gunwales. Also, the degree to which the inwale and outwale were squeezed against the bark elements and each other when they were all nailed and lashed together varies in different areas. Thus, the gunwale cap covers nearly completely the top of the gunwale unit (inwale, bark layers, and outwale) in some areas. In other areas, it leaves exposed up to 1/4 inch or more of width. This uncovered area is sometimes on the inboard side of the cap, sometimes on the outboard side, and sometimes a little on each side of the cap. The width of the cap tapers much more quickly toward the ends than the combined gunwale unit (Fig. 23). The outboard edge of the cap tends to be aligned with the outboard edge of the outwale toward the ends; thus, the area of the inwale that is exposed gradually increases toward the ends. Near the headboards, up to 1/2 inch of the width of the inwale is exposed.

The cap covers both the inwale and the outwale until 1-1/4 inches inboard of the headboards. There, the outwale in its upward sweep diverges from the inwale. The cap then follows only the outwale from there to its tip.

The gunwale cap conforms to the curvature of the outwale for its entire length. Thus, it runs horizontally over much of the length of the canoe, and then rises very gradually toward the ends. About 13 inches inboard from the end thwart, it begins to curve moderately upward. A little inboard of the headboard, the cap sweeps upward in a curve to a virtually vertical position at the tip, extending 1/8 to 1/4 inch higher than the tip of the outwale (Fig. 20). The virtually vertical tips of the outwales and caps extend 5/8 to 3/4 inch above the maximum height of the end panels.

To facilitate the bending of the upward curve and the extreme upsweep of the ends, a single horizontal saw kerf, 1/32 to 3/64 inch wide, was cut into the ends, to produce two lamination layers (Fig. 16). This kerf runs inboard for 30" from the tip of the cap; it ends two to four inches outboard of the ends of the three lamination kerfs in the inwale and the outwale. At the point where the kerf in the gunwale cap ends, one of the downward nails which attached the original gunwale cap to the inwale and the outwale was driven. This nail prevented any further splitting inboard of the lamination kerf. No lashings bind the two laminations together at the end of the kerf.

The upswept end of the gunwale cap extends upward and slightly outboard for 11 inches on the curve

past the headboard, to a point 2-1/2 inches above the adjoining stempiece edge. From the headboard to the tip, all four edges of the cap are carved moderately rounded, but the tips themselves are cut off squarely.

From headboard to headboard, the gunwale caps were originally attached to the inwale and the outwale by downward-driven nails. Since the original gunwale caps were replaced in the 1971 restoration, no original cap nails or nail holes are available for study. However, in one location where the replacement cap does not fit tightly down atop the inwale, toward the stern end on one wall, two original nail holes are visible in the top of the inwale. They are rectangular (irregular, since the nails were later pulled out), and lie 20 inches apart.

Other evidence of the original gunwale cap nails is found in one of the 1971 photos, which shows a top view of the stern end area after the original caps were removed. In the photo, one rectangular nail hole appears in the top surface of each outwale beside the headboard.

No nail holes can be observed on the underside of the inwales or outwales. This indicates that the cap nails did not extend completely through the inwale and the outwale.

No further information can be extrapolated concerning the gunwale cap nails, to determine whether they were positioned to enter the inwale and outwale in the spaces between the gunwale lashing groups, how far apart they were spaced, or whether they alternated being driven one into the inwale and the next into the outwale. The replacement restoration screws do alternate in this manner, and are usually positioned in the spaces between the gunwale lashing groups. They are 6 to 8 inches apart in the midsection, increasing to intervals of 13 to 24 inches toward the headboards. Their positions may or not reflect the positions of the original nails in the original caps.

Outboard of the headboards, no nails fasten the gunwale cap ends; the caps are attached to the outwales only by lashings in this area (Fig. 20). The tips of the two caps are joined to each other and to the tips of the two outwales by a span of wrapped lashings 1-1/4 inches long, which begins 3/4 inch below the tips. No wedge is inserted between the tips of the caps to assist in making the lashings tight, as was done between the outwale tips. Nor are the tips of the converged caps pegged or nailed to each other. Down 5-1/4 inches below the lower edge of the upper wrapped lashings, another set of lashings binds each cap to its respective outwale. This set of lashings, spanning 2-1/4 to 2-1/2 inches, extends inboard to the headboard. In all of the lashings, loose ends are tucked under two or more turns of adjacent lashing.

The 1971 photo of the original gunwale cap seems to show a moderate degree of wear to the exposed surfaces of the cap, from its period of usage. The description of the painted decoration on the caps is found on page 52.

Guard Strips

A rare feature of this fur trade canoe is its set of narrow wooden guard strips; one runs alongside the exterior face of each outwale (Figs. 2 and 21 to 24). The strip protected the exterior side of the gunwale lashings from damage, in the same way that the gunwale cap protected the top side of these same lashings. This feature would be especially useful if the canoe were sometimes loaded or unloaded beside a dock or a pier.

The guard strips found on the sides of the outwales of the Royal Canoe are by no means unique in canoe history. A series of photos taken in western Quebec in 1907 shows a fur trade canoe being paddled and portaged by six voyageurs on the Quinze River section of the upper Ottawa River. Two of the photos are presented in Figure 113 of Volume I; another photo of the same canoe appears on page 152 of Adney and Chapelle. When original prints of the photos are viewed under magnification, it is clear that the canoe in the photos is a virtual mate to the Royal canoe in nearly all of its features, including the guard strips. The strip is clearly visible on the canoe in each of the photos.

In addition, Adney recorded in great detail the features of an 18-1/2 foot Ojibwa freight canoe from Lake Temagami which bears outwale guard strips very similar to those on the Royal Canoe.[14] Lake Temagami is located about fifty miles southwest of the Quinze section of the upper Ottawa River, where the above fur trade canoe was photographed. A description of the guard strips on this canoe is presented on page 34.

Guard strips on the sides of birchbark canoes were not always confined to the outwales. Some Micmac rough-water canoes which were fitted for sailing had a wooden guard strip running from end to end on the exterior side of each wall, about six or seven inches be-low the outwales.[15] The strips, made of two sections joined at the middle, were about 3/4 inch wide and 5/16 inch thick. The lashings which fastened them to the walls were installed between the ribs.

Gunwale guard strips were originally probably bound to the outwales with a few widely spaced root lashings, like those which attached the wall guard strips on certain Micmac canoes. With the importation of iron nails, the strips could be more firmly and easily attached. Unlike gunwale caps, attachment of guard strips with wooden pegs was probably never a practical procedure. Since the strips were mounted beside the gunwale lashings rather than on top of the lashings like the caps, downward blows inflicted on the strips during usage of the canoe could break the pegs or loosen the strips.

During the 1971 restoration of the Royal canoe, its original guard strips were removed so that the gunwale lashings could be restored. Afterward, the strips were replaced with close copies of the originals. Nine of the 1971 photos show the original strips, and verify the correctness of the various features of the reconstructed copies. The only variance from the originals is the degree of taper of the ends, which will be discussed shortly.

The total length of the nearly straight guard strip is 24 feet 6-1/2 inches (3 feet 9-3/4 inches shorter than the outwale). It is made up of two pieces whose inboard ends overlap in a diagonal joint (Fig. 25). As shown in the 1971 photos, this joint occurs in the right gunwale strip a little toward the bow from the midpoint. In the reconstructed strip on the left gunwale, the joint occurs five inches rearward of the center thwart. At the midpoint, the strip is 1/2 inch wide across the top and 7/8 inch deep on the outboard face (Fig. 19). All surfaces are planed smooth and flat. The two inboard edges are square, while the two outboard ones are carved or planed very round.

The upper edge of the strip runs 3/16 to 1/4 inch below the upper edge of the outwale. Thus, it is aligned just slightly above the midline of the outwale. Below the guard strip, the outwale is exposed for 1/4 to 5/16 inch.

The strip runs horizontally for much of the length of the canoe; then it rises slightly and very gradually toward its ends. The strip ends 1/2 to 1 inch outboard of the end thwarts, before the outwale has made much of its strong upward curve to the ends. From the end of the guard strip, the outwale extends for another 23 inches at each end, measured on the outside of the curve.

The width and depth of the reconstructed guard strip taper moderately quickly over a span of 14 inches at each end, down to 1/8 inch wide across the top and 3/8 inch deep at the tips. The original strip, as shown in the 1971 photos (Fig. 24), tapers similarly in width; but in depth it tapers only slightly, to about 3/4 inch at the tips, where it is cut off squarely.

The strip is attached to its outwale by horizontal nails driven from the exterior. The original machine-cut nails were replaced with round-headed wire nails when the two strips were reinstalled after the early restoration. These replacement nails were presumably driven into the nail holes of the original machine-cut nails.

One of the 1971 photos, which shows a section of the guard strip on the right wall, provides information on the positions of these early replacement nails. At the point where the ends of the two sections of the strip join in a diagonal overlap (angling through the thickness of the two sections), one nail was driven into the end of each section (Fig. 25). These nails lie 3/4 inch and 2-3/4 inches respectively from the joint seam. Another nail was driven into the strip about 12-1/4 inches forward of the seam.

The three nails shown in the photo lie generally in the midline of the guard strip; each was driven into a group of gunwale lashings. Thus, no effort was apparently made to drive the guard strip nails into the spaces between the lashing groups, unless these replacement nails do not reflect the original positions of the original nails.

The modern nails in the reconstructed guard strips are positioned at irregular intervals of 8 to 22 inches over most of the length of the strip. These intervals reduce gradually near the ends of the strip: the outermost four nails are spaced 9, 9, and 5 inches apart. The last nail lies 1-1/4 to 1-1/2 inches from each end of the strip. Many of the nails are driven into groups of gunwale root lashings. Again, the positions of these modern nails in the replacement strips may or may not reflect the positions of the original nails in the original strips.

Several 1971 photos show that the end tips of each guard strip had been also lashed securely to the gunwales during the early restoration, by one or two turns of root at the edge of a group of gunwale lashings (Fig. 24). This would imply that the guard strips had been installed on the canoe before those particular gunwale lashings had been completed, and thus before the gunwale cap was installed (since all of the lashings had to be completed before the cap was added). The tips are not presently covered by any of the lashings installed during the 1971 restoration. At this point, it is not possible to determine whether the tips were originally lashed on the Royal canoe or not. No lashings are visible on the tips of the guard strip on the canoe which appears in the 1907 portaging photos.

The 1971 photos of the Royal canoe indicate what appears to be light to moderate wear and weathering on the surfaces of the original strips. The description of the painted decoration on the guard strips is found on page 52.

The guard strips are believed to be definitely original to the Royal canoe, rather than later additions. The strongest evidence lies in the photos taken in 1907 of the virtually identical canoe. The strips on this latter canoe are made up of two segments joined at the midpoint and fastened to the outwale with horizontal nails driven from the exterior, as on the Royal canoe. The dimensions of the strips and the locations of their ends, as shown in the 1907 photos, match almost exactly the original strips on the Royal canoe, as shown in its 1971 photos.

In addition, the guard strips on the Lake Temagami Ojibwa canoe also resemble very closely those found on the Royal canoe[16] (Fig. 26). Each of the nearly straight strips curves upward slightly over its last 11 to 12 inches, ending about 18 inches short of the tip of the outwale. Since it is about 1-1/2 inches deep, the strip covers nearly all of the depth of the outwale, until the strip tapers slightly on its lower edge over its last 10 to 12 inches. Horizontal nails driven from the exterior side attach the guard strip to the exposed face of the outwale. In addition, each tip is attached by one gunwale lashing group and one thwart lashing group. A photo from 1913 of an almost identical Ojibwa canoe clearly shows an identical guard strip. No lashings are visible along the strip in the photo; only horizontal nails driven from the exterior side can be seen.

The repairs carried out on the Royal canoe during the early restoration project were only sufficient for display, not for usage. Therefore, there is no reason to suspect that its guard strips were made and added to the canoe during the early restoration, since the craft was not being restored for usage. Also, the weathered condition of the original guard strips, as shown in the 1971 photos, appears to indicates that the age and condition of the strips matched that of the other wooden elements of the canoe when the strips were removed and replaced. Further discussion of the guard strips is found on page 56.

Reinforcement Bark Strips

The reinforcement strip of birchbark doubles the thickness of the upper edge of the bark wall where it is attached to the gunwales. Before the inwale and outwale were nailed together onto the upper edge of the bark wall, the reinforcement strip was inserted between the bark wall and the outwale, so that its top edge matched the top edge of the bark wall (Fig. 19). When the awl holes were pierced through the wall and the lashings were wrapped around the gunwales, the bark strip was pierced and lashed as well. Its presence reduced the danger of splitting of the upper bark wall, both while being sewed and during the usage of the canoe.

The strip, made of 1/16 to 1/8 inch thick bark, runs from headboard to headboard: it extends down 1-3/4 to 3 inches below the lower edge of the outwale (Fig. 21). Its width does not taper toward the outboard ends. The lower edge is generally parallel to the lower edge of the outwale for the full length of the strip; but it was cut quite irregularly and with considerable undulation. The edge was cut off in such a way that a beveled edge slanting downward was produced.

The strip was apparently cut to its present width before being installed on the canoe. There is no cut or scratch on the bark wall panel adjacent to the lower edge of the strip, which would have been produced if the strip had been cut off against the unprotected wall. However, a piece of bark could have been temporarily inserted between the wall panel and the reinforcement strip to shield the wall from knife cuts as the strip was trimmed.

The majority of the length of the strip is made up of one or two long continuous pieces of bark. In addition to these long strips, the span beneath the outwale where it curves upward to the headboard at each end is made up of two or three short pieces. The curved portion at the bow end of the left wall, spanning about 30 inches, is made up of three pieces (Fig. 21). The inboard seg-

ment is 19 inches long, while the second one is 10 inches long. (The inboard end of the second segment has cracked, producing a triangular section at its end.) The final piece, extending to a point beside the headboard, is a truncated wedge-shaped piece with a 2-1/2 inch base and a 1-1/2 inch top. These three end pieces, extending around the upward curve of the outwale, overlap each other slightly at their ends; the exposed overlapping edges face outboard, toward the end of the canoe.

At the stern end of the same wall, the distance around the upward curved area of the outwale is about 16 inches. The reinforcement strip around this curve is made up of a 6 inch piece followed by an 8 inch one. The final strip, 1-1/2 inches long, is now missing from its area directly beside the headboard. It was most likely a truncated wedge-shaped piece like the one that is found at the bow end. The ends of the two surviving segments butt against each other, rather than overlapping, in contrast to the comparable segments at the bow end. The individual pieces of bark which make up the reinforcement strip are not attached at their ends to each other or to the canoe wall in any manner.

The reinforcement strip that follows the upward curvature of the outwale on the right wall at the bow end differs in two respects (Fig. 22). It consists of only one long and one short segment; the short truncated wedge-shaped piece beside the headboard is now missing. In addition, the surviving segment has a distinctive sawtooth pattern cut into its lower edge over its end most 10 inches. This pattern is composed of a series of irregular triangular points, formed by indentations about 1/4 inch deep. The purpose of this sawtooth pattern was to show the voyageurs at a glance which end of the canoe was the bow end, whether the end panel was painted with a special design or not.

An additional strip of bark, which visually appears to be a continuation of the reinforcement bark strip, is located outboard of the headboard on each wall (Figs. 22 and 23). This piece, 7 to 8 inches long, extends beyond the outwale for 2 to 2-1/4 inches. It runs up to the root lashings which bind the tips of the outwales to the hull. The strip lies beside the area where the outwales converge, the area which is covered by the bark deck piece and the figure-eight root lashings. The strip extending beyond the outwales appears to be the outer overlapping end of the bark deck piece. But it is an additional separate strip of bark, inserted between the outwale and the hidden short end of the bark deck piece. This strip is held in place only by the pressure exerted by the outwale against the deck piece and the bark wall panel.

The outboard edge of this additional strip is usually cut parallel to the outwale, to match the lower edge of the bark reinforcement strip. But the strip on the right wall of the bow has a sawtooth edge, with 15 points cut 1/4 inch deep, to match the sawtooth pattern in the lower edge of the adjacent reinforcement bark strip.

Gunwale Lashings

The upper edge of the bark wall is sandwiched between the inwale, the reinforcement bark strip, and the outwale. It is cut off flush with the top surface of the two wooden elements. The four layers of bark and wood are nailed and lashed together with spaced groups of root lashings from headboard to headboard.

Each lashing group normally runs through six holes (sometimes five or seven) in the bark wall (Fig. 27). The holes, generally round in shape, have diameters of 3/16 to 1/4 inch, with very rough edges. They were made by an awl with a triangular or square cross section, which was inserted from the exterior side of the wall and twisted. The holes are spaced 1/4 to 1/2 inch apart. Each row of holes, spanning 2-1/2 to 3-1/2 inches, presently lies 3/8 to 1/2 inch below the lower edge of the inwale. When originally installed, the lashing holes would have been close to the lower surface of the inwale. Over time, the upward pressure exerted by the ribs forced the inwales upward somewhat, thus increasing the distance between the lashing holes and the inwale.

The original split root lashing material of the gunwales was 3/16 to 1/4 inch wide, with a half-round cross section. (The original lashings still survive in all of the sewn seams and in the area of original damage repair.)

In the series of 1971 photos, eight close-up shots show in great detail the gunwale lashings after the gunwale caps had been removed. These lashings were those that had replaced the original lashings during the early restoration. They were presumably done using the identical patterns and techniques of the originals. In 1971, the conservators copied exactly the lashings of the early restoration.

To lash the gunwales, a long length of split root was drawn to its midpoint through the first hole in the set of six holes. Then, in a single harness stitch, each of the ends of the root passed over the top of the inwale and outwale (crossing each other) and ran through the second hole, in opposite directions from each other. Since the width of the root was equal to the diameter of the hole, there was no room for the two turns of root to fit beside each other as they passed through the hole. So first one passed through, and then the other end was inserted below the first. The two ends of the root passed again around the combined inwale and outwale, and through the third hole. This pattern continued through each of the six holes, laying down ten adjacent wrappings around the gunwales. After the two ends of the root had passed through the final hole in the set, they each spanned horizontally across a distance of 3/4 to 1-1/2 inches to the first hole in the next set of holes.

Each typical group of lashings is composed of ten turns of root around the gunwales, covering a span of 2-1/4 to 3-1/2 inches of the gunwales. Normally, the first and last hole of each set of holes has a single turn of root through it and around the inwale and outwale, while each of the other holes contains two turns. An interval of 3/4 to 1-1/4 inches separates each group of lashings. The interval between each group is spanned by a single horizontal stitch, at the base of the lashing groups, on both the exterior and the interior side of the bark wall.

This lashing style, using both ends of the same root, produces a horizontal connecting stitch on both the exterior and the interior between each group of lashings. It is a rather unusual choice for lashing gunwales, although such use has been documented for a number of tribal groups.[17] By this method, every space between lashing groups has a horizontal connecting stitch on the interior side, in the place where the tips of the ribs are to be inserted behind the inwale. Generally, the lashings were done so that the connectors spanned between the groups only on the exterior side, leaving the interior clear for the rib tips. It is impossible to determine at this point whether the original lashings were done in this exact style, or whether the pattern was altered slightly at the time of the early restoration.

If the original gunwale lashings had been installed using only one end of a strand of root in a simple spiral stitch, the results would have differed slightly. In this method, after twelve turns had been wrapped around the gunwales (running twice through each hole), the single strand would usually return from hole #6 to hole #5 on the interior side. After passing through hole #5, the root would then bypass hole #6 and span across to the first hole of the next set of holes, on the exterior. Thus, every horizontal connector stitch would lie on the exterior side, leaving the spaces between the lashing groups on the interior empty, to accommodate the tips of the ribs. If the root spanned directly across from hole #6 to the first hole of the next group, the resulting connector stitches would alternate between the exterior side and the interior side, with every other one lying on the interior.

During the gunwale lashing procedure on the Royal canoe, whenever the length of root was nearly depleted, several techniques were utilized to finish off the root securely before starting a new root. In most instances, the ends were finished off atop the inwale and outwale, by being looped under the previous stitch to maintain the tension. Then they were tucked underneath several previous stitches or tightly down between the sandwiched layers of inwale, bark wall, and outwale, to hold the ends securely. The gunwale caps covered and protected all of these root ends.

In at least one instance, the end of the root, when it emerged on the exterior side of the canoe wall at hole #4, was run horizontally back through hole #3. Where it emerged on the interior, the tip was cut off rather short and inserted into hole #2. There it was held firmly in place by the two turns of root that had previously been run through the hole.

The 1971 photos also show a third root ending technique. In the area where the right outwale sweeps upward at the bow, the end of the root was simply inserted into the central lamination kerf of the outwale on the exterior side.

The thwarts were also bound into the gunwales at the same time as the gunwales were lashed. The thwart lashing groups are connected to the gunwale wrappings by the same horizontal connector stitches.

Stempieces

The stempiece, made of northern white cedar, is visible in several areas of the canoe (Fig. 28). Its heel is visible where it projects into the interior of the canoe at the base of the headboard. The laminated profile can be seen through the lashing holes in the bark walls around the entire curved perimeter of the cutwater edge, from the chin to the juncture with the outwales (since the thin restoration stitches do not completely fill the awl holes). The area of the juncture of the outboard ends of the horizontal braces and the stempiece at the cutwater edge is visible through a four inch break in the bark panel on the left side of the bow. The laminated upper end of the stempiece can be seen where it projects through the inboard face of the headboard.

The curvature of the stempiece is implied in several areas. The curve of the cutwater edge of the canoe from chin to outwales outlines the entire outer curved portion of the stempiece. Also, the stempiece is lashed to the headboard at the point where the inwales are lashed into their notches in the headboard.

The horizontal braces with their nailed ends are visible in the break in the bark in the cutwater edge area of the bow, as well as at the point where the ends of the braces are connected to the sides of the headboard.

The heel of the stempiece projects 2-3/4 inches inboard from the inboard surface of the base of the headboard. At its extreme end, it is about 1/8 inch deep (in profile) by 5/8 inch thick, with sharp corners and edges. By its juncture with the surface of the headboard, the depth of the stempiece has increased to 1-1/4 inches, while the width has remained the same. All surfaces of the heel are carved flat and smooth. The stempiece does not have a notch into which the legs of the headboard fit. On the outboard side of the headboard, the stempiece broadens in depth (profile) to 1-3/4 to 1-7/8 inches and in thickness to 11/16 inch, with sharp edges. These dimensions are maintained for the rest of its length. The cross section is straight-sided, with no taper in thickness toward the outboard edge.

The stempiece is divided by three slits into four lamination layers 3/8 to 1/2 inch thick. It is not possible to determine how near to the headboard the lamination slits run, nor whether the slits are sawn or split. But the comparable slits in the inwales, outwales, and gunwale caps are all saw kerfs; thus, it is highly likely that the slits in the stempiece are also sawn. The laminations extend from the outboard side of the headboard through the complete upper length of the stempiece to its end.

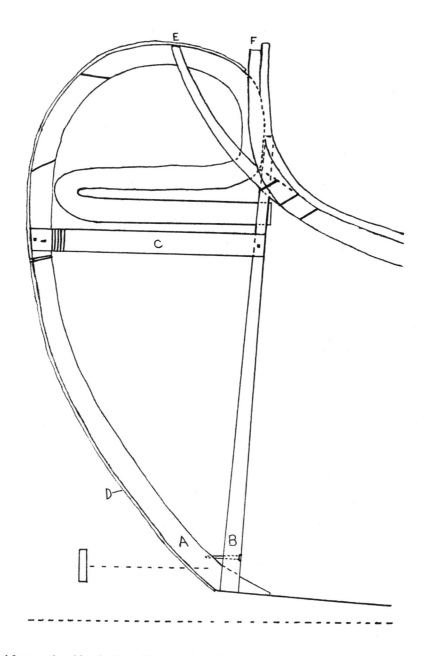

Fig. 28. Royal Canoe: End frame unit, with only the visible string wrappings indicated. A. stempiece, B. headboard, C. braces, D. batten, E. inwale, F. outwale.

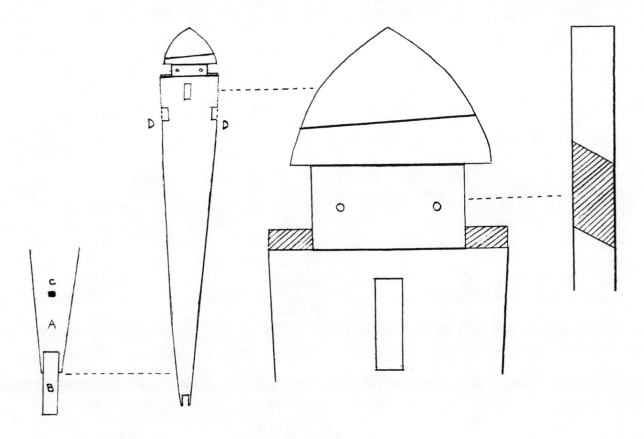

Fig. 29. Royal Canoe: Headboard. A. headboard, B. heel of stempiece, C. nail, D. braces.

The laminated portion of the stempiece is spirally wrapped with the same commercial string as was used to spirally wrap the ends of the inwales. The wraps are visible only singly; thus, it is not possible to determine the spacings between the wrappings.

The stempiece curves upward and outboard from the base of the headboard (the chin of the canoe) for 40 inches. Then it arcs in a broad curve upward and inboard for 14 inches to its maximum height at the head. At about this point, the tips of the inwales are lashed to the stempiece, one on each side. Then the stempiece curves downward and inboard for about 9-1/2 inches, to the point where it is lashed to the converged tips of the outwales. About 5 inches further down, the stempiece is also lashed to the headboard, near where the notched shoulders of the headboard receive the inwales.

The stempiece curves outboard at this point, and runs horizontally back toward the cutwater area. At some point, it doubles back very sharply on itself. In the drawing, the proximity of the sharp bend to the cutwater area is conjectural, since this area is not visible. But such a return to the outer cutwater area is extremely typical, according to all of the Adney models of Type B-1 stempieces. The degree of sharpness of this last bend may have required the breaking of some of the lamination layers (this area cannot be seen). Finally, the stempiece runs horizontally inboard to and through the headboard. The maximum horizontal distance of the curvature of the stempiece, from the cutwater edge to the outboard side of the headboard, is about 18 inches.

Down about 16 inches (measured vertically) from the highest point of the top curvature, two carved wooden braces run horizontally on each side of the stempiece, from the sides of the cutwater edge to each side of the headboard. They lie 3/4 inch below the horizontal span of the stempiece. The braces, 18 inches long and 1-5/8 to 1-3/4 inches wide (deep), have flat, planed surfaces and square edges and corners. At the headboard, they are 3/4 inch thick, tapering gradually to 1/8 inch thick at the cutwater edge.

The braces are attached to each side of the stempiece at the cutwater edge by two horizontal nails, one driven through from the left side and one from the right side. The nails extend through the midline of each brace, one back 1/4 inch from the outboard end of the brace,

and the other 3/4 inch from the outboard end. The machine-cut nails have 1/8 by 3/16 inch heads (see the nail information summary on page 53). The nail shanks are clinched over for about 5/16 inch. The opposite ends of the braces are nailed to the headboard, as described in the headboard discussion.

Possibly there are additional lashings attaching the sharply turned bend in the stempiece to its adjacent cutwater edge section, as well as binding the horizontal portion to the adjacent horizontal braces. These areas are not visible.

The form of the internal curvature of the stempiece plus its pair of horizontal braces closely resembles the "Tete de Boule" versions modeled by Adney; these appear on pages 136 and 149 at the far left in Adney and Chapelle. (Note that the correct attribution by Chapelle for the left example on page 149 should have been "Tete de Boule," to parallel the Adney model depicted on page 136.)

Headboards

The headboard, fashioned from northern white cedar, stands with its base 16 inches inboard from the outermost point of the cutwater edge (Fig. 3). It is positioned quite close to the end of the canoe: it stands at the chin, which is set close to the end due to the moderate undercut of the profile of the canoe. Its head lies beneath the upswept ends of the gunwale caps, rather than in the more usual position inboard of the cap ends. The headboard is angled slightly, so that the outboard side of the base stands at the chin of the canoe, while the head lies two inches inboard. (This two inch inboard slant of the head was also a trait of fur trade canoes that were built in the latter nineteenth century at the posts on the upper Ottawa River in western Quebec.[18]) The top of the low, bluntly pointed head fits between the converging inwales and gunwale caps at or slightly below the level of the upper surface of the caps (Fig. 20). Thus, when the canoe is viewed in profile, the headboard is not visible above the caps.

The height of the headboard is 35-1/2 inches (Fig. 29), while its maximum width is 5-1/8 inches, just below the side notches which receive the inwales. This width tapers gradually over a span of 31 inches, down to 3/4 inch at the base. The sides of this long tapered body area are bowed outward slightly, from the shoulders to the base. From the base up to the inwale notches, the headboard is 1-1/4 to 1-3/8 inches thick. Above the notches, the thickness is 7/8 inch. The flat face and all edge surfaces except those on the head are planed smooth, with all corners and edges sharp. The edges of the head are carved flat. No evidence indicates whether the headboard was originally split or sawn to thickness before it was planed. No plane marks are visible, but hand planing would not necessarily produce visible blade marks.

Below the rounded triangular head, which measures 2-3/4 inches in height and 4-1/4 inches at its maximum width, a notch is cut out of each side. The inwales fit into these notches, which are 1-5/8 to 1-3/4 inches high and 7/8 to 1 inch deep. The top and bottom surface of each notch angles upward toward the outboard side of the headboard, to accommodate the upward curve of the ends of the inwales. The notches were removed by cutting the upper and lower edges with a saw and then splitting out the wood between the two saw kerfs.

Inboard 1/2 to 5/8 inch from the midpoint of each of these inwale notches is a single hole, through which one or two turns of split roots lashed the head of the headboard to the stempiece and the inwales. The two irregularly round, tapered holes, 3/16 inch in diameter, were apparently drilled with an awl with a triangular or square cross section. Remnants of original split root lashings remain in these holes in the headboard at the bow end. (These lashings were not restored.) This root material is 3/16 inch wide by about 1/16 inch thick, with a half-round cross section. Below the notches for the inwales 5/8 inch lies a chiseled rectangular hole in the midline of the headboard. The hole is 1-7/8 inches high and 11/16 inch wide. The laminated end of the stempiece projects completely through this hole, protruding 1/4 to 3/8 inch from the inboard surface of the headboard (Fig. 28). No wooden wedge was inserted into the hole to hold the stempiece end firmly in the hole; it is held very tightly due to its close fit.

Below this central hole 3/4 inch, a notch is cut into each edge of the headboard, 1-5/8 to 1-3/4 inches high and 3/4 inch wide. These level horizontal notches were cut at the top and bottom with a saw, after which the intervening wood was chiseled out. The inboard ends

of the two horizontal braces which connect the headboard to the stempiece fit into these notches. The end surface of each brace lies flush with the surface of the headboard. Each brace is held in its notch by a single horizontal nail which runs through the thickness of the brace and into the inner side of the notch. These machine-cut nails have 1/8 by 3/16 inch heads (see the nail information summary on page 53).

The base of the headboard has a rectangular notch, 1-1/4 inches tall and 5/8 inch wide. This notch was likewise produced by two saw kerfs and chiseling. The two legs produced by the notch are each 1/8 inch wide at the tips. The legs of the notch fit over the heel of the stempiece.

Only the headboard at the bow end is decorated (Fig. 29). An irregular horizontal bar, 3/4 to 1-1/16 inch wide, is painted across the base of the head, just above and adjacent to the two inwale notches. The bar, painted a slightly brownish red color, is outlined along its full length on both the top and bottom edges by a very thin black line. An identical black line also runs horizontally across the headboard exactly at the base of the two inwale notches. These three black lines, all about 1/64 inch wide, are so narrow and consistent in width that it is clear that they were drawn with a pencil, rather than painted.

No such lines occur on the stern headboard. Thus, their occurrence on the headboard at the bow may imply simply a decorative function. But the lines quite probably indicated the positions of the top and bottom surfaces of the inwales, and thus the location of the notches that were to be cut to receive the inwales. The red bar with its black outlines on the headboard at the bow indicated to the paddlers which end of the canoe was the bow end.

The headboard is firmly attached to the stempiece in four areas: the root lashings in the neck area of the headboard, the end of the stempiece through the hole below the neck, the two braces beside the upper body, and a single nail driven horizontally through the headboard 2-3/4 inches above its base. The head of the machine-cut nail is 3/16 by 5/16 inch (see the nail information summary on page 53).

When the headboard, the stempiece, and the two horizontal braces were combined into a solid end frame unit before insertion into the canoe, the outboard ends of the two braces were also lashed together, using the same commercial string that was used to spirally wrap the laminated area of the stempiece and the ends of the inwales (Fig. 28). The five adjacent and overlapping wraps squeeze the tips of the braces tightly against the stempiece.

The same type of string was used to lightly attach the batten strip to the outboard edge of the stempiece: two adjacent wraps are visible in one area, just below the horizontal braces (Fig. 28). This was done in preparation for lashing the cutwater edges at each end of the canoe.

Cutwater Edges

A carved wooden batten runs the full length of 63-1/2 inches of the lashed cutwater edge, from chin to outwales. The batten fits between the edges of the two panels of bark which form the end of the canoe, to cover and protect the outboard edge of the stempiece (Fig. 30). In some areas, the outer face of the batten is flush with the edges of the two bark panels; in other areas it projects outward from the bark edges up to 3/16 inch.

The batten is 7/16 to 5/8 inch wide and 3/16 to 1/4 inch thick, with square edges and a slightly domed surface facing the exterior. It is made up of two separate pieces: one, 27 inches long, extends from the outwale over the curve and down to the lower end of the unpitched root stitches; the other extends from this point down 36 inches to the chin. The lower piece lies in the area of the cutwater edge which is covered by pitched fabric.

At the bow end, the batten is attached to the canoe by only root stitches. At the stern, in addition to the stitches, a single machine-cut nail was driven vertically through the batten strip and into the stempiece. The nail was installed near the top of the end panel, at a point 8-1/2 inches outboard from the tip of the outwales. The head of the nail is 3/16 by 5/16 inch (see the nail information summary on page 53).

To accommodate the stitching of the cutwater edge, a zigzag row of holes runs around the upper portion of the perimeter (Fig. 22). Beginning at the outwales, the holes extend for 27 inches around the curve. The holes are spaced at intervals ranging from 1/8 to 5/8 inch, but most are from 1/4 to 5/16 inch apart. The holes alternate in short and long distances from the outer surface of the batten: the near ones are 1/2 to 3/4 inch from the edge of the batten, while the far ones lie 1 to 1-1/4 inches from the edge.

The holes, produced by an awl with a triangular or square cross section, are 3/16 to 1/4 inch in diameter. They were all pierced from the same side of the canoe. On the entry side, the pierce and twist of the awl produced an irregular but generally round hole, with no flaring of the bark edges around the perimeter of the hole. On the opposite side of the canoe, the holes are generally diamond shaped, with the edges of the bark flaring outward.

The stitching was done with a single strand of root. It begins at the outwales with a single harness stitch, in which both ends of the root pass in opposite directions through the same hole. Thereafter, the two ends of the single root form cross stitches, in shoelace style, around the edge of the curved end for 27 inches. Wherever the length of root was depleted, the ends of the root were simply inserted into the awl holes after the new root had been pulled through and started. The span of cross stitching ends as it began, with a single harness stitch. This upper 27 inches of stitches is not covered with pitch.

On the lower 36 inch distance of the cutwater edge, extending down to the chin, the stitching holes lie in a straight row, 3/4 to 7/8 inch from the outer edge of the batten (Fig. 30). The holes, 3/16 to 1/4 inch in diameter, are placed at intervals of 5/8 to 1-1/2 inches. A single split root was used to make the simple in-and-out stitches.

In all sewing of the cutwater edge, whether crossstitch or in-and-out style, the stitches pass directly through the stempiece inside the end of the canoe, rather than around it. The root lashings run through awl holes through the stempiece. (The stempiece can be glimpsed through certain awl holes in the bark which are not completely filled by the thin replacement lashings.)

The lower portion of the cutwater edge, the area sewed with in-and-out stitches, is sealed with a strip of pitched fabric similar to that used to seal the bark panels. Glued over the cutwater edge with blackened pitch, the strip applied to the bow end of the canoe is 4-1/2 to 5-1/2 inches wide. It extends around the edge and onto the sides of the canoe for 1-1/2 to 2-1/4 inches. The total length is composed of two strips placed endto-end, one 15 inches long and the other 24 inches.

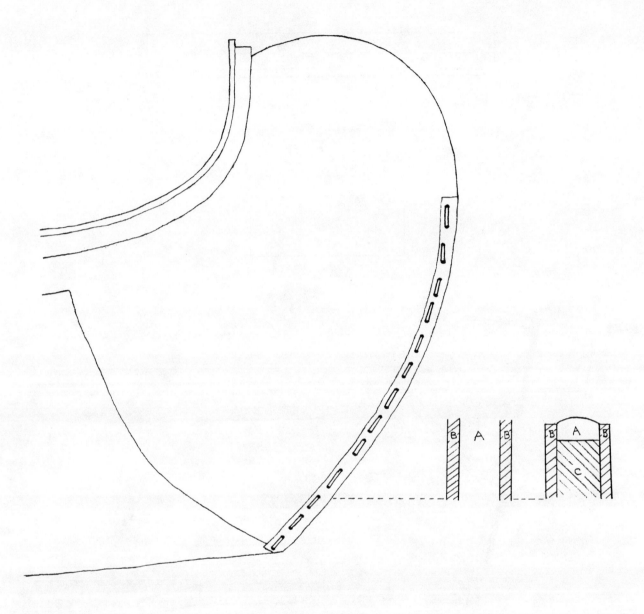

Fig. 30. Royal Canoe: Cutwater edge, with a narrow strip of pitched fabric applied over the stitches at the stern end. A. batten, B. bark wall panels, C. stempiece.

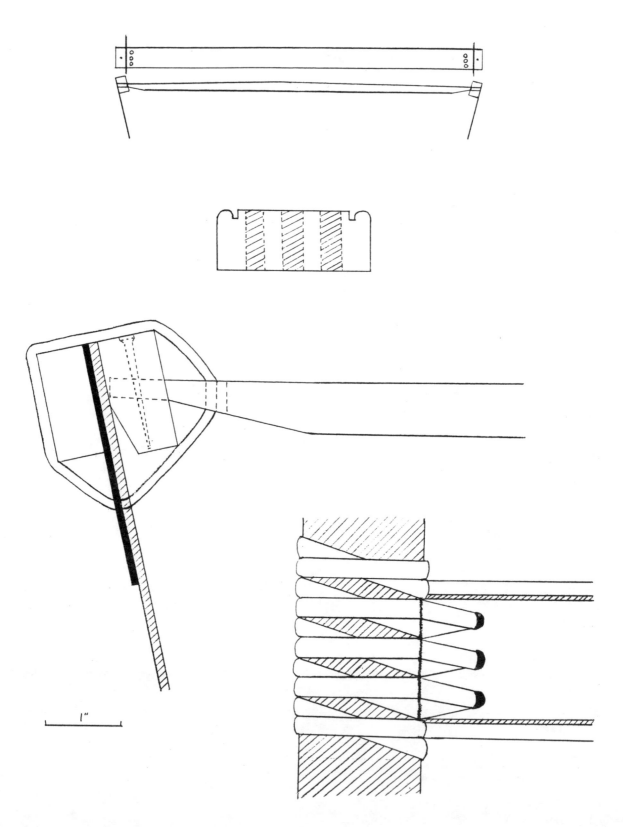

1"

Fig. 31. Royal Canoe: Thwarts.

The lower strip extends 3 inches past the chin onto the bottom of the canoe.

At the stern end, the fabric strip is much narrower, 2-1/2 to 3 inches wide; it extends onto the sides of the canoe for 7/8 to 1-1/8 inches. It is made up of three end-to-end strips, which are 13, 18, and 5 inches long. They extend down the curve of the cutwater edge, and stop at the chin.

The outer surface of the glued fabric strip is completely covered with blackened pitch, which extends past the edges of the fabric onto the bark walls for 1/4 to 1/2 inch. The edges of the pitched area are broadly curved, following the contours of the edges of the fabric strips and the cutwater edge.

The pitched portion of the lower and middle area of the cutwater edge at the bow end spans 39 inches. It begins 3 inches inboard of the chin, on the bottom of the chin, and rises to a position 14 inches below the highest point of the end. At the stern, the total length of the pitched area is 36 inches. The pitch begins at the chin, rather than inboard of the chin, and runs up to the same height as at the bow.

The upper portion of the cutwater edge, the area lashed with cross-stitches, is not sealed with pitch. This allowed unobstructed drainage of water out of the canoe when it was overturned on its side on shore.

The total thickness of the cutwater edge is 3/8 to 5/8 inch in the lower pitched area (the area of the waterline), and 3/4 to 7/8 inch thick in the unpitched cross-stitched area. This thickness includes the stempiece with its batten, the two bark panels, and the stitches, as well as the pitched cloth sealant in the lower area. The lower portion of the edge, even though it is covered by a layer of pitched fabric, is narrower than the upper portion. This is because the in-and-out root stitches of the lower area do not wrap around the cutwater edge and add thickness to it, as do the cross stitches in the upper area.

Thwarts

The thwarts are sawn or split from eastern larch (tamarack). The nine thwarts (creating an eight-place canoe) are spaced symmetrically, with the center thwart lying exactly at the midpoint of the canoe (Fig. 8). The distances between the thwarts are measured from centerline to centerline.

The positions of the thwarts seem to imply a canoe shape that tapers symmetrically at both ends. Yet this point deserves closer scrutiny. Four pairs of thwarts flank the center thwart. In three out of the four pairs (pairs A, C, and D), the thwart toward the bow is 1/4, 3/4, or 1 inch longer than its sternward counterpart.

Center: Thwart #1: 63 inches
Pair A: Thwart #2: 58-1/4 inches
         Thwart #3: 59-1/4 inches
Pair B: Thwart #4: 48 inches
         Thwart #5: 48 inches
Pair C: Thwart #6: 32-1/2 inches
         Thwart #7: 32-3/4 inches
Pair D: Thwart #8: 12 inches
         Thwart #9: 12-3/4 inches

The lengths, measured along the longest edge, do not include the hidden portion at each end which fits into the mortise hole in each inwale. The actual length of each thwart is about 1-1/2 inches longer than each of these measurements, since the additional portion at each end, which extends completely through the inwale, is roughly 3/4 inch long.

In comparing the endmost pair, the bow thwart is 3/4 inch longer than its sternward counterpart; in the next pair inboard, the bow thwart is 1/4 inch longer. In the pair nearest to the center, the thwart toward the bow is a full inch longer. These small differences may be simply variances due to measurement by eye rather than by measuring devices. But the exactness of the spacings between the thwarts indicates that some form of measuring device was used, possibly cords knotted at certain lengths or sticks notched or cut off at prescribed lengths.

Thus, there is a possibility that the builders intentionally made the thwarts slightly longer in the bow half, creating a canoe that is slightly wider in the beam toward the bow than the stern. Such a trait was commonly built into the fur trade canoes that were constructed in the latter nineteenth century at the canoe-building posts of the upper Ottawa River in western Quebec.[19] It is also a trait of the surviving Ojibwa and Varden canoes, and possibly the Catlin one as well.

Such a feature, quite widespread in traditional Indian canoe construction, may have contributed to greater efficiency of forward movement of the canoe.

Walter J. Hoffman, in his detailed 1896 study of the Menominee Indians, recorded their tendency to traditionally make the bow end of their birchbark and dugout canoes wider and more suddenly tapered than the stern end: "The bow and the stern, though apparently similarly, are still sufficiently unlike for the Indian to note which is the bow, for that end of the canoe, as in the dugout, is usually a little broader across the shoulders." In discussing their dugout canoe manufacture, he states, "The outside is chipped down...in order to make the stern narrower, and thus to give the canoe almost the shape of a cigar."[20] In addition, Johann Kohl, who lived with and studied the Ojibwas of Wisconsin and Michigan in 1855, noted, "The canoe has really a bow and stern, although the ends at first glance appear precisely similar. All canoes are slightly broader in front, although this is not so perceptible as in the body of the fish, which the Indians evidently selected as their model."[21] Thus, the slightly longer lengths of most of the thwarts in the forward half of the Royal canoe, although not noticeable to the eye, may have been intentionally made thus by the builders.

The following description applies to each of the nine thwarts (Fig. 31). The width remains constant at 2 to 2-1/8 inches over the entire length of the thwart. At the center, the thickness is 3/4 to 15/16 inch. This dimension tapers very gradually over nearly the entire span toward each inwale, by the removal of wood from the upper surface. At a point 1-1/2 to 2-1/2 inches inboard from each inwale, the thickness has tapered to 5/8 inch. The underside remains level and straight over this entire distance.* Over the remaining span of 1-1/2 to 2 1/2 inches, to the juncture with the inwales, each end of the thwart angles upward on the underside. At the point where the thwart meets the inwale, the thickness has tapered to 1/4 inch. The dimensions of 1/4 inch in thickness by 2 to 2-1/8 inches in width appear to remain constant as the end of the thwart projects through the 3/4 inch thickness of each inwale.

All four sides of the thwart are planed smooth, except in the area of the sudden underside taper at each end; here the undersurface is carved (to fit the mortise holes), with no planing. The upper two edges are planed round, with extremely even and smooth surfaces. The lower two edges are sharp.

Along the full length of both upper edges, a groove has been cut with a molding plane, 3/16 inch from each edge. This groove, 1/16 inch wide by 3/32 inch deep, has its outside edge rounded and its inside edge square. The planing has created a 3/16 inch wide bead with rounded edges, which runs along the full length of both upper edges of every thwart.

All of the thwarts match this description (varying only in length). One minor difference occurs in the relative position of thwarts # 8 and #9 (the end most pair). All of the other thwarts are positioned so that their upper and lower surfaces lie in level, horizontal planes. The endmost thwarts are positioned in the gunwales at the point where the gunwales curve upward toward the ends of the canoe. Thus, the planes of the top and bottom surfaces of these two endmost thwarts are also angled upward, with the outboard edge higher than the inboard edge.

At the point where each thwart (except the endmost ones) meets the inwale, a horizontal mortise hole is chiseled through the midline of the inwale, to receive the end of the thwart. Each hole is 2-1/8 inches long by 5/16 inch wide, with sharp edges and corners. The outboard surface of the inwale is not visible, so it is impossible to observe whether the mortise hole runs completely through the inwale; but such was commonly the case. The hole is cut at a slight angle, with its inboard end lower than its outboard end. This compensates for the slight outward angle of the inwale, since it angles outward in conjunction with the upper walls of the canoe. The angle of the hole permits the straight horizontal end of the thwart to fit into the hole in the angled inwale.

At the ends of the outermost pair of end thwarts, no mortise holes are cut through the inwales to receive the ends of the thwart. Instead, the tapered ends are forced into the central one of the three lamination kerfs in the inwales. In all other respects, the treatment of these end thwarts is identical to that of the other thwarts.

The end of each thwart is held firmly in the inwale by a single vertical nail driven downward from the upper surface of the inwale through the thwart. The machine-cut nail has a rectangular head 1/8 by 3/16 inch (see the nail information summary on page 53). The shank of the nail does not protrude through the lower surface of the inwale.

Each end of the thwart is lashed with split root to the

combined inwale and outwale. The lashings run through three vertical holes in the end of the thwart, 1/2 to 5/8 inch inboard from the inwale. The two outer holes lie 5/16 to 3/8 inch from the sides of the thwart. The round holes, irregular in shape and 1/4 to 5/16 inch in diameter, were carved with an awl or a knife. The upper edges of the holes are sharp.

Below the junction of the thwart and the gunwales, there are six awl holes in the bark wall. These lashing holes, spanning 2-1/2 to 3-1/2 inches, extend 3/16 to 3/4 inch beyond the outer edges of the thwart (Fig. 16). All of the previous information describing the lashing of the gunwale elements also applies to the lashing of the thwarts. Of the ten turns of root, two of them lie beside each edge of the thwart and two turns pass through each of the three holes in the thwart. The thwarts were lashed at the same time as the gunwales. Thus, their lashings fit into and are connected to the series of lashing groups along the length of the gunwales.

During the years of usage of the canoe, considerable wear and breakage occurred to both of the underside edges of thwarts #1, #2, #3, #4, #5, and #7; these include all of the thwarts except the endmost thwart at the bow and the endmost two thwarts at the stern. The description of the painted decoration on the thwarts is found on page 52.

* Some of the thwarts now bow upward slightly toward the middle. This appears to be due to sagging and warpage resulting from many decades of storage of the canoe in an upside down position.

Sheathing

Before the sheathing strips were laid in, a thick piece of birchbark was positioned on the floor of the canoe at each end, adjacent to (but not under) the heel of the stempiece (Fig. 16). This bark piece, rectangular with broadly rounded corners, measures about 8-1/2 to 9 inches long by about 8 inches wide. It distributes over a wide area the downward pressure of the ends of the sheathing strips which lie in the midline area of the floor, and prevents them from puncturing the bark cover when bearing heavy loads.

The sheathing strips or splints, split from northern white cedar, are 5 to 7 feet long, 3 to 5 inches wide, and 1/8 to 1/4 inch thick. On the flat faces, areas of undulating raised grain patterns indicate that the strips were split out rather than sawn. Each splint has generally parallel edges for most of its length; the endmost 4 to 6 inch span at each end is carved so that the edges gradually taper into a shape that is rounded, bluntly pointed, or sharply pointed (Fig. 32). Only the inboard edge and the tapered ends of the strips show evidence of thinning; these feathered edges and ends are carved down to 1/16 to 3/32 inch.

The pattern of overlapping ends indicates that the splints were laid into the canoe in five groups: first at each end, then two more groups inboard of the end groups, and finally, a central group in the midsection area. The two end groups, laid into the narrowest areas of the canoe, are each made up of 16 to 18 strips. The broader areas of the canoe, filled by the other three groups, required up to 26 to 28 splints. After each end group of splints had been laid in, the following three groups of splints were positioned so that they overlapped the ends of the previously-laid groups for about 2 to 6 inches.

In laying in the sheathing, the first strips were positioned along the midline of the canoe. These strips were not extended under the heel of the stempiece. Succeeding rows of sheathing splints were then added, out to and up the walls. Thus, the overlapping edge of each successive splint faces downward or inward, toward the midline of the canoe. The overlapping edge extends 1/2 to 1 inch over the previous strip.

The tips of the endmost splints extend 6 to 8 inches outboard of the headboard, to a point about 10 to 12 inches from the outer curved area of the stempiece. At the ends of the craft, additional short sheathing strips were inserted outboard of the headboard for stiffening and support. Many of these lie in very steeply angled positions, nearly vertical; they extend out to or near to the outboard edge of the stempiece. In Figure 33, one nearly horizontal strip is visible in the right wall, running inboard from the headboard to the second rib. No other material, such as wood shavings or moss, was stuffed into the ends to support the bark cover.

The successive rows of sheathing were laid up the walls to a point 1-1/4 to 1-1/2 inches below the lower edge of the inwale; this is about 1/2 to 3/4 inch below the gunwale lashing holes in the bark walls. Toward each end of the canoe, a gradually widening expanse of the upper bark wall is left exposed, not covered by the straight horizontal strips of sheathing, where the gunwales curve up-

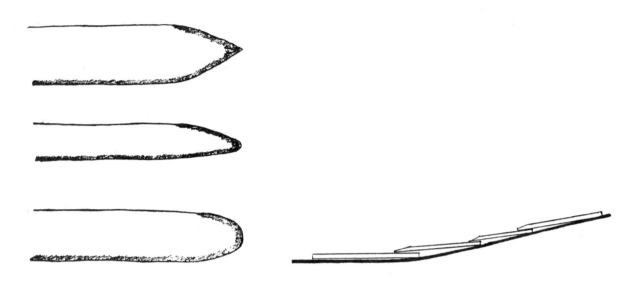

Fig. 32. Royal Canoe: Sheathing strips.

Fig. 33. Royal Canoe: Bow end, showing sheathing, ribs, headboard, and end thwart.

Fig. 34. Royal Canoe: Profile of ribs and thwarts.

Fig. 35. Royal Canoe: Curvature of ribs.

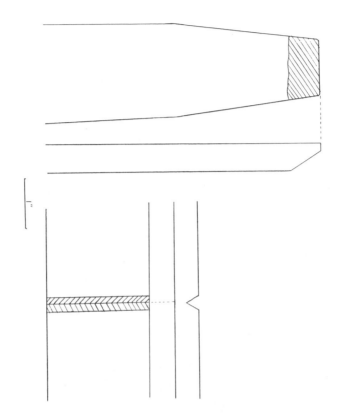

Fig. 36 (left). Royal Canoe: Ribs, with endmost ones grooved at midpoint for sharp V bend.
Fig. 37 (right). Royal Canoe: Bend of the endmost ribs.

ward (Fig. 33). These wider areas of exposed upper wall extend for about 6 to 8 inches inboard of the headboards. Beside the headboards, the area of each wall which is not covered by the sheathing splints ranges from 5-1/2 to 8 inches in height.

In 1971, the N.M.M. conservators temporarily removed the ribs and sheathing from the canoe, to record the underlying construction features. Before removing them, the staff carefully noted and the positions of the sheathing and ribs; thus, their present locations reflect the original positions in which they were installed by the builders.

Ribs

The canoe was build with a total of 78 ribs of northern white cedar (39 pairs). Throughout the length of the canoe, they are spaced at intervals of 1-1/4 to 1-7/8 inches, measured edge to edge. All but the end ribs curve upward in a very broad, gradual curve from the midline of the canoe (Fig. 34). There is no flat horizontal area in the midsection of the floor; the profile of the ribs in the floor and lower walls is entirely rounded in all areas of the canoe except at the sharp narrow ends. The curve of the ribs reflects the rounded body plan of this fast express canoe (Fig. 35).

The midsection ribs in the area of the central thwart are 86-1/2 to 87 inches long. This includes the length of about 3/8 to 5/8 inch at each tip which is hidden from view where it is inserted behind the inwale (Fig.19). The width of these ribs is 2-1/4 to 2-1/2 in the area of the floor of the canoe. They taper very slightly and gradually as they extend upward, to a width of 1-3/4 to 2 inches at a point which is 2-1/2 to 3-1/2 inches from the tips (Fig. 36). The thickness remains in the range of 1/2 to 5/8 inch over this distance. Over the uppermost 2-1/2 to 3-1/2 inches of each tip, the width tapers quite suddenly, down to 1 to 1-1/4 inches at the squared-off tip. The flat inboard surface at the end of the tip is carved in a sudden taper over the uppermost 1/2 to 3/4 inch into a chisel shape. The thickness at the tip is reduced to about 1/8 inch.

The ribs nearer to the ends, other than being shorter, are similar in dimensions to the long midsection ribs. Although they are identical in thickness, they are slightly narrower in width. But the width tapers less, so that they are generally similar to the long central

ribs in the areas near the gunwales.

The endmost rib at each end, adjacent to the headboard, is 63 to 63-1/2 inches long, including the length of 3/8 to 5/8 inch at each tip which is inserted behind the inwale. The width in the floor area is 2-1/8 to 2-3/8 inches. This width tapers very slightly and gradually as the rib extends upward, reducing by only about 1/8 to 1/4 inch as it nears the tip. The thickness remains within the range of 1/2 to 5/8 inch over this distance. In the uppermost portion of 3-1/2 to 4-1/2 inches of each tip, the width tapers quite suddenly, to 3/4 to 1 inch at the squared-off tip. The flat inboard surface at the end of the tip is carved in a sudden taper over the uppermost 1/2 to 3/4 inch into a chisel shape, reducing the thickness to 1/16 to 1/8 inch at the tip.

The flat inboard faces of all of the ribs show in some areas the characteristic raised grain pattern which was created when the ribs were split out. However, they were later carved flat and smooth on much of their flat inboard surfaces and the edges. All of the edges of the ribs were originally sharp. In most areas of the ribs, except in their uppermost tip areas, the exposed edges were worn slightly rounded during the usage of the canoe. In the floor areas, these exposed edges are worn quite round, and are splintered and dented in some areas.

The sharp V-shaped profile of the endmost five or six ribs at each end of the canoe involves an extremely sharp bend at the midpoint (Fig. 33). This rib shape reflects the sharp hull form inboard of the headboards of this fast canoe. To achieve the sharp bend without breaking completely through the rib, a V-shaped groove was cut across the width of the inboard face of the rib at its midpoint (Fig. 36). This groove, 1/8 to 1/4 inch deep and about 1/4 inch wide across its top, allowed the rib to be bent sharply at its midpoint. Some of the wood beneath the cutout groove cracked, but it did not break entirely through. The end rib adjacent to the headboard requires such a sharp V profile that its tops are nearly vertically upright, with the two tips only 6-1/2 inches from each other. Of the five or six endmost ribs that required the sharp V bend (Fig. 37), the more inboard their position, the less sharp was the required midpoint bend. Thus, the inboard two or three of these ribs required only a deeply scored line with an awl across the face at the midpoint to facilitate the bend, rather than the cutting of a deep, wide groove.

In the midsection of the canoe, the ribs stand perpendicular to the horizontal plane of the keel line (Fig. 3). Beginning at about thwarts #4 and #5 and extending to the bow and stern headboards, the keel line rises gradually as the rocker of the bottom curves upward. In these rising areas, each rib was installed at a slight angle to the gradually rising keel line. In this manner, the tops of the ribs remain vertically upright, even where the keel line of the canoe curves upward toward each chin. (If each rib had been installed perpendicular to the keel line, each rib toward the ends of the craft would stand at an angle, with its base outboard of its tips.) The headboard does stand slightly angled, following the curve of the rising floor. Thus, its base lies 2 inches outboard of its head. The headboard angles outboard at its base while the ribs stand vertically upright. Due to these differences, the distance between the endmost rib (near its tips) and the upper area of the headboard is 2-1/2 inches, while the distance between the base of this rib and the base of the headboard measures 4-1/2 inches.

On the tip area of most of the ribs, an X about 1 inch tall was scratched with an awl, just below the inwale along both walls of the canoe. These marks appear to have been applied to the ribs by the builders during manufacture. They may have been applied during a fitting stage of the ribs, to indicate the general length to which they were to be cut.[22]

Painted Decoration

The horizontal stripe or bar of brownish red paint on the head of the bow headboard has already been discussed. The same red color covers the gunwale caps and the guard strips (Fig. C-1). On each of these gunwale elements, all three exposed surfaces are painted. In addition, all of the thwarts are painted greenish blue on the upper face and both sides. The underside of each thwart is unpainted.

On the exterior of the bark cover, a long white stripe lies adjacent to the lower surface of the outwale (Fig. 21). This stripe, 2-3/4 to 3 inches wide, runs nearly the full length of the canoe, connecting the large white painted panels at each end. The stripe covers the reinforcement bark strip below the outwale as well as a narrow area of the wall panel below this bark strip.

Immediately beneath the white stripe lies a painted greenish blue stripe, 2-3/4 to 3-1/4 inches wide. This stripe also extends to the white panels at the bow and the stern. Near its bow end, a curved projection, 7 inches long, extends downward from the stripe. This projection ends in a sharp point. The horizontal portion of the greenish blue stripe ends at the outboard edge of the endmost thwart at the bow, 30 inches from the outermost edge of the cutwater at that horizontal level.

At the stern, the large white panel area covers the entire end of the canoe (Fig. 30). Its inboard edge extends in an arc upward and inboard from the chin to the white stripe below the outwale. It joins the white stripe at a point 2 inches inboard of the endmost thwart at the stern, 33 inches inboard from the outermost curve of the cutwater edge at that horizontal level. The outboard edge of the white panel extends to the edge of the pitch-covered fabric on the lower cutwater edge, and to the row of stitching holes which runs around the remaining perimeter of the end of the canoe. No further decoration was applied to the white panel on either wall at the stern end.

At the bow, the white painted panel is somewhat larger. Like the stern panel, its inboard edge also arcs upward from the chin; but it extends rearward in a horizontal extension which ends in an upward-curved ball finial. The finial runs inboard to a point 42 inches from the outermost curve of the cutwater edge at that horizontal level. The white finial is bordered on its outboard side by the curved projection which extends downward from the greenish blue stripe.

Although the large white panel is identical on both walls of the bow, each of these panels has a different design painted over the white background. The design element on the left wall panel is 12-1/2 inches in diameter, composed of two concentric circles surrounding a ball (Fig. 21). The outer circle is a brownish red stripe 2-1/4 to 2-1/2 inches wide (the same color as the painted wooden elements). Inside this circle, an area 2-1/4 to 2-1/2 inches wide is in the white background paint. In the center lies a round ball, 4 inches in diameter. It is painted a medium green color (not the greenish blue of the horizontal stripe or the thwarts). The entire design is positioned 5 inches below the upper edge of the cutwater and 3-1/2 inches inboard from the forward edge.

The design on the right wall panel of the bow (Fig. 22) is positioned 3-1/2 inches below the upper edge of the cutwater and 2-1/2 inches inboard from the forward edge. The design element is a pinwheel, 11-1/2 to 12 inches in diameter, painted in the same medium green color found on the opposite wall design. The five long slender arms are each in the form of a triangle, with the apex of each one pointing in a clockwise direction. The arms extend 5-1/2 to 5-7/8 inches from the center of the pinwheel.

All of the painted areas on the canoe which appear in the 1971 photos are extremely faded (Figs 2 and 24). Considering the great degree of the fading, there is little likelihood that the original pigments had ever been repainted. Each of the original painted areas except the red bar across the bow headboard were repainted during the 1971 restoration.

Nails

All of the nails used in the manufacture of the Royal Canoe are of the machine-cut type, in the style which was available from the 1830s on.[23] Two sizes, medium and small, were utilized (Fig. 38).

Medium size

The head is 5/16 inch long by 3/16 to 7/32 inch wide, with slightly convex sides and ends and sharp corners. The head, 1/16 inch thick, has a flat surface.

The shank is 2 to 2-1/2 inches long. It is rectangular in cross section, with a thickness of 3/32 inch for nearly its full length. Its width tapers from 3/16 inch just be-

the stempiece at the stern end (one nail); and probably the gunwale caps.

Small size

The head is 3/16 to 7/32 inch long by 1/8 to 5/32 inch wide. Its sides are straight, the ends are straight or slightly convex, and the corners are sharp. The head, 1/16 inch thick, has a flat surface.

The shank is 1-3/8 to 1-3/4 inches long. It is rectangular in cross section, with a thickness of 1/16 inch for nearly its full length. Its width tapers from about 1/8 inch below the head to 3/64 to 1/16 inch at the truncated tip. The sharp-cornered truncated tip is 1/16 inch by 3/64 to 1/16 inch.

This size was used to nail the ends of the thwarts into the inwale mortise holes; the horizontal braces to the headboard and the stempiece at both the bow and the stern; and probably the guard strips.

On some examples of both sizes of nails, the edges of the heads are somewhat irregular and the heads have a slightly domed appearance. These features are apparently due to inconsistency in manufacture, damage and distortion caused during the pounding of the nails, and later deterioration of the edge surfaces.

The modern style of wire nail, with its round head and a shank with a round cross section, appeared in widespread use by about 1879. It overtook the cut nail,

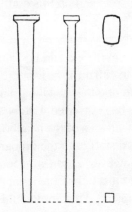
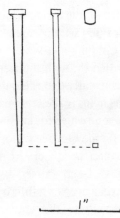

Fig. 38. Royal Canoe: Machine-cut nails.

low the head to 3/32 inch at the truncated tip. The sharp-cornered truncated tip is 3/32 inch square.

This size was used to nail the combined unit of inwale-bark wall-outwale; the cutwater batten strip at the stern end (one nail); the base of the headboard to

due to its relatively cheaper price, although some cut nails continued to be produced.[24] No examples of this modern type of nail were utilized in the manufacture or repair of the Royal canoe.

Wood Types

The types of wood used to build the Royal canoe are typical of those used for canoe construction. The stempieces, headboards, sheathing, and ribs are made of northern white cedar. The gunwale elements of the inwale and the outwale (and probably the original gunwale caps and guard strips as well) are fashioned from spruce. As discussed previously, the type of spruce most typically used in canoe construction is black spruce. The thwarts are made of eastern larch (tamarack).[25]

The lashings are fashioned of the roots of either spruce or eastern larch (tamarack). As previously discussed, if they are of spruce, the most typical type for canoe lashings would be black spruce.

The wood types that were chosen for the construction of the Royal canoe match exactly those which were used at the canoe-building posts of the upper Ottawa River region in the latter nineteenth century, as reported by the builders at those posts.[26] According to the craftsmen, when white cedar became scarce near the posts, whipsawn spruce was used instead for certain parts of the canoes. The thwarts were normally fashioned of spruce or tamarack, the latter being preferred by Christopherson at his posts. The other elements of the canoes were made of white cedar.

Miscellaneous Features
Seats

There is no evidence on the canoe which would indicate that it was ever fitted with permanent or temporary wooden seats. Canoe seats were typically flat boards with holes drilled through their ends. Adjustable suspension cords usually encircled the gunwales and passed through the holes in the seat boards.[27] Holes in the walls below the gunwales for such seat suspension cords are found on the Quebec canoe.

No areas of wear can be observed on the gunwales that would have been caused by such seat cords. Nor are any wear areas visible on the upper portions of the ribs, where the ends of the seat boards would have bumped and abraded, whether the boards were suspended by cords from the gunwales or were wedged temporarily between the upper arms of the ribs. Likewise, no evidence of seat mounting blocks is found on the ribs. No seats were installed in the canoe which appears to have been a

virtual mate of the Royal canoe, as indicated by photos of the craft taken in 1907.

Provision for Sail and Cordelling Line

No evidence can be observed which would indicate the lashing of either a mast or a cordelling (towing) line to the forward thwarts. The hardness of the eastern larch (tamarack) wood would have probably prevented any denting or abrasion from these lashings; such evidence is sometimes found on thwarts made of the softer wood of northern white cedar.

The canoe is not equipped with a permanent perforated thwart or mast step for sailing. Thus, if a sail were sometimes used, the upright mast would have been temporarily lashed to the second or third thwart at the bow end. Or a temporary perforated thwart may have been lashed to either of these thwarts, with the mast then positioned in its hole.

The base of the mast may have been placed into a drilled or carved indentation in a loose board laid down the midline, to step the mast. Sometimes merely a moccasin, a frying pan, or some other object was positioned beneath the base of a mast to protect the canoe.[28] These temporary measures of mast attachment and stepping would leave no permanent evidence that a sail had been used on the canoe. Thus, the lack of such evidence on the Royal canoe does not rule out the use of sail on this craft.

Flags

No evidence can be found for the attachment of a flag at either the bow or the stern. No space exists outboard of either headboard into which a flag staff could have been inserted. Likewise, there is no space around the head area of the headboard to permit the lashing of such a staff onto the inboard surface.

However, a light cord could have encircled the headboard just below the level of the projecting end of the stempiece. This cord could have bound a flag staff to the inboard surface of the headboard.

Bow/Stern Differences

The builders of the Royal canoe created a number of differences between the bow and the stern ends of the craft, which are listed below. Some of these features were installed for efficient performance of the canoe.

Others were added to indicate which end of the craft was the bow, to best utilize the efficiency features. Some of the differences may be only coincidental, or may reflect the difficulties of working to close tolerances in rather primitive conditions.

A. The bow end reaches a maximum height of 47 inches, compared to 46-1/4 inches at the stern. The rocker of the bottom rises to a point 2-1/4 inches above the horizontal baseline at the bow chin, compared to 2 inches at the stern chin.

B. The pitched fabric sealant strip that was applied to the cutwater edge is both longer and wider at the bow than at the stern, for greater protection of the bow edge. At the bow, the 39 inch strip begins 3 inches inboard of the chin, on the bottom of the canoe, while at the stern the 36 inch strip begins directly at the chin. At the bow, the sealant fabric extends onto the side walls beside the cutwater edge for 1-1/2 to 2-1/4 inches. The strip at the stern extends only 7/8 to 1-1/8 inches onto the side walls. Thus, the cutwater edge at the bow is protected by the pitched fabric further inboard on both the bottom and the walls than its counterpart at the stern.

C. The overall thickness of the fabric-covered lower cutwater edge is greater at the bow than at the stern. This may have been intentionally done at the time of manufacture, or it may simply be the result of a greater number of reapplications of pitch at the bow due to more frequent damage at that end.

D. The thwarts of the bow half may have been intentionally made slightly longer than their mates in the stern half. This would create a slightly broader beam at the gunwale level in the forward area of the craft, for greater efficiency of forward travel.

E. All of the overlapping edges of the various bark panels are lapped so that the edge that is exposed on the exterior side faces sternward. This increased the efficiency and reduced the likelihood of catching on obstructions.

F. Before any painted decoration was applied to the canoe, the builders had already signified the bow end on the right wall by the sawtooth pattern cut into the edge of the bark strips extending outboard from the outwale at the bow.

G. The painted decorations at the bow end are more elaborate than those at the stern. The greenish blue stripe has an additional downward projection near its bow end, while the white bow panel has an added rear-ward extension and finial. Also, a pattern of concentric circles and a pinwheel are painted over the white panels on the bow end panels, while the panels at the stern are plain white expanses.

H. A brownish red bar is painted across the head of the headboard at the bow end. At the stern, the headboard is undecorated.

Usage and Wear

The physical evidence indicates that the canoe saw considerable usage in North America before it became the property of the Royal Family. The bark cover has many scrapes and gouges, as well as a patched and sewn repair which was applied during the period of usage. In addition, nearly all of the ribs show a considerable degree of worn roundness on their exposed edges. Finally, all of the thwarts except the endmost thwart at the bow and the endmost two at the stern show a considerable amount of worn roundness and breakage on their underside edges. This wear would have been caused by repeated loading and unloading of packs, wooden chests and cases, etc. beneath the thwarts.

Construction Tools, Methods, and Materials

The Royal canoe was manufactured from the traditional forest materials of birchbark, wood, tree roots, and pine or spruce gum mixed with animal fat and pulverized charcoal. It was painted afterward with Euroamerican commercial paints.

The builders of the canoe used the typical array of tools normally employed in canoe manufacture during the nineteenth century. These include an axe, knife, crooked knife, drawknife, awl, rib-setting mallet, pitch melting and applying implements, and paint containers and brushes.

In addition, they utilized a number of tools and techniques that have generally been considered less traditional in the canoe construction of that era. A saw (rather than a knife) was used to cut the sides of the notches in the headboards, as well as to cut the lamination slits in the upward curved ends of the gunwale elements (which were traditionally split). A smoothing plane (instead of a knife, crooked knife, or drawknife) smoothed the flat surfaces of all of the gunwale elements, headboards, and thwarts. A molding plane cut the long bead running along each upper edge of the thwarts. A chisel (rather than a knife or a crooked knife) appears to have been used to remove the wood from the sawn notches in the headboards, to carve the mortise holes in the inwales, and to cut out the hole in each headboard which holds the end of the stempiece. (In each of these cutouts, no carving marks extend beyond the corners of the cutout area, as would usually occur if they were made with a knife rather than a chisel. However, a rasp or file may have been used to cleanly trim these areas rather than a knife.)

Commercial string was substituted for the traditional strips of basswood or cedar inner bark or split roots for the spiral wrapping of the laminations of the bent stempieces and inwales and for the binding of the stempiece braces. Traditionally, thin strips of birchbark were often glued with pitch onto the interior side of all of the seams in the bark cover, as a sealant, as well as onto the exterior of the lower cutwater edges.[29] Strips of fabric replaced the traditional bark strips at these locations, as well as on all of the other gummed seams below the waterline.

One of the most visually obvious departures from traditional canoe construction involves the substitution of iron nails for carved wooden pegs, driven with an iron hammer. Nails fasten the gunwale elements together; they also hold the ends of the thwarts into the inwale mortise holes, as well as fastening the ends of the braces to the headboard and stempiece units. Two nails appears to have been installed to tighten loose elements, rather than as actual steps of construction. These include the single nail which holds the cutwater edge batten strip to the stempiece at the stern, and the one which fastens the base of the stern headboard to its stempiece. These two nails did not replace any usual attachments that had formerly been held by wooden pegs (although the very base of the headboard was occasionally pegged to the stempiece[30]). The use of nails in birchbark canoe construction became quite widespread in the early nineteenth century, being used in many areas of North America before 1850.[31]

The final feature of the Royal canoe which has not been considered traditional is its pair of outwale guard strips. These have not been formerly reported on fur trade canoes. As has been previously discussed, the strips on the Royal canoe are considered to be definitely original to the construction of the craft. An apparently identical set of guard strips can be observed on another fur trade canoe, the virtual mate to the Royal canoe, which was photographed in 1907 while being paddled and portaged by voyageurs on the upper Ottawa River. These two canoes match each other so closely that it is suspected that they are related: they may have been constructed at the same canoe-building post, or in separate locations by builders who had been trained in an identical style. The canoes of this model, fitted with gunwale guard strips, may be possibly considered a latter development in the evolution of fur trade canoes, or they may represent an upper Ottawa Valley local variant, possibly from a single post or builder.

Many of the above "nontraditional" features of the Royal canoe represent practical, labor-saving substitutions and improvements; these elements probably produced a canoe with equal or better performance qualities, with less labor and in less time. Since these traits have been observed on a surviving example of a fur trade canoe, they may in fact reflect standard manufacturing techniques used to build such canoes in the mid-to-latter nineteenth century, rather than "nontraditional" variations.

Condition

The bark cover and the wooden elements of the canoe are in sound, stable condition. But the bark cover has at least two areas of modern breakage which have not been sealed with tar. One is a break in the left wall at the bow end, beside the cutwater edge in the white painted area. Another is a round hole two inches in diameter through the bottom near the stern.

The original root lashings remain intact in all of the original bark panel seams and slits, as well as in the original damage repair. Apparently original paint still decorates the bow headboard. Much of the original sealant pitch (with its fabric strips) remains, although it is covered in some areas with tar from the 1971 restoration. The 1971 replacement gunwale caps, guard strips, gunwale lashings, cutwater edge stitches, and paint are in excellent condition.

Numerous procedures were carried out on the Royal canoe during its many years of display before 1971. Thus, the following resultant features do not apply to the original construction or usage of the canoe.

A. Three or four round holes were drilled at intervals

completely through the midline of the floor, extending through the bark cover, the sheathing, and the ribs. The canoe was apparently at one time bolted to a display pedestal through these holes; or it may have been suspended from bolts.

B. A number of wood screws were driven downward into the inboard faces of several ribs in the floor area in scattered locations. These screws presumably fastened the wide board which once ran down the midline of the floor from headboard to headboard. (The plank appears in one of the 1971 photos.) It may have been associated with the midline holes and bolts, as a stabilizer.

C. A wide stripe of dark black stain with straight, even sides extends down the midline of the bottom, from chin to chin. Sand or grit adheres to the staining substance. This may also relate to a former display pedestal beneath the midline of the canoe.

D. A number of ribs have been cracked in the lower wall areas. No areas of damage in the bark cover relate to the locations of these broken ribs. Thus, the cracks presumably occurred during handling or storage of the canoe in England, rather than during its earlier period of usage. Some of the broken ribs have been left untreated, while a few have been repaired with glue.

One cracked rib, in the middle of the right wall just forward of the center thwart, was repaired with a sheet metal patch. The small rectangular patch, 1 5/8 by 4 inches, was nailed onto the inboard face of the rib with eight wire nails. These nails had shanks with a round cross section 3/32 inch in diameter. The patch has since been removed, leaving a dark stain (which indicates the dimensions of the former patch) and a series of round nail holes.

E. At the ends of every thwart except the endmost one at the bow and the stern, one or two modern wood screws were inserted at a downward angle through the thwart and into the mortise hole area of the inwale. The screws, with 5/16 inch diameter heads, were installed to tighten the ends of the thwarts in their mortise holes.

F. Various wood screw holes are found in the upper surfaces of a number of the thwarts. Canoe paddles were at one time screwed to the tops of the thwarts for display.

G. Wood screws with 1/8 inch diameter shanks were inserted horizontally at some point into the inboard surface of both of the headboards. One screw was in-

stalled into the head area of the stern headboard, while three were inserted into the neck area of the bow one. Their function is not known. They may have fastened a wooden or sheet metal plate to each headboard, possibly as an informational plaque.

Notes: Royal Canoe

1. Adney and Chapelle, p. 141.
2. Ibid., pp.143, 134.
3. Ibid., pp. 28-29,102,149.
4. Ibid., pp. 134,138.
5. Ibid., p. 146.
6. Santucci, p. 11; Hume, pp. 253-54.
7. Christensen, personal communication of December 5, 1994.
8. Adney and Chapelle, pp. 15-16.
9. Ibid., pp. 138, 141, 147.
10. Adney and Chapelle, pp. 17, 25.
11. James, p. 92.
12. Christensen, op. cit. October 14, 1994.
13. Adney and Chapelle, pp. 17, 19.
14. Ibid., pp. 124-25.
15. Ibid., pp. 63, 64, 66.
16. Ibid., pp. 124-25, 131.
17. Ibid., pp. 44-45.
18. Ibid., p. 140.
19. Ibid., p. 147-48.
20. Hoffman, pp. 292-294.
21. Kohl, p. 35.
22. Ritzenthaler, pp. 33-34, 38; Gidmark, p. 54.
23. Santucci, p. 11; Hume, pp. 253-54.
24. Ibid.
25. Christensen, op. cit. October 14 and 26, 1994.
26. Adney and Chapelle, pp. 148, 150.
27. Ibid., pp. 135, 137.
28. Sha-Ka-Nash, pp. 6-7.
29. Adney and Chapelle, pp. 50, 53.
30. Ibid., p. 150.
31. Ibid., p. 56.

The Ojibwa Canoe

Contents

Ojibwa Canoe

Several features of the Ojibwa canoe suggest that it is an Ojibwa/Cree style of voyaging canoe, the Type B-2 style. These traits include the extended height and breadth of the ends in relation to the height of the walls in the midsection, the considerable degree of undercut in the profile of the ends, and the form of the interior curvature of the stempieces. The canoe was built in the moderately large, six-place (seven-thwart) format, in the size category of either a North canoe or a half-size canoe.

Overall Dimensions

Length: 23' 7".

Distance between the outboard sides of the tips of the outwales: 20' 3-1/2" (Fig. 40).

Distance between the inboard faces of the heads of the headboards: 19' 9-1/4".

Depth at the midpoint, from the top of the gunwale caps to the top of the ribs on the floor: 18-3/4".

Height above the baseline: at the midpoint 19-3/4". Due to many years of storage and display of the canoe in an upright position without support of the ends, each end has sagged an estimated two inches. The bow is presently 42-1/2" high (projected original height ca. 44-1/2"); the stern is presently 40" high (projected original height ca. 42").

Beam at the midpoint: 3' 11" (Fig. 41).

Interior beam, inside the gunwales: 3' 7-1/2".

Total girth around the hull, from gunwale top to gunwale top: 5' 10".

Adney based the drawings and model of his Ojibwa fur trade canoe on a photo taken of such a canoe at Lake Temagami in eastern Ontario in about 1895.[1] (Lake Temagami lies about twenty miles west of the upper Ottawa River, north of Lake Nipissing.) In comparing the dimensions of the surviving 23' 7" Ojibwa canoe to Adney's shorter 20'10" version, the beam is identical in both craft. The existing canoe, built slightly narrow, has an interior beam which equals 15.37 percent of the overall length of the craft. The surviving Ojibwa canoe has slightly low walls in the midsection, 1-1/4 inches lower than those of the shorter Lake Temagami canoe. The projected original heights of its ends, 44-1/2 inches at the bow and 42 inches at the stern, are 6-1/2 and 4 inches higher than those on the canoe portrayed by Adney. Although the ends of the Ojibwa canoe are especially high compared to the Lake Temagami example, this height appears even greater in conjunction with the slightly low midsection walls. In addition, the outwales and gunwale caps on the Ojibwa canoe sweep upward at their ends to a nearly vertical position, in contrast to the considerably more angled position in Adney's representations. This further enhances the sense of extreme height of the ends. Five detailed drawings of fur trade canoes are presented in Adney and Chapelle. Of the various forms of prows which are depicted, the height of each end rises above its respective midsection height by an increase of 41 to 100 percent. The projected original heights of the prows of the Ojibwa canoe rise above the height of the slightly low midsection walls by 110 percent at the stern and 125 percent at the bow. It must be noted that even the projected original height of 44-1/2 inches of the bow end is still 2-1/2 inches lower than the bow end of the larger Royal canoe.

The high ends of voyaging canoes have often been interpreted as serving to deflect high waves in larger bodies of water and when running rapids; in reality, their primary function was to provide ample head room when the canoe was overturned on its side on shore as an instant shelter. The height of the ends was not determined by the length of the canoe: it was guided by the tastes and traditions of the individual builders, as well as by the above-stated functions of the ends. Smaller fur trade canoes had generally higher ends in proportion to the canoe length than larger craft,[2] since the purpose of the ends for deflecting waves and providing head room remained the same whatever the size of the canoe. The ends of the Ojibwa canoe may appear to be very high on the moderately long (23' 7") canoe; but the identical ends would not seen proportionately high on a longer canoe.

The high prow form of this surviving Ojibwa canoe

Fig. 39. Ojibwa Canoe, with bow to left.

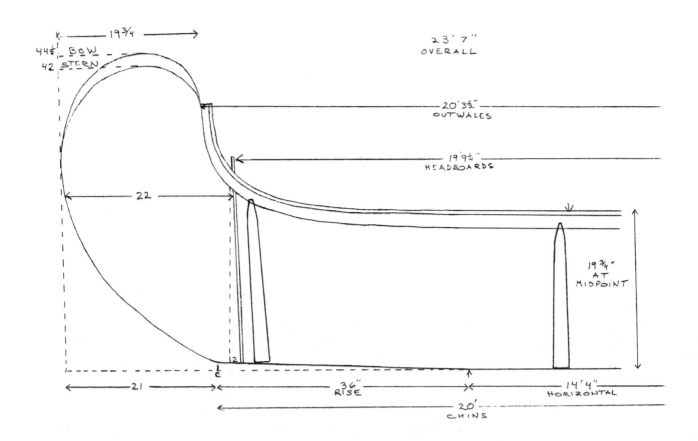

Fig. 40. Ojibwa Canoe: Hull profile and dimensions.

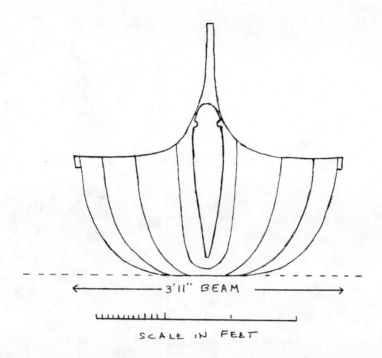

Fig. 41. Ojibwa Canoe: Body plan (freight canoe).

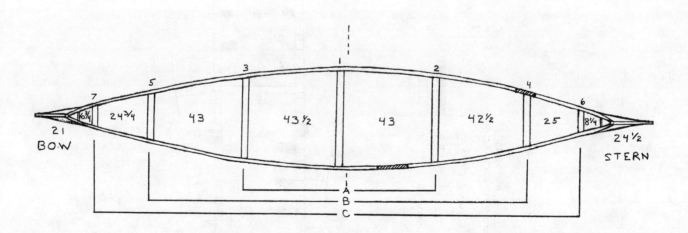

Fig. 42. Ojibwa Canoe: Hull form, thwart positions, and gunwale repair locations.

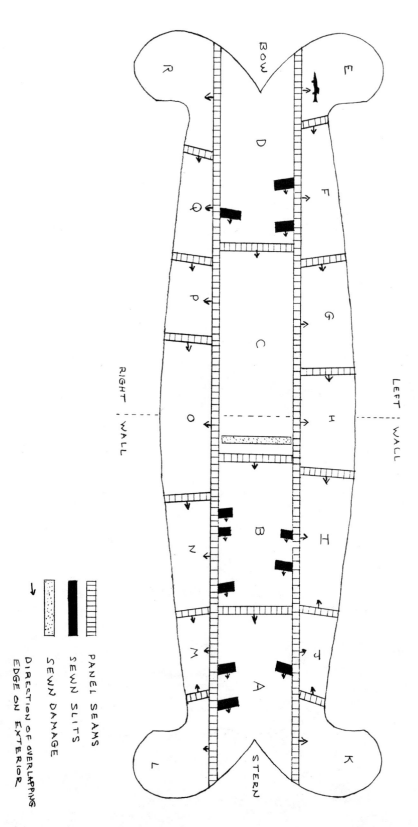

Fig. 43. Ojibwa Canoe: Bark cover.

- 62 -

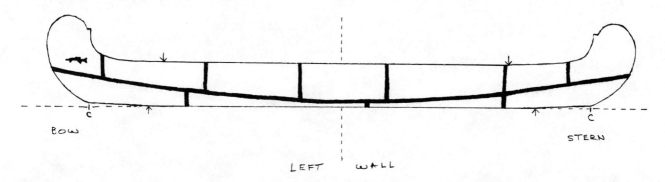

BOW   STERN

LEFT WALL

Fig. 44. Ojibwa Canoe: Bark panels.

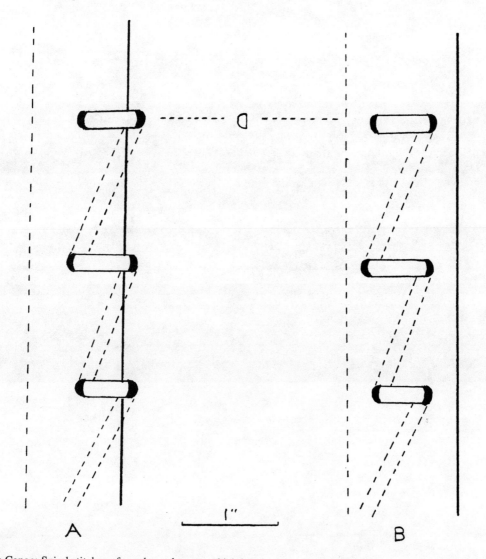

A   1"   B

Fig. 45. Ojibwa Canoe: Spiral stitches of overlapped seams which join bottom panels together and close gore slits (A) and which join side panels together (B).

– 63 –

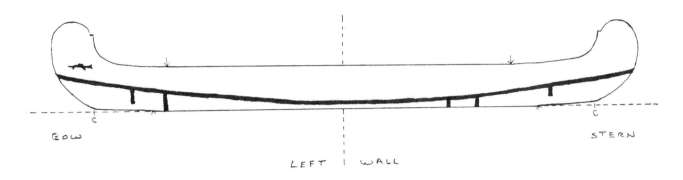

BOW   LEFT | WALL   STERN

Fig. 46. Ojibwa Canoe: Gore slits.

Fig. 47. Ojibwa Canoe: Harness stitches which join side panels to bottom panels.

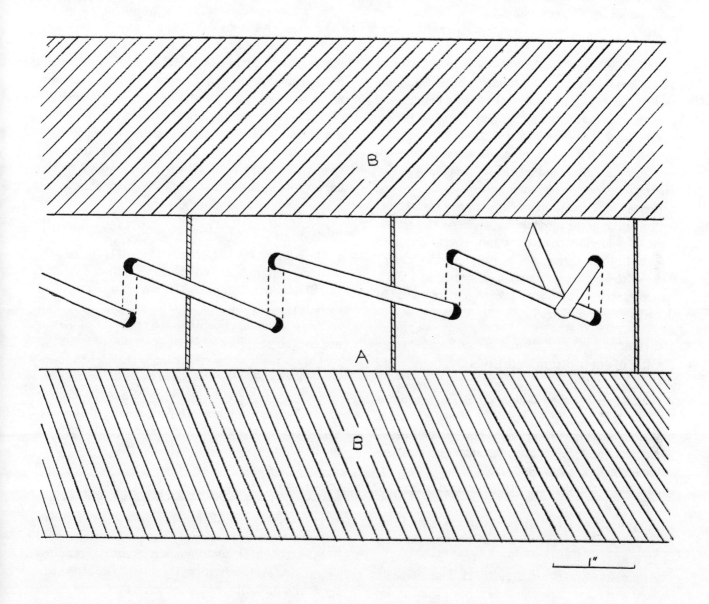

Fig. 48. Ojibwa Canoe: Interior view of bottom repair. A. sheathing strips, B. ribs.

may have been an unusual variation, out of the norm, the result of the judgement and taste of one particular builder or group of builders. On the other hand, it may have been one of the common forms of voyaging canoes: note the great similarity to the high end form of the Catlin Ojibwa model of the late 1830s. Far too few such canoes now survive to make a solid judgement.

In the rapids-running painting by Hopkins, the canoe has very high prows which extend well above the upswept gunwale tips. Hopkins' artworks are considered to be accurate and reliable portrayals of actual fur trade canoes. It has long been assumed that the extremely high end forms depicted by numerous other period artists of the fur trade era were gross exaggerations. Considering the high end forms of the surviving Ojibwa full size canoe and the Catlin Ojibwa model, some of these portrayals may have been only moderate exaggerations of the canoes that were observed by the artists.

Hull Form
Profile of the Bottom and Ends

The horizontal span of the bottom extends for 14 feet 4 inches, between a point about 36 inches inboard of the bow chin and a point about 32 inches inboard of the stern chin (Fig. 40). From the bow end of the horizontal section, a 36 inch span of moderate rocker (measured on the horizontal base line) gradually rises to a moderately rounded chin (to the point where the stitches of the cutwater edge begin). At the stern, a 32 inch span of moderate rocker gradually rises to the chin. The total length of the bottom between the chins is 20 feet.

As previously mentioned, each end of the canoe has sagged down over the years, due to inadequate support. Each chin presently lies only about 1/2 inch above the horizontal baseline. The chins of the Ojibwa canoe portrayed by Adney stand 2-1/2 inches above the baseline.[3] Thus, the amount of sagging of the surviving Ojibwa canoe is estimated to be about 2 inches, projecting the original rocker at the chins to have been about 2-1/2 inches in height.

From the chin, each end extends 21 inches outboard (measured on the baseline) to the outermost point of the end. The cutwater edge at each end curves upward from the moderately rounded chin, beginning three inches outboard of the foot of the headboard. At the bow, it extends upward and outward for 33 inches (measured on the curve) to the point of maximum length of the canoe, creating a considerably undercut profile. Then it curves upward and inboard over 24 inches to the highest point of the prow, and finally downward and inboard over a span of 12-1/2 inches to meet the outwales. At the stern prow (which stands 2-1/2 inches lower than the bow), the cutwater edge measures 34 inches, 21 inches, and 12-1/2 inches in its comparable spans. The total length of the edge, measured on the curve from chin to outwales, is 69-1/2 inches at the bow and 67-1/2 inches at the stern.

Body Plan

The bottom is flat and narrow (Fig. 41). The bilge is moderately rounded, while the upper walls are straight and flare outward slightly. The four cross sections in the end-view drawing illustrate the contours of the hull and its gradual taper between the midpoint of the canoe and the headboards. The four sections correspond roughly to the four thwart positions between the midpoint and the headboards (Fig. 42).

The widest area of the bottom appears to lie at about the midpoint of the length of the canoe. This width appears to taper gradually and symmetrically from the midpoint to each end of the canoe.

The Ojibwa canoe was built in a form designed for moderately fast paddling with ample cargo capacity. Its features, including a narrow flat bottom, moderately rounded bilge, slightly narrow beam, long slender taper to the ends, and very narrow U form inboard of the headboards, contributed to its ease of paddling yet provided generous room for cargo.[4] The canoe was built with the hull form of the standard freight canoe of the period, although the undercut area of the bilge extends well toward the midline, in the usual Ojibwa-Cree style.[5] The contours of the bilge areas of the full size Ojibwa canoe match those of the Adney-Chapelle drawing of an Ojibwa voyaging canoe, while the upper walls flare outward to a lesser degree than those portrayed by Adney and Chapelle.

The bottom of most voyaging canoes is slightly to moderately rounded. Only a narrow area along the midline of the bottom of the Ojibwa canoe is flat, with a corresponding flat area of 8 or 9 inches in the center of the midsection ribs. The slightly rounded form of the adjacent areas of the bottom and the ribs suggests that the original form of the entire bottom and ribs may have been slightly rounded. It is not possible to determine now whether the present narrow flat area which runs along the midline of the bottom and the midsection ribs may be warpage that was caused by long-term storage of the canoe in an upright position on a flat surface. This premise is supported by the considerable sag of each end of the craft, which is attributed to many years of such upright-position storage.

On the other hand, Adney did fashion a model of an Ojibwa 18 foot hybrid freight canoe from Lake Temagami in eastern Ontario which had a flat bottom. This craft, which he observed in 1925, is described and drawn on pages 124-25 of Adney and Chapelle. Although this craft, with its abruptly cutoff ends and narrow plank stempieces, appears to have been built in a late hybrid style based on canvas canoes, it does provide an example of an Ojibwa freight craft with a truly flat bottom.

Bark Cover

The diagram of the bark cover (Fig. 43) portrays the canoe as if it had been placed in an upside down position and flattened by unsewing the end seams. The drawing is not to exact scale or proportion, and the locations and dimensions of the seams are approximate. All of the seams and the repair have been widened for ease of identification.

Color and Thickness

Most of the panels of bark are light golden tan in color. But at least two panels, side panels G and H in the midsection of the left wall, are reddish brown "winter bark." After more than a century of fading, it is not possible to determine now whether some of the other panels may have originally also been reddish brown. The thickness of the bark ranges from 3/32 to 1/8 inch, in both the bottom panels and the wall panels. (The thickness profile is visible in several locations.)

Panels

On the diagram, the seams joining the eighteen panels of bark are marked with crosshatching. The arrows indicate the direction of the exposed overlapping edges on the exterior of the canoe.

Exact measurements of the individual panels cannot be taken, since the pitch covering the seams in many cases hides from view the exact positions of the edges of the panels. Only the portions of bark visible on the exterior of the canoe were measured, making no allowance for hidden overlaps. The measurement of the height of the side panels runs to the top of the outwale, where the bark was cut off flush with the top of the outwale. Each side panel was measured at its widest point.

Bottom Panels
A. 68 inches long x 32 inches wide
B. 61" L   x   32" W
C. 80" L   x   32" W
D. 77" L   x   32" W

Left Wall Panels (including the two high end panels)
E. 27" L   x   28" W
F. 53" L   x   14" W
G. 43" L   x   19" W
H. 36" L   x   19" W
I. 55" L   x   18" W
J. 34" L   x   14" W
K. 39" L   x   26" W

Right Wall Panels (including the two high end panels)
L. 40" L   x   26" W
M. 34" L   x   14" W
N. 43" L   x   18" W
O. 60" L   x   19" W
P. 31" L   x   18" W
Q. 35" L   x   14" W
R. 44" L   x   28" W

If the bark cover were flattened, as in the diagram, the maximum width in the midsection would be 5' 10" (the total girth of the bark of the canoe). The width near the ends measures 14 and 18 inches more. The length would be 23' 11" at the level of the gunwales. This total length of the side and end panels of each wall of the canoe is four inches longer than the length of the assembled canoe, because the side panels follow the curvature of the broadening midsection of the canoe, rather than a straight line down the midline.

The bottom of the canoe was made of four long panels of bark, while each wall was formed by joining two high end panels and five side panels (Fig. 44). In the profile drawing, the panels and seams are positioned exactly as they lie on the canoe.

The canoe builders apparently had no concern about creating weak points in the hull by positioning vertical wall seams directly opposite each other across the hull of the canoe. The seams which attach the side of the two high end panels at the stern (seams J-K and L-M) lie directly opposite each other. (Those attaching the high end panels at the bow are offset from each other by about seventeen inches.) The seams between panels F-G and P-Q as well as those between panels I-J and M-N likewise lie opposite each other. The vertical seams between side panels G-H and O-P are offset from each other by thirteen or fourteen inches, while those between side panels H-I and N-O are offset by eleven or twelve inches from each other.

The builders positioned most of the seams in the walls well distant from seams B-C and C-D in the bottom. No wall seams were placed closer than about seven or eight inches from these two bottom seams. However, the pair of wall seams I-J and M-N, which lie directly opposite each other at a point 73 inches forward of the stern, are directly aligned with the bottom seam A-B. If this alignment of two wall seams and a bottom seam created a weak point in the hull, it was apparently not a concern of the builders of the Ojibwa canoe.

Sewn Seams

The original lashing material still survives in all of the sewn seams. A minute sample of this original lashing root was analyzed microscopically. It has been identified as either spruce or eastern larch (tamarack). When analyzing only a sample of root material, without any accompanying trunkwood, it is impossible to differentiate between these two tree types.[6] If the roots were spruce, they would most likely be black spruce, which is the best and most common type of root for canoe construction.[7]

It is not possible to determine on any of the seams the amount of overlap of one side over the other, since no interior views are available. The only tucked-under ends of seam lashing roots which are visible for observation and description are those on the repair seam of the bottom, all of the others having been finished on the hidden interior side. No evidence suggests that a batten strip of wood or root was incorporated into any of the seams for added reinforcement, either on the exterior or the interior side of the bark cover.

Bottom Seams

The three seams connecting the four panels of the bottom to each other were the first seams that were sewed in building the canoe. They are overlapped so that the exposed edge on the exterior faces toward the stern. These seams are sewn with split roots in a series of widely spaced spiral stitches, with one stitch per hole (Fig. 45). The portion of each stitch on the exterior side of the canoe is horizontal, while the connector portion running to the next stitch on the interior of the canoe is diagonal. The stitches run through pairs of awl holes: on the overlapping side of the seam, one hole lies about 3/8 to 1/2 inch from the edge of the bark; on the opposite side of the seam, the other hole is immediately adjacent to the overlapping edge. The visible horizontal portions are about 1/2 to 5/8 inch long, and are spaced about 1-1/4 to 1-1/2 inches apart.

The lashing roots are 1/8 to 3/16 inch wide (about the same as the diameter of the awl holes) and about 3/32 inch thick, with a half-round cross section (Fig. 45). The rounded side, which was scraped somewhat flat, is the side of the root lashing which faces the exterior.

Gore Slits

After the four bottom panels were joined together, the long span of bottom bark was laid out on the building bed, and the building frame was placed upon it. As previously discussed, this frame determined the general outline of the bottom of the canoe, particularly the shape of the taper toward the ends. The building frame was about as long as the bottom of the canoe, from chin to chin. After the bark was bent upward around the perimeter of the frame, a number of gore slits were sliced at intervals along the sides of the bottom panels. These slices ran from the edges of the bark inboard nearly to the building frame. At each of these slits, one edge of the bark was made to overlap the other edge, with the exposed edge on the exterior facing toward the stern. (No slice of bark was removed to create a seam with butting edges). The overlapping edge was thinned considerably, so that the exposed edges of the gore slits are lower and less prominent than all of the other overlapping seams on the canoe, which were not thinned.

The slits are stitched closed with split roots in a series of widely spaced spiral stitches, in a manner identical to that which was used to connect the four bottom panels together (see above and Fig. 45). But in the gore slit seams, the stitches lie slightly closer together, at intervals of 1 to 1-1/4 inches.

The gore slits in the bottom panels are positioned at irregular intervals outboard of the midsection of the canoe and well inboard of the chins (Figs. 43 and 46). They are located on the profile drawing exactly as they lie on the canoe. Five slits are found in the left wall and six in the right wall. The majority lie in the stern half of the canoe. Only two of the slits in each wall have a mate located nearly exactly opposite (having been cut on the opposite side of the building frame). These two pairs occur in panels A and B. In traditional building methods, gore slits do not always appear in equal numbers on both sides of the canoe or always lie directly opposite one another.[8] Whether intentionally or not, the builders installed the gore slits in the bow half so that they begin much further from the midpoint of the canoe and extend slightly closer to the end of the canoe than the series in the stern half.

When the canoe is viewed in side profile, the gore slits extend downward from the longitudinal main seam, which runs the full length of each side of the canoe (Fig. 46) In the central, widest area of the canoe, this seam curves down close to the horizontal baseline of the canoe. Here, the gore slits are barely visible in a profile view; they extend down nearly to the flat bottom of the canoe in this area. Toward the ends of the canoe, where the main seam rises, the full length of the endmost gore slit at each end is visible, running down the curved bilge area of the lower walls and ending two to six inches above the bottom.

The length of each gore slit cannot be measured exactly, since each is covered by a coating of pitch. This pitch extends inboard toward the midline of the canoe beyond the end of each slit. Measurement can be made of the length of each pitch strip, which implies the general length of the gore slit which it covers. The pitch strips closest to the midsection are the shortest; they measure five to six inches in length. The strips become gradually longer toward the ends of the canoe: the endmost ones are eight to nine inches long.

Bottom panel B contains the pair of opposing gore slits which lies closest to the midpoint of the canoe. The length of each of these pitch strips is five inches, creating a span of 22 inches between the inboard tips of the two strips. The pair of opposing gore slits closer to the stern end, in panel A, has slits seven inches long; the span between their tips measures 18 inches.

Since the gore slits were sliced from opposite edges of the bottom bark panels inboard nearly to the building frame, the spans between the opposing pairs of slits across the bottom of the canoe ought to reflect the shape and dimensions of the building frame. As previously mentioned, the strip of pitch sealing each gore slit extends further inboard than the actual end of the gore slit itself. Thus, the span measured between the tips of a pair of opposing pitch strips is shorter than the actual span between the tips of the slits, and likewise shorter than the span across the building frame. Also, the pitch was not applied to the gore slits in a precise fashion. The gore slits are presented in the diagram according to the length of their pitch strips.

Some generalities may be deduced concerning the form of the building frame. It was presumably about 20 feet long, since that is the length of the bottom (the distance between the chins). No gore slits were cut in the entire midsection of the canoe. Thus, the area of maximum width of the building frame at its midpoint may have approximated nearly all of the 32 inch width of the bottom panels. The maximum width of the building frame that was used to construct slightly rounded and nearly flat-bottomed fur trade canoes was often two-thirds of the interior beam of the gunwales.[9] In the case of the Ojibwa canoe, this ratio would produce a measurement of about 29 inches. The span between the pitched pair of strips nearest to the stern end measures 18 inches. This represents in a general manner the degree of taper from the wide midpoint of the building frame to its pointed ends.

Side Panels to Bottom Panels

After the gore slits were cut and stitched along the side edges of the bottom panels, the side panels were attached to the bottom panels. The seam connecting the side and bottom panels to each other is the prominent longitudinal seam which arcs across the full length of the canoe on each wall. When the side panels were attached to the bottom panels, a wider panel was installed at each end of both walls, to create the high upswept prows of the canoe.

The lower edges of the side panels are positioned inside the edges of the bottom bark panels. Thus, the edges of the bottom panels are exposed on the exterior of the canoe, facing upward toward the gunwales (Fig. 47). The seams are sewn with split roots in a harness stitch, with the two ends of a single root running in opposite directions through the same hole, one stitch per hole (Fig. 18). The end-to-end stitches, 7/8 to 1 inch long, are composed of the same 1/8 to 3/16 inch diameter awl holes and split roots described above for the bottom seams and gore slits. The horizontal row of stitches lies 3/8 to 1/2 inch below the exposed edge of the bottom bark panel.

Side Panels to Side Panels

The seams which join the side panels to each other are all overlapping seams. In each instance, the exposed edge which overlaps on the exterior faces toward the stern, with the following three exceptions. On each wall at the stern, the seam that joins the high end panel to its adjacent side panel overlaps toward the bow (seams J-K and L-M). This may have been done to facilitate the sewing procedure. The forward direction of these two overlaps is not critical, since these sternmost seams are the ones least likely to receive abrasion during use of the canoe.

The only other overlapping edge which faces toward the bow is found in the seam joining wall panels I and J, in the left wall well toward the stern. This seam lies six feet forward of the stern. There appears to be no logical explanation for this feature; it probably was an oversight of the builders during construction.

The root sewing which joins the side panels to each other is nearly the same as that used in the bottom panels and the gore slits: spiral stitches 1/2 to 5/8 inch long lie at intervals of 1-1/4 to 1-5/8 inches (Fig. 45). However, the placement of the stitches in relation to the overlapping edge of bark is unusual. The stitches do not pass over the edge; instead, they lie about 1/4 inch from the edge.

Seam Sealing

All of the seams in the canoe were coated with charcoal-blackened melted pitch or gum from spruce or pine trees, of the same description as the gum found on the Royal canoe. The remaining original pitch is now very brittle; it does not indent under thumb pressure.

A coating of gum was presumably applied to all of the seams on the interior side of the canoe, with the canoe in the upright position, a typical procedure. But no interior views between or beneath the sheathing strips are visible to verify this assumption.

With the canoe turned upside down, all of the seams were sealed on the exterior of the canoe. The position of the canoe is indicated by the runs of melted pitch, which extend toward the gunwales. The swaths of melted gum which cover the longitudinal main seams are 2 to 2-1/2 inches wide, while those sealing the bottom and wall panel seams are 2 to 2-1/4 inches in width. The pitched areas which cover the gore slits are narrower, 1 to 1-1/2 inches wide. The gum sealing the wall panel seams extends up to the lower edge of the reinforcement bark strip. After repeated reapplications during usage of the canoe, the pitch is up to 1/8 inch thick in some areas.

Exterior Hull Surface

The discussion concerning the disruptions in the smooth, even surface of the bark cover of the Royal canoe also applies to the Ojibwa canoe as well. Overlapping panel edges and applications of sealant pitch up to 1/8 inch thick have produced seams which stand out from the flat surface of the hull.

In addition, three wall panel seams overlap toward the bow. However, these overlapping edges which face forward all lie above the waterline; thus, they would not impede the forward flow of the canoe through the water.

Damage and Repairs

During the early period of usage of the canoe (while it apparently still belonged to the Ojibwas), a major crack occurred across the bark bottom. The damage is located about nine inches space of the midpoint of the canoe, just forward of the bottom seam B-C (Fig. 43). The crack was repaired with a series of root stitches spanning nearly the entire bottom of the canoe, covering a length of 27-1/2 inches.

The standard procedure for repairing major damage on a canoe normally began with the moving of a sufficient number of ribs and strips of sheathing to expose the interior side of the damaged bark shell for repair. (Such a procedure was followed in the repair of the Royal canoe.) On the Ojibwa canoe, the location of the damage in the midsection plus its extent across the entire bottom would have required the removal of the entire course of sheathing in the midsection, together with its series of ribs. The decision was made to sew the crack in the bottom through the bark and the sheathing, rather than to remove the ribs and sheathing strips and execute the repair on the interior side of the bark. The sheathing would function in this instance like an interior bark patch, stiffening the broken edges of bark. Sewing the bark bottom to the sheathing strips precluded the possibility of future movement or adjustment of the strips; but it also eliminated considerable labor in the repair procedure, which may have taken place en route, under circumstances in which time was limited. The author has documented a very similar example of a root-sewn repair, spiral-stitched through the bottom bark and the sheathing strips, on a full size Type A-1, four-place Ojibwa canoe which was collected in Wisconsin in 1893 for the Smithsonian Institution.

To repair the six-place Ojibwa canoe, pairs of irregular round holes about 3/16 inch in diameter were made with an awl from the exterior side of the bottom (the only side on which the crack in the bark was visible) (Fig. 48). The holes pass through the bark cover and the sheathing strips inside, in the space between two ribs. The pairs of holes are 5/8 to 3/4 inch apart center to center, and lie at intervals of 1-5/8 to 2 inches. Split roots about 3/16 inch wide and 3/32 inch thick, with a half-round cross section, form the series of widely spaced spiral stitches. The short longitudinal spans of the stitches lie on the bottom of the canoe, while the long diagonal connector spans are visible on the interior between the ribs, atop the sheathing strips. On the interior side, the loose ends of the lashing root return over the adjacent stitch and are then tucked underneath that stitch. The seam is sealed with a swath of melted blackened pitch across the bottom on the exterior of the canoe.

Since this area of major damage was repaired using the traditional methods of split root stitches and pitch sealant, it is believed that the repair was carried out by the Ojibwas while they still owned and used the canoe, before its acquisition by Jay Cooke.

Gunwale Elements

The wood which was used to fashion the inwales, outwales, and gunwale caps of this canoe has been microscopically identified from minute samples as northern white cedar.[10] All of the gunwale elements are angled slightly outward, at the same degree of outward flare as the top of the bark walls to which they are attached (Fig. 49).

Inwales

The total length of the inwale on the curve is 21 feet 7 inches. This is about 10 inches shorter than the outwale, since the ends of the inwale rise considerably less than the outwale (Fig. 59). In the midsection, the inwale strip is 1 inch wide across the top and 1-5/8 inches deep (Fig. 49). The bottom surface is only 5/8 to 3/4 inch across, since the lower outboard edge is planed off into a beveled surface 5/8 inch wide; this produces a space about 1/2 inch high into which the tips of the ribs fit. Beginning about 7 inches outboard of the third thwart from each end, the inwale tapers very gradually toward each end over a span of about 74 inches. At a point 1-1/2 inches from the tip of the inwale, the width (thickness) has tapered down to 1/2 inch and the depth has reduced to 1 inch. Over the final 1-1/2 inches, the width tapers suddenly to 1/4 inch at the tip, while the depth of 1 inch is maintained.

All surfaces of the inwale are planed flat and smooth. The outboard edges are sharp, while the two inboard edges have a single narrow bevel 1/8 to 3/16 inch wide carved on the edge. At the tips, the ends are cut off square.

The inwale runs nearly horizontally over much of the length of the canoe, and then rises very gradually toward the ends. About each end thwart, it begins to curve up moderately toward its ends. At the headboard, it has risen 3-3/4 inches above its height in the midsection. Just outboard of the headboard, the inwale diverges from the outwale; it extends about 5 inches further, while angling gradually upward (Fig 59). The tips of the inwales do not extend in the usual manner to the outboard portion of the stempiece. Instead, they end beside the inboard pair of vertical stempiece braces.

To facilitate the bending of the upward curve of the ends of the inwale, three splits were made in the ends, to produce four lamination layers. The slits extend inboard from the tip of the inwale for about 26 inches, to a point

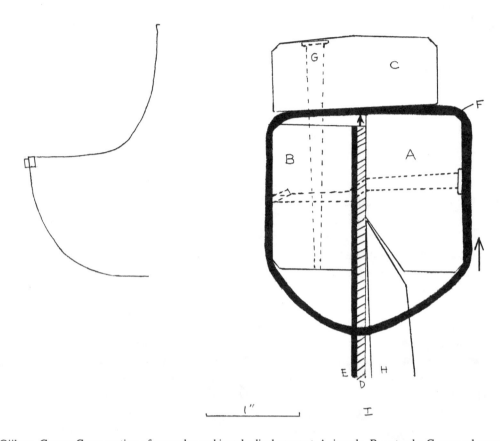

Fig. 49. Ojibwa Canoe: Cross section of gunwales and inwale displacement. A. inwale, B. outwale, C. gunwale cap, D. bark wall, E. reinforcement bark strip, F. root lashings, G. nails, H. rib, I. sheathing begins two inches lower.

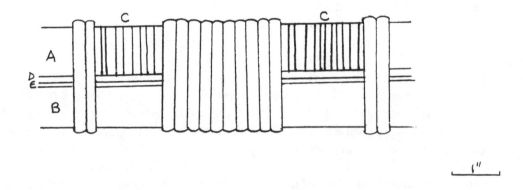

Fig. 50. Ojibwa Canoe: Top view of scored inwale, minus the gunwale cap. A. inwale, B. outwale, C. scored areas, D. bark wall, E. reinforcement bark strip.

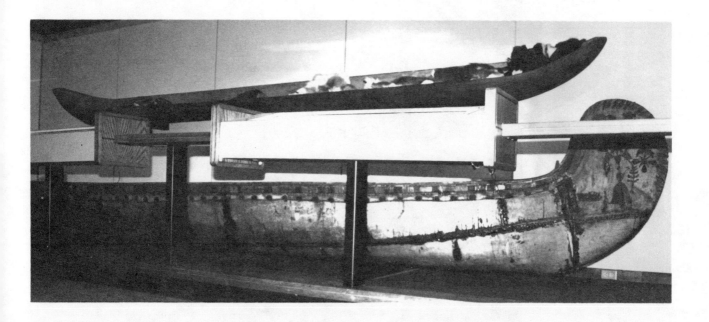

Fig. 51. Ojibwa Canoe: Stern portion of left wall.

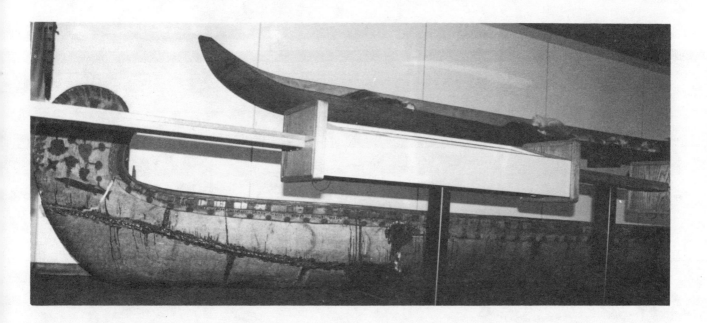

Fig. 52. Ojibwa Canoe: Bow portion of left wall.

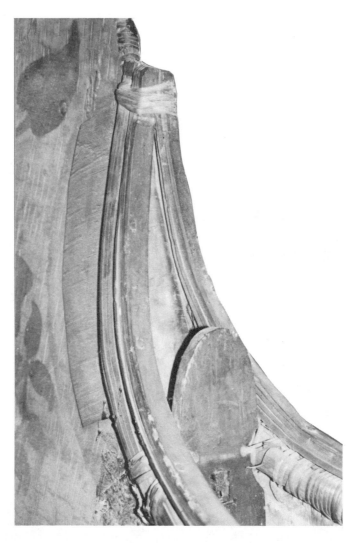

Fig. 53. Ojibwa Canoe: Gunwale ends, bark deck piece, and headboard at stern.

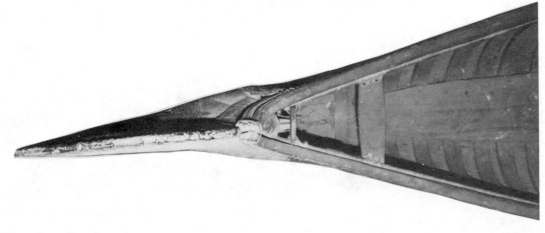

Fig. 55. Ojibwa Canoe: Top view of stern.

- 74 -

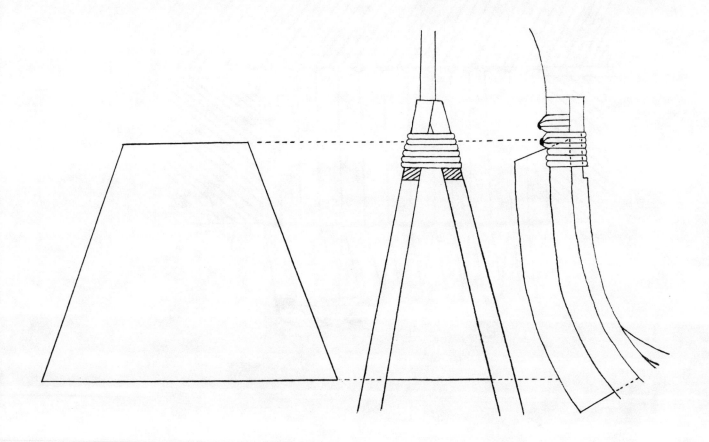

Fig. 54. Ojibwa Canoe: Gunwale ends and bark deck piece.

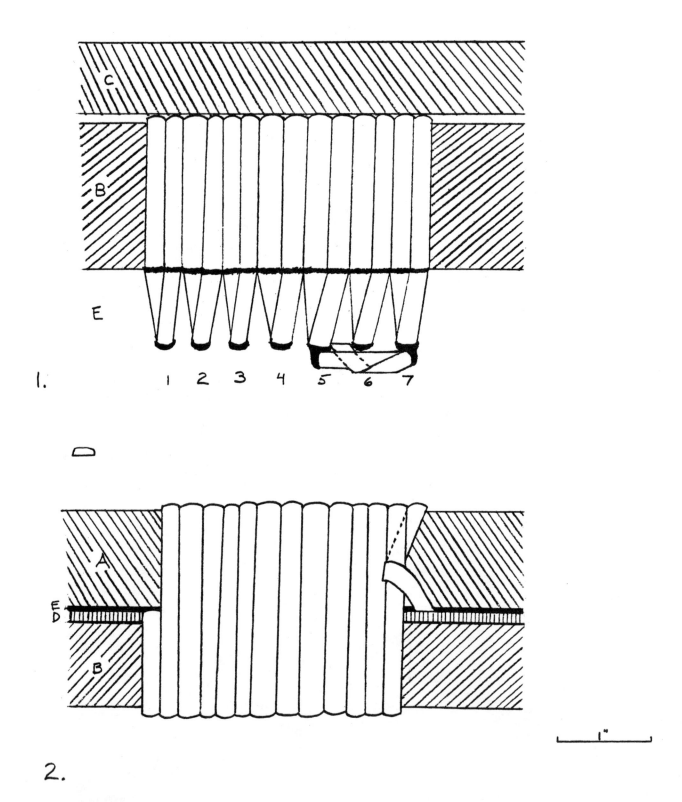

Fig. 56. Ojibwa Canoe: Side view of gunwale lashings from interior (upper), and top view minus gunwale cap (lower). A. inwale, B. outwale, C. gunwale cap, D. bark wall, E. reinforcement bark strip.

Fig. 57. Ojibwa Canoe: Gunwale lashings, with gunwale nail visible where lashings now missing.

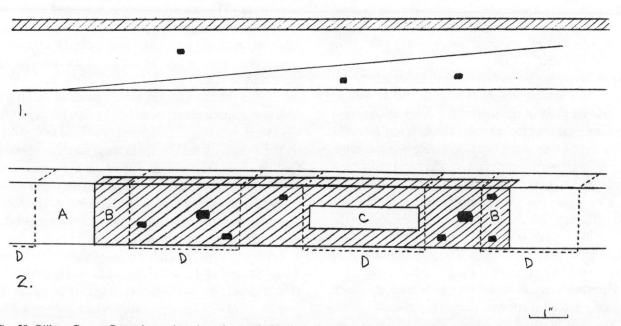

Fig. 58. Ojibwa Canoe: Gunwale repairs minus the root lashings. 1. Exterior view of outwale nailed repair. 2. Interior view of inwale wooden patch repair. Nails are not shown in exact original positions. A. inwale, B. wooden patch, C. mortise hole for thwart, D. locations of gunwale root lashings.

about 20 inches inboard of the headboard. The lamination layers, 3/32 to 3/16 inch thick near the tips, gradually widen as they extend inboard, up to 3/8 inch. The lashings which bind the inwale to the outwale cover the area where the three lamination slits ends. These lashings prevent the slits from splitting further inboard.

The inwale fits into a notch which is cut into the side of each headboard (Fig. 60). Two turns of split root bind the inwale to the headboard at the notch. The tips of the inwale are also firmly bound in place. At the juncture of the pair of converging inwale tips and the pair of vertical stempiece braces, two turns of heavy string wrap around the pair of inwales, squeezing them tightly against the braces. The commercial string, light brown in color, is 1/16 inch in diameter. Before the installation of the inwale onto the canoe, its laminated ends were bent upward and spirally bound with widely spaced wrappings of a single strand of the same commercial string. Remnants of the spiral wrappings are visible to a point just inboard of the end thwart.

The inwale is nailed to the outwale over nearly the entire distance in which the two strips run parallel. The row of nails ends about 11 to 12 inches inboard of the headboards. The endmost 9 to 10 inch span of nails lies in the portion of the gunwales which is laminated. The nailed inwale and outwale strips have sandwiched between them the top edge of the bark wall (cut off flush with the top surface of the outwale) and a strip of reinforcement bark (Fig. 49). Most of the nails were driven horizontally from the interior side of the inwale; the endmost four nails at each end as well as occasional nails in the midsection were driven from the exterior side of the outwale. The nails run generally down the midline of the two wooden elements, at intervals of 5-1/2 to 9 inches. The machine-cut nails have heads which are 9/32 to 5/16 inch long by 3/16 to 1/4 inch wide (see the nail information summary on page 108). The tips of the nail shanks protrude throughout the face of the outwale or inwale up to 1/8 to 3/16 inch; they are clinched over horizontally. The gunwale nails were later covered by the groups of gunwale lashings.

From headboard to headboard, the entire length of each inwale is scored at intervals on its top surface (Fig. 50). The prominent parallel scratches, about 1/16 inch wide and about 1/32 inch deep, were made with an awl or other sharp implement across the width of the inwale,

at intervals of 1/8 to 1/4 inch. The scored areas, 1-1/2 to 1-3/4 inches long, correspond to the spaces between the gunwale lashing groups. No comparable marks are found in the areas which were originally covered by the gunwale lashings (many of which are now exposed, due to broken and missing root wrappings) or on the outwale. The top of the inwale was probably scored before the gunwale lashings were installed, to indicate the intended locations of the root wrappings (between the scored areas).[11] The scoring may instead be a decorative element, added after the gunwale lashings had been applied but before the gunwale caps were installed. This is less likely to have been the original purpose of the scoring, however, since the marks are often hidden beneath the caps.

Outwales

The total length of the outwale on the curve is 22 feet 5 inches, measured on the outside of the curve. In the midsection, it is 7/8 inch wide across the top and 1-1/2 inches deep (Fig. 49). In both width and depth, the outwale is 1/8 inch less than the inwale. Over the entire span between the headboards, the outwale is positioned so that its top surface lies 1/8 to 1/4 inch below the top surface of the inwale. (Usually the two top surfaces are at the same level.) The bottom surface either matches that of the inwale or extends up to 1/8 inch below it. This unusual relationship of positions was caused by the constant upward pressure on the inwale by the ribs, forcing the inwale gradually upward in spite of the nails which attach it to the outwale. On some canoes in which the inwale was attached to the outwale by wooden pegs, this upward rib pressure caused the pegs to bend in the midsection.[12] Such a bend is noted in the gunwale pegs of the Quebec canoe. The midsections of the inwale-outwale nails in the Ojibwa canoe presumably have comparable bends, which are not visible on the exterior. The Sault canoe also exhibits very similar upward warpage of the inwales and bent inwale-outwale nails.

Beginning 10 to 12 inches inboard of the second thwart from each end of the canoe, the width and depth of the outwale taper very gradually over a span of 56 inches, to a width of 5/8 inch and a depth of 7/8 inch at the tips. The outwale begins this gradual end taper about 18 to 20 inches further outboard than its parallel inwale.

All surfaces of the outwale are planed flat and

smooth. The two inboard edges are sharp, while the two outboard edges have a narrow bevel 1/8 to 3/16 inch wide carved on the edge. At the tips, the ends are cut off square. The horizontal machine-cut nails which fasten the outwale to the inwale have already been discussed in the inwale information. The description of the painted decoration on the outwales is found on page 106.

The outwale runs nearly horizontally over much of the length of the canoe, and then rises very gradually toward the ends (Figs. 51 and 52). At about each end thwart, it begins to curve up moderately toward its ends. At the headboard, it has risen 3-3/4 inches above its height in the midsection (Fig. 59). Just outboard of the headboard, the outwale diverges from the inwale; it sweeps upward in a strong curve to reach a nearly vertical position at the tips. (The ends are slightly more angled than the virtually vertical outwale ends of the Royal canoe.) The ends of the outwale sweep outboard and upward beyond the headboards for 13 inches on the curve. From the headboard to the tip, the outwale rises about 10 inches in height. The tip reaches a point 6 inches below the maximum height of the prow of the canoe.

The length and degree of upward sweep of the tips of the outwales and gunwale caps outboard of the headboards are within the standard range as represented in surviving canoes and early photos, as well as in Adney's models. The fact that these elements on the Ojibwa canoe end so far below the top of the bark end panels is due to the unusual height of the panels. See the discussion of a similar example on the Catlin model. As has been previously mentioned, Hopkins depicted canoes which had comparable high prows, extending well above the tips of the outwales and caps.

At the bow end, the ends of the outwales and gunwale caps presently curve inboard well past the vertical position. This is presumably the result of warpage of the entire bow section caused by improper storage, since the corresponding gunwale elements at the stern end sweep upward only to the nearly vertical usual position.

To facilitate the bending of the upward curve and the extreme upsweep at the tips, the same lamination procedure was done as on the inwales: five slits were made, to produce six lamination layers (Fig. 51). The

lamination slits extend from the tips inboard for a distance of 26 to 28 inches, to a point about 12 to 15 inches inboard of the headboards. (This is about 5 to 8 inches outboard of the point at which the inwale lamination slits end.) The lamination layers, 1/8 to 3/16 inch thick near the tips, gradually thicken as they extend inboard, up to 1/4 inch. The lashings which bind the outwale to the inwale cover the area where the five lamination slits end. These lashings prevent the slits from splitting further inboard. The six lamination layers are cut off at the tip of the outwale to form a generally square, horizontal end.

The tips of the two converged outwales are joined to each other by a series of wrapped root lashings (Fig. 54). There is no wooden or bark wedge inserted between the tips of the two strips to assist in making the lashings tight. Nor are the tips pegged or nailed to each other. The split root lashings, beginning 5/8 inch below the tips, wrap in three adjacent spiral turns around the two joined outwales, covering a distance of 5/8 inch. The three wraps also run through one hole in the adjacent bark wall, passing through the stempiece inside the bark wall as well. The split root lashing material is 3/16 to 1/4 inch wide and 1/16 to 3/32 inch thick, with a half-round cross section. After being split, each side of the root was scraped somewhat flat.

Immediately below the root lashings which bind the tips of the outwales to the hull, the triangular area between the two converging outwales is covered by a bark deck (Figs. 53 and 54). The piece of bark, of the same thickness as the bark of the hull, is cut in a truncated pyramid shape. It extends downward for ten inches, to a point one inch from the headboard. Its ends extend over the edge of the bark walls so that they are visible below the outwales for 1-1/4 to 2 inches. Each end is cut in such a manner that it appears to be a continuation of the reinforcement strip of bark.

The bark deck appears to be held in place by only the pressure of the outwales, which squeeze the bark down against the bark end panels. No root stitches are visible that may have fastened the piece of bark.

Although the bark deck fills all but one inch of the gunwale area outboard of each headboard (Fig. 55), there is a possibility that a slender flagstaff could have been inserted adjacent to the outboard side of the headboard, beside the stempiece, at either the bow or the stern. Likewise, there is enough space between the head of the headboard and the gunwale caps for the wrapping of a cord around the headboard, to bind a flagstaff to the outboard or inboard face of the headboard, at both the bow and the stern.

Gunwale Caps

The total length of the gunwale cap is 22 feet 1 inch, measured on the top of the curve. (This is four inches shorter than the outwale, which was measured on the under side of the outwale.) In the midsection, the cap is 1-3/4 inches wide by 3/4 inch deep (thick) (Fig. 49). Beginning about 6 to 8 inches inboard of the second thwart from each end, the width and depth of the cap gradually taper over a distance of 53 inches, to a width of 5/8 inch and a depth of 5/8 inch at the tips.

All surfaces are flat and smooth. The top surface is smoothed in two bevels 3/4 to 1 inch wide (probably from a drawknife or a plane), with a very slight median ridge between the bevels. The lower two edges are sharp, while the upper two have a narrow bevel 1/8 to 3/16 inch wide carved on the edge. At the tips, the ends are cut off square. The interior side of one cap is tapered slightly in width over its endmost inch, so that it merges with the opposite cap (Fig. 54).

The combined width of the inwale (1 inch) and the outwale (7/8 inch) is 1/8 inch greater than the width of the gunwale cap (Fig. 49). In addition, the bark wall and the reinforcement bark strip which are sandwiched between the inwale and the outwale add about 1/8 to 5/32 inch more of thickness to the combined gunwales. Also, the degree to which the inwale and outwale were squeezed against the bark and each other when they were all nailed and lashed together varies in different areas. Thus, the gunwale cap is about 1/4 to 5/16 inch narrower than the top of the gunwale unit (inwale, bark layers, and outwale) in most areas of the midsection. Its width tapers much more quickly toward the ends than the combined gunwale unit. Since its outboard edge is aligned with the outboard edge of the outwale for its full length, the area of the inwale that is exposed gradually increases toward the ends. Near the headboards, up to 3/4 of the width of the inwale is exposed (Fig. 55).

The gunwale cap conforms to the curvature of the outwale for its entire length. Thus, it runs horizontally over much of the length of the canoe, and then rises very gradually toward the ends. At about each end thwart, it begins to curve up moderately toward its ends. At the headboard, it has risen 3-3/4 inches above its height in the midsection. Just outboard of the headboard, it sweeps upward in a strong curve to reach a nearly vertical position at the tips. The ends of the cap sweep outboard and upward beyond the headboards for 12 inches, ending exactly at the tips of the outwale. From the headboard to the tip, the cap rises about 10 inches in height. The tip reaches a point 6 inches below the maximum height of the prow of the canoe. Since the nearly vertical tips of the outwales and caps end 6 inches below the tops of the end panels, the high bark ends would rest on the ground rather than on the gunwale tips when the canoe was overturned on its side as a shelter.

To facilitate the bending of the upward curve and the extreme upsweep of the ends of the cap, two splits were made in the ends, to produce three lamination layers. These laminations run inboard about 32 inches from the tip of the cap; they end 4 to 6 inches inboard of the ends of the lamination splits in the outwale and about 1 to 3 inches outboard of the ends of the splits in the inwale. The lamination layers, 3/32 to 1/8 inch thick near the tips, gradually thicken as they extend inboard, to 3/16 inch. At the point where the splits in the gunwale cap end, one of the nails which attach the cap to the outwale is driven. This nail prevented any further splitting inboard of the lamination splits. No lashings bind the three lamination layers together at the end of the splits.

From headboard to headboard, the gunwale caps are attached to the outwales by nails of the same description and medium size as those which were used to nail the inwales and outwales together (see the nail information summary on page 108). Driven at intervals of 10 to 13 inches, the nails often enter the outwale by passing through the gunwale root lashings, rather than in the spaces between the lashings. Outboard of the headboards, two to four small nails fasten each upswept cap to its outwale. The nails, at intervals of 3/4 to 2-1/4 inches, extend outboard to within 4-1/2 to 7 inches of the tips of the caps. The machine-cut nails have heads 3/16 to 7/32 inch long by 5/32 inch wide (see the nail information summary on page 108). The tips of their shanks do not protrude through the outboard surface of the outwale.

The tips of the two converged caps are joined to each other and to the tips of the two outwales by a series of wrapped root lashings (Fig. 54). No wedge is inserted between the tips of the caps to assist in making the lashings tight. Nor are the tips of the converged caps pegged or nailed to each other. The split root lashing material is 3/16 to 1/4 inch wide and 1/16 to 3/32 inch thick, with a half-round cross section. After being split, each side of the root was scraped somewhat flat.

Beginning 1-1/4 inches below the tip of each cap, a shallow notch is carved into its upper face, 1-3/4 inches long. The uppermost three turns of split root lie adjacent to each other in the upper end of the notch, immediately below the lashings which bind the tips of the outwales together. They encircle in a simple spiral both pairs of outwales and caps, running through one hole in the adjacent bark wall and passing through the stempiece inside the bark wall as well. Below these three turns, three or four more adjacent turns encircle the caps and outwales, extending downward for about 3/4 inch. These wrappings do not pass through a hole in the wall. The gunwale cap lashings span about 1-1/4 inches, leaving the lowest area of up to 1/2 inch of the carved notch empty. The description of the painted decoration on the gunwale caps is found on page 99.

Reinforcement Bark Strips

The reinforcement strip of birchbark increases the thickness of the bark wall where it is lashed to the gunwales. Before the inwale and outwale were nailed together onto the upper edge of the bark wall, the reinforcement strip was inserted between the bark wall and the outwale (Fig. 49). Its top edge, like that of the bark wall, was cut off at the level of the top of the outwale. When the awl holes were pierced through the wall and the lashings were wrapped around the gunwales, the bark strip was pierced and lashed as well.

The strip, made of thin bark about 1/32 inch thick, runs from headboard to headboard and to a point 1-1/2 to 3 inches beyond the headboards (Fig. 52). It extends down 2-1/2 to 3-1/2 inches below the lower edge of the outwale in the midsection area. This width gradually tapers toward the ends, reducing to about 1-3/8 to 1-1/2 inches near the ends. Three of the four tips of the two bark strips

are now broken off. The surviving original tip, at the bow end of the left wall strip, tapers over a distance of about two inches to a blunt point approximately 3/4 inch wide (Fig. C-10). The lower edge of the reinforcement strip generally runs parallel to the lower edge of the outwale for the full length; but it was cut quite irregularly and with considerable undulation. The strip was cut to its present width after being installed on the canoe. There is a knife cut or scratch on the bark wall panel immediately adjacent to the lower edge of the strip along its full length; this was produced when the strip was trimmed off against the unprotected wall.

The majority of the length of the strip is made up of five long pieces of bark, measuring 77, 48, 45, 39, and 27 inches. In addition to these long strips, the span beneath the outwale where it curves upward to the headboard is made up of one short piece at each end, 11 inches long at the bow and 6 inches at the stern.

The individual pieces of bark which make up the reinforcement strip overlap each other at their ends, from 1/4 to 1-1/4 inches. The exposed overlapping edges face sometimes outboard toward the ends of the canoe and sometimes inboard, in no discernible pattern. The pieces are not attached at their ends to each other or to the canoe wall in any manner.

The bark deck piece is bent down on either side between the bark hull and the outwale, and is trimmed to appear to be a continuation of the reinforcement bark strip, outboard of the headboard (Figs. 53 and C-10). This deck piece, 10 inches long, extends below the outwale for 1-1/4 to 2 inches. Its edge is cut parallel to the outwale to match the lower edge of the bark reinforcement strip. The description of the painted decoration on the reinforcement bark strips and the bark decks is found on page 106.

Gunwale Lashings

The upper edge of the bark wall is sandwiched between the inwale, the reinforcement bark strip, and the outwale (Fig. 49). It is cut off flush with the top surface of the outwale. The four layers of bark and wood are nailed and lashed together with spaced groups of root lashings from headboard to headboard.

Each lashing group normally runs through six or seven holes in the bark wall (sometimes eight holes) (Fig. 56). The holes, generally round in shape, have diameters of 1/8 to 3/16 inch, with irregular edges. They are now slightly elongated at the top, due to the upward pull of the root lashings. The holes were made by an awl with a square cross section, which was inserted from the exterior side of the wall and twisted.

The holes are spaced 3/16 to 1/4 inch apart. Each row of holes, spanning 2-1/2 to 3 inches, lies about 5/8 inch below the lower edge of the inwale. When originally installed, these lashing holes would have been considerably closer to the inwale, before it was forced upward by the pressure of the ribs.

The split root lashing material is 3/16 to 1/4 inch wide and 1/16 to 3/32 inch thick, with a half-round cross section. After being split, each side of the root was scraped somewhat flat. In addition to these split roots, narrower unsplit roots, about 1/8 inch in diameter, were utilized for some of the lashings.

To lash the gunwales, a long length of split root was drawn nearly to its end through the first hole in the set of six or seven holes. The short end of the root was drawn up to the top surface of the combined gunwales on the exterior and inserted down between two of the sandwiched layers of wood and bark. Then, in a simple spiral stitch, the long end of the root passed over the top of the inwale and outwale and again through the same first hole. The root then passed around the combined inwale and outwale a second time, and through the second hole. This pattern continued through each of the six or seven holes, with usually two turns per hole, laying down twelve or fourteen wrappings around the gunwales. Sometimes three turns were made per hole, when the root was narrower than usual.

Several techniques were used to finish off the root securely before starting a new group of lashings (Fig. 56). Sometimes the end was finished off atop the inwale and outwale, by being looped under the previous stitch to maintain the tension. Then it was tucked underneath a previous stitch or tightly down between the sandwiched layers of inwale, bark wall, and outwale, to hold the end securely. The gunwale caps covered and protected all of these tucked root ends.

In other instances, when the end of the root emerged on the exterior side of the canoe wall at the last hole (#7), it was run horizontally back through an enlarged hole #6, #5, or #4 (Fig. 57). Where it emerged on the interior, the tip was cut off rather short. It was held

firmly in place by the two turns of root that had previously been run through the hole.

Sometimes the strand returning horizontally from hole #7 to hole #6 or #5 was run on the interior side (Fig. 56). After passing through the enlarged hole #6 or #5, it returned horizontally to hole #7 on the exterior side, passed through it, and then was tucked under the horizontal span on the interior side.

Each typical group of lashings is composed of twelve to fourteen turns of root around the gunwale, covering a length of 2-1/2 to 3 inches of the gunwale. An interval of 1-1/2 to 1-3/4 inches separates each group of lashings. The interval between each group is not spanned by a connector stitch; each group begins and ends independently.

The endmost group of lashings at each end of each gunwale is considerably longer than the majority of the lashings (Fig. C-13). Extending inboard from a point beside the headboards, each of these groups is composed of about 25 to 30 turns of split root. They pass through a correspondingly greater number of holes, with usually two turns per hole.

The thwarts are bound into the gunwales with root lashings that fit into the pattern of the gunwale wrappings. The thwart lashing groups are not joined to the gunwale lashings by connector stitches.

Damage and Repairs

The outwale of the left wall and the inwale of the right wall were both broken early in the life of the Ojibwa canoe (Fig. 42). In each instance, the damaged area was repaired using machine-cut nails and split root lashings which match well the nails and lashings that were used in the original manufacture of the craft. The materials and techniques which were utilized to make the repairs imply that the damage occurred and was repaired during the period when the canoe was still in the possession of the Ojibwas.

A crack in the outwale of the left side begins 17 inches in back of the center thwart. Angling upward from the bottom surface of the outwale, it extends 13 inches to the rear while rising one inch, to end 1/2 inch below the top surface (Fig. 58).

To repair the crack, the root lashings were removed from the damaged area, and three nails were driven horizontally from the outside face of the outwale. The nails lie in an irregular row spanning 7-1/2 inches, with intervals of 2-3/4 and 4 inches between them. The machine-cut nails match the small ones that were used to attach the tips of the gunwale caps to the outwales (see the nail information summary on page 108). The tips of the shanks do not protrude through the inboard face of the inwale.

After the nails were driven in, the split root lashings were replaced on the gunwales, to match those that had been installed during the original manufacture. The new lashings covered and hid from view the three repair nails. A number of the lashings have since been broken, exposing to view the crack and its repair nails.

The breakage in the inwale of the right side was apparently more severe, requiring a more complicated repair procedure. The damage occurred in the area where the right end of the second thwart from the stern fits into its mortise hole in the inwale. To repair the breakage, the root lashings were first removed from the damaged area, including those binding the right end of the thwart.

The inboard surface of the inwale was then sawed completely across its face in two locations, to a depth of 3/8 inch (about halfway through the thickness at this location). The piece of wood between the two vertical saw kerfs, 10-5/8 inches long by 1-1/2 inches high, was neatly chiseled out. The cutout area extends to a point 2-3/8 inches outboard of the rear edge of the thwart and to a point 5-1/2 inches inboard of the forward edge of the thwart.

A wooden replacement patch of the same dimensions as the cutout area was neatly sawed and trimmed to shape so that it fit flush with the surfaces and the sawed edges of the adjoining original inwale. A mortise hole was carved into the wooden patch to receive the end of the thwart. The patch was nailed into place with eight horizontal nails from the inboard side. The machine-cut nails match the two sizes of nails which were used to attach the gunwale caps to the outwales in the original construction of the canoe (see the nail information summary on page 108). Of the eight nails, one medium size one and three small ones were driven into the wooden patch on both the forward side and the rear side of the mortise hole and thwart. The two medium nails protruded about 1/8 inch on the exterior surface of the outwale, where they were clinched over.

As in the repair on the outwale, the split root gunwale lashings were then replaced to match those installed in the original manufacture. The replacement lashings covered all but one small nail in the area forward of the thwart and all but one medium and one small nail in the area to the rear of the thwart. A number of these replacement lashings have since been broken, exposing to view the wooden patch repair.

In both of the gunwale repair procedures, the nailed gunwale cap was probably raised slightly to facilitate the initial removal and later replacement of the gunwale lashings. It was tapped back down into place after the repair was completed.

The damage to the left wall outwale and the right wall inwale may have resulted from the same or separate accidents. Both areas of damage lie in the stern half of the canoe, with a span of about fifty inches between the rear end of the crack in the outwale and the forward end of the cutout patch in the inwale.

Stempieces

The stempiece, made of northern white cedar, is visible in several areas of the canoe (Fig. 59). Its heel is visible where it projects into the interior of the canoe at the base of the headboard. Most of the upper half of the bow stempiece with its braces is clearly visible behind the unlashed and cracked bark end panel on the right side of the bow; views of the rest of the stempiece are available via this damaged area as well. The bark deck outboard of the bow headboard is also broken, affording a view of the wooden elements beneath the deck. The laminated upper end of the stempiece and the inboard ends of its pair of horizontal braces can be seen where they project through the headboard.

The curvature of the stempiece is implied in several areas. The curve of the cutwater edge of the canoe, from chin to outwales, outlines the entire outer curved portion of the stempiece. Also, the stempiece is lashed to the outwales and gunwale caps just below their tips.

The total length of the stempiece is about 98 inches, measured on the outboard edge. The heel of the stempiece projects 1-1/8 inches inboard from the inboard surface of the base of the headboard. At its end, it is 2-1/8 inches deep (in height) by 1/2 inch thick, with sharp corners and edges (Fig. 59). All surfaces of the heel are carved flat and smooth. The top surface of

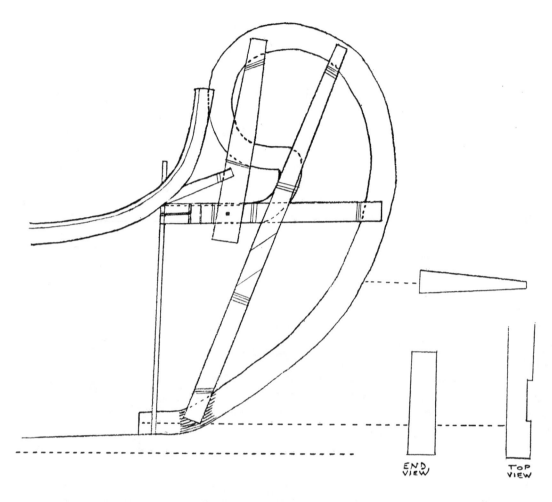

END
VIEW

TOP
VIEW

Fig. 59. Ojibwa Canoe: End frame unit. The spiral wrappings of the stempiece are not shown.

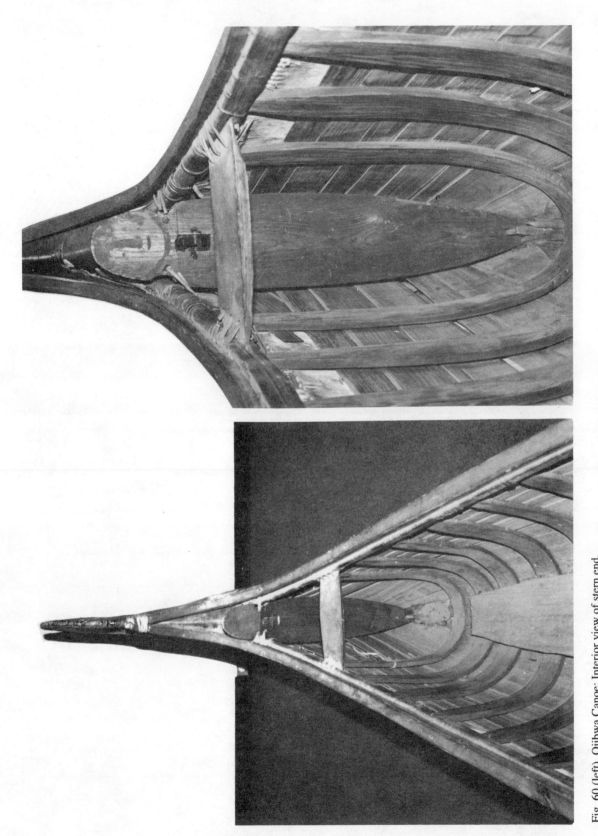

Fig. 60 (left). Ojibwa Canoe: Interior view of stern end.
Fig. 62 (right). Ojibwa Canoe: Painted headboard at bow end. This is the only known surviving headboard from an original voyaging canoe which is decorated with a human figure.

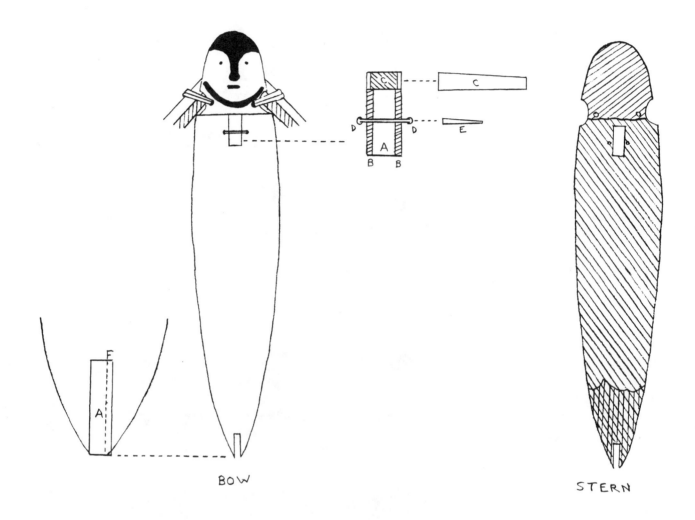

BOW

STERN

Fig. 61. Ojibwa Canoe: Headboards. A. stempiece, B. braces, C. wedge, D. holes and strings, E. pegs, F. notch in stempiece.

the heel remains horizontally level as it extends inboard to the headboard. The heel has a notch carved into its side, 3/4 inch from its tip. The notch, 7/8 inch wide and 1/8 inch deep, runs down the full height of 2-1/8 inches. The notch on the bow stempiece faces the right wall, while the one on the stern stempiece faces the left wall. The legs of the headboard straddle this notched area of the heel.

On the outboard side of the base of the headboard, the stempiece broadens slightly in depth (height) to 2-1/4 inches. This is a rather deep, robust stempiece, compared to the various ones modeled by Adney. The thickness at the inboard edge is 3/8 to 1/2 inch, tapering to 1/8 inch at the outboard edge; this taper creates a triangular cross section. All surfaces are flat and all edges are sharp. These dimensions are maintained over the entire broad curve of the stempiece, to its junction with the outwales.

Beginning about 2-1/2 inches outboard of the headboard, at a point about 4 inches from the tip of its heel, the stempiece is divided by eleven splits into twelve lamination layers 1/8 to 3/16 inch thick. The lamination splits extend through the complete upper length of the stempiece to its end. (In the Figure 59 diagram, they are portrayed only in the lowest portion.) The entire laminated portion of the stempiece is spirally wrapped at intervals of about 1/2 to 3/4 inch with the same heavy commercial string as that which binds the laminated end areas and the tips of the inwales. The string, light brown in color and 1/16 inch in diameter, was wrapped around the stempiece before the stempiece braces were added; the tips of some of the braces cover string-wrapped areas.

The stempiece angles slightly upward from the headboard to the rounded chin, the point at which the stitching of the end begins. From the chin, which lies about 3 inches outboard of the base of the headboard, the stempiece curves upward and outboard for 33 inches. Then it arcs in a broad curve upward and inboard for 24 inches to its maximum height at the head. From there, the stempiece curves downward and inboard for about 12-1/2 inches, to the point where it is lashed to the converged tips of the outwales and gunwale caps. The stempiece continues its curve outboard at this point until about halfway toward the cutwater edge, where it bends very sharply downward. The degree of sharp-

ness of this bend required the breaking of three of the lamination layers on the inside of the curve. Finally, the stempiece makes a moderately hard curve inboard and runs horizontally to and through the headboard. The maximum horizontal distance of the curvature of the stempiece, from the cutwater edge to the outboard side of the head of the headboard, is about 22 inches.

Below the junction with the outwales, the cross section of the stempiece becomes rectangular (rather than triangular) for the remainder of its length, with a thickness of 3/8 to 1/2 inch. Below the outwale junction, the profile (depth) also tapers gradually, reducing to 2 inches by the very sharp turn in the stempiece and to 1-1/2 inches where it projects through the headboard.

Three pairs of carved wooden braces add stability to the tall stempiece and thus to the high prow. One pair runs nearly horizontally, on each side of the stempiece, from the sides of the cutwater edge to and through the hole in the headboard. The braces, 21 inches long and 1-1/2 to 1-3/4 inches wide (deep), have flat surfaces and sharp edges. At the headboard, they are 1/8 inch thick; as they extend outboard for about 4 inches, the thickness increases to 1/2 inch. This measurement continues for about 8 inches, after which it tapers gradually over a span of 9 inches to a thickness of 1/16 inch at the outboard end.

The inboard ends of this pair of braces, on each side of the end of the stempiece in the hole in the headboard, are held firmly in place by a wooden wedge (which is described in the headboard discussion). The outboard ends are attached to each side of the stempiece at the cutwater edge by several wraps of the same brown string around the braces, which squeeze the braces tightly against the sides of the stempiece. In addition, these two braces are bound to the stempiece with string in four locations within the span in which they run parallel to the end of the stempiece (Fig. 59). This series of four wrappings appears to be made from one doubled length of string; the three inboard sets are each composed of just one double wrap.

From the most inboard set of these wraps, one doubled strand runs inboard alongside the midline of the brace to the headboard; it passes through a small hole in the headboard, crosses over the ends of the stempiece and the pair of braces, and returns through a second small hole back to the opposite side of the endmost brace wrappings. The string is held firmly in each of the holes in the bow headboard by a carved wooden peg that is inserted in each hole from the inboard side of the headboard. (These pegs are described in the headboard discussion.)

This doubled strand of string could not have had any practical strength. But to the builders of the canoe it may have served a traditional or symbolic function, uniting the stempiece, braces, and headboard together into a single solid frame unit for each end of the canoe. One of the traditional styles of Great Lakes Indian end frame units which was modeled by Adney features an identical set of lashing holes flanking the stempiece hole in the headboard (Fig. 19, No. 2, Vol. I). One or two turns of the split root or inner bark which spirally wraps the stempiece runs through the two holes. The builders of the Ojibwa canoe continued this traditional form of attachment of the head of the stempiece to the headboard, even though the string which they used to spirally wrap the stempiece had little strength.

After the horizontal pair of braces was installed, two more pairs were added. One of these sets extends diagonally upward for 41 inches from the chin to a point just outboard of the highest area of the stempiece. Each of these braces measures 1-1/2 inches in width and 3/8 inch in thickness in the span from its base up to the juncture with the stempiece below the sharp bend. Above the juncture, the width gradually tapers to 1 inch at the tip. In the same upper span, the thickness also tapers gradually to 1/4 inch near the end; over the last 2-1/4 inches, it reduces more suddenly, to 1/16 inch at the tip. The braces have flat surfaces and sharp edges and ends.

Wrappings of the same brown string squeeze the ends of this pair of long braces firmly against the stempiece; three turns are found at the lower end, and eleven turns at the upper end. Three wraps of string also bind the two braces to the stempiece just below its sharp bend. Below the horizontal braces, the wrapping string spirals widely twice around the diagonal braces and then makes six adjacent turns around them. This appears to have been done simply to take up the extra length of the string, rather than as a useful wrapping.

The third pair of stempiece braces, nearly vertical, spans 21 inches, running from the pair of horizontal braces to the top of the stempiece. These, the widest of the braces, measure 2-1/2 inches in width by 1/2 inch in thickness in the span from the base up to the juncture with the

stempiece near the sharp bend. Above the juncture, the width gradually tapers to 1-1/4 inches at the tip. Over the same upper span, the thickness also tapers gradually to 1/4 inch near the end; over the last 1-1/2 inches, it reduces more suddenly, to 1/16 inch at the tip. The braces have flat surfaces and sharp edges and ends.

This set of braces likewise has turns of string squeezing the two of them tightly against the sides of the stempiece: three wraps encircle them near the tips and another set of two wraps is positioned just below the juncture with the stempiece near its sharp bend. The lowest fastener is unique in the entire series of braces. A single horizontal nail extends from the right side through the pairs of vertical and horizontal braces and the stempiece. The medium size nail, with its 2-1/2 inch shank, penetrates through the combined thickness of nearly 2-1/2 inches of the wooden elements (see the nail information summary on page 108).

The tips of the converged pair of inwales lie adjacent to the set of vertical braces. The tips of the inwales, as previously described, are bound tightly together with string to squeeze them against the outside surfaces of the two braces.

None of the turns of string which join together the stempiece, braces, and inwales pass through holes in the wooden elements. In each instance, the lashings only pull together the outer elements, applying squeezing pressure to the inside element to hold the unit firmly together. All of these lashings are of heavy commercial string of 1/16 inch diameter, rather than split roots.

The form of the internal curvature of the stempiece plus its horizontal braces closely resembles the old Algonkin version modeled by Adney; it appears on page 151 at the far left in Adney and Chapelle. (Note that the numerals 1 and 3 beneath the photo have been reversed by Chapelle: the example at the far left matches the early Algonkin form of cutwater edge, while the example at the far right parallels the Adney "Tete de Boule" model depicted on pages 134-35.)

Headboards

The headboard, fashioned from northern white cedar, stands at the bow end with its base 24 inches inboard of the outermost point of the cutwater edge (Fig. 40). The stern headboard is positioned 3-1/2 inches further inboard than its bow end counterpart. Each is positioned well inboard from the end of the canoe: the headboard stands inboard of the chin, which is set well in from the end due to the considerable undercut of the profile. At the bow, the outboard side of the base falls three inches inboard of the chin of the canoe. The headboard is angled slightly, so that its head lies two inches outboard of its base. (This is the opposite direction of the two-inch slant of the headboards of the Royal canoe.) The side notches beneath the head fit between the converging inwales. When the canoe is viewed in profile, the rounded head of the headboard projects about three inches above the caps.

The overall height of the headboard (Figs. 60 to 62) is 26 inches; the height from the shoulders to the base is 21-1/2 inches. Its maximum width is 5-3/16 inches, at a point 5-1/2 inches below the side notches. This maximum width tapers slightly to 4-1/4 inches at the base of the notches, and also tapers gradually over a span of 16 inches down to the base, where it is 1/2 inch. From the base up to the inwale notches, the headboard is 1/2 inch thick. Above the notches, the thickness is 3/8 inch. The flat inboard surface is planed smooth, all edge surfaces are carved flat, and all corners and edges are sharp. The headboard appears to have been sawn to thickness before it was planed. No plane marks are visible, but hand planing would not necessarily produce visible blade marks.

Below the rounded head, which measures 3-5/8 inches at its maximum width, a notch is cut out of each side. The inwales fit into these notches, which are 1-1/2 inches high and 1/2 inch deep. (In a later restoration, the lower side of each of the notches in the stern headboard was carved lower; this was apparently done to accommodate the downward sag of the ends of the gunwales.) The top and bottom surface of each notch are level, rather than angling upward toward the outboard side of the headboard to accommodate the upward curve of the ends of the inwales.

A horizontal line, scored shallowly with the tip of an awl, runs across the headboard at exactly the base of the two notches, This scored line is found on the headboard at both the bow and the stern. It appears to have been an indicator of the height of the lower edge of the inwales, and thus the location of the lower edge of the notches that were to be cut out to receive the inwales.

Inboard 3/8 inch from the midpoint of each of these inwale notches is a single hole, through which two turns of split roots lash the inwales to the neck of the headboard. (These lashings have been restored.) The two irregularly round, tapered holes, about 1/4 inch in diameter, were apparently drilled with an awl with a triangular or square cross section.

A chiseled rectangular hole lies in the midline of the headboard, at the level of the bases of the inwale notches. The hole is 1-7/8 inches high and 3/4 inch wide. The laminated end of the stempiece, flanked by the ends of its pair of horizontal braces, projects through this hole. All three elements end flush with the surface of the headboard. The end of the stempiece measures 1-1/2 inches tall by 1/2 inch thick, while each of the brace ends is 1-1/2 inches tall by 1/8 inch thick. A wooden wedge, 2 inches long, is inserted into the hole above the end of the stempiece, to hold the stempiece and braces firmly in the hole. The flat exposed inboard end of the wedge measures 3/8 inch in height by 5/8 inch in width. At its outboard end, the 5/8 inch width remains the same, while the 3/8 inch height (thickness) has tapered slightly.

About 1/8 inch outboard of each side of the rectangular hole lies an irregularly round tapered hole, drilled by an awl with a triangular or square cross section. Between the two 1/8 inch diameter holes runs the doubled strand of string which lashes together the stempiece and its braces. (This string running through the headboard is described in the stempiece discussion.) At the bow headboard, the doubled strand is held firmly in the holes by a carved rectangular wooden peg inserted into each hole from the inboard side. The head of each peg, cut off irregularly, measures 1/8 by 1/4 inch. Over the 7/8 inch length of the peg, all four sides taper. The tip, cut off bluntly, is 1/16 by 1/8 inch. The head of each peg projects about 1/8 inch from the inboard surface of the headboard, while its tip projects 1/4 inch beyond the outboard surface. The outboard tips of the two pegs, positioned beside each of the horizontal stempiece braces, do not make contact with any wooden elements. The only function which is served by the two pegs in the bow headboard appears to be to hold the doubled strand of string in place within the two holes. An identical doubled strand passes through the two comparable holes in the stern headboard, but no pegs are inserted into these holes.

The base of the headboard has a rectangular notch cut out, 1-3/4 inches tall and 3/8 inch wide. The two legs produced by the notch each taper to a sharp point at the base. The legs fit over the notch in the heel of the stempiece.

The headboard at each end of the canoe is decorated. On the bow headboard has been painted a simple face, 4-1/2 inches high (Fig. C-8). Most of the face is depicted in slightly brownish red color, with the mouth and a dot in the center of each red eye in black. In addition, the entire carved flat edge around the head is painted black. This red and black face on the headboard at the bow possibly served as an indication to the paddlers of which end of the canoe was the bow end. This is the only known surviving headboard from an original voyaging canoe which is decorated with a human figure.

At the stern, the entire head and the upper half of the neck area of the headboard are entirely painted with the same brownish red paint (Fig. 60). The entire flat carved edge around the head is painted black. From the halfway point of the notches downward, the body is completely painted black. The division between the red and black areas is a moderately even horizontal line. The lowest quarter of the body area is entirely painted deep green over the coat of black. The division between the black and green areas is a moderately even line composed of two unequal scallops.

Cutwater Edges

No wooden batten was built into the stitched cutwater edge to cover and protect the outboard edges of the two bark panels or the stempiece. The edges of the bark panels are cut off flush with the edge of the stempiece (Fig. 63).

To accommodate the stitching of the cutwater edge, a single row of holes runs around the perimeter for four inches outboard from the outwales. The holes, spaced at intervals of 1/32 to 1/16 inch edge to edge, lie 1/4 to 3/8 inch inboard from the cutwater edge. Produced by an awl with a triangular or square cross section, the holes are 3/32 to 1/8 inch in diameter. They were all pierced from the same side of the canoe. On the entry side, the pierce and twist of the awl produced an irregular but generally round hole, with no flaring of the bark edges around the perimeter of the hole. On the opposite side of the canoe, the edges of the holes flare outward slightly.

The split lashing roots, 3/32 to 1/8 inch wide and about 1/16 inch thick, have a half-round cross section. After being split, each side of the root was scraped a little flat. The stitching was done with a single strand of root in a continuous spiral stitch, with one turn per hole. The stitches lie adjacent to each other, almost completely covering the cutwater edge.

The following distance of 35 inches around the curve is lashed in a pattern of stitches composed of a series of graceful concave arcs. The narrow section of each arc points outboard or downward depending on its position along the curve. Each individual arc is made up of a series of 9 to 13 adjacent stitches. The holes, 3/32 to 1/8 inch in diameter, lie at intervals of 1/32 to 3/32 inch edge to edge. The first hole in each series is positioned 1-3/8 to 1-3/4 inches inboard from the cutwater edge; the following 6 to 8 holes each lie progressively nearer to the edge. These are followed by 2 to 4 holes which are 1/8 to 3/16 inch from the edge. The series of holes is sewn with a single root the same size as those described above, in a continuous spiral stitch with one turn per hole. Each unit of 9 to 13 adjacent stitches covers a span of about 1-3/4 to 2 inches of the cutwater edge.

On the lowest 28 inch span of the cutwater edge, extending down to the chin, the stitching holes are in a single row, parallel to the edge and 1/4 to 3/8 inch from it. The holes, 3/32 to 1/8 inch in diameter, are placed at intervals of 3/8 to 1/2 inch edge to edge. A single split root about the same size as those described above forms cross stitches, in which the two ends of the root pass through each hole in opposite directions, after crossing each other like shoe laces on the cutwater edge. The holes are spaced considerably more widely than those in the upper two lashing areas of the cutwater edge (where the continuous spiral stitches lie adjacent to each other). Thus, even with two turns of cross stitching per hole, there are intervals of 1/8 to 1/4 inch between each of the pairs of turns in which the cutwater edge is not covered with stitches.

In all sewing of the cutwater edge, the stitches pass directly through the stempiece inside the end of the canoe, rather than around it. The root lashings run through awl holes through the stempiece. (The stempiece can be clearly seen behind the broken high end panel at the bow end of the right wall.)

The lower portion of the cutwater edge (the area in which spaces occur between the pairs of stitches) is sealed

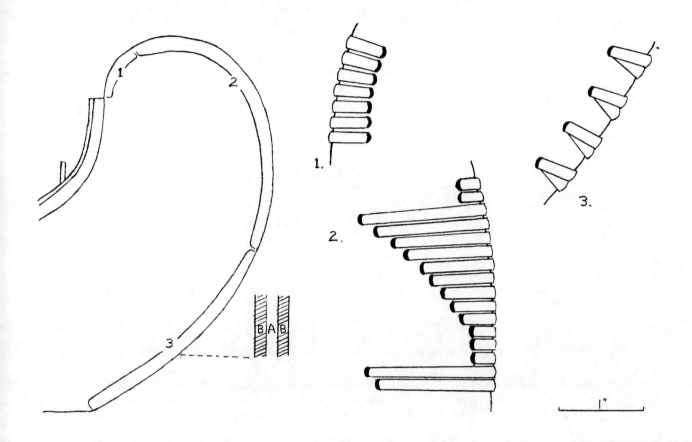

Fig. 63. Ojibwa Canoe: Root lashings of cutwater edge. A. stempiece, B. bark wall panels.

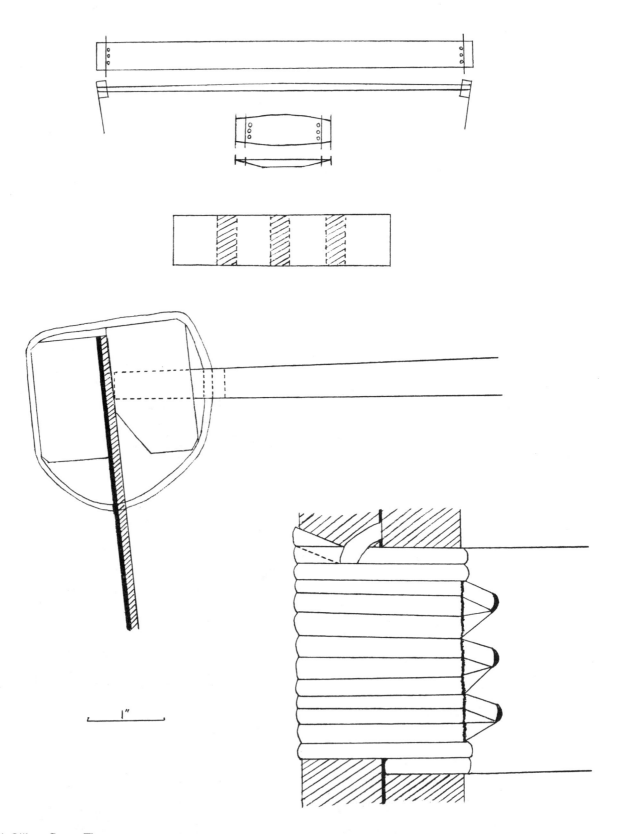

Fig. 64. Ojibwa Canoe: Thwarts.

1"

with blackened pitch in the same manner as the bark panel seams are sealed. The swath of pitch begins 1-1/2 inches inboard of the chin, on the bottom of the canoe. It extends upward for 29-1/2 inches on the curve, covering the entire area of cross stitches up to the arc pattern stitches. The pitch extends from the outer edge of the prow onto the bark walls for 3/4 to 1 inch. The edges of the pitched area are broadly curved, following the contour of the outer edge of the canoe. The upper portion of the cutwater edge is not sealed with pitch. This allowed unobstructed drainage of water out of the canoe when it was overturned on its side on shore.

The total thickness of the cutwater edge is 1/2 to 9/16 inch in the lower pitched area (the area of the waterline), and 7/16 to 1/2 inch thick in the unpitched upper area. This thickness includes the stempiece, the two bark panels, and the stitches, as well as the pitch in the lower area.

Thwarts

The thwarts, of northern white cedar, appear to have been fashioned from sawn boards. The seven thwarts (creating a six-place canoe) are not spaced exactly symmetrically (Fig. 42). The distances between the thwarts are measured from centerline to centerline. Their positioning indicates a canoe shape that tapers slightly asymmetrically toward the two ends at the gunwale level, with the bow half a little wider and more suddenly tapered near the end than the stern.

The center thwart lies two inches forward of the exact midpoint of the canoe. In comparing the distance to each of the adjacent thwarts (pair A), the bow span is 1/2 inch greater than the stern counterpart. The distance from the pair A thwarts to pair B is likewise 1/2 inch greater in the bow half than in the stern. The spans from pair B to pair C (the endmost thwarts) reflect the more sudden taper of the bow near its end: the bowward span is 1/4 inch shorter than the sternward counterpart. The end thwart at the bow end lies 1-1/2 inches closer to its headboard than does the stern end thwart to its headboard, another indicator of the quicker bow taper. Likewise, the bow headboard is positioned 3-1/2 inches nearer to the end of the canoe compared to the same span at the stern. Thus, the end thwart at the bow lies a total of 5 inches closer to its tip of the canoe than the end thwart at the stern. These measurements im-

ply a hull shape in which the bow half has slightly greater width and a more sudden taper near the end compared to the narrower stern half with its longer and more gradual taper.

The lengths of the thwarts also imply the same asymmetry. Three pairs of thwarts flank the center thwart. In two out of the three pairs (pairs B and C), the thwart toward the bow is slightly longer than its stern counterpart.

Center: Thwart #1: 43-1/4 inches
Pair A: Thwart #2: 38-1/2 inches
           Thwart #3: 38-1/4 inches
Pair B: Thwart #4: 22-3/4 inches
           Thwart #5: 23-3/8 inches
Pair C: Thwart #6: 8-5/8 inches
           Thwart #7: 9-1/2 inches

The lengths, measured along the longest edge, do not include the hidden portion at each end which fits into the mortise hole in each inwale. The actual length of each thwart is about two inches longer than each of these measurements, since the additional portion at each end, which extends completely through the inwale, is roughly one inch long.

In comparing the endmost pair, the bow thwart is 7/8 inch longer than its stern counterpart; in the next pair inboard, the bow thwart is 5/8 inch longer. These small differences may be simply variances due to measurement by eye rather than by measuring devices. But there is a possibility that the builders intentionally made the thwarts slightly longer in the bow half, to create a canoe that is slightly wider in the beam toward the bow than the stern, for greater efficiency of forward movement of the canoe. Considering the positions of the thwarts and headboards in the Ojibwa canoe, such asymmetry would have been produced even if the thwarts in the bow half had been exactly the same lengths as their counterparts in the stern (since the bowward thwarts are positioned slightly closer to the end of the canoe). This slightly widened bow form, also found in the Royal and Varden canoes and possibly the Catlin canoe, was commonly built into the fur trade canoes that were constructed in the latter nineteenth century at the canoe-building posts of the upper Ottawa River in western Quebec[13]. It was also quite widespread in traditional Indian canoe construction, as has been previously discussed.

The following description applies to five of the seven thwarts (Fig. 64). (The endmost pair of thwarts are discussed afterward.) The width remains constant at 2-11/16 to 2-3/4 inches over the entire length of the thwart. At the center, the thickness is 5/8 to 11/16 inch. This dimension tapers very gradually over nearly the entire span toward each inwale, by the removal of wood from the upper surface. At the point where the thwart meets the inwale, the thickness has tapered to 3/8 inch. The dimensions of 3/8 inch thick by 2-11/16 to 2-3/4 inches wide appear to remain constant as the end of the thwart projects through the one inch thickness of each inwale. The underside remains level and straight over the entire length. All four sides of the thwart are planed smooth, and all four edges are sharp.

All but the endmost pair of thwarts match this description (varying only in length). The width of each end thwart measures 2-7/8 to 3 inches for much of the length; toward the inwales, it tapers slightly, to reach 2-3/8 to 2-3/4 inches at the inwales. The width continues to taper gradually as the end of the thwart projects through the inwale. At the center, the thickness is 5/8 to 11/16 inch. This dimension tapers rather quickly over a distance of 1-1/2 to 2 inches near each inwale, by the removal of wood from the underside. At the point where the thwart meets the inwale, the thickness has reduced to 1/8 inch. This tapering continues as the thwart projects through the inwale, reaching a sharp edge at the tip of the thwart. The upper surface remains level and straight over the entire length.

Another minor difference occurs in these endmost pair of thwarts. All of the other thwarts are positioned so that their upper and lower surfaces lie in level, horizontal planes. The endmost thwarts are positioned in the gunwales at the point where the gunwales curve upward toward the ends of the canoe (Fig. 62). Thus, the planes of the top and bottom surfaces of these two endmost thwarts are also angled upward, with the outboard edge higher than the inboard edge.

At the point where each thwart (except the endmost ones) meets the inwale, a horizontal mortise hole is cut through the midline of the inwale, to receive the end of the thwart (Fig. 64). Each hole is 3 inches long by 1/2 inch wide, with sharp edges and corners. The sides of the holes are smoothly cut, while the ends are somewhat roughly cut and split out. The mortise hole runs completely through the inwale. The hole is cut at a slight angle, with its inboard end lower than its outboard end. This compensates for the slight outward angle of the inwale, since it angles outward in conjunction with the upper walls of the canoe. The angle of the hole permits the straight horizontal end of the thwart to fit into the hole in the angled inwale.

At the ends of the outermost pair of end thwarts, a section is cut out from one of the central lamination layers in the inwale as a   hole. At the bow end, the length of the cutout segment measures 3 to 3-1/2 inches, while at the stern the removed section is 4 to 4-1/2 inches long. In all other respects, the treatment of these end thwarts is identical to that of the other thwarts.

No vertical nail or wooden peg was driven downward from the upper surface of the inwale through any of the thwarts to hold the end of the thwart firmly in the inwale. The ends of the thwarts now rest loosely in the holes, since the thwart has shrunk somewhat.

Each end of the thwart is lashed with split root to the combined inwale and outwale. The lashings run through three vertical holes in the end of the thwart, 1/8 to 3/16 inch inboard from the inwale. The two outer holes lie 1/2 to 3/8 inch from the sides of the thwart. The neatly drilled round holes are 1/4 inch in diameter. The upper edges of the holes are sharp rather than rounded.

Below the junction of the thwart and the gunwales, there are six or seven awl holes in the bark wall. These lashing holes, spanning 2-1/2 to 3 inches, sometimes end slightly short of the outer edges of the thwart, and in other instances extend up to 1/8 inch beyond the outer edges (Fig. 64). All of the previous information describing the lashing of the gunwale elements also applies to the lashing of the thwarts. In the present replacement lashings, two turns of root lie beside each edge of the thwart while three turns pass through each of the three holes in the thwart. The thwarts were lashed at the same time as the gunwales. Thus, their lashings fit into the series of lashing groups along the length of the gunwales.

During the years of usage of the canoe, moderate wear occurred to the edges of the thwarts. The description of the painted decoration on the thwarts is found on page 106.

Sheathing

The sheathing strips or splints, split from northern white cedar, are 8 to 8-1/2 feet long, 2-1/2 to 4 inches wide, and very thin, 1/16 to 3/32 inch. On the flat faces, areas of undulating raised grain patterns indicate that the strips were split out rather than sawn. Each splint has generally parallel edges for most of its length; the edges are carved rather straight. The endmost 4 to 5 inches at each end is carved so that it gradually tapers into a sharp point or occasionally a truncated sharp point (Fig. 65). Only inboard edge of each of the tapered ends is feathered; these edges of the ends are thinned down to 1/32 to 1/16 inch.

The pattern of overlapping ends indicates that the splints were laid into the canoe in three groups: first at each end, and then a central group in the midsection area. The two end groups, laid into the narrowest areas of the canoe, are each made up of 16 to 18 strips. The broader area of the canoe, filled by the midsection group, required 24 to 26 splints. After each end group of strips had been laid in, the central group was positioned so that the splints overlapped the ends of the previously-laid groups for about 8 to 10 inches.

In laying in the sheathing, the first strips were positioned near the top of each wall of the canoe, 2-3/4 to 4 inches below the lower edge of the inwale. This is about 2 to 3-1/4 inches below the gunwale lashing holes in the walls. Succeeding rows of sheathing splints were then added down the walls and across the floor. Thus, the overlapping edge of each successive splint faces upward or outward, away from the midline of the canoe. The overlapping edge extends 1/2 to 1-1/2 inches over the previous strip.

The final splint to be installed in each group was the wide strip down the midline of the floor. In each of the end groups of splints, this central strip runs up to but not underneath the base of the headboard (Fig. 62). The tapered outboard tip of each of these central strips is split down its midline for about 1-1/2 to 2 inches. The split fits over the heel of the stempiece which projects inboard from the base of the headboard; the split halves of the sheathing strip lie along each side of the heel.

Toward each end of the canoe at the top of the walls, a gradually widening expanse of the upper bark wall is left exposed, not covered by the straight horizontal strips of sheathing where the gunwales curve upward (Fig. 62). These wider areas of exposed upper wall extend for about 6 to 8 inches inboard of the headboards. Beside the headboards, the area of each wall which is not covered by the sheathing splints ranges from 3 to 5-1/2 inches in height.

The tips of the endmost splints extend outboard of the headboard for a distance: in some cases, they may run to or beside the stempiece. To stiffen and support the bark cover at both of the high ends of the canoe, additional short sheathing strips were inserted outboard of the headboard (Fig. 66). Seven such strips are visible via the damaged right end panel at the bow. From 20 to 24 inches long and 2 to 3-1/2 inches wide, these strips have rounded or sharply squared tips. They lie in various angled positions, some very steeply angled. Most of them extend out to or near to the outboard edge of the stempiece. The inboard ends of these splints fit between the main sheathing strips and the bark wall panels. Thus, they were installed in the ends of the canoe before the main splints were laid in, or they were inserted later via the open cutwater edge at the end of the canoe before it was stitched closed. The inboard ends of some of the added strips are visible inside the canoe, in the expanse of upper bark wall which is left exposed above the main sheathing splints (Fig. 62); they lie in an angled position, extending up to 3 to 4 inches inboard of the headboard. No other material, such as wood shavings or moss, was stuffed into the ends of the canoe to support the bark cover.

Ribs

The canoe was built with a total of 54 ribs of northern white cedar (27 pairs). Throughout most of the length of the canoe, they are spaced at intervals of 1-1/2 to 2-1/4 inches, measured edge to edge. Near the ends of the canoe, the spacing reduces to 1 to 2-1/4 inches.

The profile of the midsection ribs is composed of a narrow flat area about 8 to 9 inches long in the midline of the floor, from which the bilge areas curve moderately upward; the upper sections flare slightly outward (Fig. 67). The width of the flat central area gradually reduces toward each end of the canoe; by the endmost rib, the profile is a narrow U form. The curve of the ribs reflects the body plan of the canoe (Fig. 68).

The midsection ribs in the area of the central thwart are 64-1/2 to 65 inches long. This includes the length

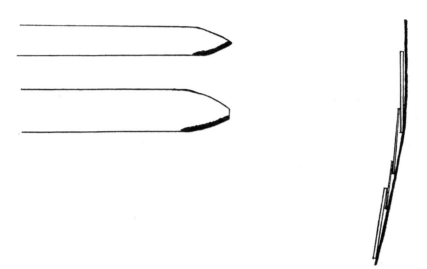

Fig. 65. Ojibwa Canoe: Sheathing strips.

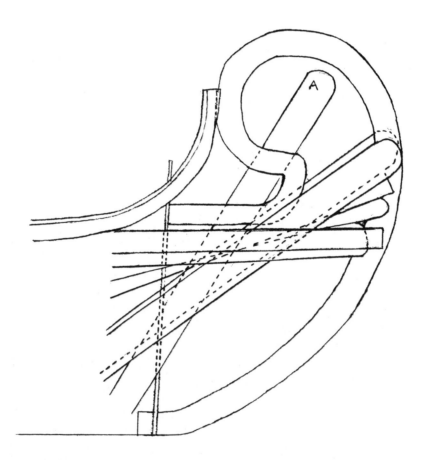

Fig. 66. Ojibwa Canoe: Additional sheathing strips installed in the ends.

Fig. 67. Ojibwa Canoe: Profile of ribs and thwarts. The plank running down the midline of the floor is a modern addition, not original to the craft.

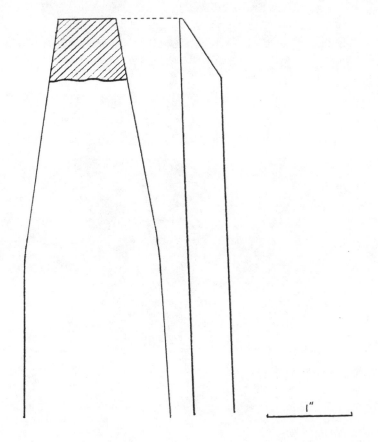

Fig. 69. Ojibwa Canoe: Ribs.

Fig. 68. Ojibwa Canoe: Interior view from the bow.

of about 3/8 to 5/8 inch at each tip which is inserted behind the inwale (Fig. 49). The width of these ribs is 2 to 2-3/4 inches in the midline of the floor of the canoe. They taper gradually as they extend outward and upward, to a width of 7/8 to 1-1/8 inches at about the point where they are inserted behind the inwales (which is 5/8 to 3/4 inch from the tip) (Fig. 69). The taper is somewhat quicker in the uppermost 2 to 3 inch span below the inwale. The thickness in the floor area is 1/2 to 5/8 inch; as the tops rise, the thickness reduces very slightly and gradually by about 1/8 inch. Over the uppermost 5/8 to 3/4 inch of each tip (the area mostly behind the inwale), the width tapers further, down to 5/8 to 3/4 inch at the squared-off tip. The inboard surface at the end of the tip is carved in a sudden taper over the same uppermost 5/8 to 3/4 inch span into a chisel shape. The tip has a sharp edge about 1/32 to 1/16 inch thick.

The ribs nearer to the ends, other than being shorter, are similar in dimensions to the long midsection ribs. Although they are identical in width and taper, they are about 1/8 inch thinner. But the thickness does not taper, so they are identical to the long central ribs in the areas near the gunwales. The endmost rib at each end, adjacent to the headboard, is 43-1/2 to 44 inches long, including the length of about 3/8 to 1/2 inch at each tip which is inserted behind the inwale. The width in the midline of the floor is 2 to 2-3/4 inches. This width tapers gradually as the rib extends outward and upward, reducing to 7/8 to 1-1/8 inches at about the point where it is inserted behind the inwales (which is 5/8 to 3/4 inch from the tip). The thickness remains within the range of 3/8 to 1/2 inch over this distance. In the uppermost portion of 5/8 to 3/4 inch of each tip, the tapered forms and dimensions are identical to those described above for the midsection ribs. This sharply tapered area at the tips of all of the ribs lies mostly behind the inwales.

The flat inboard face of a few of the ribs shows in scattered areas the characteristic raised grain pattern which was created when the ribs were split out. But the ribs were later carved very flat and smooth on virtually all of their flat inboard surfaces as well as the edges. All of the edges of the ribs were originally sharp. In most areas of the ribs, except in their uppermost tip areas, the exposed edges are now worn slightly to mod-

erately rounded from usage of the canoe.

The narrow U-shaped profile of the endmost ribs at each end of the canoe did not require an extremely sharp bend at the midpoint (Fig. 60). Thus, no groove or scoring was necessary across the midpoint to facilitate the bend. The end rib adjacent to each headboard has such a narrow U profile that its tops are vertically upright, with the two tips only about 8 inches from each other.

In the midsection of the canoe, the ribs stand perpendicular to the keel line (Fig. 40). Toward the ends of the canoe, the keel line rises gradually, as the rocker of the bottom curves upward. Outboard of thwarts #2 and #3, each rib was installed at a slight but ever-increasing angle to the gradually rising keel line; the tops of the ribs angle more and more outboard from their bases. (If each rib had been installed perpendicular to the keel line, each rib would angle in the opposite direction, with its base outboard of its tips.) The headboard also stands slightly angled, in the same direction and degree as the angled adjacent ribs; its base lies 2 inches inboard of its head. The distance between the endmost rib at the bow (near its tips) and the upper area of the headboard is 2 inches; the distance between the base of this rib and the base of the headboard is about the same. At the stern end, these distances each measure 6 inches.

Painted Decoration

All of the painted decoration on the canoe appears to be original from the period of Ojibwa construction. The shade of each color and its degree of fading is consistent throughout the entire canoe, implying that all of the pigments were applied at the same time, rather than some having been added at a later date. No restoration is discernible on any of the painted surfaces.

The decoration on the headboards (in black, slightly brownish red, and deep green) has been previously described. Many other surfaces of the wooden elements are also painted (Figs. C-8 to C-13). Along the full length of the gunwale caps, the upper surface is painted black while the outboard edge is a slightly brownish red. The ends of the tips are also black. A coat of deep green was added over the black paint on the upper surface of their tips at each end, over a span of 1-5/8 to 1-3/4 inches. Much of this green area was later covered by the root lashings which bind the tips of the gunwale caps to the

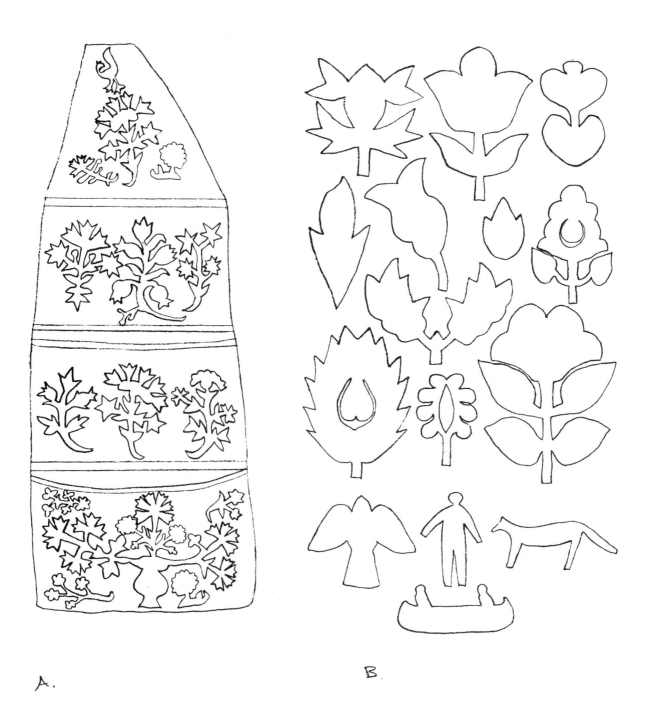

A.

B.

Fig. 70. Traditional native decorative motifs of the Great Lakes region: A. quillwork on deerskin pouch of Charles Langlade, B. Ojibwa beadwork patterns and toy figures, cut from birchbark.

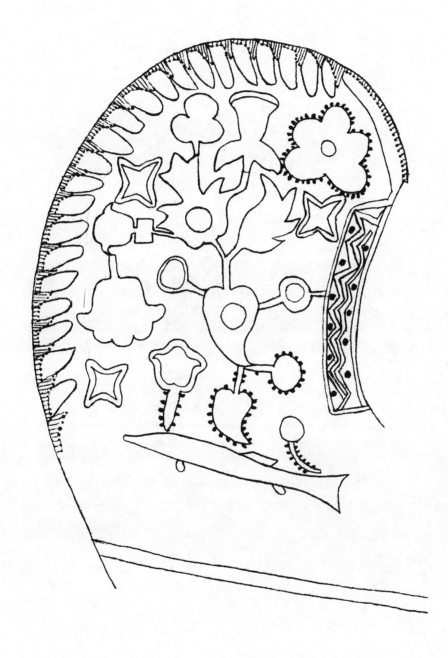

Fig. 71. Ojibwa Canoe: Painted designs on left wall of bow.

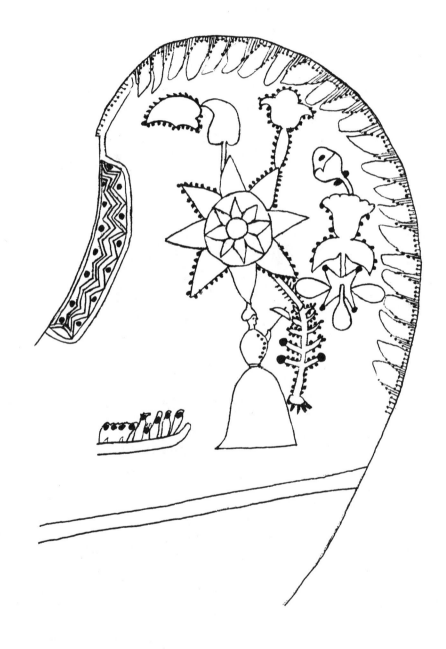

Fig. 72. Ojibwa Canoe: Painted decorations on left wall of stern.

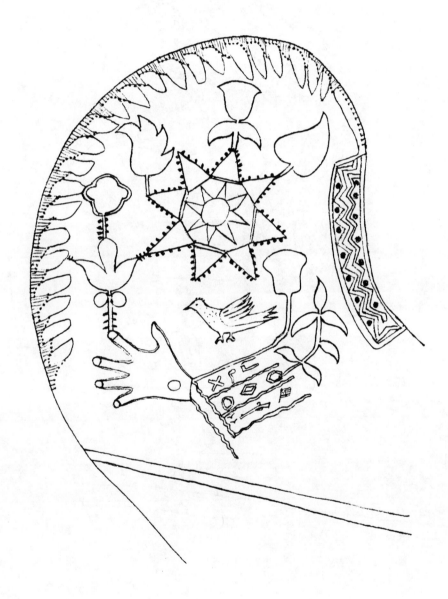

Fig. 73. Ojibwa Canoe: Painted designs on right wall of stern.

Fig. 74. Ojibwa Canoe: Painted decorations on right wall of bow.

Fig. 75. Ojibwa Canoe: Detail of painted designs on right wall of stern.

Fig. 76. Ojibwa Canoe: Detail of painted decorations on right wall of bow, partially obscured by repairs of pitch and tar.

outwales. Most of these lashings have since broken, exposing the green paint underneath. The location of the green pigment beneath the lashings indicates that the caps were painted before the tip lashings were installed. All of the thwarts are painted black on the upper surface over the full length.

The outwales are painted on the outboard side and the top surface at each interval between the gunwale lashings. The intervals are in alternating colors: one interval is a slightly brownish red, while the following one is deep green. The outboard side of the outwale is painted black in the endmost areas, which extend from the lashings beside each headboard to the tips of the outwale. This black end area the stern end of the left wall also has an additional overcoating of deep green. (The other three outwale ends are left in black.) The ends of the tips are also black.

On the reinforcement bark strip, a black disc is painted below each interval between the gunwale lashings. The discs, irregularly round with diameters of 1-1/4 to 1-1/2 inches, lie on the lower edge of the bark strip.

Rather elaborate painted decoration occurs on the ends of the bark deck at each end of the canoe, where the deck ends project below the outwales. With minor variations, the pattern is composed of a slightly brownish red outline around all four sides of the bark flap plus two long parallel zigzag lines in the same color which fill the midsection within the outline. A row of seven or eight black dots lies in the series of triangular areas formed by each of the two zigzag lines and its adjacent outline. A considerable part of the red outline around the deck ends often lies on the bark wall panel adjacent to the deck ends.

An extensive series of painted figures is found on each of the four high end panels (Figs. 71 to 74 and C-10 to C-13). They were executed in the identical hues of slightly brownish red and black which were used on the other painted surfaces of the canoe. Dark brown was also utilized, while deep green was only used on two small elements. The figures were applied directly onto the plain bark panels rather than onto a painted background of a solid color. Painting designs directly onto the bark was a rather common technique in the decoration of end panels of traditional Indian canoes as well as voyaging canoes.[14]

On all four panels, the same series of elements borders the area containing the figures. A brownish red bar, 5/8 to 3/4 inch wide, runs parallel to the span of 4 inches of the edge which is sewn with simple adjacent spiral stitches, beginning at the tips of the gunwales. The distance along the edge which is sewn with stitches in arc patterns is decorated with a series of 22 or 23 lozenge or leaf shaped forms, alternating in brownish red and black. The irregularly shaped painted areas, 2 to 2-1/2 inches long by 3/4 to 1 inch wide, conform generally to the arc shape of each set of stitches. These perimeter decorations, plus the painted end of the bark deck, encircle an area about 20 inches high and 15 inches wide, on which the series of painted figures was applied above the waterline area.

The design patterns on the four end panels are very different from each other, although a number of individual figures are repeated on more than one panel. In addition, certain elements are repeated within the same panel in some cases.

The outlines of the individual figures were applied to the bark panels using two techniques: pattern tracing and freehand painting. Very fine scored lines may be observed on the bark wall around the perimeter of at least five different types of stylized floral and leaf motifs (including their long stems) plus the curved heart or leaf motif. This indicates that these figures were first cut out of a thin but firm material, presumably bark; these patterns were then traced around their perimeter onto the canoe wall with a very sharply pointed implement, probably an awl. Sometimes the patterns were inverted right-to-left or upside down. With the scored lines as guides, the artist then painted the outlines of each figure with a very thin dark line. Finally, the outlined area was filled in with paint, often less darkly than the thin outlines.

Other figures were painted freehand onto the bark panels, without scored guidelines: usually a thin dark outline was first applied, which was then filled in. There is the possibility that some of these apparently freehand figures may have been produced by first painting a fine outline around the perimeter of bark patterns. A few of the figures were painted in true freehand style, without preliminary outlines.

In Figure 70 is illustrated a series of patterns for bead work as well as toy figures, cut from birchbark.

They were collected by Frances Densmore from Ojibwas in northern Minnesota, Wisconsin, and adjacent Ontario between 1905 and 1925.[15] The similarity of these forms to many of the painted figures on the Ojibwa canoe is striking. Comparable bark patterns were presumably used in the decoration of the Ojibwa canoe. Figure 70 also presents the decorative patterns which are found on a deerskin pouch from the second half of the 18th century.[16] The pouch belonged to Charles Langlade, a prominent Metis (Ottawa and French) trader who resided at Michilimackinac from his birth in 1729 until about 1765, and at Green Bay, Wisconsin until at least 1800.[17] The stylized floral motifs are oulined on the pouch in quill work. The virtually exact repetition of two different motifs, reversed right-to-left, indicates the use of bark patterns in the application of these decorations. Another feature of the lowest design area on the pouch is the connected aspect of a number of the forms. This is also very common on the Ojibwa canoe. On some of its end panels, nearly all of the figures are joined. Connected stylized floral motifs were very popular decorative elements among the native populations of the Great Lakes region from at least the second half of the 1700s into the twentieth century.[18]

On the end panels of the Ojibwa canoe, the figures are usually filled in with the same color as their painted outlines. But in some cases, dark brown outlines are filled in with black, reddish brown, or dark green, and black outlines are sometimes filled with dark brown. Most of the figures are composed of two main colors (besides the outline); but some are executed in a single color or in three colors.

The left panel at the bow (Figs. 70 and C-10) contains eight types of stylized floral and leaf motifs, two sizes of a curved heart or leaf pattern, a four-pointed star (repeated three times), and a long slender fish (sturgeon?). The left panel at the stern (Figs. 72 and C-11) displays four or five floral and leaf patterns, the smaller size of curved heart or leaf, a tree, and a small eight-pointed round star or sun within a larger eight-pointed version. A woman holding a parasol is wearing a European style brown dress with a hoop skirt and a row of six black buttons down the bodice. In the lower left appears a red canoe containing nine (?) human, animal, or spirit individuals. On each of the black figures, the artist added

a daub of brownish red, possibly to indicate the facial area. The inboard end of the canoe motif is no longer visible, now covered by tar repairs.

The right panel at the stern (Figs. 73 and C-12) is decorated with six floral and leaf designs, the larger size of curved heart or leaf, a small eight-pointed round star or sun within a larger version, a bird, and a black outstretched hand (outlined widely in brown) which bears a dark brown disk on it near the wrist. At the bottom is found a series of dark brown items contained within a grid of undulating brown lines (Fig. 75). The upper row has a pair of crossed sticks (?), a ball-headed club, and a pipe emitting smoke from its bowl. The middle row contains three shapes: a circle, a diamond, and a hexagon. In the bottom row is portrayed a long arm pointed toward two flying birds, and a flag with five or six stripes plus a field for stars in the upper left corner. Only one central star is depicted in this field.

The right panel at the bow (Figs. 74 and C-13) exhibits the greatest number of human figures of the four end panels. At the top is found a rectangle within an eight-pointed rectangular star or sun. The large central figure, an archer, appears to be clothed in a black shirt, red breech clout, black leggings or trousers, and black footwear. His long black hair and red (roach?) headdress imply a native individual. In front of him stands another apparently Indian figure, with long black hair and an upright feather headdress. He wears a red and black shirt, brown breech clout, and red moccasins. He stands smoking a pipe and holding a long firearm by its muzzle.

The potbellied red figure to the far left is more enigmatic. It is not clear whether the individual is human, animal, or spirit. If he faces toward the right, he appears to wear a single red feather at the back of his head. In addition, he has four red lines cascading down over his face, possibly representing a bleeding head wound. If he faces toward the left, he appears to have a long downward-curving beak as well as hair flowing down the back of his head.

The individual in the lower left wears a wide-brimmed Euro-American style hat. He has received five or six wounds to the chest, from which blood is streaming down his chest and legs. To the left is a large black object resembling an iron pot hook used for suspending a kettle over a fire. To the right, a dog stands attentively, with ears and tail erect, in low foliage. Nearly every one of the creatures painted on the canoe was depicted facing toward the nearby end of the canoe.

Beneath the seven figures on the right panel at the bow, the artist painted block letters and numbers, using the identical slightly brownish red pigment as on all of the decorative elements on the canoe (Figs. 74 and 76). The paint of the letters and numbers has faded to the identical shade as that of the other red painted surfaces. Thus, the writing definitely appears to have been applied at the same time as all of the painted decoration on the canoe.

Two successive applications of tar on a modern repair now hide from view one or two letters in the first line and one number in the second line. The top line, P__ONE, is composed of simple block capital letters about 3/4 inch tall. The letters N and E were made backwards. The numbers in the middle line, 1_58, are of the same style and size as the letters of the upper line. The number 5 was painted backwards. A rather narrow horizontal red line separates the second line from the bottom line, on which is painted the word OSAUGIE. It is made up of larger capital letters, about one inch high, in a more formal stencil style. The last three letters, GIE, were formed backwards. All of the letters and numbers appear to have been applied freehand; no preliminary outlining is visible.

The upper two lines of red letters and numbers on the bow appear to represent the name of the canoe builder, P__one, and the year of manufacture, 1_58. Due to the tar repair, the complete name of the canoe builder may never be known. The oral history which survived with the canoe indicates that it was built by Ojibwas in about 1855. The painted date of 1(8)58 on the canoe clearly corroborates this information.

The word Osaugie has not yet been identified. It may indicate the place of manufacture; however, a search of the hundreds of village names in the *Atlas of Great Lakes History* by Helen Tanner did not yield any similar place names. John Steckley, the noted linguistic specialist of native languages of the Great Lakes region, has suggested that a logical explanation of the three lines of text would be the maker's name, the date, and his clan. But the name Osaugie does not suggest any known clan names.[19] Considering the initial letter O, Steckley rules out the possibility of the word Osaugie referring to the Missisauga Ojibwa village of Saugeen or Sauking on the shore of Lake Huron in southwestern Ontario.[20]

He also notes that Osaugie is the name by which the Ojibwas and other speakers of the Algonquian language family referred to the Sauk people. Often the initial letter O was dropped from many Algonquian tribal names, especially in more recent eras. The Sauk referred to themselves as *Asa-Ki-Waki*, essentially the same name.[21] Thus, there is a possibility that the builder of the Ojibwa canoe may have been identifying himself as having originated with the Sauk people. No definite identification of the inscription Osaugie has as yet come to light.

The selection of figures which were painted on each end panel certainly must have had significance for the Ojibwa builders and users of the canoe.[22] The copious number and rich variety of figures exceeds the usual devices applied to native and fur trade canoes to identify the builders or owners or to invoke spiritual protection. The figures on this canoe many include representations of exploits of one or more individuals, or certain significant events in their lives over a number of years. The figures may also include some spiritual symbols, reflecting the Ojibwa world view as well as personal protective totems. The connected aspect of so many of the figures may imply their concept of the interconnectedness of the various elements of the world. However, such speculation is beyond the scope of this study.

Nails

All of the nails used in the manufacture and repair of the Ojibwa canoe are of the machine-cut type, in the style which was available from the 1830s on.[23] Two sizes, medium and small, were utilized. The illustrations of the two sizes of nails which are found in the Royal canoe also apply to the Ojibwa canoe nails. The only difference is that the tip of the large nail in the Ojibwa canoe tapers slightly more in width at the tip, to 1/16 inch, compared to the 3/32 inch tip on the Royal canoe nail.

Medium size

The medium size nails have heads that are 9/32 to 5/16 inch long by 3/16 to 1/4 inch wide. The sides of the heads are straight or slightly convex, the ends are slightly convex, and the corners are sharp. The head, 1/16 inch thick, has a generally flat surface.

The shank, rectangular in cross section, is 2-1/4 to 2-1/2 inches long. The thickness of 3/32 inch is maintained for nearly its full length. Its width tapers from 3/16 inch below the head to 1/16 inch at the tip. The sharp-cornered truncated tip is 1/16 by 3/32 inch.

This size was used to nail the unit of inwale-bark wall-outwale; the gunwale caps; the unit of stempiece, horizontal braces, and vertical braces (one nail at each end of the canoe); and the wooden repair patch on the inwale (two nails).

Small size

The head is 3/16 to 7/32 inch long by 5/32 inch wide. The sides of the heads are straight or slightly convex, the ends are straight or slightly convex, and the corners are sharp. The head, 1/16 inch thick, has a flat surface.

The shank is not observable, but it is 1-1/2 inches or less in length. Presumably it is rectangular in cross section and has a sharp-cornered truncated tip, as is usual on machine-cut nails. This size was used to nail the tips of the gunwale caps outboard of the headboards, the repair of the cracked outwale, and the wooden repair patch on the inwale.

On some examples of both sizes of nails, the edges of the heads are somewhat irregular and the heads have a slightly domed appearance. These features are apparently due to inconsistency in manufacture, damage and distortion caused during the pounding of the nails, and later deterioration of the edge surfaces. The nails found on the Ojibwa canoe resemble very closely those found on the Royal canoe, in terms of the method of manufacture, the form, and the two sizes.

The modern style of wire nail, with its round head and a shank with a round cross section, appeared in widespread use by about 1879. It overtook the cut nail, due to its relatively cheaper price, although some cut nails continued to be produced.[24] No examples of this modern type of nail were utilized in the manufacture or repair of the Ojibwa canoe.

Wood Types

The type of wood used to build the Ojibwa canoe is very typical for canoe construction. The inwales, outwales, gunwale caps, thwarts, stempieces, headboards, sheathing, and ribs are all fashioned of northern white cedar.[25]

The lashings are made of the roots of either spruce or eastern larch (tamarack).[26] As previously discussed, if they are of spruce, the most typical type for canoe lashings would be black spruce.

Miscellaneous Features
Seats

As on the Royal canoe, there is no evidence on the Ojibwa canoe which would indicate that it was ever fitted with permanent or temporary wooden seats. No areas of wear can be observed on the gunwales or the upper portions of the ribs that can be attributed to the use of such seats.

Provisions for Sail and Cordelling Line

Likewise, no evidence can be observed which would indicate the lashing of a mast or a cordelling (towing) line to the forward thwarts. This is in spite of the fact that the thwarts were made of northern white cedar, a rather soft wood susceptible to the dents and abrasions of such lashings.

The canoe is not equipped with a permanent perforated thwart or mast step for sailing. Thus, if a sail were sometimes used, the upright mast would have been temporarily lashed to the second or third thwart at the bow end. Or a temporary perforated thwart may have been lashed to the second or third thwart, with the mast then positioned in its hole.

The base of the mast may have been placed into a drilled or carved indentation in a loose board laid down the midline, to step the mast. These temporary measures of mast attachment and stepping would leave no permanent evidence that a sail had been used on the canoe. Thus, the lack of such evidence on the Ojibwa canoe does not rule out the use of sail on the craft.

Flags

No evidence can be found for the attachment of a flag at either the bow or the stern. But sufficient space exists outboard of both headboards into which a slender flag staff could have been inserted. Likewise, there is space around the base of the head of each headboard to permit the lashing of such a staff. A light cord could have encircled the headboard between the edges of the head and the gunwale caps, to bind a flag staff to either the outboard surface or the inboard surface of the headboard.

Bow/Stern Differences

The builders of the Ojibwa canoe created a number of differences between the bow and the stern ends of the craft, which are listed below. Some of these features were installed for efficient performance of the canoe, such as the direction of the overlap of the bark panels. Others may have been added to indicate which end of the craft was the bow, to best utilize the efficiency features. Some of the differences may be only coincidental.

A. The prow at the bow presently reaches a maximum height of 42-1/2 inches, compared to 40 inches at the stern.

B. The rocker of the bottom rises to the chin over a span of about 36 inches at the bow compared to about 32 inches at the stern. It is not possible to accurately compare the degree of rise of the rocker at the chins, since both ends of the canoe have sagged somewhat; each chin presently lies about 1/2 inch above the horizontal baseline.

C. The positions and lengths of the thwarts create in the bow half a slightly broader beam and a more sudden taper near the end (at the gunwale level) compared to the narrower stern half, with its longer and more gradual taper.

D. All of the overlapping edges of the various bark panels (except the two high end panels at the stern and one adjacent upper wall panel) are lapped so that the edge that is exposed on the exterior side faces sternward. This increases the efficiency and reduces the likelihood of catching on obstructions.

E. The painted decorations on the exterior of the high end panels are equally abundant and elaborate at both ends of the canoe; human figure motifs occur at both ends. Painted names and dates, however, are found only at the bow end, on the right wall.

F. The tip area of the outwale on the left wall at the stern is overcoated with green paint over its black paint, while the tip area at the bow is left in black. On the right wall, both of the tips of the outwale are left black.

G. A brownish red face is painted on the head of the headboard at the bow end, while its counterpart at the stern is entirely covered with solid areas of brownish red, black, and green.

Usage and Wear

The physical evidence indicates that the canoe saw considerable usage by the Ojibwas before it became the property of Jay Cooke. The bark cover has a major sewn repair across the bottom, which was applied in the traditional native manner. In addition, repairs to both the inwale and the outwale were also carried out using materials and methods which match well those of the original construction of the canoe. Each of these three repairs appears to have been done during the period of usage of the Ojibwas.

The bark cover has a number of scrapes and gouges on the bottom and walls. The ribs and thwarts show a light to moderate degree of worn roundness on their upper edges, while the upper outside edge of each gunwale cap is quite heavily worn in most areas except near the ends. It is not possible to determine whether this wear occurred before or after Mr. Cooke acquired the canoe from the Ojibwas.

Construction Tools, Methods, and Materials

The Ojibwa canoe was manufactured from the traditional forest materials of birchbark, wood, tree roots, and pine or spruce gum mixed with animal fat and pulverized charcoal. It was painted afterward with Euro-American commercial paints.

The builders of the canoe used the typical array of tools normally employed in canoe manufacture during the nineteenth century. These include an axe, knife, crooked knife, drawknife, awl, rib-setting mallet, pitch melting and applying implements, and paint containers and brushes.

In addition, they utilized a few techniques and tools that have generally been considered less traditional in the canoe construction of that era. The use of vertical and diagonal braces on the end frame unit of stempiece and headboard does not appear to have been previously reported in the birchbark canoe literature. Likewise, the tips of the inwales ending at these vertical braces rather than extending out to the stempiece is also rare. As previously mentioned, the extreme number and the variety of the painted figures on each of the high end panels is also rare on traditional native canoes as well as fur trade craft.

A smoothing plane (instead of a knife, crooked knife, or drawknife) smoothed the flat surfaces of all of the gunwale elements, headboards, and thwarts. A brace and bit or a gimlet (a small hand auger) was used instead of an awl or a knife tip to drill the lashing holes in the ends of the thwarts. Commercial string was substituted for the traditional strips of basswood or cedar inner bark or split roots for the spiral wrapping of the laminations of the inwales and stempieces and for the binding of the stempiece braces.

One of the most visually obvious departures from traditional canoe construction involves the substitution of iron nails for carved wooden pegs, driven with an iron hammer. Nails fasten the gunwale elements together; they also fasten (with a single nail) certain braces to the headboard and stempiece unit. In addition, nails were installed to repair damage to the inwale and the outwale. The use of nails in canoe construction and repair became quite widespread in the early nineteenth century, being used in many areas of North America before 1850.[27]

Many of the above "nontraditional" features of the Ojibwa canoe construction represent practical, labor-saving substitutions and improvements; these elements probably produced a canoe with equal or better performance qualities, with less labor and in less time. Since these traits have been observed on a surviving example of a voyaging canoe, they may in fact reflect standard manufacturing techniques used to build such canoes in the middle of the nineteenth century, rather than "nontraditional" variations.

Condition

The bark cover and the wooden elements of the canoe are in sound, stable condition. However, the bark cover has several areas of modern breakage which were never sealed with tar as a restoration measure. One is a very long vertical break in the high end panel of the right wall at the bow. A second crack is located in the end panel on the opposite wall of the bow. Another long crack extends downward from the longitudinal main seam near the stern end. The bark deck outboard of the bow headboard is also partially broken.

The original root lashings remain intact in all of the original bark panel seams and slits, in the original damage repair across the bottom, and in scattered locations on the gunwales and cutwater edges. Much of the original sealant pitch remains, although it is covered in some areas with tar from later restorations. The original painted decoration remains intact, only moderately faded.

Several restoration procedures were carried out on the canoe during its many years of use at the summer home of Jay Cooke as well as during its subsequent display period. Thus, the following resultant features do not apply to the original Ojibwa construction and usage of the canoe.

A. The root lashings in many areas of the gunwales were replaced with lashings of furniture cane strips. These include all of the lashings which bind the thwarts and the headboards to the gunwales.

B. The center thwart and the adjacent bowward thwart were replaced (and left unpainted).

C. A portion of the lower cutwater edge at the stern, extending outboard from the chin, became unstitched. The lowest span was resewn with light-colored cord, which has since become unstitched.

D. To add stability and to reduce the sagging of the ends of the canoe when on display, a long sawn board was fastened down the midline of the floor, atop the ribs. The board, 18 feet 2 inches long, 9-1/2 inches wide, and 3/4 inch thick, tapers over the endmost 23 to 24 inches at each end to a width of 4 inches at the tips. The board is attached to the ribs with downward wood screws at intervals of 5 to 7 inches. The board has no wear on its flat face or edges, while the edges of the ribs adjacent to the board are moderately worn. This indicates that the board was installed after the period of usage of the canoe.

E. Over the years, tar has been applied as a sealant to cover the original pitched seams as well as later breakage in the bark cover. At one point, a coat of tar was applied to virtually all of the original seams of the canoe. The tar was generally applied only on the seams themselves, not covering much of the original pitch sealant which spread beyond the seams. The direction of the runs indicates that the tar was added while the canoe was in an upside down position. Little care was taken to apply the tar in a neat fashion: in many areas, it runs from the longitudinal main seam nearly the full distance to the gunwales, over a span of up to fifteen inches. This tar application, which has lost its shine, appears to date to the period of usage of the canoe at the Cooke summer home. Its untidy appearance implies a utilitarian rather than a cosmetic purpose.

More recent applications of tar (still shiny) were added to cover numerous breaks in the bark cover. These coats of tar, more carefully applied, were added in conjunction with a strip of fabric in five locations on the canoe. The rather finely woven cloth, dark tan in color, was cut into strips about 1-1/2 inches wide. The strips were glued to the canoe with tar and were then covered over with a second coat of tar. In at least three additional locations, only a coat of tar was added to cover the break, without a strip of fabric. None of the above breaks in the bark that were repaired with either tar alone or tar and fabric were ever sealed with pitch.

Notes: Ojibwa Canoe

1. Adney, correspondence of June 17,1925; McFee, tenth drawing in Adney Portfolio; Adney and Chapelle, pp.137, 139, 147.
2. Adney and Chapelle, pp. 141-42.
3. Ibid., p.139.
4. Ibid., pp. 28, 29, 102, 149.
5. Ibid., pp. 134, 136, 139, 140, 143.
6. Christensen, personal communication of December 5, 1994.
7. Adney and Chapelle, pp. 15-16.
8. Ibid., p. 57.
9. Ibid., pp. 138, 141, 147.
10. Christensen, October 14, 1994.
11. Guy, pp. 21, 26; Ritzenthaler, pp. 27-28; Adney and Chapelle, p. 118.
12. Hadlock and Dodge, illustrations.
13. Adney and Chapelle, p. 147.
14. Ibid., pp. 76-77, 137, 153.
15. Densmore, pp. 281, 390, p. 57.
16. Gerin- Lajoie, p. 9.
17. Drummer, p. 372, n. 4; Thwaites, pp. 130-132, n. 68.
18. Flint institute of Arts, pp. 3, 41, 55, 69, 83, 107.
19. Steckley.
20. Tanner, pp. 33-34, 58-59, 127, 164-65, 176-77.
21. Callender, p. 648.
22. Ketemer.
23. Santucci, p. 11; Hume, pp. 253-54.
24. Ibid.
25. Christensen, October 14, 1994.
26. Ibid.
27. Adney and Chapelle, p. 56.

The Sault Canoe

Contents

The Sault Canoe

Certain features of the Sault canoe suggest that it is an Ojibwa/Cree style of fur trade canoe, the Type B-2 style. These traits include the considerable degree of undercut in the profile of the ends and the upright plank stempiece. The canoe was built in the moderately large, six-place (seven-thwart) format, in the size category of a half-size or 16-piece-capacity canoe.

Overall Dimensions

Length: 20' 9-3/4".
Distance between the outboard sides of the tips of the outwales: 19' 1-3/4" (Fig. 78).
Distance between the inboard sides of the tips of the gunwale caps: 19'.
Distance between the inboard faces of the heads of the headboards: 18' 5-7/8".
Depth at the midpoint, from the top of the gunwale caps to the top of the ribs on the floor: 21-1/4".
Height above the baseline: at the midpoint 22-5/8", at the bow 32-3/4", at the stern 32-7/8".
Beam at the midpoint: 3' 11-1/4" (Fig. 79).
Interior beam, inside the gunwales: 3' 8-1/8".
Total girth around the hull, from gunwale top to gunwale top: 5' 8-1/4".

The ends of the canoe are rather modest in height. In contrast to the extremely high ends of the Ojibwa canoe, those of the Sault canoe rise above the midsection height by an increase of only 45 percent. This is the same degree of rise as that of the Royal canoe.

The beam is quite broad in relation to the overall length of the craft. The interior beam equals 17.72 percent of the length. Of the four full size surviving craft, only the Royal canoe is proportionally wider, with an interior beam equal to 18.30 percent of the overall length.

Hull Form
Profile of the Bottom and Ends

Along the keel line, the horizontal span of 11 feet 7 inches appears to lie exactly centered within the total length of the canoe (Fig. 78). From each end of the horizontal section, a 40 inch span of moderate rocker (measured on the horizontal base line) gradually rises to a moderately rounded chin (to the point where the stitches of the cutwater edge begin). The total length of the bottom between the chins is 18 feet 3 inches. At the chins, the rocker has risen 3-7/8 inches above the horizontal baseline.

The length of the two spans of rising rocker are quite long for a craft of this size; the Royal canoe is 8 feet longer, yet its rocker areas are only one inch longer than those of the Sault canoe. In addition, the height of the chins above the baseline is by far the highest of the four surviving full size canoes. The considerable length and height in the rise of the rocker to the chins provided greater maneuverability to the Sault canoe.

From the chin, each end extends 15-1/2 inches outboard (measured on the baseline) to the outermost point of the end. The cutwater edge at each end curves upward from the moderately rounded chin, beginning 2-1/8 inches outboard of the foot of the headboard. At each end, it extends upward and outward for 29-1/8 inches (measured on the curve) to the point of maximum length of the canoe, creating a considerably undercut profile. Then it curves upward and inboard over 9-1/4 inches to the highest point of the end, and finally inboard and only very slightly downward over a span of 3-3/4 inches to meet the outwales. This latter span is nearly horizontal, with almost no downward curve; this is an unusual trait on fur trade canoes. The total length of the edge, measured on the curve from chin to outwales, is 42-1/8 inches at each end of the canoe.

Body Plan

The bottom is narrow and moderately rounded (Fig. 79). The bilge is gradually rounded, while the upper walls are straight and flare outward slightly. The four cross sections in the end-view drawing illustrate the contours of the hull as it gradually tapers between the midpoint of the canoe and the headboards. The four sections correspond roughly to the four thwart positions between the midpoint and the headboards (Fig. 84).

The widest area of the bottom appears to lie directly at

Fig. 77. Sault Canoe, with bow to right.

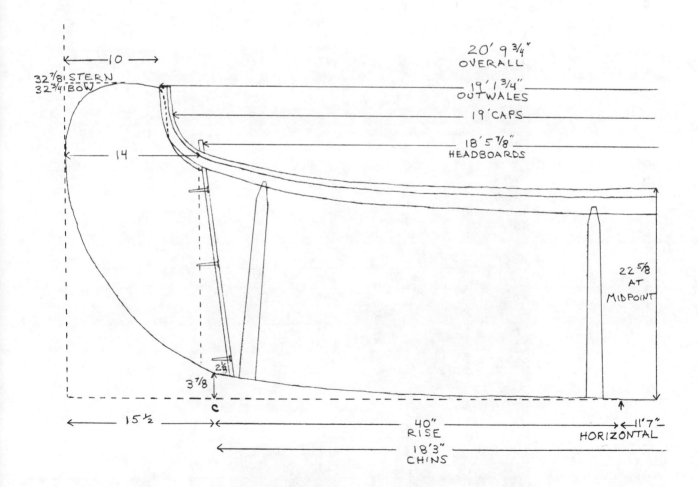

Fig. 78. Sault Canoe: Hull profile and dimensions.

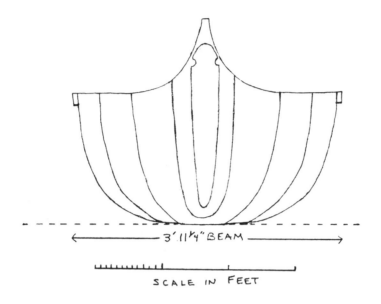

3' 11¼" BEAM

SCALE IN FEET

Fig. 79. Sault Canoe: Body plan (express/freight canoe).

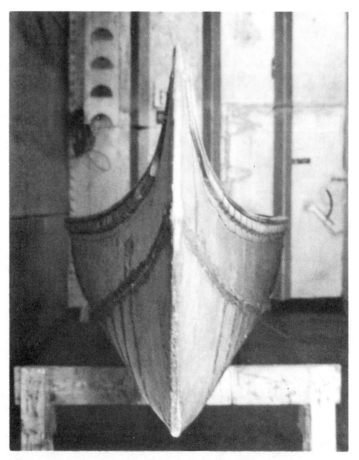

Fig. 80. Sault Canoe: End view of stern.

Fig. 81 (left). Sault Canoe: Lower end view of stern.
Fig. 82 (right). Sault Canoe: Bottom view of stern.

Fig. 83. Sault Canoe: Hull form and thwart positions.

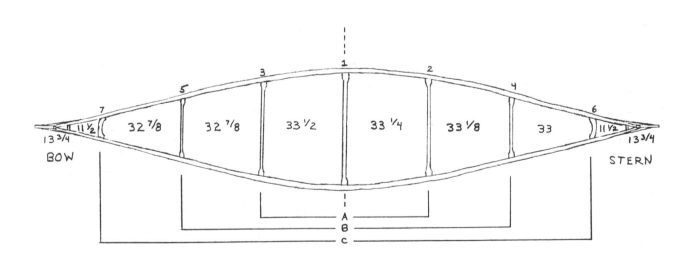

Fig. 84. Sault Canoe: Hull form and thwart positions.

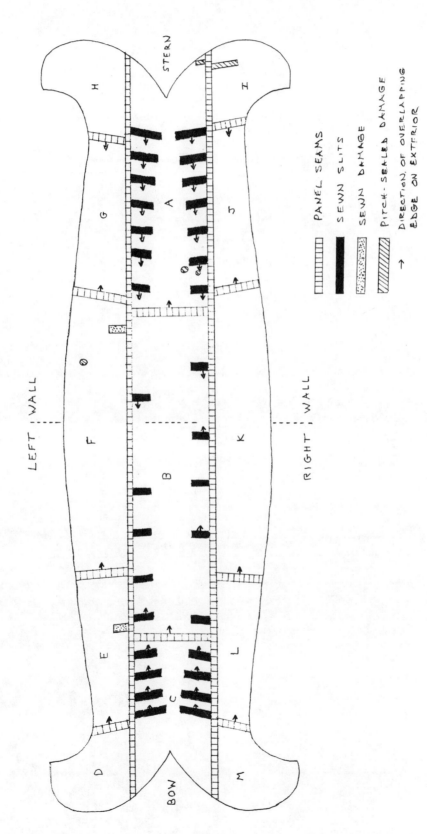

Fig. 85. Sault Canoe: Bark cover.

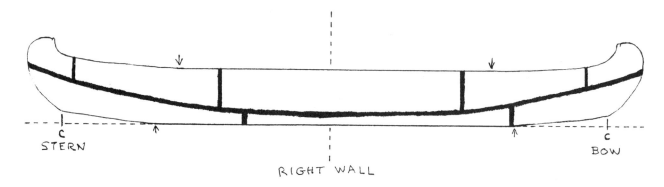

Fig. 86. Sault Canoe: Bark panels.

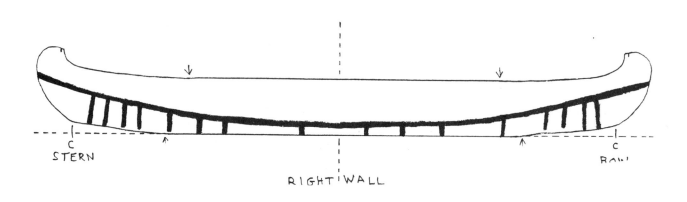

Fig. 87. Sault Canoe: Gore slits.

Fig. 88 (left). Sault Canoe: Harness stitches of longitudinal main seam and cutwater edge.
Fig. 89 (right). Sault Canoe: Sheathing strips, ribs, repair stitches through bark cover and sheathing, and folded birchbark fillers over two of the rib tips.

the midpoint of the length of the canoe. This width tapers gradually and symmetrically from the midpoint to each end of the canoe.

The Sault canoe was built in a style designed for fast paddling. Its features, including a narrow moderately rounded bottom and a gradually rounded bilge, a long slender taper to the ends, and a sharp V form inboard of the headboards all contributed to its speed.[1] (See the description of the sharp V form of the endmost ribs in the ribs discussion.)

Yet its beam at the gunwales is unusually wide in relation to its length: the interior beam is equal to 17.72 percent of the overall length, only slightly less than the 18.30 percent of the Royal canoe. In addition, its depth is very generous in relation to the beam, much more so than that of the Royal canoe. This generous width and depth increased the roominess, which otherwise would have been reduced by the narrow speed features that were built into the canoe. However, the spaciousness was added at the gunwale and upper wall level, rather than in the floor and bilge area.

The moderately rounded bottom of the canoe is much narrower and the bilge area is considerably more undercut (thus a faster craft) than the standard cargo canoes of the period as portrayed by Adney, with their slightly rounded or nearly flat bottoms. In addition, it has a generous depth and an oversize beam at the gunwale level in proportion to its length (although the degree of outward flare of the upper walls is slight). This form would provide generous space for paddlers sitting on raised seats, as well as cargo stacked well above the floor. Its design suggests that this craft was built to serve as an express canoe, transporting fur trade, military, governmental, or clerical personnel as well as mail and cargo. Nearly all period photos and artistic depictions of fur trade canoes show the passengers sitting low, on the floor of the canoe. Possibly passengers in the Sault canoe sat on raised seats of some sort, to take advantage of the roominess in the upper areas of the hull. In contrast to the Sault canoe, some other express canoes of the same era were built relatively narrow at both the bottom and the gunwales.[2]

Bark Cover

The diagram of the bark cover (Fig. 85) portrays the canoe as if it had been placed in an upside down position and flattened by unsewing the end seams. The drawing is not to exact scale or proportion, and the locations and dimensions of the seams are approximate. All of the seams and the repairs have been widened for ease of identification.

Color and Thickness

All of the panels of bark are light golden tan to brownish tan in color. The thickness of the bark ranges from 1/8 to 5/32 inch in the bottom panels and 1/16 to 3/32 inch in the wall panels. (The thickness profile is visible in several locations.)

Panels

On the diagram, the seams joining the thirteen panels of bark are marked with crosshatching. The arrows indicate the direction of the exposed overlapping edges on the exterior of the canoe.

Exact measurements of the individual panels cannot be taken, since the pitch covering the seams in many cases hides from view the exact positions of the edges of the panels. Only the portions of bark visible on the exterior of the canoe were measured, making no allowance for hidden overlaps. The measurement of the height of the side panels runs to the top of the outwale, where the bark was cut off flush with the top of the outwale. Each side panel was measured at its widest point.

Bottom Panels
A. 93-1/2 inches long x 32 inches wide
B. 102-1/2" L x 35" W at the midpoint of the canoe, tapering toward the ends
C. 60-1/2" L x 32" W

Left Wall Panels (including the two high end panels)
D. 26" L x 13-1/4" W
E. 57-1/2" L x 13-1/4" W
F. 86-3/4" L x 16-1/2" W
G. 56-3/4" L x 15-1/4" W
H. 29" L x 12-1/2" W

Right Wall Panels (including the two high end panels)
I. 21-3/4" L x 12-5/8" W
J. 62-1/2" L x 14-1/4" W
K. 89-1/2" L x 16-3/4" W
L. 56-1/2" L x 13-3/4" W
M. 25-1/2" L x 13-1/2" W

If the bark cover were flattened, as in the diagram, the maximum width in the midsection would be 5' 8-1/4" (the total girth of the bark of the canoe). The width near the ends measures 10 and 11-1/8 inches less. The length would be 21' 4" at the level of the gunwales. This total length of the side and end panels of each wall of the canoe is 6-1/4 inches longer than the length of the assembled canoe, since the side panels follow the curvature of the broadening midsection of the canoe, rather than a straight line down the midline.

The bottom of the canoe was made with three panels of bark (two long and one rather short), while each wall was formed by joining two high end panels and three side panels (Fig. 86). An unusual feature is the taper in width of the central bottom panel toward the ends of the craft. In the profile drawing, the panels and seams are positioned exactly as they lie on the canoe.

The canoe builders apparently had no concern about creating weak points in the hull by positioning vertical wall seams directly opposite each other across the hull of the canoe. The seams which attach the side of the two high end panels at the bow (seams D-E and L-M) lie directly opposite each other. (Those attaching the high end panels at the stern are offset from each other by about four inches.) The seams between panels E-F and K-L as well as those between panels F-G and J-K lie nearly opposite each other, offset by only 1-1/4 to 1-1/2 inches.

The builders positioned the seams in the walls well distant from the seams in the bottom. The sternward wall seams lie 10 and 10-1/2 inches from seam A-B, while the bowward wall seams were placed 20-1/2 and 23 inches from seam B-C.

Sewn Seams

The original lashing material still survives in all of the sewn seams. A minute sample of this original lashing root was analyzed microscopically. It has been identified as either spruce or eastern larch (tamarack). When analyzing only a sample of root material, without any accompanying trunkwood, it is impossible to differentiate between these two tree types.[3] If the roots were spruce, they would most likely be black spruce, which is the best and most common type of root for canoe construction.[4]

The only tucked-under ends of seam lashing roots

which are visible for observation and description are those on the resewn seams of the bottom and walls, all of the others having been finished on the hidden interior side. No evidence suggests that a batten strip of wood or root was incorporated into any of the seams for added reinforcement, either on the exterior or the interior side of the bark cover.

Bottom Seams

The two seams connecting the three panels of the bottom to each other were the first seams that were sewed in building the canoe. They are overlapped so that the exposed edge on the exterior faces toward the stern, with an overlap of about 2 to 3-1/4 inches. These seams are sewn with split roots in a series of widely spaced spiral stitches, with one stitch per hole. The portion of each stitch on the exterior side of the canoe is horizontal, while the connector portion running to the next stitch on the interior of the canoe is diagonal. The stitches run through pairs of awl holes: on the overlapping side of the seam, the hole lies about 1/4 to 3/8 inch from the edge of the bark; on the opposite side of the seam, the other hole is immediately adjacent to the overlapping edge. The visible horizontal portions are about 7/16 to 1/2 inch long, and are spaced about 1-3/8 to 1-5/8 inches apart.

The lashing roots are 3/32 to 1/8 inch wide (about the same as the diameter of the awl holes) and about 1/16 to 3/32 inch thick, with a half-round cross section. The rounded side, which was scraped somewhat flat, is the side of the root lashing which faces the exterior.

Gore Slits

After the three bottom panels were joined together, the long span of bottom bark was laid out on the building bed, and the building frame was placed upon it. As previously discussed, this frame determined the general outline of the bottom of the canoe, particularly the shape of the taper toward the ends. The building frame was about as long as the bottom of the canoe, from chin to chin. After the bark was bent upward around the perimeter of the frame, a number of gore slits were sliced at intervals along the sides of the bottom panels. These slices ran from the edges of the bark inboard nearly to the building frame.

At nearly all of these slits, one edge of the bark was

made to overlap the other edge by about 1/4 to 1-1/2 inches, with the exposed edge on the exterior facing toward the midpoint of the canoe. In five cases (all in the bowward half), a slice of bark was removed to create a seam with beveled butting edges. These five slits are those in the diagram of the bark cover which have no directional arrow. Each overlapping edge was thinned considerably, so that the exposed edges of the gore slits are lower and less prominent than all of the other overlapping seams on the canoe, which were not thinned.

It is not common to find the exposed overlapping edges facing toward the midpoint of the canoe rather than toward the stern; but such a feature is also found on the Quebec canoe. In addition, it has been reported on a Tete de Boule medium sized craft built north of Trois-Rivieres, as well as on some Algonkin canoes.[5] With this method of construction, no matter which end of the canoe was used as the forward end, the exposed overlaps in the forward half would face rearward, slightly facilitating the movement of the canoe.

The slits are stitched closed with split roots in a series of moderately spaced spiral stitches, in a manner nearly identical to that which was used to connect the three bottom panels together. But in the gore slit seams, the stitches are slightly longer, 9/16 to 5/8 inch long; they also lie slightly closer together, at intervals of 3/4 to 1-1/4 inches. In addition, the awl holes in each pair of holes lie equidistant from the seam, 1/8 to 3/16 inch from it.

The gore slits in the bottom panels are positioned at irregular intervals from the midsection of the canoe to a point 8-1/2 to 9 inches inboard of the chins (Figs. 85 and 87). They are located on the profile drawing exactly as they lie on the canoe. In general, the intervals between the slits gradually reduce from the midsection toward each end of the craft.

Sixteen slits are found in each wall, with an equal number of slits in each half of the canoe. In the stern half are found seven pairs of rather closely-spaced pairs of slits, lying directly opposite each other. These pairs, spaced at intervals of 6-1/2 to 12-1/2 inches, extend to a point 27 inches from the end of the craft. Inboard from these seven pairs, a single slit is found in each edge of bottom panel B. In the bow half are found five pairs of rather closely-spaced pairs of slits, lying directly opposite each other. These pairs, at intervals of

7-1/2 to 10-1/2 inches, reach a point 28 inches from the end of the canoe. Inboard from these five pairs, three slits were cut into each edge of panel B. Of these, only two lie as a pair directly opposite each other; the remaining slits occur singly, two in each edge of the panel. It may be significant that four of the five butted gore slit seams in the canoe are found in these six midsection slits in the bow half. (All but one of the other gore slits on the craft are overlapping seams.)

In traditional building methods, gore slits do not always appear in equal numbers on both sides of the canoe or always lie directly opposite one another.[6] Whether intentionally or not, the builders installed the gore slits in the bow half so that they begin somewhat closer to the midpoint of the canoe and extend to a point one inch closer to the end of the canoe than the series in the stern half.

When the canoe is viewed in side profile, the gore slits extend downward from the longitudinal main seam, which runs the full length of each side of the canoe (Fig. 87) In the central, widest area of the canoe, this seam curves down close to the horizontal baseline of the canoe. Here, the gore slits are barely visible in a profile view where they extend down to the rounded bottom of the canoe. Toward the ends of the canoe, where the main seam rises, the slits become gradually longer. The full length of the slits toward each end is visible, running down the curved bilge area of the lower walls up to a length of 12-1/2 inches, to reach the rounded bottom.

The length of each gore slit cannot be measured exactly, since each is covered by a coating of pitch. This pitch extends inboard toward the midline of the canoe beyond the end of each slit. Measurement can be made of the length of each pitch strip, which implies the general length of the gore slit which it covers. The pitch strips closest to the midsection are the shortest; they measure 8-1/2 to 10-1/2 inches in length. The strips in general become gradually longer toward the ends of the canoe: the endmost ones are 11 to 12-1/2 inches long.

Bottom panel B contains the pair of opposing gore slits which lies closest to the midpoint of the canoe, about 18 inches bowward from the midpoint. The length of these pitch strips is 8-1/2 and 9-1/4 inches, creating a span of 19 inches between the inboard tips of the two strips. The next pair of opposing gore slits, 14 inches closer to the bow end in panel B, has slits 6-1/2 and 8-1/2 inches long; the span between their tips measures 20 inches.

Since the gore slits were sliced from opposite edges of the bottom bark panels inboard nearly to the building frame, the spans between the opposing pairs of slits across the bottom of the canoe ought to reflect the shape and dimensions of the building frame. As previously mentioned, the strip of pitch sealing each gore slit extends further inboard than the actual end of the gore slit itself. Thus, the span measured between the tips of a pair of opposing pitch strips is shorter than the actual span between the tips of the slits, and likewise shorter than the span across the building frame. Also, the pitch was not applied to the gore slits in a precise fashion. The gore slits are presented in the diagram generally according to the length of their pitch strips.

Some generalities may be deduced concerning the form of the building frame. It was presumably about 18 feet 3 inches long, since that is the length of the bottom (the distance between the chins). The maximum width of the building frame that was used to construct slightly rounded and nearly flat-bottomed fur trade canoes was often two-thirds of the interior beam of the gunwales.[7] In the case of the Sault canoe, this ratio would produce a measurement of about 29-1/2 inches. There are no gore slits at the midpoint; the bottom span measures 19 and 20 inches between the pairs of slits which lie nearest to the midpoint. The span between the pitched pair of strips nearest to each end measures 4-1/4 and 5-1/2 inches. This represents in a general manner the degree of taper from the wide midpoint of the building frame to its pointed ends.

Side Panels to Bottom Panels

After the gore slits were cut and stitched along the side edges of the bottom panels, the side panels were attached to the bottom panels. The seam connecting the side and bottom panels to each other is the prominent longitudinal seam which arcs across the full length of the canoe on each wall. When the side panels were attached to the bottom panels, a wider panel was installed at each end of both walls, to create the high upswept ends of the canoe.

The lower edges of the side panels are positioned inside the edges of the bottom bark panels. Thus, the edges

of the bottom panels are exposed on the exterior of the canoe, facing upward toward the gunwales (Fig. 88). The seams are sewn with split roots in a harness stitch, with the two ends of a single root running in opposite directions through the same hole, one stitch per hole. The end-to-end stitches, 1/2 to 3/4 inch long, are composed of 3/16 to 1/4 inch diameter split roots, considerably wider than those described above for the bottom seams and gore slits. The horizontal row of stitches lies 1/4 to 3/16 inch below the exposed edge of the bottom bark panel. This edge was cut off after the seam was stitched, as evidenced by a knife slit in the wall panels along the full length of the longitudinal main seam. The seam undulates considerably as it spans the length of the canoe; one seam often rises higher than its counterpart on the opposite wall.

An unusual touch was added by the builders when they sewed this seam. Toward each end of the canoe, the stitches gradually shorten, reaching a length of 1/4 to 3/8 inch near the ends. As the stitches shorten, slightly narrower strands of lashing roots were also utilized; those near the ends measure 1/8 to 3/16 inch in width. These touches added a delicate appearance to the seam, which is visible in the photo.

Side Panels to Side Panels

The seams which join the side panels to each other are all overlapping seams, with the edges overlapping about 1 to 1-1/2 inches. In each instance, the exposed edge which overlaps on the exterior faces toward the stern, with two exceptions. On each wall at the stern, the seam that joins the high end panel to its adjacent side panel (seams G-H and I-J) overlaps toward the bow. This may have been done to facilitate the sewing procedure. The forward direction of these two overlaps is not critical, since these sternmost seams are the ones least likely to receive abrasion during use of the canoe.

The root sewing which joins the side panels to each other is nearly the same as that used in the bottom panels. The spiral stitches are made of split roots 3/16 inch wide, with the rounded side scraped somewhat flat. The stitches measure 3/8 to 1/2 inch in length; they lie at intervals of 1-1/4 to 1-1/2 inches. The holes in the overlapping panel of the bark are positioned 1/8 to 3/16 inch from the edge, while those on the under panel lie adjacent to the edge of the overlap. The two seams in the midsection of each side which join side panels to side panels are stitched together. In contrast, the endmost seams at both ends of each wall were not stitched; they were sealed only with pitch. These end panel seams are the only seams on all four of the full size fur trade canoes in this study which are not stitched together. In contrast, a number of seams are unstitched, sealed only with pitch, on the Assiginack, Varden, and Catlin model canoes.

Seam Sealing

All of the seams on the exterior of the canoe were coated with charcoal-blackened melted pitch or gum from spruce or pine trees, of the same description as the gum found on the Royal canoe. The remaining original pitch is now very brittle; it does not indent under thumb pressure.

A coating of plain unblackened gum was applied to all of the seams on the interior side of the canoe. Interior views of this pitch are visible between displaced sheathing strips in several areas.

In addition, all of the seams were sealed on the exterior of the canoe. No runs of melted pitch indicate the position of the canoe at the time of its application. The swaths of gum which cover the longitudinal main seams are 1-1/4 to 2-1/2 inches wide, while those sealing the bottom and gore slit seams are 1-1/2 to 2 inches in width. The pitched areas which cover the main wall panel seams are somewhat narrower, 1 to 1-1/2 inches wide. The gum sealing the main wall panel seams extends up to the lower edge of the reinforcement bark strip. The swath of pitch which seals each of the four unstitched end panel seams is even narrower, only 1/4 to 7/8 inch wide. Some of these swaths extend up to the reinforcement bark strip, while others end 3/4 to 1-1/8 inch below the bark strip. After repeated reapplications of melted gum during usage of the canoe, the sealant is up to 1/8 to 3/16 inch thick in most areas of the canoe.

Exterior Hull Surface

The discussion concerning the disruptions in the smooth, even surface of the bark cover of the Royal canoe also applies to the Sault canoe as well. However, the builders of the Sault canoe abraded down many of the larger growths which projected from the surface, so that they became flush with the surface of

the bark. This was not done on any of the other craft in this study.

Overlapping panel edges and applications of sealant pitch up to 3/16 inch thick have produced seams which stand out from the flat surface of the hull. In addition, two wall panel seams overlap toward the bow. But these overlapping edges which face forward lie above the waterline; thus, they would not impede the forward flow of the canoe through the water.

Damage and Repairs

During the period of usage of the canoe, a series of repairs was carried out on the bark cover. These include five repairs of damage using only blackened pitch, the stitching of two breaks in the cover, and the relashing of the four main wall seams and one of the bottom seams (Fig. 85).

Two small areas of damage in the forward portion of bottom panel A were repaired utilizing only gum. The smaller area is located about 80 inches forward of the stern tip and 4-1/2 inches below the longitudinal main seam. It is covered with a small oval swath of pitch about 3/4 by 1 inch. About 3 inches sternward from the first damage area and a little lower on the bilge area lies the second gummed repair, measuring 1-1/4 by 2 inches. Another damage area sealed with only pitch is found in the upper portion of the left wall, in the sternward half of panel F. Located 6 inches below the gunwale cap, the oval swath measures 1-1/4 by 2-5/8 inches. The remaining two pitched repairs lie close to each other on the right wall at the stern, extending from the longitudinal main seam. One crack, 4 inches from the end of the canoe, extends downward from the main seam. It is covered by gum in an area 1 by 4 inches. The other crack, 9 inches forward of the end of the canoe, extends upward from the main seam. It was sealed with pitch in a swath that measures 1-1/2 by 5 inches.

Two areas in which cracks extended upward from the main seam in the left wall were lashed with root stitches and sealed with blackened pitch. One is located in panel E, 59 inches from the bow end of the canoe. The vertical crack, 5-1/2 inches long, was closed with four spiral stitches 5/8 to 3/4 inches long. These lashings, made with split roots 1/8 inch wide, run through holes which lie 1/8 to 3/16 inch from each side of the crack. The stitches are spaced at intervals of 1-1/8 to 1-3/4 inches. The area of the crack and its lashings was then sealed on the exterior with a swath of blackened melted gum about 1-1/2 inches wide and 6 inches long.

The second crack occurred in wall panel F, at a point 94-1/2 inches forward of the stern tip. It extends vertically upward from the main seam for 4 inches. The damaged area was closed with split roots 1/8 to 3/16 inch in diameter, running through awl holes which lie 3/16 to 1/4 inch from each side of the crack. The three stitches, 5/8 to 3/4 inch long, are placed at intervals of 1 to 1-1/8 inches. The damaged area was then covered with a swath of blackened pitch measuring 1-1/2 by 4-1/2 inches.

During the course of the usage of the canoe, all four of its main wall seams (E-F, F-G, J-K, and K-L) and the bottom seam B-C were relashed. The five seams appear to have been redone during a single repair procedure, in order to bind the two end courses of sheathing strips firmly in place. The repair was carried out after many years of rib pressure had gradually warped the inwales upward, thus decreasing the holding pressure of the ribs against the sheathing strips. Sewing the bark cover to the sheathing strips would preclude the possibility of future movement or adjustment of the strips; but it would hold the sheathing in position.

To relash the five seams of the Sault canoe, the midsection ribs and the central course of sheathing strips were removed from the craft; the original lashing roots were also taken out of the five seams. Then an awl was inserted from the exterior side of the craft through the preexisting holes of the former stitches. The awl drilled through the sheathing strips inside, in the space between two ribs (Fig. 78). The pairs of irregular round holes in the sheathing are about 1/8 to 3/16 inch in diameter. Split roots, about 1/8 to 3/16 inch wide and 1/16 to 3/32 inch thick, with a half-round cross section, form the series of widely spaced spiral stitches. The short horizontal spans of the stitches lie on the exterior of the canoe, while the long diagonal connector spans are visible on the interior between the ribs, atop the sheathing strips. On the interior side, the loose ends of the lashing roots are tucked underneath an adjacent stitch. The photo shows that, in one of the seams, the uppermost long diagonal stitch, under which the upper end of the root was tucked, has broken away

and is now missing. Each resewn seam was resealed with a swath of melted blackened pitch on the exterior of the canoe.

After the five seams were relashed, the central course of sheathing strips and the midsection ribs were restored to their former positions in the craft. The ends of the strips in some instances covered a number of the replacement stitches, as is shown in the photo. The tips of many of the midsection ribs were covered with folded strips of birchbark before reinstallation; these strips filled the gap between the rib tips and the raised warped inwale. (Two such fillers are visible in the photo.) The fillers are described and illustrated with the rib information.

Gunwale Elements

The wood which was used to fashion the inwales, outwales, and gunwale caps of this canoe has been microscopically identified from minute samples as northern white cedar.[8] All of the gunwale elements are angled slightly outward, at the same degree of outward flare as the topsides of the bark walls to which they are attached (Fig. 90).

Inwales

The total length of the inwale on the curve is 20 feet 7-1/4 inches. This is the same length as the outwale, since the ends of the inwale rise and end in exact parallel with the outwale (Fig. 78). In the midsection, the inwale strip is 7/8 inch wide across the top and 1-1/4 inches deep (Fig. 90). The bottom surface is only 1/2 inch across, since the lower outboard edge is planed off into a beveled surface about 1/2 inch wide; this produces a space into which the tips of the ribs fit. Beginning at about the second thwart from each end, the inwale tapers very gradually toward each end over a span of about 58 inches. At the tip of the inwale, the width (thickness) has tapered down to 3/32 to 5/32 inch, and the depth has reduced to 11/16 to 3/4 inch.

All surfaces of the inwale are carved flat and smooth. All edges are sharp, and the ends are cut off squarely at the tips. Nearly all of the edges are now much worn in a series of narrow indentations in the locations where the gunwales were lashed together. These worn areas were caused by the rubbing of the flat side of the split root wrappings, as the canoe flexed during usage.

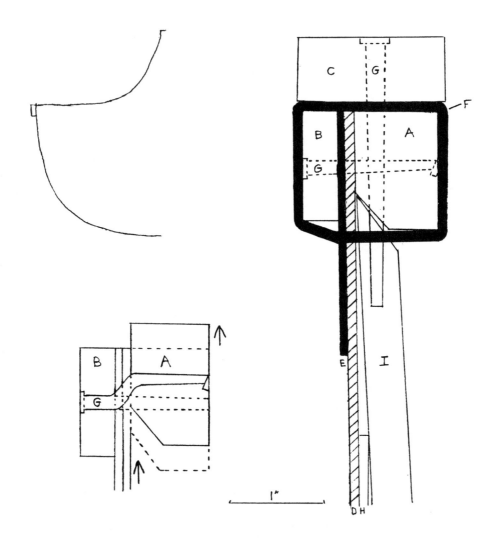

Fig. 90. Sault Canoe: Cross section of gunwales and inwale displacement. A. inwale, B. outwale, C. gunwale cap, D. bark wall, E. reinforcement bark strip, F. root lashings, G. nails, H. sheathing, I. rib.

Fig. 91 (left). Sault Canoe: Lashings of gunwale ends and cutwater edge.
Fig. 92 (right). Sault Canoe: Lashings of gunwale ends. Edge of plank stempiece is visible between the inwales, behind the headboard.

Fig. 93. Sault Canoe: Top view of gunwale tips and cutwater edge lashings.

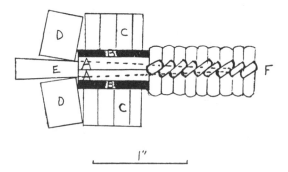

1"

Fig. 94. Sault Canoe: Top view of gunwale tips and cutwater edge lashings. A. inwale tips, B. bark walls, C. laminated outwale tips, D. gunwale cap tips, E. wedge or peg, F. cutwater edge lashings, with decorative "beads" down midline.

Fig. 95 (left). Sault Canoe: Stern end interior. Diagonal supplemental sheathing strips extend inboard from the headboard.
Fig. 96 (right). Sault Canoe: Top view of stern end. Edge of plank stempiece is clearly visible outboard of the headboard.

–131–

Fig. 97. Sault Canoe: Top view of nailed inwale-outwale (now loosened) and gunwale cap, and machine- cut nail from gunwales.

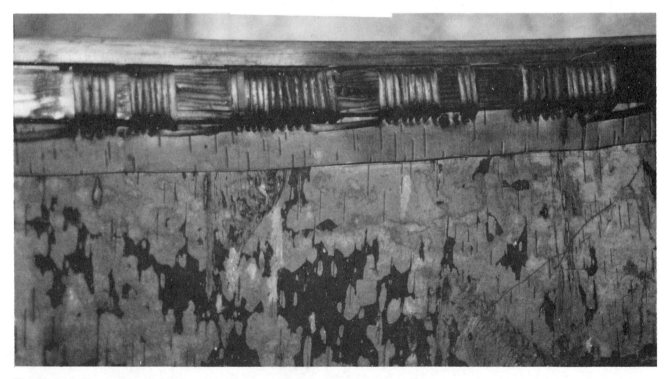

Fig. 98. Sault Canoe: Gunwale lashings and nails, and reinforcement bark strip.

Fig. 99. Sault Canoe: Gunwale and thwart lashings, ribs, and sheathing.

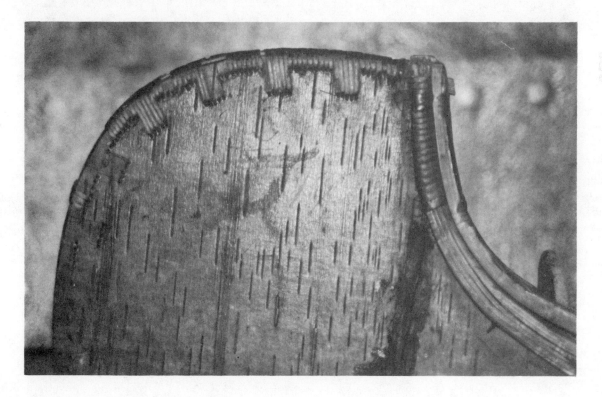

Fig. 100. Sault Canoe: Lashings of gunwale ends and cutwater edge, and painted decoration.

The inwale runs nearly horizontally over much of the length of the canoe, and then rises very gradually toward the ends (Fig. 78). At about each end thwart, it begins to curve up moderately toward its ends. Just outboard of the headboard, the inwale sweeps upward in a strong curve to reach a nearly vertical position at the tips. It does not diverge from the outwale, as is usually the case, but instead remains parallel with the outwale to the tips. The upswept ends of the inwale extend outboard and upward beyond the headboards for 9-1/2 inches. From the headboard to the tip, the inwale rises about 6 inches in height. The tip extends 3/32 to 1/8 inch above the ends of the outwales and gunwale caps, reaching a point at about the same height as the maximum height of the end panel of the canoe.

To facilitate the bending of the upward curve of the ends of the inwale, three splits were made in the ends, to produce four lamination layers. The slits extend inboard from the tip of the inwale for about 10 to 16 inches. Inboard of the headboard, the area where the three lamination slits end is covered by the 6 to 6-1/2 inch span of lashings which bind the inwale to the outwale. These lashings prevent the slits from splitting further inboard.

The inwale fits into a notch which is cut into the side of each headboard (Fig. 95). Two turns of split root bind the inwale to the headboard at the notch. The tips of the inwales, sandwiched between the tips of the outwales, are also firmly bound to the outwales by a series of 16 spiral lashings (Figs. 91 to 94). These lashings are described in the outwale section. Below the inwale-outwale lashings 1/4 inch, 3-1/2 inches below the tips, the converging inwales are bound together. Three wraps of split roots 1/8 inch wide encircle the inwales, just inboard of the edge of the stempiece. These were tightened by two turns of the root around the midpoint of the encircling three wrappings.

The inwale is nailed to the outwale over the entire distance between the headboards. The endmost nail in each gunwale at the stern end was driven into the edge of the headboard; the endmost one in each gunwale at the bow end lies in the portion of the gunwales which is covered by the span of gunwale lashings just inboard of the headboard. The endmost nail in each case was driven into the portion of the gunwales which is laminated. The nailed inwale and outwale strips have

sandwiched between them the top edge of the bark wall (cut off flush with the top surface of the outwale) and a strip of reinforcement bark (Fig. 90). The nails were driven horizontally from the exterior side of the outwale. The nails run generally down the midline of the two wooden elements, at intervals of 4-1/2 to 9 inches. These intervals vary irregularly, not in relation to the location along the gunwales. The machine-cut nails have heads which are 3/16 to 7/32 inch long by 5/32 inch wide (Fig. 90). (See the nail information summary on page 148.) The tips of the nail shanks in some cases barely protrude throughout the face of the inwale. In other instances, they protrude up to 1/8 inch; these are clinched over horizontally. About half of the gunwale nails were later covered by the groups of gunwale lashings; the remainder are visible between the lashing groups.

From headboard to headboard, the entire length of each inwale is scored at intervals on its top surface. The parallel scratches, about 1/32 inch wide and about 1/32 inch deep, were made with an awl or other sharp implement across the width of the inwale and the outwale. The scored areas, separated by intervals of 2-3/8 to 2-5/8 inches, correspond to the locations of the gunwale lashing groups. They are now visible where the lashings are broken and missing and the gunwale cap has been raised due to upward rib pressure. The tops of the inwale and outwale were scored before the gunwale lashings were installed, to indicate the intended locations of the root wrappings.[9]

Outwales

The total length of the outwale on the curve is 20 feet 7-1/4 inches, measured on the outside of the curve. In the midsection, it is 3/8 inch wide across the top and 1-1/8 inches deep (Fig. 90). In width (thickness), the outwale is 1/2 inch less than the inwale, and in depth it is 1/8 inch less than the inwale. The thickness is unusually slight for a craft of this size.

Over nearly the entire span between the headboards, the outwale is now positioned so that its top surface lies about 1/4 inch below the top surface of the inwale. (Usually the two top surfaces are at the same level.) The bottom surface extends up to 1/8 inch below that of the inwale. This unusual relationship of positions was caused by the constant upward pressure on the inwale by the ribs, forcing the inwale gradually upward, in spite of the nails which attach it to the outwale. Such warpage is found on the Ojibwa and Quebec canoes as well. On some canoes in which the inwale was attached to the outwale by wooden pegs, this upward rib pressure caused the pegs to bend in the midsection.[10] Such a bend is noted in the gunwale pegs of the Quebec canoe. The midsections of the inwale-outwale nails in the Sault canoe presumably have comparable bends, which are not visible from the exterior (Fig. 90). Such bends are also present in the gunwale nails of the Ojibwa canoe.

Beginning at about the second thwart from each end of the canoe, the depth of the outwale tapers very gradually over a span of about 58 inches, to 9/16 to 5/8 inch at the tips. The width (thickness) of 3/8 inch remains unchanged over the full length.

All surfaces of the outwale are carved flat and smooth. All of the edges are sharp, and the ends are cut off squarely at the tips. As on the inwale, nearly all of the edges in the locations of the gunwale lashings are now much worn in a series of narrow indentations; this wear was caused by the rubbing of the flat side of the split root lashings. The horizontal machine-cut nails which fasten the outwale to the inwale have already been discussed in the inwale information.

The outwale runs nearly horizontally over much of the length of the canoe, and then rises very gradually toward the ends (Figs. 77 and 78). At about each end thwart, it begins to curve up moderately toward its ends. Just outboard of the headboard, the outwale sweeps upward in a strong curve to reach a nearly vertical position at the tips. (The ends are angled nearly identically to those on the Ojibwa canoe, slightly more angled than the virtually vertical outwale ends of the Royal canoe.) The ends of the outwale sweep outboard and upward beyond the headboards for 9-1/2 inches on the curve. From the headboard to the tip, the outwale rises about 6 inches in height. The tip reaches a point 1/8 inch below the maximum height of the prow of the canoe.

To facilitate the bending of the upward curve and the extreme upsweep at the tips, the same lamination procedure was done as on the inwales: three slits were made, to produce four lamination layers. The lamination slits extend from the tips inboard for a distance of 10 to 16 inches. The lashings which bind the outwale to the inwale just inboard of the headboards cover the area where the lamination slits end. These lashings prevent the slits from splitting further inboard. The four lamination layers are cut off at the tip of the outwale to form a generally square, horizontal end.

The tips of the two converged outwales are joined to each other and to the inwale tips by a series of lashings made of split roots 3/16 inch wide (Figs. 91 to 94). The tips are not pegged or nailed to each other. The lashings, beginning 1/2 inch below the tips, wrap in 16 adjacent spiral turns around the two joined outwales and inwales, covering a span of 3-3/8 inches. The 16 wraps also run through an equal number of holes in the adjacent bark wall, passing through the stempiece inside the bark wall as well. Of these spiral lashings, the lower 12 each have a short turn around the midpoint of the large encircling wrap, which pulls the upper and lower spans of the wrap toward each other. Each short turn around the midpoint was added after the root had completely encircled the outwales and inwales, before beginning the next large circular wrapping.[11] The series of short central turns adds strength and rigidity to the rather wide span of split roots which fills the area between the converging outwales. This technique was also used by the builders of the Quebec canoe. In contrast, the builders of the Royal canoe filled the comparable expanse with wrappings in a figure-eight pattern, to provide the required strength and rigidity for the rather wide span of roots.

After the lashings of the inwale-outwale tips were completed, a long slender cedar wedge was driven horizontally between the tips of the inwales and outwales, to tighten the lashings further. The tapered peg or wedge is 2-3/8 inches long. It measures 3/8 by 1/4 inch at its exposed wide end, tapering gradually to 1/8 by 1/16 inch at the tip. Over its full length, the peg has flat sides and rounded edges. At its broad end, it is cut off sharply. The narrow end was inserted between the first and second uppermost root wrappings which encircle the inwales and outwales, 5/8 to 11/16 inch below their tips. The peg was driven between the tips of the inwales and outwales and about 3/4 inch into the edge of the plank stempiece. In the process, the second and third uppermost root lashings were broken. The broad end of the peg projects about 1/4 inch inboard from the inboard surface of the gunwale caps. When the caps were later lashed together with the inwales and outwales, the tips of the caps were squeezed tightly against the sides of the projecting peg.

The triangular area between the converging outwales and inwales outboard of the headboards is not covered by a bark deck. There is a possibility that a slender flagstaff could have been inserted adjacent to the outboard side of the headboard, beside the stempiece, at either the bow or the stern (Fig. 96). However, there is not enough space between the head or upper body of the headboard and the gunwales or sheathing strips for the wrapping of a cord around the headboard, to bind a flag staff to the outboard or inboard face of the headboard, at either the bow or the stern.

Gunwale Caps

The total length of the gunwale cap is 20 feet 2-1/2 inches, measured on the inside of the curve. (This is 4-3/4 inches shorter than the outwale, which was measured on the opposite side of the curvature.) In the midsection, the cap is 1-9/16 inches wide by 5/8 inch deep (thick) (Fig. 90). Beginning at about the midpoint of the cap, its width and depth gradually taper over a distance of 10 feet, to a width of 1/2 inch and a depth of 3/8 inch at the tips.

All surfaces are carved flat and smooth, and all edges are sharp. The ends are cut off squarely at the tips. Through usage, the upper outboard edge has been worn round in all areas except near the tips of the caps.

The combined width (thickness) of the inwale (7/8 inch) and the outwale (3/8 inch) is 5/16 inch less than the width of the gunwale cap (Fig. 90). But the bark wall and the reinforcement bark strip which are sandwiched between the inwale and the outwale add about 5/16 inch more of thickness to the combined gunwales. Also, the degree to which the inwale and outwale were squeezed against the bark and each other when they were all nailed and lashed together varies in different areas. Thus, the gunwale cap is about the same in width as the top of the gunwale unit (inwale, bark layers, and outwale) in most areas of the midsection. Its width tapers toward the ends at about the same rate as the combined gunwale unit, until a point about 9 inches inboard of each end thwart. From there to the ends, the cap tapers more quickly than the rest of the gunwale unit. Since its outboard edge is aligned with the outboard edge of the outwale for its full length, the area of the inwale that is exposed gradually increases

toward the ends. Near the headboards, up to 1/4 inch of the width of the inwale is exposed (Fig. 96). Outboard of the headboards, the full 3/8 inch width (thickness) of the inwale is exposed, not covered by the cap.

The gunwale cap conforms to the curvature of the outwale for its entire length. Thus, it runs horizontally over much of the length of the canoe, and then rises very gradually toward the ends. At about each end thwart, it begins to curve up moderately toward its ends. Just outboard of the headboard, it sweeps upward in a strong curve to reach a nearly vertical position at the tips. The ends of the cap sweep outboard and upward beyond the headboards for 7-1/2 inches on the curve, ending exactly at the tips of the outwale. From the headboard to the tip, the cap rises about 5 inches in height. The tip reaches a point 1/8 inch below the maximum height of the end panel of the canoe. Since the nearly vertical tips of the outwales and caps end very slightly below the level of the tops of the end panels, the high bark ends would rest on the ground when the canoe was overturned on its side as a shelter. No lamination splits were made in the ends of the caps to facilitate the bending of the upward curve and the extreme upsweep of the ends.

From headboard to headboard, the gunwale caps are attached to the gunwale unit by downward-driven nails (Figs. 90 and 97). Driven generally along the midline of the cap, the nails are positioned in the spaces between the gunwale root lashings. Over most of the length of the cap, the intervals between the nails measures 9 to 11-1/2 inches. Beginning about 12 to 13 inches inboard of each end thwart, the endmost eight nails lie closer together, in the curved end portions of the cap. The intervals between the endmost five nails measure 2-1/4 to 3-1/4 inches, the next one inboard is 4-1/2 to 5-1/2 inches, and the seventh interval spans 7 inches. The endmost nail in each cap lies 1 to 1-1/2 inches outboard of the headboard, at a point 5-1/2 to 6 inches from the tip of the cap (Fig. 92).

The machine-cut nails which were used over most of the length are medium size, with heads 1/4 to 5/16 inch long by 3/16 to 7/32 inch wide. The endmost five or six nails at each end of the cap are of the small size which was used to join the inwales and outwales together. These have heads which measure 3/16 to 7/32 inch long by 5/32 inch wide (see the nail information summary on page 148). Many of the medium-size nails which lie inboard of the midline of the cap project through the underside of the inwale. Up to 7/8 inch of these nail tips are visible beside the bark wall. Near the ends of the caps, the small nails were driven into the outwale rather than the inwale. In these areas, the tips of the nail shanks sometimes protrude through the underside of the outwale up to 1/4 inch.

The tips of the two converged caps are joined to each other and to the tips of the two outwales by a span of 1/4 inch wide split root lashings (Figs. 91 to 94). The tips of the converged caps are not pegged or nailed to each other. The peg which was inserted between the tips of the inwales and outwales has been described above. The caps are squeezed against the sides of this peg. Beginning 1 inch below the tips of the caps, 1/2 inch below the top of the inwale-outwale lashings, three turns of split root encircle in a simple spiral all of the caps, outwales, and inwales. These wrappings, immediately below the projecting wooden peg, run through a single 1/4 inch hole in the adjacent bark wall, passing through the stempiece inside the bark wall as well. The three wraps cover a span of 5/8 to 11/16 inch. Below these three turns 2-1/8 inches, four more turns of 1/4 inch root encircle each cap and its outwale. These lashings, spanning about 5/8 to 3/4 inch, pass through two 1/4 inch holes in the adjacent bark wall, two turns per hole.

Reinforcement Bark Strips

The reinforcement strip of birchbark increases the thickness of the upper edge of the bark wall where it is attached to the gunwales. Before the inwale and outwale were nailed together onto the upper edge of the bark wall, the reinforcement strip was inserted between the bark wall and the outwale (Fig. 90). Its top edge, like that of the bark wall, was cut off at the level of the top of the outwale. When the awl holes were pierced through the wall and the lashings were wrapped around the gunwales, the bark strip was pierced and lashed as well.

The strip, made of bark about 1/16 inch thick, runs from headboard to headboard and to a point 3/4 to 1-1/4 inches outboard of the headboards. It extends down 1-1/4 to 1-3/8 inches below the lower edge of the outwale in the midsection area. This width gradually tapers toward the ends, reducing to 1/8 to 9/16 inch at

the narrow, bluntly pointed ends. The strip is unusually narrow along its full length. The lower edge of the reinforcement strip generally runs parallel to the lower edge of the outwale for the full length; it was cut quite evenly, with little undulation. The strip was cut to its present width after being installed on the canoe. There is a knife cut or scratch on the bark wall panel immediately adjacent to the lower edge of the strip along its full length; this was produced when the strip was trimmed off against the unprotected wall. The edge had been also sliced off previously, as evidenced by a second knife cut along the full length of the strip 1/8 to 3/8 inch below the present edge and its adjacent knife cut.

The majority of the length of the strip is made up of three long pieces of bark, measuring 68-1/2, 79, and 57 inches. In addition to these long strips, the span beneath the outwale where it curves upward to the headboard is made up of one short piece at each end, 13-1/2 inches long at the bow and 14 inches at the stern.

The individual pieces of bark which make up the main length of the reinforcement strip butt against each other, while the strip at each end of both walls overlaps the adjacent strip, from 1/8 to 3/16 inch. The exposed overlapping edges face inboard toward the midpoint of the canoe. The pieces are not attached at their ends to each other or to the canoe wall in any manner.

Gunwale Lashings

The upper edge of the bark wall is sandwiched between the inwale, the reinforcement bark strip, and the outwale (Fig. 90). It is cut off flush with the top surface of the outwale. The four layers of bark and wood are nailed and lashed together with spaced groups of root lashings from headboard to headboard.

Each lashing group normally runs through 12 to 15 holes in the bark wall (occasionally as few as nine holes when the root is especially wide) (Figs. 98 and 99). The holes, generally square or triangular in shape, have diameters of 1/8 to 3/16 inch, with rather regular edges. The holes were made by an awl with a square or triangular cross section, which was inserted from the exterior side of the wall but was not twisted to round out the holes.

The holes are spaced 1/16 to 1/8 inch apart. Each row of holes, spanning 2-3/8 to 2-5/8 inches, lies about 1/8 inch below the lower surface of the outwale and immediately below the lower surface of the inwale. The split root lashing material is 3/16 to 1/4 inch wide and 1/16 to 3/32 inch thick, with a half-round cross section. After being split, each side of the root was scraped somewhat flat.

To lash the gunwales, a long length of split root was drawn nearly to its end through the first hole in the set of 12 to 15 holes. The short end of the root was drawn up to the top surface of the combined gunwales on the exterior side and inserted down between two of the sandwiched layers of wood and bark. Then, in a simple spiral stitch, the long end of the root passed over the top of the inwale and outwale and through the second hole. The root then passed around the combined inwale and outwale another time, and through the third hole. This pattern continued through each of the 12 to 15 holes, with one turn per hole, laying down 12 to 15 wrappings around the gunwales.

After the 15 turns had been wrapped around the gunwales, the strand returned from hole #15 to hole #12 or 13 on the interior side (Fig. 99). After passing through hole #12 or 13, the root then spanned across to the first hole of the next set of holes, on the exterior (Fig. 100). Thus, every horizontal connector stitch lies on the exterior side, leaving the spaces between the lashing groups on the interior empty, to accommodate the tips of the ribs.

Several techniques were used to finish off the root securely whenever it reached the end of its length. Usually the end was finished off atop the inwale and outwale, by being looped under the previous stitch to maintain the tension. Then it was tucked underneath a previous stitch or tightly down between the sandwiched layers of inwale, bark wall, and outwale, to hold the end securely. The gunwale caps covered and protected all of these tucked root ends.

In some instances, when the end of the root emerged on the interior side of the canoe wall in the middle of a lashing group, it was run horizontally back through an enlarged hole which was two holes distant. Where it emerged on the exterior, the tip was cut off short, to be held firmly in place by the turn of root that had previously been run through the hole. On occasion, this end was left somewhat long and was tucked beneath a long horizontal connector stitch. Sometimes the tip of the above described strand was not ended on the exterior,

but was instead run through another hole to the interior again. There it was tucked under the horizontal span of root on the interior side.

Each typical group of lashings is composed of 12 to 15 turns of root around the gunwale, covering a length of 2-3/8 to 2-5/8 inches of the gunwale. An interval of 1-1/8 to 1-1/4 inches separates each group of lashings. The interval between each group is spanned by a connector stitch running beneath the outwale on the exterior side.

The endmost group of lashings at each end of each gunwale is considerably longer than the majority of the lashings. Extending inboard from a point beside the headboards, each of these groups is composed of about 36 to 37 turns of split root, passing through a corresponding number of holes, one turn per hole. These long lashing groups span 5-3/4 to 6-1/2 inches.

The thwarts are bound into the gunwales with root lashings that fit into the pattern of the gunwale wrappings. The thwart lashing groups are joined to the gunwale lashings by connector stitches.

Damage and Repair

During the manufacture or usage of the Sault canoe, the outside edge of the gunwale cap of the left wall was damaged. Eight inches forward of the center thwart, a crack 1-1/4 inches long extends diagonally inboard from the outer edge. The crack was repaired with a small machine-cut nail identical to those which were used to attach the inwale and outwale together. The nail was driven diagonally downward and inboard from the upper outboard edge of the cap, through the cap and into the outwale.

Stempieces

The upright plank stempiece, made of northern white cedar, is visible in two areas of the canoe. Much of its curved upper inboard edge and side surfaces are visible outboard of the headboard between the converging gunwale ends, since this area is not covered by a bark deck piece (Figs. 92 and 96). In addition, a portion of its outboard edge and side surfaces can be seen along the cutwater edge in the area of maximum outward arc of the bow end of the canoe. Here, a number of the lashings are missing and a small area of the bark wall panel has broken away, exposing the stempiece.

The form of the stempiece is implied in two areas (Fig. 78). The curve of the cutwater edge of the canoe, from chin to outwales, outlines the entire outer curved portion of the stempiece. Also, the stempiece is fitted along its entire straight inboard edge to the straight outboard surface of the headboard.

The plank stempiece was fashioned with its grain running in a vertical position. Its maximum height is 27-1/4 inches, from the base of the headboard to the level of the topmost edge. The width at the point of maximum outward arc is 14 inches. The long, straight inboard edge measures 20 inches in height. Due to the angle at which the headboard stands, the top of this straight edge of the stempiece stands about 2-1/2 inches outboard of the base of this edge. The curved edge of the plank in the area between the converging gunwales outboard of the headboard measures 10-1/4 inches in length, on the curve. The lower portion of this edge lies up to 7/8 inch below the lower surface of the outwales.

The outboard edge of the stempiece angles slightly upward from the headboard to the rounded chin, the point at which the stitching of the end begins. From the chin, which lies about 2-1/8 inches outboard of the base of the headboard, it curves upward and outboard for 29-1/8 inches. Then it arcs in a moderate curve upward and inboard for 9-1/4 inches, to its maximum height at the head. From there, the edge curves inboard and very slightly downward for 3-3/4 inches, to the point where it extends between the converged tips of the gunwales.

The plank is thickest along its inboard edge, both in the portion which fits against the headboard and in the upper area that is visible outboard of the headboard. This entire edge measures 5/8 inch in thickness. The flat sides of the plank were trimmed with a drawknife, so that the thickness gradually tapers toward all portions of the cutwater edge (from chin to gunwales). The cutwater edge is 3/16 inch thick in all areas.

All surfaces of the stempiece are flat, and all of its edges are sharp, except the curved upper inboard edge between the converging gunwales. This curved area has a single bevel 1/8 to 3/16 inch wide carved onto both of its edges. Three machine-cut nails, driven horizontally from the inboard face of the headboard, fasten the headboard to the stempiece. The description

and placement of these nails is discussed in the headboard section.

The vertical plank stempiece in the Sault canoe is very similar to that which is found in the Bell canoe model, in both its form and in the method of attachment to the headboard. It is equally similar, in both form and attachment, to the plank stempiece which is found in a 13-1/2 foot, 4-place Ojibwa Type A-1 canoe that was collected in Wisconsin for the Smithsonian Institution in 1893.[12] These surviving canoes indicate that it was not an uncommon practice in 19th century Ojibwa canoe construction in the upper Great Lakes region to install very broad upright plank stempieces. These planks extend the full distance from the cutwater edge to the headboard, where they are attached with horizontal machine-cut nails to the headboard.

Headboards

The headboard, fashioned from northern white cedar, stands with its base 17-5/8 inches inboard of the outermost point of the cutwater edge (Fig. 78). The outboard side of the base falls 2-1/8 inches inboard of the chin of the canoe. The headboard is angled moderately, so that its head lies 2-5/8 inches outboard of its base. (This is the same direction of the two-inch slant of the headboards of the Ojibwa canoe.) The side notches beneath the head fit between the converging inwales. When the canoe is viewed in profile, the rounded head of the headboard projects 1-1/4 inches above the caps.

The overall height of the rather slender headboard is 23-1/2 inches (Fig. 95). The height of the head measures 1-3/4 inches, while the span from the shoulders to the base is 20-3/4 inches. Its maximum width is 3-5/8 inches, at a point 5-1/2 inches below the side notches. This maximum width tapers slightly to 3-1/8 inches at the base of the notches, and also tapers gradually over a span of 15-1/4 inches down to the base, which ends in a rounded blunt point. In all areas of the headboard, the thickness measures 5/16 inch. The flat inboard surface is planed smooth. The headboard appears to have been sawn to thickness before it was planed. No plane marks are visible, but hand planing would not necessarily produce visible blade marks. All edge surfaces are carved flat, and all corners and edges are sharp. The upper edges of the head are now worn moderately

Chapter 3—The Sault Canoe

round in many areas.

Below the rounded head, which measures 1-3/4 inches in height and 3 inches at its maximum width, a rounded notch is cut out of each side. The inwales fit into these notches, which are 1 inch high and 1/4 inch in maximum depth. The top and bottom surface of each notch angle upward toward the outboard side of the headboard, to accommodate the upward curve of the ends of the inwales.

Inboard 5/16 inch from the midpoint of each of these inwale notches is a single hole, through which two turns of split root lash the inwales to the neck of the headboard. The two irregularly round, tapered holes, about 3/16 inch in diameter, were apparently drilled with an awl with a triangular or square cross section. The split root, 3/16 inch wide, encircles the inwale twice; then it ends by running into one of the lamination slits in the inwale.

The headboard is attached to the straight inboard edge of the upright plank stempiece with three horizontal machine-cut nails. The nails, positioned along the midline of the headboard, are of medium size, with heads that measure 1/4 to 5/16 inch long by 3/16 to 7/32 inch wide. (See the nail information summary on page 148.) The uppermost nail lies about 1/2 inch below the side notches, the lowest one is 1-1/4 inches above the base, and the third nail is positioned in the midsection. Neither of the headboards is decorated.

Cutwater Edges

No wooden batten was built into the stitched cutwater edge to cover and protect the outboard edges of the two bark panels or the stempiece. The edges of the bark panels are cut off generally flush with the edge of the stempiece, but in some areas the bark edges now lie up to 1/16 inch inboard of the stempiece edge.

Before the cutwater edge was stitched, two horizontal wooden pegs were inserted through the two bark panels and the stempiece near the outboard edge, to hold the three elements together during the lashing of the edge. One peg was installed at exactly the end of the longitudinal side seam, while the other was inserted one inch higher. The two holes, 3/16 inch in diameter, were drilled 1/4 to 5/16 inch inboard of the edge. Each peg was made from a 1/2 inch long segment of sapling with a diameter of 3/16 inch. The ends of the pegs

were cut off flush with the outer surface of the bark panels. The cutwater edge at the bow was broken off at some time, in a vertical line with the grain along the two peg holes; but the pegs have remained in position.

To accommodate the stitching of the cutwater edge, a single row of holes runs around the perimeter outboard from the gunwale tips, over a span of 13 inches on the curve. The holes, produced by an awl with a triangular or square cross section, are 1/8 to 3/16 inch in diameter. They are spaced at intervals of 1/32 to 1/16 inch edge to edge.

A block pattern, made up of groups of long and short stitches, was formed by varying the distance between the holes and the cutwater edge (Fig. 100). Groups of 9 or 10 holes positioned 3/8 to 7/16 inch from the edge alternate with groups of 5 or 6 holes that lie 1-1/8 to 1-3/16 inch from the edge. Six blocks of long stitches, each about 1/2 to 5/8 inch wide, were installed along the cutwater edge. During the lashing procedure, the areas which were to be covered by the long blocks were delineated by lines scratched onto the bark panel with the tip of an awl.

The split lashing roots, 1/8 to 3/16 inch wide and about 1/16 to 3/32 inch thick, have a half-round cross section. After being split, the round side of the root was scraped somewhat flat. The stitching was done with a single strand of root in a continuous spiral stitch, with one turn per hole. The stitches lie adjacent to each other, completely covering the cutwater edge. After each turn of root was completed, the root was made to encircle the newly-completed wrap at the midline of the cutwater edge before beginning the next wrap (Fig. 93). This created a row of delicate beads about 3/32 inch thick along the upper 13 inch span of the edge.

The following distance of 5 inches around the curve is lashed in a pattern of cross stitches. The holes are in a single row, parallel to the edge and 3/8 to 7/16 inch from it. The holes, 1/8 to 3/16 inch in diameter, are placed at intervals of 3/8 to 5/8 inch edge to edge. A single split root about the same size as those described above forms cross stitches, in which the two ends of the root pass through each hole in opposite directions, after crossing each other like shoe laces on the cutwater edge. The holes are spaced considerably more widely than those in the upper lashing area of the cutwater edge (where the continuous spiral stitches lie adjacent to each other). Thus, even with two turns of cross stitching per hole, there are intervals of 1/8 to 3/8 inch between each of the pairs of turns in which the cutwater edge is not covered with stitches.

The lowest 23-3/4 inch span of the cutwater edge, extending from the longitudinal side seam down to the chin, is lashed with harness stitches (Fig. 88). The awl holes, of the same diameter of 1/8 to 3/16 inch as those described above, lie at intervals of 5/8 to 7/8 inch, inboard from the cutwater edge 1/4 to 3/8 inch. The harness stitches were made with the two ends of a single root running in opposite directions through the same hole, one stitch per hole. The end-to-end stitches measure 5/8 to 7/8 inch in length.

In all sewing of the cutwater edge, the stitches pass through the plank stempiece inside the end of the canoe, running through awl holes through the stempiece. (The stempiece can be clearly seen where a portion of the bark end panel at the bow end of the left wall has broken from the cutwater edge.)

The lower portion of the cutwater edge (the area which is lashed with harness stitches) is sealed with a strip of fabric and gum. The single layer of fine-weave cloth, 2-1/4 inches wide, is now brownish tan in color. It may have originally been white or light tan. The fabric was first glued to the hull with unblackened gum, after which it was coated with the same blackened gum as that used to seal bark panel seams. The pitch and cloth begins 1-1/2 inches inboard of the chin, on the bottom of the canoe. It extends upward for 26 inches on the curve, covering the entire area of harness stitches, up to the longitudinal side seams. The sealant extends past the cutwater edge onto the bark walls for 1-1/8 to 1-1/2 inches. The edges of the pitched area are broadly curved, following the contour of the outer edge of the canoe. The upper portion of the cutwater edge is not sealed with pitch. This allowed unobstructed drainage of water out of the canoe when it was overturned on its side on shore.

The total thickness of the cutwater edge is 1/2 to 5/8 inch in the lower pitched area (the area of the waterline), and 1/2 inch thick in the unpitched upper area. This thickness includes the stempiece, the two bark panels, and the stitches, as well as the fabric and pitch in the lower area.

Thwarts

The thwarts were made from either eastern larch (tamarack) or spruce, more likely larch. They appear to have been fashioned from sawn boards. The seven thwarts (creating a six-place canoe) are spaced exactly symmetrically, with the intervals between the pairs varying by only 1/8 to 1/4 inch (Fig. 84). The distances between the thwarts are measured from centerline to centerline. Their positioning indicates a canoe shape that tapers symmetrically toward the two ends at the gunwale level. The center thwart lies at the exact midpoint of the canoe.

The lengths of the thwarts also imply the same symmetry. Three pairs of thwarts flank the center thwart. In two out of the three pairs (pairs B and C), the lengths are within 1/8 inch of each other. In pair A, the thwart #3 toward the bow appears to have been 1-1/2 inches longer than its sternward counterpart #2. But thwart #3 is now missing. Its apparent original length, the measurement across the canoe from inwale to inwale, has presumably splayed outward somewhat due to the lack of a thwart to hold the gunwales firmly in place. Thus, the original length of thwart #3 was probably very similar to that of thwart #2.

Center: Thwart #1: 43-7/8 inches
Pair A: Thwart #2: 37-3/8 inches
         Thwart #3: 38-7/8 inches
Pair B: Thwart #4: 24 inches
         Thwart #5: 24-1/8 inches
Pair C: Thwart #6: 8-1/4 inches
         Thwart #7: 8-1/8 inches

The lengths, measured along the longest edge, do not include the hidden portion at each end which fits into the mortise hole in each inwale. The actual length of each thwart is about 1-3/4 inches longer than each of these measurements, since the additional portion at each end, which extends completely through the inwale, is roughly 7/8 inch long. The small differences in the lengths appear to be simply variances due to measurement of the builders by eye rather than by measuring devices.

Each of the thwarts in the Sault canoe is quite slender and delicate for the size of the craft. The following description applies to four of the seven thwarts (Figs. 101 to 103). (The center thwart and the endmost pair are discussed afterward.) The width measures 1-1/16 inch at the midpoint. This dimension tapers very slightly and gradually toward the ends, reaching 7/8 to 1 inch at a point 4-1/8 inches inboard of each inwale. From this location, the width increases fairly quickly to the shoulders, over a span of 2-3/4 inches. The sharp shoulders measure 1-5/8 inches across. This dimension remains constant over the final distance of 1-3/8 inches to the inwales, and also as the thwart extends through the 7/8 inch width (thickness) of the outwale.

At the center, the thickness is 3/4 inch. This dimension remains constant over most of the length of the thwart. Beginning about 2-1/2 to 3-1/2 inches inboard of the inwales, it tapers fairly quickly toward each inwale, by the removal of wood from the lower surface. At the point where the thwart meets the inwale, the thickness has tapered to 5/16 inch. The dimensions of 5/16 inch thick by 1-5/8 inches wide appear to continue as the end of the thwart projects through the 7/8 inch thickness of each inwale. The top surface remains level and straight over the entire length. All four sides of the thwart are planed smooth. The upper two edges are sharp, while the lower two each have a wide carved bevel along the distance between the shoulders. These bevels taper in width from 3/8 inch at the midpoint to 1/8 inch at the shoulders. Thwarts #2, 3, 4, and 5 match this description (varying only in the length of the midsection area).

The center thwart has the same form, but with somewhat greater dimensions. The width at the midpoint is 1-3/8 inches, which tapers gradually to 1-1/16 inches at a point 4-1/2 inches inboard of each inwale. From this location, the width increases over a span of 2-3/4 inches to the shoulders, where it measures 1-7/8 inches. This dimension remains constant over the final distance of 1-3/4 inches to the inwale, and also as the thwart extends through the inwale.

At the center, the thickness measures 1 inch; this remains constant over most of the length of the thwart. Over the endmost span of 2-1/2 to 3-1/2 inches to each inwale, the thickness tapers moderately, reaching 5/16 to 3/8 inch at the inwale. The dimensions of 5/16 to 3/8 inch thick by 1-7/8 inches wide remain constant as the thwart extends through the inwale for 7/8 inch. The top surface remains level and straight over the full length of the thwart. The upper two edges are sharp; the wide bevel carved along the two underside edges tapers in width from 1/2 inch at the midpoint to 3/16 to 1/4 inch at the shoulders. The span

between the shoulders measures 40-1/4 inches.

In contrast to the five main thwarts, the pair of end thwarts are asymmetrical in shape (Fig. 96). The outboard edge is very slightly convex, while the inboard edge has a long shallow central concavity with a maximum depth of 1/4 inch. Shoulders are found only on the inboard edge, positioned 4-3/8 inches apart. The width of each end thwart is narrowest at the midpoint, where it measures 1 inch. Over the span of 2-3/16 inches to each shoulder, the width increases to 1-1/2 inches at the shoulder. This dimension increases slightly over the distance of 2-1/8 inches to the inwale, where it measures 1-5/8 inches. The thickness taper on the underside is very similar to that of thwarts #2, 3, 4, and 5. But due to the short length of the end thwart, the taper begins at about the midpoint of the thwart. The upper two edges are sharp, while the lower two each have a carved bevel which tapers in width from about 1/2 inch at the midpoint to zero at the shoulders.

Another minor difference occurs in these endmost pair of thwarts. All of the other thwarts are positioned so that their upper and lower surfaces lie in level, horizontal planes. The endmost thwarts are positioned in the gunwales at the point where the gunwales curve upward toward the ends of the canoe (Fig. 101). Thus, the planes of the top and bottom surfaces of these two endmost thwarts are also angled upward, with the outboard edge higher than the inboard edge.

At the point where each thwart meets the inwale, a horizontal mortise hole is cut through the midline of the inwale, to receive the end of the thwart (Fig. 99). Each hole is 1/16 to 3/32 inch longer than the width of the respective thwart, and is the same width as the thickness of the thwart. The surfaces of the holes are smoothly cut, with sharp edges and corners. The mortise hole runs completely through the inwale. (A full view is available of the two empty mortise holes that formerly held thwart #3.) The hole is cut at a slight angle, with its inboard end lower than its outboard end. This compensates for the slight outward angle of the inwale, since it angles outward in conjunction with the upper walls of the canoe. The angle of the hole permits the straight horizontal end of the thwart to fit into the hole in the angled inwale.

No vertical nail or wooden peg was driven downward from the upper surface of the inwale through any of the thwarts to hold the end of the thwart firmly in the inwale. (Several thwart end areas are visible beneath the loosened gunwale caps.)

Each end of the thwart is lashed with split root to the combined inwale and outwale. The lashings run through four vertical holes in the end of the thwart, 1/4 to 5/16 inch inboard from the inwale and 3/32 to 1/8 inch apart. The outer two holes lie 3/16 inch from the sides of the thwart. The neatly drilled round holes are 3/16 inch in diameter. The lack of taper of these holes indicates that they were drilled with an auger or a gimlet, rather than with a tapered awl. The upper edges of the holes are sharp rather than rounded.

Below the junction of the thwart and the gunwales, there are 12 to 15 awl holes in the bark wall. These lashing holes, spanning 2-3/8 to 2-5/8 inches, extend up to 3/4 inch beyond the outer edges of each thwart (Fig. 99). All of the previous information describing the lashing of the gunwale elements also applies to the lashing of the thwarts. One to four turns of root lie beside each edge of the thwart while two (occasionally three) turns pass through each of the four holes in the thwart. The thwarts were lashed at the same time as the gunwales. Thus, their lashings fit into and are connected to the series of lashing groups along the length of the gunwales.

During the years of usage of the canoe, light to moderate wear occurred to the upper edges of all of the thwarts except the endmost pair. These end thwarts have very light wear on their upper edges.

Sheathing

The sheathing strips or splints, split from northern white cedar, are 7 to 8 feet long, 2-1/2 to 3-3/4 inches wide, and very thin, 1/16 to 3/32 inch. On the flat faces, areas of undulating raised grain patterns indicate that the strips were split out rather than sawn. Each splint has generally parallel edges for most of its length; the edges are carved rather straight. The endmost 4 to 5 inches at each end is carved so that it gradually tapers into a sharp point (Fig. 89). The inboard edges of each of the tapered ends are feathered in a bevel about 1/16 to 1/8 inch wide; these edges of the ends are thinned down to 1/32 to 1/16 inch.

The pattern of overlapping ends indicates that the splints were laid into the canoe in three groups: first at

each end, and then a central group in the midsection area. The two end groups, laid into the narrowest areas of the canoe, are each made up of 16 to 19 strips. The broader area of the canoe, filled by the midsection group, required 27 splints. After each end group of strips had been laid in, the central group was positioned so that the splints overlapped the ends of the previously-laid groups for about 8 to 10 inches. The ends of the middle group of splints lie about 66 to 80 inches from the bow tip of the canoe and about 80 to 90 inches from the stern tip.

In laying in the sheathing, the first strips were positioned along the midline of the canoe. These strips were not extended under the heel of the stempiece. Succeeding rows of sheathing splints were then added, out to and up the walls. Thus, the overlapping edge of each successive splint faces downward or inward, toward the midline of the canoe. The overlapping edge extends 1/2 to 1 inch over the previous strip.

The successive rows of sheathing were laid up the walls to a point 2 to 2-1/4 inches below the lower edge of the inwale. Toward each end of the canoe, a gradually widening expanse of the upper bark wall is left exposed, not covered by the straight horizontal strips of sheathing, where the gunwales curve upward (Fig. 95). These wider areas of exposed upper wall extend well inboard of the headboards. Beside the headboards, the area of each wall which is not covered by the sheathing splints ranges from 4-3/4 to 5 inches in height.

The tips of the endmost splints extend 2 to 7 inches outboard of the headboard, to a point about 3 to 8 inches from the outer curved area of the stempiece. To stiffen and support the bark cover at both ends of the canoe, two additional short sheathing strips were inserted in each wall outboard of the headboard (Fig. 95). From 25 to 30 inches long and 3-1/2 to 4 inches wide, these strips have pointed tapered tips similar to those on the main sheathing splints. Lying in an angled position, they extend out to within 1/2 inch of the outboard edge of the stempiece. The inboard ends of these splints fit between the main sheathing strips and the bark wall panels. Thus, they were installed in the ends of the canoe before the main splints were laid in, or they were inserted later via the open cutwater edge at the end of the canoe before it was stitched closed. The inboard ends of the added strips are visible inside the canoe, in the expanse of upper bark wall which is left exposed above the main sheathing splints. They lie in an angled position, extending 13 to 17 inches inboard of the headboard, and up to 10 to 14 inches outboard of the headboard. No other material, such as wood shavings or moss, was stuffed into the ends of the canoe to support the bark cover.

Ribs

The canoe was built with a total of 58 ribs of northern white cedar (29 pairs). Throughout the full length of the canoe, they are spaced at intervals of 1-1/2 to 1-3/4 inches, measured edge to edge. All but the end ribs curve upward in a very broad, gradual curve from the midline of the canoe (Figs. 101 and 102). There is no flat horizontal area in the midsection of the floor; the profile of the ribs in the floor and lower walls is entirely rounded in all areas of the canoe except at the sharp narrow ends. The curve of the ribs reflects the rounded body plan of this fast express canoe (Fig. 79).

The midsection ribs in the area of the central thwart are 64-1/4 inches long. This includes the length of about 1/8 to 3/8 inch at each tip which is inserted behind the inwale (Fig. 90). (Before the upward warpage of the inwales, each tip probably fit behind the inwale 3/8 to 1/2 inch or more.) The width of these ribs is 2-1/8 to 2-1/2 inches in the midline of the floor of the canoe. They taper slightly and gradually as they extend outward and upward, to a width of 1-5/8 to 2 inches at a point which is 2-5/8 to 2-7/8 inches from the tip (Figs. 89 and 99). The thickness remains in the range of 3/8 to 7/16 inch over this distance. Over the uppermost 2-5/8 to 2-7/8 inches of each tip, the width tapers quite suddenly, down to 11/16 to 3/4 inch at the squared-off tip. The two sides are slightly beveled in this tapered span. The flat inboard surface at the end of the tip is carved in a sudden taper over the uppermost 3/8 to 7/8 inch span into a chisel shape. The tip has a sharp edge about 1/32 inch thick.

The ribs nearer to the ends, besides being shorter, are also narrower and thinner than the long midsection ribs. The endmost rib at each end, adjacent to the headboard, is 38-3/4 inches long, including the length of about 3/8 to 7/16 inch at each tip which is inserted behind the inwale. The width in the midline of the floor is 1-3/4 inches. This width tapers slightly and gradually as the rib extends outward and upward, reducing

to 1-3/8 inches at a point which is 2-1/2 to 2-5/8 inches from the tip. The thickness remains within the range of 1/4 to 5/16 inch over this distance. In the uppermost portion of 2-1/2 to 2-5/8 inches of each tip, the tapered forms and dimensions are identical to those described above for the midsection ribs.

The flat inboard face of a few of the ribs shows in scattered areas the characteristic raised grain pattern which was created when the ribs were split out. But the ribs were later carved very flat and smooth on virtually all of their flat inboard surfaces as well as the edges. All of the edges of the ribs were originally sharp. In most of the floor areas of the ribs, the exposed edges are now worn moderately rounded from usage of the canoe.

The sharp V-shaped profile of the endmost rib at each end of the canoe involves an extremely sharp bend at the midpoint (Fig. 95). This rib shape reflects the sharp hull form inboard of the headboards of this fast canoe. To achieve the sharp bend without breaking completely through the rib, a V-shaped groove was cut across the width of the inboard face of the rib at its midpoint. The groove is very similar to that which is illustrated for the Royal canoe ribs. This wide groove, about 3/32 inch deep, allowed the rib to be bent sharply at its midpoint. The end rib adjacent to the headboard requires such a sharp V profile that its tops are nearly vertically upright, with the two tips only 6-1/4 inches from each other.

In the midsection of the canoe, the ribs stand perpendicular to the horizontal plane of the keel line (Fig. 78). Toward the ends of the canoe, the keel line rises gradually, as the rocker of the bottom curves upward. Throughout the length of the canoe, each rib was installed perpendicular to the gradually rising plane of the keel line; thus, toward the ends of the craft, the tops of the ribs angle slightly more and more inboard from their bases. The headboard stands moderately angled, in the opposite direction of the slightly angled adjacent rib; its base lies 2-5/8 inches inboard of its head. The distance between the endmost rib (near its tips) and the upper area of the headboard is 5-1/4 inches; the distance between the base of this rib and the base of the headboard measures 1-1/8 inches.

In the majority of the midsection area of the canoe, most of the ribs have a horizontal line scored across the inboard face of the right tip. The lines, scored with an awl tip, lie 6-3/4 to 7-3/4 inches below the inwale. These

Fig. 101. Sault Canoe: End view of the interior from the stern.

Fig. 102. Sault Canoe: Profile of ribs and thwarts.

Fig. 103. Sault Canoe: Top view of thwart and ribs.

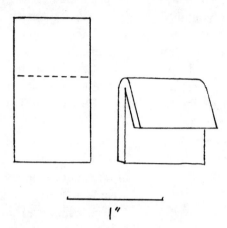

Fig. 104. Sault Canoe: Rib tip fillers or spacers of folded birchbark.

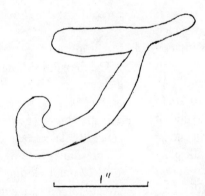

Fig. 105. Sault Canoe: Painted decoration on right wall at stern.

marks appear to have been applied to the ribs by the builders during manufacture. They were probably applied when the ribs were removed from their temporary settings in the canoe, where they had been inserted to dry and set after being bent to shape. The marks would indicate which tip of each rib was to be fitted against the right wall when the ribs were installed permanently.[13]

Over the years of usage of the Sault canoe, the upward pressure of the ribs on the inwales eventually forced the inwales to a location well above their original position. This in turn caused the ribs to become loose, so that the usual pressure of the ribs was reduced and no longer sufficient to hold the ribs and sheathing strips in position.

Two antidotes were installed to remedy this situation. The four main wall seams in the midsection and the bottom seam B-C were resewed, with the root lashings passing through holes in the two end courses of sheathing strips, to hold the strips in position. This repair has already been described. In addition, fillers or spacers of folded strips of birchbark were installed onto the tips of most of the midsection ribs, to fill the space between the ribs and the inwales.

Each filler is fashioned from a thick strip of bark which measures 1-3/8 to 1-5/8 inches in length, 3/4 to 7/8 inch in width, and 3/32 inch in thickness. One end of the strip is folded over at a point 1/2 to 5/8 inch from the end (Fig. 104). The long portion of the strip, which extends 7/8 to 1 inch below the fold, was inserted between the end of the rib and the bark wall, so that the short folded end fit over the chisel-shaped tip of the rib. Two such bark spacers are shown in Figure 89. Some of the ribs required two filler strips, stacked one atop the other, to fill an especially wide gap between the rib tip and the adjacent inwale. The 13-1/2 foot Ojibwa Type A-1 canoe which was collected in Wisconsin in 1893 for the Smithsonian Institution has very similar birchbark spacer strips over a number of its rib tips.[14]

Painted Decoration

The Sault canoe was not decorated by painting in the usual manner. Several other types of decoration were applied to the craft during its manufacture. These are discussed in the section on manufacturing methods.

There is one painted item on the craft; it appears to have been applied for identification purposes rather than for decoration. Near the top of the high end panel of the right wall at the stern, a single letter was painted (Fig. 100). It appears to be a florid capital J or T, executed in dark brown paint, which is now considerably faded (Fig. 105). Centered in the upswept end panel, 2-1/2 inches below the cutwater edge, the letter stands 1-3/8 inches high. The brush strokes vary from 1/4 to 3/8 inch in width.

Nails

All of the nails used in the manufacture and repair of the Sault canoe are of the machine-cut type, in the style which was available from the 1830s on.[15] Two sizes, medium and small, were utilized. The photo in Figure 97 shows a medium-sized nail fully exposed, and another with its head visible in the gunwale cap. In addition, a small-sized nail can be seen as it runs horizontally through the outwale and the inwale. The illustrations of the two sizes of nails found in the Royal canoe also apply to the Sault canoe nails. The only major differences are that the shank of the large nail in the Sault canoe is 1/4 to 5/16 inch longer, and its tip tapers slightly less in width at the tip, to 1/8 inch, compared to the 3/32 inch tip on the Royal canoe nail.

Medium size

The medium size nails have heads that are 1/4 to 5/16 inch long by 3/16 to 7/32 inch wide. The sides and ends of the heads are straight or slightly convex, and the corners are sharp. The head, 1/16 to 3/32 inch thick, has a generally flat surface.

The shank, rectangular in cross section, is 2-3/4 to 2-13/16 inches long. The thickness of 1/8 inch is maintained for its full length. Its width tapers from 7/32 inch below the head to 1/8 inch at the tip. The sharp-cornered truncated tip is 1/8 inch square. This size was used to nail most of the length of the gunwale caps, as well as to fasten the headboards to the stempieces.

Small size

The head is 3/16 to 7/32 inch long by 5/32 inch wide. The sides and ends of the heads are straight or slightly convex, and the corners are sharp. The head, 1/16 inch thick, has a flat surface.

The shank, rectangular in cross section, is 1-1/2 to 1-5/8 inches long. The thickness remains at 3/32 inch along its full length. The width tapers from 5/32 inch below the head to 3/32 inch at the tip. The sharp-cornered truncated tip is 3/32 inch square. This size was used to nail the unit of inwale-bark wall-outwale, the end areas of the gunwale caps, and the repair of the cracked gunwale cap.

On some examples of both sizes of nails, the edges of the heads are somewhat irregular and the heads have a slightly domed appearance. These features are apparently due to inconsistency in manufacture, damage and distortion caused during the pounding of the nails, and later deterioration of the edge surfaces. The nails found on the Sault canoe resemble very closely those found on the Royal and Ojibwa canoes, in terms of the method of manufacture, the form, and the two sizes.

The modern style of wire nail, with its round head and a shank with a round cross section, appeared in widespread use by about 1879. It overtook the cut nail, due to its relatively cheaper price, although some cut nails continued to be produced.[16] No examples of this modern type of nail were utilized in the manufacture or repair of the Sault canoe.

Wood Types

The types of wood used to build the Sault canoe are very typical for canoe construction. The inwales, outwales, gunwale caps, stempieces, headboards, sheathing, and ribs are all fashioned of northern white cedar. The thwarts are made of either spruce or eastern larch (tamarack), more likely of the latter.[17]

The lashings are made of the roots of either spruce or eastern larch (tamarack).[18] As previously discussed, if they are of spruce, the most typical type for canoe lashings would be black spruce.

Miscellaneous Features
Seats

There is no evidence on the Sault canoe which would indicate that it was ever fitted with permanent or temporary wooden seats. No areas of wear can be observed on the gunwales or the upper portions of the ribs that can be attributed to the use of such seats.

Provisions for Sail and Cordelling Line

Likewise, no evidence can be observed which would indicate the lashing of a mast or a cordelling (towing) line to the forward thwarts. This is in spite of the fact that the thwarts were made of northern white cedar, a rather soft wood susceptible to the dents and abrasions of such lashings.

The canoe is not equipped with a permanent perforated thwart or mast step for sailing. Thus, if a sail were sometimes used, the upright mast would have been temporarily lashed to the second thwart at the bow end. Or a temporary perforated thwart may have been lashed to the second thwart, with the mast then positioned in its hole.

The base of the mast may have been placed into a drilled or carved indentation in a loose board laid down the midline, to step the mast. These temporary measures of mast attachment and stepping would leave no permanent evidence that a sail had been used on the canoe. Thus, the lack of such evidence on the Sault canoe does not rule out the use of sail on the craft.

Flags

No evidence can be found for the attachment of a flag at either the bow or the stern. But sufficient space exists outboard of both headboards into which a slender flag staff could have been inserted. There is no space around the base of the head or beside the upper body of either headboard to permit the lashing of such a staff.

Bow/Stern Differences

The Sault canoe contains a few differences between the bow and the stern ends of the craft, which are listed below.

A. All of the overlapping edges of the various bark panels (except the two high end panels at the stern) are lapped so that the edge that is exposed on the exterior side faces sternward. This increases the efficiency and reduces the likelihood of catching on obstructions.

B. A painted letter is found on the exterior of the high end panel on the right wall at the stern. Its purpose is unknown at this time.

C. The high end panel at the bow presently reaches a maximum height of 32-3/4 inches, compared to 32-7/8 inches at the stern. This minor difference of 1/8 inch apparently has no significance.

Usage and Wear

The physical evidence indicates that the canoe saw considerable usage over many years. The bark cover has a great many scrapes and gouges on most areas of the bottom and walls. Many of these run longitudinally along the bottom.

Five areas of damage of the bark cover were repaired with only pitch, while two breaks were sewed with root stitches before being sealed with pitch. In addition, all four of the main wall seams and one of the bottom seams were relashed, with the stitches extending through the sheathing strips. These latter root stitches were installed after the ribs had become too loose to hold the sheathing firmly in place, due to upward warpage of the inwales from many years of upward pressure by the ribs. Birchbark filler pieces were installed between the tips of many of the ribs and the inwales, to fill the gap and tighten the ribs. Finally, a short crack in one of the gunwale caps was repaired with a single machine cut nail. Each of these repairs was done during the period of usage of the craft.

The upper edges of all but the endmost thwarts are worn lightly to moderately round, while the upper edges of the ribs in most of the floor areas are worn moderately round. The exposed edges of the inwales and outwales are worn lightly to moderately round. In addition, the outwales and inwales are heavily worn along most of their length where each of the groups of gunwale root lashings rubbed against the wooden elements as the craft flexed during usage.

Nearly all areas of the upper edges of the gunwale caps are worn round, except near their ends; the outer edge is moderately to heavily worn, while the inboard edge is moderately worn. In addition, very heavy wear is found on the upper outer edge of each cap near the stern, where the paddle shaft of the *gouvernail* abraded during steering procedures. Beginning about six to seven inches forward of the stern thwart (the seat of the stern paddler), this heavily worn area of the outer edge extends forward over a span of 12 to 13 inches. These areas of rounded wear on the outer edges of the caps at the stern paddler's position provide a graphic, tangible link with the voyageurs who earned their living paddling the Sault canoe.

Construction Tools, Methods, and Materials

The Sault canoe was manufactured from the traditional forest materials of birchbark, wood, tree roots, and pine or spruce gum mixed with animal fat and pulverized charcoal. It was painted afterward with Euroamerican commercial paints.

The builders of the canoe used the typical array of tools normally employed in canoe manufacture during the nineteenth century. These include an axe, knife, crooked knife, drawknife, awl, rib-setting mallet, pitch melting and applying implements, and paint container and brush.

In addition, they utilized a few techniques and tools that have generally been considered less traditional in the canoe construction of that era. The most striking departure from 'traditional' building practices is the installation of upright broad plank stempieces which extend from the cutwater edge to the headboard, instead of narrow laminated bent stempieces. This type of stempiece does not appear to have been previously reported in the birchbark canoe literature of the fur trade. Virtually identical upright plank stempieces are found in the full size Sault canoe, the Bell miniature fur trade canoe, and the 13-1/2 foot Type A-1 Ojibwa canoe which was collected for the Smithsonian Institution in Wisconsin in 1893. These three examples indicate that this building technique was much more widely practiced in the upper Great Lakes region in the mid-to-latter 19th century than has been previously reported.

A brace and bit or a gimlet (a small hand auger) was used instead of an awl or a knife tip to drill the 3/16 inch lashing holes in the ends of the thwarts. Traditionally, thin strips of birchbark were often glued with pitch onto the exterior of the lower cutwater edges. Strips of fabric replaced these traditional bark strips on the cutwater edges of this craft.

Another practice of the Sault canoe builders which is not often reported in the birchbark canoe literature involved abrading down the larger of the projecting growths which were found on the bark cover. These growths were reduced so that they became flush with the surface of the bark.

One of the most visually obvious departures from traditional canoe construction involved the substitution of iron nails for carved wooden pegs, driven with an iron hammer. Nails fasten the gunwale elements together; they also fasten the headboard and stempiece unit together. In addition, a single nail was installed to repair damage to the gunwale cap. The use of nails in canoe construction and repair became quite widespread in the early nineteenth century, being used in many areas of North America before 1850.[19]

Many of the above "non-traditional" features of the Sault canoe construction represent practical, labor-saving substitutions and improvements; these elements probably produced a canoe with equal or better performance qualities, with less labor and in less time. Since these traits have been observed on a surviving example of a fur trade canoe, they may in fact reflect standard manufacturing techniques used to build such canoes in the mid-to-latter nineteenth century, rather than "non-traditional" variations.

Although the Sault canoe was not decorated with paint like six of the other seven fur trade canoes in this study, a number of decorative features were built into the craft during its manufacture. First, the thwarts, headboards, and reinforcement bark strips are especially slender in relation to the size of the craft. In addition, the longitudinal side seams were installed with gradually shortened stitches and gradually narrower roots toward each end of the seam. This imparted a graceful touch to these seams. Finally, a row of "beads" was created along the top of each cutwater edge by a turn of the root around the previous stitch after each round of wrapping. This also added a purely decorative feature to the craft which is seldom observed on birchbark canoes. Since the root lashing procedures of canoe construction were traditionally done by native women, it may be suggested that the artistic execution of the side seams and the cutwater edges of the Sault canoe may be women's touches.

Condition

The bark cover and the wooden elements of the canoe are in sound, stable condition. However, the bark cover has several small areas of modern breakage which were sealed with tar as a restoration measure. Two such sealed cracks are found in the left wall, and five in the right wall. In addition, a few areas of original seams which were sealed with blackened pitch were also touched up with tar in the recent era.

Back 38 inches from the bow tip, a small hole runs through the bark cover of each wall, at a point 11 inches below the gunwales. The hole in the right wall, an oval measuring 1/4 by 1/2 inch, extends through both the bark wall and the sheathing strips. The hole in the left wall, 1/4 inch in diameter, runs through only the bark cover. The third thwart from the bow is now missing. In addition, three ribs are cracked in the midline area of the floor. Two of these ribs are located about 17 and 20 inches forward of the stern, while the third example is the second rib toward the stern from the center thwart. In each case, the crack extends across the full width of the rib, but only through about the upper half of its thickness. It is not possible to determine whether these cracks occurred during the period of usage of the canoe or later during its years of storage and display; but none of the cracks appears to have a related area of damage on the bark cover, which would often occur if the damage had occurred during usage.

On the central area of the bow cutwater edge, a strip 7 inches long by a maximum width of 3/8 inch has broken away from the edge of the plank stempiece. This break occurred along the vertical grain in line with the two horizontal pegs which were installed to hold the bark panels to the stempiece before the cutwater edge was lashed. A narrow area of the bark on the left wall adjacent to this break is also missing, over a vertical span of 8 inches and up to 1-1/2 inches in width.

The original root lashings remain intact in all of the original bark panel seams, slits, and repairs; in the original repairs across the bottom and up the walls which pass through the sheathing splints; and in about 75 percent of the areas of the gunwales and the cutwater edges. The root lashings are dry but not excessively brittle in most areas. The high rate of survival of the original roots is presumably related to the cold, moist environment in which the craft has been stored and displayed year round over the previous two decades or more, in the hold of the floating freighter museum.

The majority of the original sealant pitch remains, although it is covered in some areas with tar from later restoration. On the cutwater edges, nearly all of the fabric strips and much of the pitch are now missing. The original painted letter at the stern remains intact, only moderately faded.

No restoration procedures appear to have been carried out on the canoe during its many years of storage and display, other than the small applications of tar. At some point during its modern history, a series of undeciphered letters and/or numbers were painted on the bark cover on the bottom of the craft. These moderately large figures were added with modern reddish brown oil paint, which still retains much of its original shine.

Trade Bead

Some time during the usage of the Sault canoe, a broken half of a moderately large glass trade bead became lodged in the space between the gunwale cap and the inwale-outwale unit. The globular bead, medium blue in color, measures 9/32 inch in length by 5/16 inch in maximum width at the midsection. The large central hole is 5/32 inch in diameter. The translucent glass contains many air bubbles; several tiny chips have broken from the exterior surface.

The bead most closely resembles in form and color the round blue bead reported from excavations at Ft. Michilimackinac which is identified as Type 3, Variety e.[20] The dimensions of the two beads are very similar; however, the diameter of the hole of the Sault bead is about three times greater than that of the Michilimackinac example. In form and color, the Sault bead is closely represented in the Kidd Classification System for Glass Beads as Class II, Type a, Variety 36, as illustrated in Kidd's color plate 6.[21]

The trade bead lodged in the Sault canoe appears to be the only known example of actual period trade goods still associated with a surviving fur trade canoe. This is true if one does not consider as trade goods the nails, commercial cordage, fabric, and commercial paints which were used in the construction of the eight craft included in this study.

Notes: Sault Canoe

1. Adney and Chapelle, pp. 28-29, 102, 149.
2. Ibid., p. 146.
3. Christensen, personal communication of June 18, 1996.
4. Adney and Chapelle, pp. 15-16.
5. Guy, p. 23; Gidmark, pp. 43-44.
6. Adney and Chapelle, p. 57.
7. Ibid., pp. 138, 141, 147.
8. Christensen, op. cit.
9. Guy, pp. 21, 26; Ritzenthaler, pp. 27-28; Adney and Chapelle, p. 118.
10. Hadlock and Dodge, illustrations.
11. Adney and Chapelle, p. 33 model.
12. Smithsonian Institution, Anthropology Department, No. 160,387.
13. Ritzenthaler, pp. 38, 40.
14. Smithsonian, op. cit.
15. Santucci, p. 11; Hume, pp. 253-54.
16. Ibid.
17. Christensen, op. cit.
18. Ibid.
19. Adney and Chapelle, p. 56.
20. Stone, p. 93, and specimen K, Figure 48, p. 94.
21. Kidd and Kidd, p. 56.

The Quebec Canoe

Contents

The Quebec Canoe

The data in the following description of the Quebec canoe is derived from close scrutiny under 5X magnification of a series of large photos taken by Richard Nash in 1972, in addition to his field notes and extensive interviews with him. The data is necessarily incomplete, since the canoe has since been destroyed and is thus not available for a complete study by the author. But Nash, an accomplished bark canoe builder, spent five days restoring the canoe in 1972, and made additional trips to observe the craft in 1978, 1980, and finally in 1986. His observations from these visits are preserved in his notes, and are reflected in the fur trade canoes he has built based on the Quebec canoe. To avoid confusion, the present description has been written in the present tense, as if the canoe were still in existence.

Numerous features of the Quebec canoe indicate that it is an Algonkin/Great Lakes Indian style of fur trade canoe, the Type A-1 style. These traits include the narrow upswept ends with level horizontal tops, the shortness of the undercut in the profile of the ends, and the form of the stempieces. The canoe was built in the large eight-place (nine-thwart) format, in the size category of a North canoe.

Overall Dimensions
Length: 24' 9".
Distance between the outboard sides of the tips of the outwales: ca. 24' 3" (Fig. 108).
Distance between the inboard faces of the heads of the headboards: 23' 1".
Depth at the midpoint, from the top of the gunwale caps to the top of the ribs on the floor: ca. 18-1/2".
Height above the baseline: at the midpoint 19-1/4", at the bow and the stern ca. 35-3/4".
Beam at the midpoint: 4' 4-1/4" (Fig. 109).
Interior beam, inside the gunwales: 4' 3/4".

The Quebec canoe was built in a large size format but in the standard traditional form and proportions of the small and medium sized versions of Algonkin/ Great Lakes canoes.[1] In form and proportions, it is vir-tually identical to certain models of these canoes which were fashioned by Adney (Figs. 18 and 19, Vol. I). The ends of the Quebec canoe rise above the height of the walls at the midpoint by an increase of about 86 percent. Of the seven Adney models of Algonkin/Great Lakes Indian canoes which are represented in Chapelle drawings (Fig. 18), six have ends which rise by a factor of 47 to 63 percent, while one rises by 100 percent. Thus, the height of the ends of the Quebec canoe fall within the upper range of Algonkin/Great Lakes canoe forms.

The canoe has an interior beam which equals 16.33 percent of the overall length of the craft. This compares to the 15.37 percent of the slightly narrow full size Ojibwa canoe, the 17.72 percent of the wide-beamed Sault canoe, and the 18.30 percent of the wide-beamed Royal canoe. The longest standard Algonkin/Great Lakes canoes which Adney reproduced in model form represent canoes 15-1/2 to 19 feet long. These rather wide-beamed craft have interior beams which range from 16.8 to 18.3 percent of the overall length of the canoe.

Hull Form
Profile of the Bottom and Ends
Along the keel line, the horizontal span appears to lie exactly centered within the total length of the canoe (Fig. 108). A span of moderate rocker gradually rises from each end of the horizontal area, extending to very gradually rounded chins. The total bottom length between the chins is about 23 feet 1 inch (measured on the horizontal baseline). At the chins, the rocker has risen above the baseline about 2-1/2 to 3 inches. The length of the rising span and the height of the chin appears to be about equal at both ends of the canoe. Each end extends about 10 inches outboard from the chin (measured on the baseline) to the outermost point of the ends.

The cutwater edge at each end curves upward from the very gradually rounded chin. It extends upward and outward in a moderate curve to the point of maximum length of the canoe, creating a rather short undercut profile. Then the virtually straight upper span

Fig. 106. Quebec Canoe, from the stern end (photo courtesy of Richard Nash).

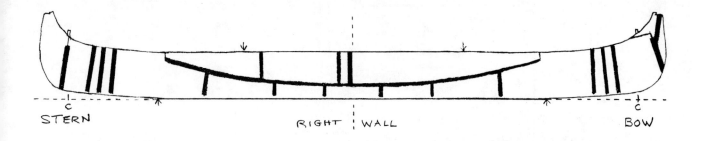

Fig. 107. Quebec Canoe.

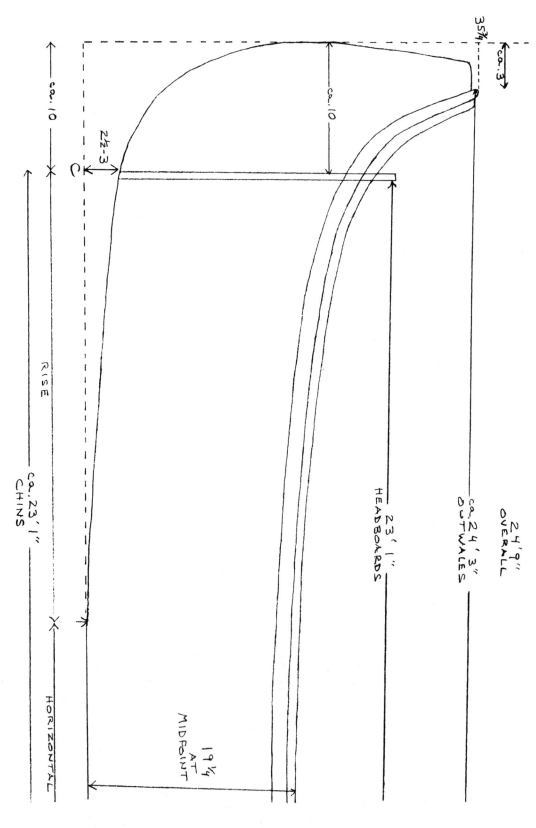

Fig. 108. Quebec Canoe: Hull profile and dimensions.

ca. 3

24' 9"
OVERALL

ca. 24' 3"
OUTWALES

35¾"

ca. 10

ca. 10

2½-3

C

RISE

ca. 23' 1"
CHINS

HORIZONTAL

23' 1"
HEADBOARDS

19¼
AT
MIDPOINT

—156—

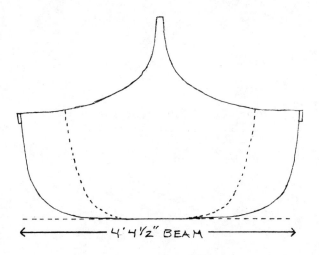

Fig. 109. Quebec Canoe: Body plan (freight canoe). Broken line indicates the approximate position of the longest rib in Figure 124 (p. 181).

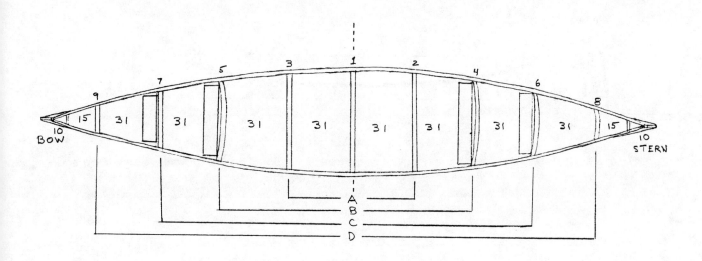

Fig. 110. Quebec Canoe: Hull form, thwart positions, and locations of crew seats.

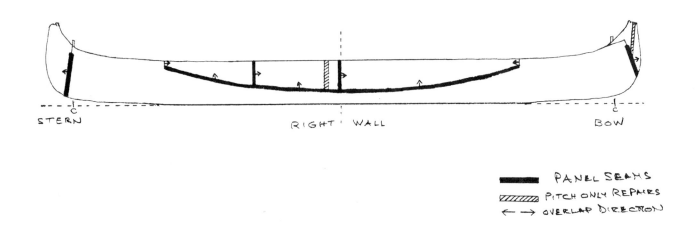

STERN   RIGHT WALL   BOW

▬▬▬▬ PANEL SEAMS
▨▨▨▨ PITCH ONLY REPAIRS
← → OVERLAP DIRECTION

Fig. 111. Quebec Canoe: Bark panels and repairs.

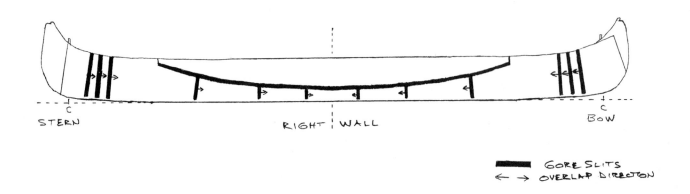

STERN   RIGHT WALL   BOW

▬▬▬▬ GORE SLITS
← → OVERLAP DIRECTION

Fig. 112. Quebec Canoe: Gore slits.

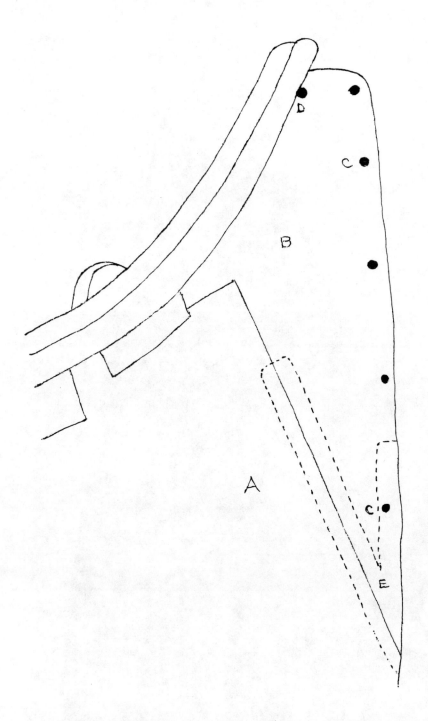

Fig. 113. Quebec Canoe: Supplemental bark pieces held by pegs before cutwater edge lashings installed. A. main bark panel,
B. supplemental bark piece of right wall at bow, C. wooden pegs along cutwater edge, D. support peg for outwales and gunwale caps,
E. outlines of swaths of pitch applied after lashings installed.

Fig. 114. Quebec Canoe: Detail view of right wall of bow, with gunwale end lashings, bark deck piece, headboard, reinforcement bark strip, supplemental bark piece, and cutwater edge lashings (photo courtesy of Richard Nash).

Fig. 115. Quebec Canoe:Detail of side view. Maple leaf outline appears to right of painted crown decoration. Boathouse in background is that of Buffalo Canoe Club, which burned with the canoe (photo courtesy of Richard Nash).

angles inboard slightly, at an angle of about 7 degrees from the upright position, as it rises to the highest point of the end. After making a sharp turn inboard, it extends over a very short straight span of about 1-1/2 inches to meet the outwales. The total length of the cutwater edge, measured on the curve from chin to outwales, is about 41 inches at each end of the canoe.

Body Plan

The bottom is narrow and very slightly rounded (nearly flat) (Fig. 109). The bilge is moderately rounded, while the upper walls are straight and flare outward slightly. The widest area of the bottom appears to lie at about the midpoint of the length of the canoe. This width appears to taper gradually and symmetrically from the midpoint to each end of the canoe.

The Quebec canoe was built in a form designed for rather fast paddling with ample cargo capacity. Its features, including a narrow very slightly rounded (nearly flat) bottom, moderately rounded bilge, medium beam, long slender taper to the ends, and a sharp V form inboard of the headboards, contributed to its ease of paddling yet provided generous room for cargo.[2] (See the description of the sharp V form of the endmost ribs in the ribs discussion.) The canoe was built with the hull form of the standard freight canoe of the period, as depicted in Adney's models.[3]

Bark Cover
Color and Thickness

The color of the bark is light brownish tan in generally all of the panels. The thickness ranges from about 3/32 to 1/8 inch. (The thickness profile is visible in several locations.)

Panels

The drawing in Figure 111 shows the seams which join the seven panels of bark plus the four supplemental end pieces (one at each end on both walls). The arrows indicate the direction of the exposed overlapping edges on the exterior of the canoe.

The majority of the canoe was made with a single large panel of bark roughly 24 feet long. To it were added three side panels on each wall in the wide midsection area. In addition, the highest portion of each end of the canoe was formed by adding a supplemental piece to each end of both walls.

The three side panels span about 13-1/2 to 14 feet of the midsection of each wall. The individual panels are not of equal lengths. They extend downward from the gunwale edge to the longitudinal side seam, spanning a maximum of about 13 inches at the midpoint of the craft.

The two supplemental pieces at each end extend outboard and upward from the ends of the main panel of bark. At the bow, the horizontal distance from the upper corner of the main panel to the cutwater edge is about 6 inches. The height of the visible portion of the two supplemental bow pieces measures about 21 inches. The stern end required two somewhat larger extension pieces to produce the desired length and height of the end of the canoe. The pieces there measure about 11 inches horizontally between the upper corner of the main panel and the cutwater edge, and about 30 inches in height.

The canoe builders apparently had no concern about creating weak points in the hull by positioning vertical wall seams directly opposite each other across the ends of the canoe. The seams which attach the side of the two supplemental end pieces at each end lie directly opposite each other.

Sewn Seams

The original lashing material still survives in all of the sewn seams and in many areas of the gunwales. The lashing root was visually identified by Richard Nash as either spruce or eastern larch (tamarack). (Even when analyzing microscopically, with only a sample of root material, without any accompanying trunkwood, it is impossible to differentiate between these two tree types.[4]) If the roots were spruce, they would most likely be black spruce, which is the best and most common type of root for canoe construction, as has been discussed.

There is no evidence that suggests that a batten strip of wood or root was incorporated into any of the seams for added strength, on either the exterior or the interior side of the bark cover. Since the bottom of the canoe was made of a single panel of bark, there are no bottom seams on the craft.

Gore Slits

After the long span of bark was laid out on the building bed, the building frame was placed upon it and weighted down. This frame determined the general outline of the bottom of the canoe, particularly the shape of the taper toward the ends. The building frame was about as long as the bottom of the canoe, from chin to chin. After the bark was bent upward around the perimeter of the building frame, a number of gore slits were sliced at intervals along the sides of the panel. These slices ran from the edges of the bark inboard nearly to the building frame. At each of these slits, one edge of the bark was made to overlap the other edge, with the exposed edge on the exterior facing toward the midpoint of the canoe (Fig. 112). (No slice of bark was removed to create a seam with butting edges.) The overlapping edge was thinned considerably, so that the exposed edges of the gore slits are lower and less prominent than all of the other overlapping seams on the canoe, which were not thinned.

It is not common to find all of the exposed overlapping edges facing toward the midpoint of the canoe rather than toward the stern; but such a feature is also found on the Sault canoe. In addition, it has been reported on a Tete de Boule medium sized craft built north of Trois-Rivieres, as well as on some Algonkin canoes.[5] With this method of construction, no matter which end of the canoe was used as the forward end, the exposed overlaps in the forward half would face rearward, facilitating the movement of the canoe.

The slits are lashed closed with split roots in a series of widely spaced spiral stitches, with one stitch per hole. The portion of each stitch on the exterior side of the canoe is horizontal, while the connector portion running to the next stitch on the interior of the canoe is diagonal. The stitches run through pairs of opposing awl holes which lie about 3/16 to 1/4 inch from the edges of the slit. The visible horizontal portions are about 3/4 to 7/8 inch long, and are spaced about 1-1/4 to 1-1/2 inches apart.

The lashing roots are about 3/16 to 7/32 inch wide (the same as the diameter of the awl holes) and about 3/32 inch thick, with a half-round cross section. The rounded side is the side of the split root which faces the exterior.

The gore slits are found in three distinct areas on each wall. The major group of slits lies beneath the series of side panels in the midsection. There are six slits in this area of the right wall and eight slits in the left wall, all positioned at rather regular intervals. This series of slits ends well inboard of the ends of the side panels.

Near each end of the canoe is a set of three closely spaced gore slits. These slits, found on both walls, lie in the outboard half of the rise of the rocker to each chin. They are about 3-1/2 to 7 inches apart, in a 10 to 12 inch span of the wall.

When the canoe is viewed in side profile, the gore slits extend downward either from the gunwales or from the longitudinal main seam, which runs the full length of the series of side panels. In the central, widest area of the canoe, this seam curves down to a point about 5 inches above the horizontal baseline of the canoe. The full length of each gore slit on the canoe is visible, running down the curved bilge area of the lower walls to the slightly rounded bottom of the canoe.

Some generalities may be deduced concerning the form of the building frame. It was presumably about 23 feet long, since the length of the bottom (the distance between the chins) is about 23 feet 1 inch. The span across the bottom between the various pitched pairs of gore slits was not measured by Nash, but he estimates that the maximum width of the building frame at its midpoint would have been roughly 34 to 35 inches. The maximum width of the frame that was used to construct slightly rounded or nearly flat-bottomed fur trade canoes was often two-thirds of the interior beam at the gunwales.[6] In the case of the Quebec canoe, this ratio would produce a measurement of 32 inches. The span between the pitched pair of gore slits nearest to each end of the canoe is very short. This represents in a general manner the degree of taper from the wide midpoint of the building frame to its pointed ends.

Side Panels to Main Panel

After the gore slits were cut and stitched along the side edges of the main panel, the side panels were attached to the main panel. The seam connecting the side and main panels to each other is the prominent longitudinal seam which arcs across the midsection of the canoe on each wall.

This seam curves downward toward the middle of the canoe because there, at its widest beam, most of the width of the main bark panel is used to form the bottom of the canoe. There is very little width remaining in the panel to extend up the walls. Toward each end, as the canoe becomes gradually narrower, the main panel has gradually more and more excess bark beyond the width of the bottom to extend up the side walls. Near the ends, this panel covers the full height of the walls.

The lower edges of the side panels are positioned inside the edges of the main bark panel. Thus, the edges of the main panel are exposed on the exterior of the canoe, facing upward toward the gunwales. The seams are sewn with split roots in a harness stitch, with the two ends of a single root running in opposite directions through the same hole, one stitch per hole. The end-to-end stitches, about 3/4 to 7/8 inch long, are composed of the same 3/16 to 7/32 inch diameter awl holes and split roots described above for the gore slits. The horizontal row of stitches lies about 1/2 to 5/8 inch below the exposed edge of the main bark panel.

Side Panels to Side Panels

The seams which join the side panels to each other are all overlapping seams. The exposed edge on the exterior faces toward the midpoint of the canoe in each instance, in the same manner as the overlapping gore slits. The root sewing which connects the side panels to each other is identical to the spiral stitches which close the gore slits in the main panel.

Supplemental End Pieces

Before the two supplemental pieces of bark were lashed to each end of the main bark panel, they were pegged to the stempiece near its outboard edge (Fig. 113). Wooden pegs about 1/4 inch in round diameter run through five holes drilled through the stempiece and the bark pieces. The holes lie about 3/16 to 5/16 inch inboard of the cutwater edge. The topmost peg is positioned in the upper outboard corner of the canoe tip, about 7/16 inch below the top edge of the bark and about 1-1/2 inches outboard of the support peg which supports the outwales and gunwale caps. Progressing downward, the spans between the pegs measure about 2-1/4, 3-1/2, 3-15/16, and 4-1/2 inches. The lowest peg in the row lies about 5 3/8 inches above the bottom of the supplemental bark piece. Each peg is cut off flush with the outer surface of the bark.

Ritzenthaler reported a nearly identical sequence in the building of an Ojibwa canoe. The builder first attached the supplemental pieces to the ends of the canoe with pegs, after which the women sewed the pieces to the main bark panel with root stitches. [7]

At each end of the canoe, the supplemental extension pieces are inserted inside the edges of the main bark panel (Fig. 115). Thus, the edges of the main panel are exposed on the exterior of the canoe, facing outboard toward the nearby cutwater edge.

The long angled vertical seams are lashed with spiral stitches much like those which close the gore slits and wall panel seams. The stitches here are also made of roots about 3/16 inch wide, and are spaced at intervals of about 1-1/4 to 1-1/2 inches. But these stitches do not straddle the seam evenly. On the overlapping inboard side of the seam, each hole lies about 3/16 inch from the edge of the bark; on the opposite side of the seam (the outboard side), the other holes are placed immediately adjacent to the overlapping edge. The horizontal spans of the stitches measure about 3/8 to 1/2 inch. In the Figure 115 photo, the three spiral stitches which lie above the pitch-sealed area have broken, and the bark pieces have shifted slightly. All of the intact stitches which are covered by pitch match the above description.

The short span of the nearly horizontal seam which is found on the two extension pieces at the bow is lashed with harness stitches. The end-to-end stitches, about 1/2 to 5/8 inch long, are made with split roots about 3/16 inch wide. The row of stitches runs about 1/4 to 5/16 inch below the exposed edge of the main bark panel.

Seam Sealing

All of the seams in the canoe were sealed with a coating of charcoal-blackened melted pitch or gum from spruce or pine trees, of the same description as the gum found on the Royal canoe. The remaining original pitch is now very brittle; it does not indent under thumb pressure. No gum has been restored on the canoe since its acquisition by the Buffalo Canoe Club. Thus, all of the sealant pitch which is visible in the photos is original.

With the canoe turned upside down, all of the seams were sealed on the exterior of the canoe. The position of the canoe is indicated by the runs of melted pitch, which extend toward the gunwales. In addition, most

of the seams later received additional applications of
gum while the canoe was in an upright position, as
indicated by the runs of melted pitch which extend
toward the baseline. The swaths of gum are about 2 to
2-1/2 inches wide on the longitudinal side seams, and
about 1-1/8 to 2 inches wide on the other seams. There
is considerable variation in width within most of the
swaths; this may be the result of the later reapplications. On all of the upper seams, the gum extends up
to the lower edge of the reinforcement bark strip. No
fabric strips were applied with the pitch sealant on any
of the seams.

Exterior Hull Surface

The discussion concerning the disruptions in the
smooth, even surface of the bark cover of the Royal
canoe also applies to the Quebec canoe as well. Overlapping panel edges and applications of sealant pitch
up to about 3/32 inch thick have produced seams which
stand out from the flat surface of the hull.

In addition, all of the gore slit seams and wall panel
seams in the stern half of the canoe overlap toward the
bow. Finally, the seams which join the supplemental
pieces of bark to the main panel at the bow end overlap toward the bow cutwater. These unthinned overlapping edges lie very near the bow cutwater edge, the
entry point of the canoe; they would tend to create a
considerable disruption in the even surface of the bark
in this critical position, even though much of the length
of the two seams is above the general waterline area
(Fig. 115).

Damage and Repairs

At some point before the canoe was acquired by the
Buffalo Canoe Club, two rather major cracks occurred
in the bark cover (Fig. 111). One crack runs vertically
down the midline of the supplemental piece of bark at
the bow end of the left wall. (In the drawing, it is portrayed on the visible right wall.) The crack angles
downward and slightly inboard over a span of about
15 inches, from the top of the cutwater edge down to
the end of the main bark panel.

Another crack is found in one of the side panels of
the right wall, a little rearward of the center thwart
and its adjacent wall panel seam (Figs. 106 and 111).
The crack spans the 12 to 13 inch height of the panel,
from the gunwales down to the longitudinal side seam.

Both of these rather long cracks were repaired using only melted blackened pitch. Neither was stitched
closed to prevent movement of the broken bark edges.
Most of the length of each crack lies above the general
waterline area, but in some circumstances both locations would receive considerable water and flexing
movement. Thus, the repairs of melted pitch alone,
without root stitches, could not have been intended to
withstand heavy or prolonged usage. The evidence
suggests that these two repairs may have been made
to prepare the canoe for short-term use on ceremonial
occasions, or possibly when the canoe was readied to
be transferred from government storage to the possession of the Canoe Club for display.

Damage also occurred at some point to a section of
the longitudinal side seam on one of the walls. In the
span where the bark and/or the root stitches were broken, the bark is nailed to the adjacent sheathing strips
and ribs with small machine-cut nails driven from the
exterior side. The flat heads of the nails are square or
rectangular in shape. The entire nailed area was covered with melted blackened pitch. Some of this gum
has since broken away, exposing the nailed repair.
Unlike the repair of the long cracks in the bark cover
using only pitch, as described above, this repair with
nails and melted pitch was applied to the canoe in a
manner which could withstand heavy or prolonged use.

The type of machine-cut nail which was used for
the seam repair was available from the 1830s on. The
wire nail type, with its round head, appeared in widespread use by about 1879. It overtook the cut nail, due
to its relatively cheaper price, although some cut nails
continued to be produced. Thus, the presence of the
cut nails establishes the earliest date of the seam repair as the 1830s. However, the continued limited pro-
duction of cut nails, even after wire nails gained as-
cendancy, does not permit the suggestion of a final
cutoff date for the repair.[8]

Gunwale Elements

The wood which was used to fashion the inwales,
outwales, and gunwale caps of the Quebec canoe has
been visually identified by Nash as northern white cedar. All of the gunwale elements are angled outward
very slightly, at the same degree of outward flare as

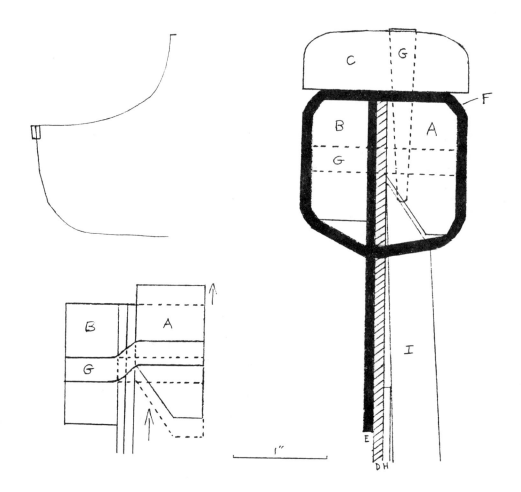

Fig. 116. Quebec Canoe: Cross section of gunwales and inwale displacement. A. inwale, B. outwale, C. gunwale cap, D. bark wall, E. reinforcement bark strip, F. root lashings, G. wooden pegs, H. sheathing, I. rib.

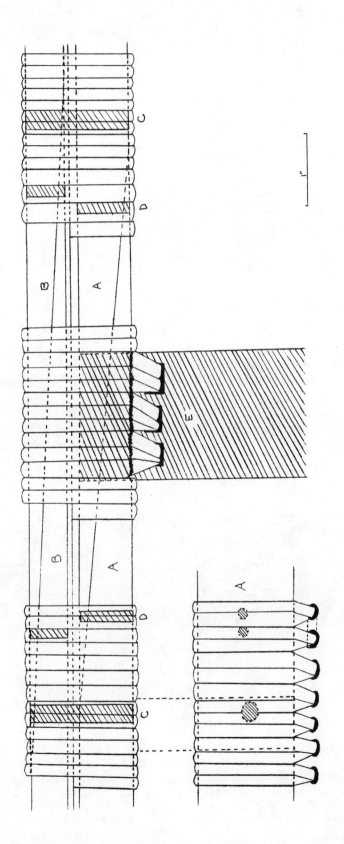

Fig. 117. Quebec Canoe: Gunwale splicing, top and interior views. A. inwale, B. outwale, C. main gunwale pegs, D. splicing pegs, E. center thwart.

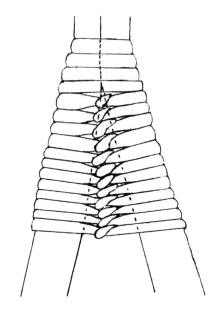

Fig. 118. Quebec Canoe: A portion of the lashings of the converging outwales.

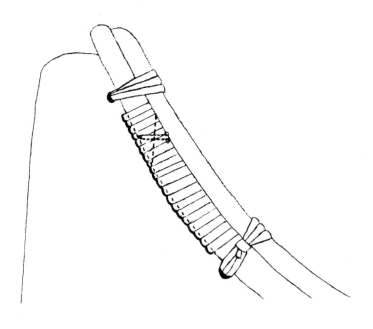

Fig. 119. Quebec Canoe: Outwale tip replacement at stern.

the topsides of the bark walls to which they are attached (Fig. 116).

Inwales

The total length of the inwale on the curve is 24 feet 9 inches (the same length as the outwale). This includes the portion of its length which is visible between the headboards plus the length at each end that is normally hidden from view outboard of the headboards (Fig. 120). (A clear view of the inwales to their tips, as well as nearly all areas of the stempiece, is visible at the stern end due to broken and missing root lashings which span the area between the converging outwales.) In the midsection, the inwale strip is 3/4 inch wide across the top and 1-3/8 inches deep (Fig. 116). The bottom surface is only about 1/4 to 3/8 inch across, since the lower outboard edge is planed off into a beveled surface to produce a space into which the tips of the ribs fit.

Beginning at about the second thwart from each end of the canoe, the width and depth of the inwale taper very gradually over a span of about 5 feet to the tips. At the ends, the width has tapered down to 5/8 inch and the depth has reduced to 5/8 inch. The tips are rather rounded. All surfaces of the inwale are carved flat and smooth. The outboard edges are sharp, while the two inboard edges are rounded by a rather wide bevel about 3/16 to 1/4 inch wide which is carved along the full length of the edge.

The inwale runs nearly horizontally over a portion of the midsection of the canoe, and then rises very gradually toward the ends. Over the span from the center thwart to the second thwart from the center, its height rises slightly, 1/2 to 1 inch. Between the second and third thwarts from the center, the inwale rises an additional 1-1/4 to 1-1/2 inches. Well inboard of each end thwart, it begins to curve up moderately. Between the third thwart and the end thwart, the inwale rises 1-3/4 to 2 inches. Outboard of the headboard, the inwale continues its moderate upward curve, extending to the cutwater edge of the stempiece (Fig. 120). The outwale curves upward considerably more strongly, diverging from the inwale outboard of the headboard. No lamination splits were made in the ends of the inwales to facilitate the bending of the upward curve of the ends.

The inwale fits into a notch which is cut into the side of each headboard. Two turns of split root bind the inwale to the headboard at the notch. The ends of the inwales are also bound into place. Just inboard of the junction of the inwales and the inboard portion of the stempiece, the two converging inwales are bound to each other. Three wraps of a rather narrow strip of cedar inner bark encircle the outwales, firmly squeezing them against the flat sides of the stempiece. These spiral bindings are further tightened by the ending of the lashing, which encircles the middle of the three wraps and then passes through this central wrap. No lashings are visible at the tips of the inwales which would bind the tips directly to the stempiece.

The inwale is attached to the outwale with wooden pegs over nearly the entire span from headboard to headboard. The two wooden strips have sandwiched between them the top edge of the bark wall and a strip of reinforcement bark (Fig. 116). The pegs run generally down the midline of the two wooden elements, at intervals of about 8 inches on center. They are all positioned beneath the groups of lashings between the ribs, under every other lashing group. The endmost pegs lie about 12 inches inboard of each headboard. The carved pegs have a generally round diameter of about 1/4 inch, which does not taper toward either end. The pegs run completely through the inwale and outwale, spanning about 1-1/2 inches. The ends are cut off flush with the surface of each of these gunwale elements. Nash has visually identified the wood of the gunwale pegs as ash; both black and white ash were used in bark canoe construction.[9]

Due to the constant upward pressure of the 68 ribs on the inwale for more than a century, the inwale has been gradually displaced upward. The top surface of the inwale, originally level with the top surface of the outwale, now stands 3/16 to 1/4 inch above it. The wooden pegs have bent in their midsection area, where they pass through the bark wall and the reinforcement bark strip, in response to the upward pressure of the ribs and the displaced inwale. The degree of bend of the pegs, offset by 3/16 to 1/4 inch, is about the same as that which has been illustrated for a Penobscot canoe from Maine.[10] Nash observed a number of the bent pegs, which had become disattached from the Quebec canoe.

The inwales and outwales of the Quebec canoe, unlike those of the other three full size canoes in this study, are each made of two strips of wood, which are spliced at the midpoint (Fig. 117). The diagonal seam of the splice of each inwale spans eight inches, while that of each outwale measures ten inches. These two sets of splices lie directly opposite each other across the exact midpoint of the canoe.

The eight-inch inwale splice fits exactly between two of the large horizontal inwale-outwale pegs. One small carved peg, about 1/8 inch in round diameter, runs horizontally through the diagonal splice near each of its ends. The untapered end of each peg is cut off flush with the surface of the inwale. The center thwart extends in its mortise hole completely through the middle of the spliced area of the inwale, functioning as a huge peg to firmly hold the diagonal splice.

The outwale splice, spanning ten inches, is held by one of the main inwale-outwale pegs very near each of its ends. In addition, one 1/8 inch diameter round peg runs horizontally through each end of the diagonally spliced area. The untapered ends of these pegs are cut off flush with the surface of the outwale.

Three spaced groups of gunwale lashings cover all of the pegs in the spliced area and hold the center thwart in place. These lashings, fitting into the overall pattern of the gunwale lashings, bind together the two inwale sections and the two outwale sections into a single solid unit. The two main gunwale pegs also add much overall strength to the spliced area.

The ends of all of the splices are covered by the lashing groups; the gunwale caps cover the two areas of the diagonal seams which are left exposed on the top surface of the inwale and outwale between the three lashing groups. Thus, no evidence of these inwale and outwale splices would have been visible when the root lashings were intact. Now, the roots are brittle and much broken, and a great many wrappings are gone, exposing to view all of the details of the splicing techniques.

The four pegs in the splices are very small and light; in addition, they are positioned so that they only hold the thin end tips of the diagonal splices. Thus, they seem to have been installed primarily to fasten the two inwale sections to each other and the two outwale sections to each other during the installation, before the gunwale lashings were added. Provisional lashings may also have been installed in the two spaces between the three lashing group locations, to help hold the pieces in place until the permanent gunwale lashings were installed. The three groups of split root gunwale lashings, plus the center thwart acting as a huge peg, appear to have been perceived by the builders as the main permanent fastening elements of the spliced area of the gunwales. The four small pegs offered minimal permanent fastening strength.

The builders of the Quebec canoe apparently did not feel that fashioning both the inwales and the outwales of two sections spliced together would create weak points in the framing structure of the canoe, even though the inwales were the main strength members of the frame.[11] Nor did they make an effort to distribute these splices at various locations along the gunwales: all four splices are positioned at the exact midpoint of the canoe. Very similar splicing of the inwales at the midpoint has been documented as a rather common building practice among the western Cree.[12]

Outwales

The total length of the outwale is 24 feet 9 inches, measured on the outside of the curve. In the midsection, it is 9/16 inch wide across the top and 1-1/4 inches deep; these dimensions are about 1/8 inch less in both directions than the inwale (Fig. 116). Beginning about 18 inches outboard of the second thwart from each end of the canoe, the outwale tapers very gradually over about 5 feet, to a width of 1/2 inch and a depth of 3/4 inch at the tips. All surfaces are carved flat and smooth. The inboard edges are sharp, while the two outboard edges are rounded by a rather wide bevel about 3/16 to 1/4 inch wide which is carved along the full length of the edge. The horizontal wooden pegs which fasten the outwale to the inwale, as well as the central splices, have already been discussed in the inwale information.

The outwale runs nearly horizontally over a portion of the midsection of the canoe, and then rises very gradually toward the ends. Over the span from the center thwart to the second thwart from the center, its height rises slightly, 1/2 to 1 inch. Between the second and third thwarts from the center, the outwale rises an additional 1-1/4 to 1-1/2 inches. Well inboard of each end thwart, it begins to curve up moderately. Between the third thwart and the end thwart, the outwale rises 1-3/4 to 2 inches.

Outboard of the headboard, it diverges from the parallel curvature of the inwale; the ends sweep upward in a moderate curve to reach a considerably angled position at the tips (Figs. 114-115 and 120).

The ends of the outwale sweep upward and outboard for about 14 inches on the curve beyond the headboards. The tips reach a point about 1-1/8 inches higher than the maximum height of the prow. The corners and edges of the tips are rounded. No lamination slits were made in the ends of the outwales to facilitate the bending of the upward curve of the ends.

At each end of the canoe, a single wooden peg runs horizontally through the hull near the tip of the outwales (Figs. 115 and 120). Each peg, adjacent to the outboard edge of the outwale, lies about 1-3/4 to 2-1/2 inches below the tip of the outwale, and about 3/4 to 1-1/2 inches below the height of the bark wall panel. The carved peg, about 1/4 inch in round diameter, runs through a drilled hole through the stempiece and the bark walls; it projects outward from each wall about 1/2 to 5/8 inch. This support peg at each end of the canoe adds support to the upward-bent outwales and gunwale caps.

Such pegs are not commonly found in the bark canoe literature. But they have been reported, in one case in a Tete de Boule medium size canoe built north of Trois-Rivieres.[13] These support pegs were of some importance in canoes in which the outwales and caps were not laminated to facilitate the upward curve of their ends. In these cases, in which the bent ends would have a tendency to straighten, the support pegs would assist in holding the end curves of the gunwale elements; this would relieve some strain from the gunwale lashings in maintaining the shape of the bends.

At the juncture of the tips of the two outwales, no bark or wooden wedge assists in making the root lashings tight. Nor does a peg or a nail join the outwale tips together. The split root lashings, beginning about 2-5/8 inches below the ends, wrap around the two converged outwales for a span of about 6-1/2 inches (Figs. 114 and 118). Each wrap runs through a hole in the adjacent bark wall, one turn per hole. The awl holes for these lashings have the triangular or square shape of the awl; this indicates that the awl was not twisted after each insertion, which would have made the holes round. The uppermost two or three wraps also pass through the stempiece inside the bark wall as well. The

split lashing root is about 1/4 inch wide, with a half-round cross section. The triangular area between the two outwales is filled with 21 root wraps that encircle the outwales in a simple spiral pattern.

Of these spiral wrappings, the lower 17 or 18 each have a short turn around the midpoint of the large encircling wrap, which pulls the upper and lower spans of the wrap toward each other. Each short turn around the midpoint was added after the root had completely encircled the outwales, before beginning the next large circular wrapping.[14] The series of short central turns adds strength and rigidity to the rather wide span of split roots which fills the area between the converging outwales. In contrast, the builders of the Royal canoe filled the comparable expanse with wrappings in a figure-eight pattern, to provide the required strength and rigidity for the rather wide span of roots.

The remaining area between the converging gunwales extends from the lower edge of the spiral root lashings inboard for about 3-3/4 inches to the headboard. This area is covered by a bark deck. The rectangular piece of bark, measuring about 3-5/8 inches vertically, is very thick, about 3/16 inch. Beginning immediately outboard of the headboard, it covers the span of open area between the converging inwales; it does not run underneath any portion of the span of spiral root lashings. The ends of the deck piece extend over the bark walls and beneath the outwales; they are visible on the exterior of the canoe below each outwale for about 1-1/8 to 1-1/4 inches.

The deck appears to be held in place by only the pressure of the outwales, which squeeze the bark down against the top edges of the bark wall panels. No root stitches are visible that may have fastened the piece of bark. A single awl hole is found in the bow deck piece, adjacent to the inboard edge of the left gunwale cap and near the forward edge of the deck (Fig. 114). The hole lies beside a set of three cap-and-outwale lashing wraps, and is of the same diameter as these adjacent lashing roots. The builders may have intended to run one of these wraps through the awl hole, but such a root binding was not installed; the condition of the edges of the hole indicates that the hole was never used.

Since the bark deck and the span of spiral root lashings completely fill the area outboard of the headboard, there is no possibility that a flag staff or any other item could have ever been inserted outboard of the head-board, at either the bow or the stern.

Gunwale Caps

The total length of the gunwale cap is about 24 feet 6 inches, measured on the inside of the curve. (This is three inches shorter than the outwale, which was measured on the opposite side of the curvature.) In the midsection, the cap is 1-3/4 inches wide by 5/8 inch thick (Fig. 116). Beginning at about the second thwart from each end, the width of the cap gradually tapers over a distance of about 5 feet, to a width of 3/4 inch at the tips. The 5/8 inch thickness of the cap is maintained for its full length. All surfaces are carved flat and smooth. The lower two edges are sharp, while the upper two are broadly rounded. As the width of the cap tapers toward its extremities, the cross section becomes completely half-round well inboard of the headboards.

The combined width of the inwale (3/4 inch) and the outwale (9/16 inch) is 7/16 inch less than the width of the gunwale cap. The bark wall and the reinforcement bark strip sandwiched between the inwale and the outwale add as much as 3/16 to 1/4 inch of thickness to the combined gunwales. Also, the degree to which the inwale and outwale were squeezed against the bark elements and each other when they were all pegged and lashed together varies in different areas. In spite of these additions to the thickness of the gunwale unit, the wide gunwale cap completely covers the top of the unit (inwale, bark layers, and outwale) in all areas of the midsection. The width of the cap tapers much more quickly toward the ends than the combined gunwale unit (Fig. 114). Thus, the area of the gunwales that is exposed gradually increases toward the ends. Since the cap is aligned generally down the midline of the gunwales toward the ends, the uncovered area increases on each side of the cap. Near the headboards, up to about 1/4 inch of the thickness of both the inwale and the outwale is exposed.

The cap covers both the inwale and the outwale until a point outboard of the headboards. There, the outwale in its upward sweep diverges from the inwale. The cap then follows only the outwale from there to its tip.

The gunwale cap conforms to the curvature of the outwale for its entire length. Thus, it runs nearly hori-zontally over a portion of the midsection of the canoe, and then rises very gradually toward the ends. Over the span from the center thwart to the second thwart from the center, its height rises slightly, 1/2 to 1 inch. Between the second and third thwarts from the center, the cap rises an additional 1-1/4 to 1-1/2 inches. Well inboard of each end thwart, it begins to curve up moderately. Between the third thwart and the end thwart, the cap rises 1-3/4 to 2 inches. Outboard of the headboard, it diverges from the parallel curvature of the inwale; the ends sweep upward in a moderate curve to reach a considerably angled position at the tips. The tips extend to a point 1/4 inch lower than the tips of the outwales. The angled tips of the outwales and caps extend about 1-1/8 inches above the maximum height of the end panels.

No lamination slits were made in the ends of the caps to facilitate the bending of the upward curve of the ends. The upswept ends of the cap extend upward and outboard for about 13 inches on the curve past the headboard. The tips are well rounded.

From nearly headboard to headboard, the gunwale caps are attached to the inwale and the outwale by downward-driven wooden pegs. At regular eight-inch intervals, round holes about 3/16 to 1/4 inch in diameter were drilled downward through the caps and the inwales, between every other gunwale lashing group. The intervals between the holes do not vary over the length of the cap. Nearly all of the holes lie slightly inboard of the midline of the cap, and angle slightly inboard into the inwale. A scattered few lie outboard of the midline and angle into the outwale. The endmost holes lie about 1 inch outboard of the endmost thwart at each end, at about the beginning of the strongest upsweep of the outwales and caps.

The long slender pegs, about 1-3/4 inches long, are about 3/16 to 1/4 inch in diameter at the head (Fig. 116). Many of the pegs taper to a rounded point at the tip, while some retain the full diameter for their full length and are only rounded at the tip. The sides of the pegs are carved with a number of bevels to round them, to fit tightly in the holes. The pegs were driven snug through the cap and the inwale and then trimmed so that the surface of the head lies flush with or barely above the surface of the cap. Most of the tips protrude slightly from the underside of the inwale, in the area into which the rib tips fit.

From the headboards to the tips of the caps, no pegs fasten the gunwale cap ends; they are attached to the outwales only by three sets of lashings in this area (Fig. 114). The tips of the two caps are joined to each other and to the tips of the two outwales by three wraps of split root which span about one inch. These three wraps completely fill a shallow notch which is carved into the upper surface of each cap, beginning about 2-1/4 inches below the tips. The notch is about one inch long and about 3/32 to 1/8 inch deep. No wedge is inserted between the tips of the caps to assist in making the lashings tight. Nor are the tips of the converged caps pegged or nailed to each other.

About 5-3/4 inches below the lower edge of the upper wrapped lashings, another set of lashings binds each cap to its respective outwale. This set of lashings, spanning about one inch, is also composed of three turns of root. To finish, the end of the lashing root encircles the three turns of root on the outboard side of the wrappings. It then ends by passing under this central wrap, effectively locking the end in position. About 4-1/4 inches below the lower edge of the middle set of lashings, about 1-1/4 inches inboard of the headboard, a third set of lashings binds each cap to its respective outwale. This lower set of lashings matches exactly the description of the middle set. The three turns of root in each of these gunwale cap lashings pass through a single hole in the bark wall, about 3/8 to 7/16 inch in diameter.

Reinforcement Bark Strips

The reinforcement strip of birchbark increases the thickness of the upper edge of the bark wall where it is attached to the gunwales. Before the inwale and outwale were pegged together onto the upper edge of the bark wall, the reinforcement strip was inserted between the bark wall and the outwale, so that its top edge matched the top edge of the bark wall (Fig. 106). When the awl holes were pierced through the wall and the lashings were wrapped around the gunwales, the bark strip was pierced and lashed as well. Its presence reduced the danger of splitting of the upper bark wall, both while being sewed and during the usage of the canoe.

The strip, made of bark about 1/16 to 1/8 inch thick, runs from headboard to headboard: it extends down 2 to 2-1/8 inches below the lower edge of the outwale (Fig. 106). Its width does not taper toward the outboard ends. The lower edge is generally parallel to the lower edge of the outwale for the full length of the strip; but it was cut somewhat irregularly and with considerable undulation.

The strip was apparently cut to its present width before being installed on the canoe. There is no knife cut or scratch on the bark wall panel adjacent to the lower edge of the strip, which would have been produced if the strip had been cut off against the unprotected wall. However, a piece of bark could have been temporarily inserted between the wall panel and the reinforcement strip to shield the wall from knife cuts as the strip was trimmed.

The majority of the length of the strip is made up of several long pieces of bark. In addition to these long strips, the span beneath the outwale where it curves upward to the headboard at each end is made up of two shorter pieces. The individual pieces of bark which make up the reinforcement strip are not attached at their ends to each other or to the canoe wall in any manner.

The bark deck piece is bent down on either side between the bark hull and the outwales. Its end may appear to be a continuation of the reinforcement bark strip, although there is a gap between the two pieces of bark (Figs. 114 and 115). This deck piece, about 3-5/8 inches long, extends beyond the outwale for about 1-!/8 to 1-1/4 inches. It runs up to the long span of root lashings which bind the tips of the outwales to the hull. The outboard edge of the deck is cut parallel to the outwale, to match the lower edge of the bark reinforcement strip. But the deck end, since it is obviously narrower than the reinforcement strip, does not truly appear as a continuation of that strip.

Gunwale Lashings

The upper edge of the bark wall is sandwiched between the inwale, the reinforcement bark strip, and the outwale. It was cut off flush with the top surface of the two wooden elements, which were originally on the same level at the time of construction. The four layers of bark and wood are pegged and lashed together with spaced groups of root lashings from headboard to headboard.

Each lashing group normally runs through seven

holes in the bark wall (Fig. 117). The holes, generally round in shape, have diameters of about 3/16 to 1/4 inch, with rather even edges. They were made by an awl with a triangular or square cross section, which was inserted from the exterior side of the wall and twisted. The holes are spaced about 1/8 to 1/4 inch apart. Each row of holes, spanning about 2-1/2 to 2-5/8 inches, lies about 3/16 to 1/4 inch below the lower edge of the outwale. This is slightly below the original location of the inwale, before it was forced upward. The split root lashing material of the gunwales is about 3/16 to 1/4 inch wide, with a half-round cross section.

To lash the gunwales, a long length of split root was drawn nearly to its end through the first hole in the set of seven holes. The short end of the root was drawn up to the top surface of the combined gunwales on the interior and inserted down between two of the sandwiched layers of wood and bark. Then, in a simple spiral stitch, the long end of the root passed over the top of the outwale and inwale and again through the same first hole. The root then passed around the combined outwale and inwale a second time, and through the second hole. This pattern continued through each of the seven holes, with two turns per hole, laying down fourteen wrappings around the gunwales.

One technique was consistently used to finish off the root securely before starting a new group of lashings. When the end of the root emerged on the exterior side of the canoe wall at the last hole (#7), it was run horizontally back through hole #6. Where it emerged on the interior, the tip was cut off rather short. It was held firmly in place by the two turns of root that had previously been run through the hole.

Each typical group of lashings is composed of fourteen turns of root around the gunwale, covering a length of about 2-1/2 to 2-5/8 inches of the gunwale. An interval of about 1-1/2 inches separates each group of lashings. The interval between each group is not spanned by a connector stitch, since each group begins and ends independently.

The endmost group of lashings at both ends of each gunwale is considerably longer than the majority of the lashings (Fig. 106). Extending inboard from a point about one inch inboard of the headboard, each of these groups is composed of about 40 turns of split root,

passing through 20 holes, two turns per hole.

The thwarts are bound into the gunwales with root lashings that fit into the pattern of the gunwale wrappings. The thwart lashing groups are not joined to the gunwale lashings by connector stitches.

Damage and Repairs

During the period in which the Quebec canoe belonged to the British and Canadian governments, the tips of both of the outwales at the stern end were replaced. In these original repairs, made during the usage period of the canoe, the damaged five-inch span of each outwale tip was cut off at a diagonal (Fig. 119). Each of the carved replacement sections has a matching diagonal end, and contours and dimensions which match the surviving original outwale tips at the bow. Each replacement segment is attached to its outwale by a single small nail, driven horizontally through the diagonal seam from the inboard side. The nails are of the wire nail type, with round heads.

The lower span of the two replacement sections is covered by the spiral root lashings which encircle the converged outwale ends. The weathered condition of these lashings and the exposed upper ends of the wooden replacement segments match that of the rest of the canoe. The original root wrappings, having become brittle and broken, were removed and replaced during the 1972 restoration. At that time, the details of the outwale repairs were exposed to view.

The two nails which hold the two replacement segments in position are of the wire nail variety. This type generally replaced machine-cut square headed nails by about 1879, although some machine-cut products were made thereafter.[15] Thus, the nail data appears to place the outwale repairs into the period between about 1879 and 1908, when the canoe was deaccessioned by the government and acquired by the Canoe Club.

The position of the replacement sections, at the stern tips of both outwales, would create weak points in the upswept gunwales at the stern (although the adjacent lashed gunwale caps would add some stability). This would interfere with the overturning of the canoe on its side on shore to produce an instant shelter for its occupants. But this deficit probably did not hinder the usage of the Quebec canoe. The craft was government property reserved for official occasions involving Queen

Victoria and the British Royal Family. The detailed official reports of the daily activities of the Royal Party during the 1860 and 1901 visits to Canada by the Prince of Wales and the Duke of Cornwall and York do not mention any usage of overturned canoe shelters.[16]

Stempieces

The stempiece is made of northern white cedar, according to Nash's visual identification. It is visible in several areas of the canoe (Fig. 120). Its heel is visible where it projects into the interior of the canoe at the base of the headboard. Nearly all areas of its upper half plus the brace are visible at the stern end, where many of the root lashings between the converging ends of the outwales are broken and missing. The laminated upper end of the stempiece can be seen where it projects through the inboard face of the headboard.

The curvature of the stempiece is implied in several areas. The curve of the cutwater edge of the canoe, from chin to outwales, outlines the entire outer curved portion of the stempiece. Also, the stempiece is lashed to the outwales and gunwale caps near their tips, just below the support peg which runs through the stempiece. The single horizontal brace is visible where its inboard end projects through the inboard face of the headboard.

The total length of the stempiece is about 62 inches, measured on the outboard edge. The heel of the stempiece projects 1/2 inch inboard from the inboard surface of the base of the headboard. At its end, it is 1-1/2 inches deep (in profile) by 3/4 inch thick, with sharp corners and edges. All surfaces of the heel are carved flat and smooth. The heel has a notch in its upper surface as well as on each side, into which the legs of the headboard fit. The square notch on the upper surface lies 1/2 inch from the tip; it is 5/8 inch long, and extends about 1/4 inch below the upper surface of the end of the heel. The tapered notches on the sides gradually deepen over a span of about 7/8 inch, to a maximum depth of about 5/32 inch. On the outboard side of the headboard, the depth (profile) of the stempiece is 2 inches, while the thickness of 3/4 inch remains the same, with sharp edges. These dimensions are maintained to about the sharp bend at the top. The cross section is straight-sided, with no taper in thickness toward the outboard edge.

The stempiece is divided by about seven slits into about eight lamination layers, beginning a little outboard of the headboard. The laminations extend through the complete upper length of the stempiece to its end. (In the drawing, they are portrayed only in the lowest area.) The laminated portion of the stempiece is spirally wrapped with a rather narrow strip of cedar inner bark.

The stempiece curves upward and outboard from the base of the headboard (the chin of the canoe) in a moderate curve. Then the virtually straight upper span angles inboard slightly, at an angle of about 7 degrees from the upright position, as it rises to its maximum height at the head. The length from the chin to the top measures about 38-1/2 inches. At the highest point, the stempiece makes a quick hard curve until it points downward and slightly inboard. This curve spans about 2 inches. The degree of sharpness of this bend may have required the breaking of some of the lamination layers on the inside of the curve. The tips of the inwales lie on each side of the stempiece a little below its top. The converged tips of the outwales rest on the support peg and are lashed to the stempiece on the inboard side of the sharp bend. From the bend, the stempiece curves downward and inboard for about 20 inches, running to and through the headboard. Over this section, the depth (profile) reduces from 2 inches to about 1-1/8 inches, while the thickness tapers from 3/4 inch to 1/2 inch. The maximum horizontal distance of the curvature of the stempiece, from the cutwater edge to the outboard side of the headboard, is about 10 inches.

Immediately below the upper end of the stempiece, a single carved wooden brace runs horizontally from the outer arc area to the headboard. The brace, about 1/2 inch thick and about 9 inches long, gradually tapers in depth (profile) over its full length. It is about 1 inch deep where it is set into the inboard edge of the stempiece; its inboard end, projecting through the headboard, measures about 1/4 inch in depth. The outboard end of the brace is not lashed to the stempiece.

The form of the internal curvature of the stempiece and its single horizontal brace closely resembles the Algonkin/Great Lakes versions modeled by Adney in Figure 18 (numbers 1 and 3) and Figure 19 (number 5) of Volume I.

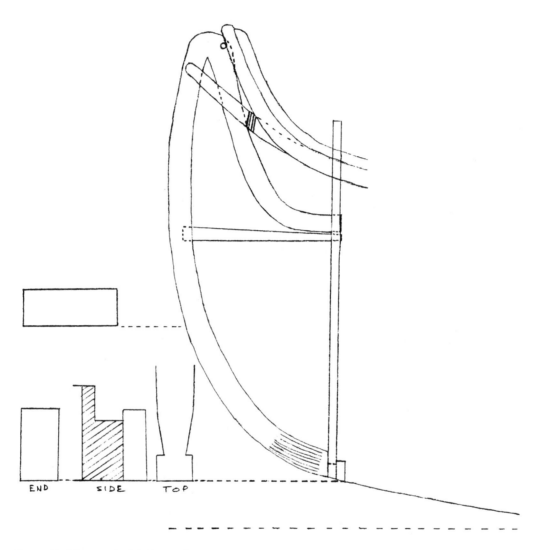

Fig. 120. Quebec Canoe: End frame unit. Spiral wrappings not shown.

END   SIDE   TOP

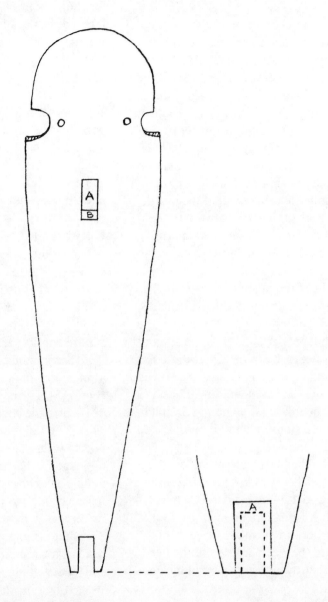

Fig. 121. Quebec Canoe: Headboard. A. stempiece, B. brace.

Headboards

The headboard is fashioned from northern cedar, according to Nash's identification. It stands exactly upright, with its base 10 inches inboard from the outermost point of the cutwater edge (Fig.108). Of the seven Adney models of Algonkin/Great Lakes canoes which are represented in Chapelle drawings, half of the headboards stand straight upright, while half of them have the head leaning slightly inboard. The Quebec headboard is positioned quite close to the end of the canoe: it stands at the chin, which is set close to the end due to the quite short undercut of the profile. The side notches beneath the head fit between the converging inwales. When the canoe is viewed in profile, the rounded head of the headboard projects about 2 to 2-1/2 inches above the caps.

The overall height of the headboard is 27 inches (Fig. 121), while its maximum width is 5 inches, just below the side notches which receive the inwales. This width tapers gradually over a span of about 23 inches, down to 1-1/4 inches at the base. The sides of this long tapered body area are bowed outward slightly, from the shoulders to the base. In all areas of the headboard, the thickness is 5/8 inch. The flat face is planed smooth, and all corners and edges are carved flat and sharp.

Below the rounded head, which measures about 3 inches in height and 4-3/8 inches at its maximum width, a notch is cut out of each side. The inwales fit into these notches, which are about 1-1/4 inches high. The top and bottom surfaces of each notch angle upward toward the outboard side of the headboard, to accommodate the upward curve of the ends of the inwales.

Inboard about 1/2 inch from the midpoint of each of these inwale notches is a single hole, through which two turns of split roots lash the inwales to the neck of the headboard. The two round holes are about 1/4 inch in diameter. The original split root lashings remain in these holes. The root material is about 3/16 to 1/4 inch wide, with a half-round cross section.

About 1-1/2 to 2 inches below the notches for the inwales lies a neatly chiseled rectangular hole in the midline of the headboard. The hole is 1-3/8 inches high and 1/2 inch wide. The laminated end of the stempiece and the end of its brace project completely through this hole; both of these elements end flush with the inboard surface of the headboard. No wooden wedge was inserted into the hole to hold the stempiece and brace ends firmly in the hole; they are held tightly due to the close fit.

The base of the headboard has a rectangular notch, 1-1/4 inches tall and 1/2 inch wide. The two legs produced by the notch are each 3/8 inch wide at the tips, which are cut off squarely. The legs of the notch fit over the heel of the stempiece, which is notched on the top and both sides. Neither of the two headboards is decorated, nor are they shaped differently from each other.

Cutwater Edges

No wooden batten was built into the stitched cutwater edge to cover and protect the outboard edge of the two bark panels and the stempiece. The edges of the panels extend slightly outboard of the stempiece. Thus, none of the outboard edge of the stempiece is exposed on the cutwater edge of the canoe.

To accommodate the stitching of the cutwater edge, a single row of holes runs around the entire perimeter (Fig. 115). The holes, spaced at intervals of about 3/8 to 1/2 inch, lie about 1/2 to 5/8 inch from the cutwater edge. The holes are positioned further inboard from the cutwater edge than the wooden pegs which attach the edge of the bark to the stempiece. Three to five lashing holes lie in the span between each peg. The round holes, about 1/4 to 5/16 inch in diameter, were produced by an awl with a triangular or square cross section. The split lashing roots, about 3/16 to 1/4 inch wide, have a half-round cross section.

The stitching was done with a single strand of root. It begins at the outwales, with the root being drawn to its midpoint through the first hole. The two ends of the root encircle the cutwater edge and pass in opposite directions through the second hole, forming cross stitches, in shoelace style, along the edge. Then end A of the root encircles the cutwater edge again and passes through the same hole. The two ends pass around the cutwater edge a second time, while crossing each other, and pass through the third hole. Then end B of the root makes its additional turn around the cutwater edge, and again runs through the third hole. The additional turn by one end of the root after each set of cross stitches fills the space on the cutwater edge which is normally left uncovered between each cross of the stitches. This upper span of stitches, not covered with pitch, extends down about 13 inches vertically from the height of the end of the canoe.

On the lower span of the cutwater edge, extending down to the chin, the stitching holes and roots are identical to those described above. This section is sewn with standard cross stitches, without the additional turn of root between each set of cross stitches.

In all sewing of the cutwater edge, whether plain or supplemented cross stitch style, the stitches pass directly through the stempiece inside the end of the canoe, rather than around it. The root lashings run through awl holes through the stempiece.

The lower portion of the cutwater edge, the area sewed with plain cross stitches, is sealed with a swath of pitch similar to that used to seal the bark panels. The pitch extends around the edge and onto the sides of the canoe for about 3/4 to 7/8 inch. The swath does not extend inboard of the chin onto the bottom of the canoe. The edges of the pitched area are broadly curved, following the contours of the cutwater edge.

The upper portion of the cutwater edge, the area lashed with supplemented cross stitches, is not sealed with pitch. This allowed unobstructed drainage of water out of the canoe when it was overturned on its side on shore.

The total thickness of the cutwater edge is made up of the two bark panels and the stitches, as well as the pitch sealant in the lower area. (The stempiece does not extend completely to the edge.) The lower portion of the edge is a little thicker than the upper portion, since it is covered by the layer of pitch.

Thwarts

The thwarts are sawn from ash, as visually identified by Nash. The nine thwarts (creating an eight-place canoe) are spaced symmetrically, with the center thwart lying exactly at the midpoint of the canoe (Fig. 110). The distances between the thwarts are measured from centerline to centerline. The positions of the thwarts indicate a canoe shape that tapers symmetrically at both ends.

Four pairs of thwarts flank the center thwart. In each of the pairs, the bow thwart is about the same length as its sternward counterpart.

Center: Thwart #1: 48-1/2 inches
Pair A: Thwart #2: 46 inches
Thwart #3: 46 inches
Pair B: Thwart #4: 37-1/4 inches
Thwart #5: 37-1/4 inches
Pair C: Thwart #6: 24-1/2 inches
Thwart #7: 24-1/2 inches
Pair D: Thwart #8: 10 inches
Thwart #9: 10 inches

The lengths, measured along the longest edge, do not include the hidden portion at each end which fits into the mortise hole in each inwale. The actual length of each thwart is about 1-1/2 inches longer than each of these measurements, since the additional portion at each end, which extends completely through the inwale, is about 3/4 inch long.

The following description applies to each of the nine thwarts (Fig. 122). At the center, the thickness is 3/4 inch. This dimension tapers very gradually over the entire span toward each inwale, by the removal of wood from the upper surface. The underside remains level and straight over nearly this entire distance. Over a distance of several inches at each end of the thwart, the underside angles moderately upward to the juncture with the inwales. At the point where the thwart meets the inwale, the thickness has tapered to 1/4 to 3/8 inch. The dimensions of 1/4 to 3/8 inch in thickness by 1-3/4 inches in width probably remain constant as the end of the thwart projects through the 3/4 inch thickness of each inwale.

The upper and lower surfaces of the thwart are planed smooth, except in the area of the underside taper at each end; here the under surface is carved flat (to fit the mortise holes). The two vertical sides are carved flat, but unevenly. All four edges are carved with a wide bevel which runs along the full length of each edge.

All of the thwarts match this description (varying only in length). But two distinct styles of thwarts are found in the canoe, with different treatment of the side contours. Thwarts #1, 2, 3, 7, and 9 have straight sides over the entire length of the thwart (Fig. 110). Their width remains constant at 1-3/4 inches for the full length. In contrast, the builders crafted gracefully curved sides on thwarts #4, 5, 6, and 8. The outboard side is slightly convex, from inwale to inwale. The

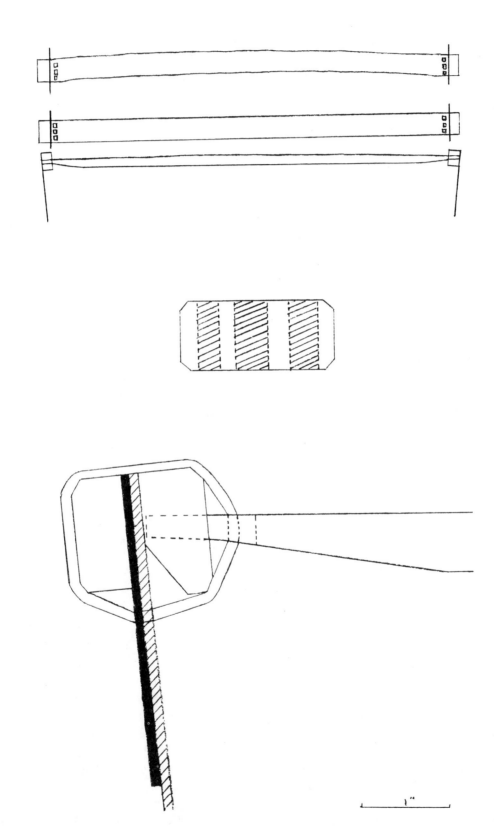

Fig. 122. Quebec Canoe: Thwarts.

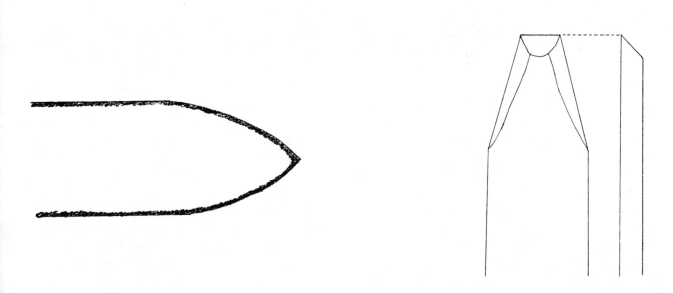

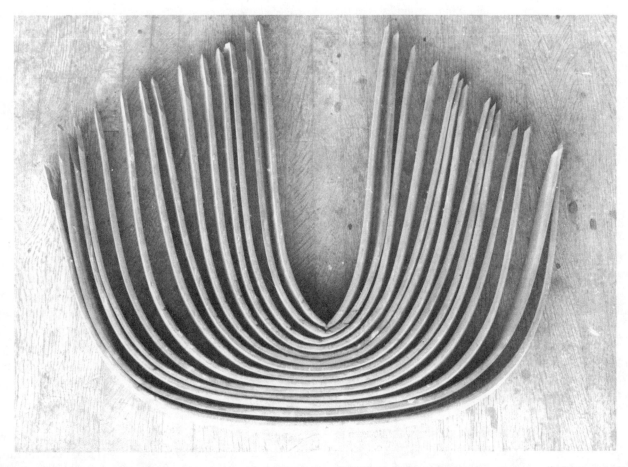

Fig. 123. Quebec Canoe: Sheathing.
Fig. 124. Quebec Canoe: Profile view of the endmost fourteen ribs (photo courtesy of Richard Nash).
Fig. 125. Quebec Canoe: Rib tips.

inboard side is straight at each end to a point 3/4 inch inboard from the inwale. The span between these two points is slightly concave, parallel to the curvature of the outboard side. The junctions of the straight portions and the central concave span are slight but sharp shoulders. The width of about 1-3/4 inches is maintained over the length of these curved thwarts. Thwarts with a nearly identical curved form are found in one of the Algonkin canoe models made by Adney.[17] The degree of curvature is portrayed accurately in the topmost drawing in Figure 122; in the canoe drawing in Figure 110, the curvature is accentuated slightly, for ease of identification.

One minor difference occurs in the relative position of thwarts # 8 and #9 (the endmost pair). All of the other thwarts are positioned so that their upper and lower surfaces lie in level, horizontal planes. The endmost thwarts are positioned in the gunwales at the point where the gunwales curve upward toward the ends of the canoe. Thus, the planes of the top and bottom surfaces of these two endmost thwarts are also angled upward, with the outboard edge higher than the inboard edge.

At the point where each thwart meets the inwale, a horizontal mortise hole is carved through the midline of the inwale, to receive the end of the thwart. Each hole, running completely through the inwale, is 2 to 2-1/4 inches long by 3/8 inch wide. The edges and corners are somewhat irregular; they may have been shaped with a flat file on the interior. The hole is cut at a slight angle, with its inboard end lower than its outboard end. This compensates for the slight outward angle of the inwale, since it angles outward in conjunction with the upper walls of the canoe. The angle of the hole permits the straight horizontal end of the thwart to fit into the hole in the angled inwale. No vertical peg or nail was driven downward from the upper surface of the inwale through the thwart to hold the end of each thwart firmly in its mortise hole.

Each end of the thwart is lashed with split root to the combined inwale and outwale. The lashings run through three vertical holes in the end of the thwart, about 3/16 to 1/4 inch inboard from the inwale (Fig. 117). The outer two holes lie about 3/16 inch from the sides of the thwart. The rectangular or square holes, carved with a knife, are irregular in shape. They are about 1/4 to 7/16 inch long

by about 1/4 to 5/16 inch wide, with sharp upper edges.

Below the junction of the thwart and the gunwales, there are seven awl holes in the bark wall. These lashing holes, spanning about 2-1/2 inches, extend about 3/8 to 1/2 inch beyond the outer edges of the thwart. All of the previous information describing the lashing of the gunwale elements also applies to the lashing of the thwarts. Of the fourteen turns of root, two or three of them lie beside each edge of the thwart and three turns pass through each of the three holes in the thwart. The thwarts were lashed at the same time as the gunwales. Thus, their lashings fit into the series of lashing groups along the length of the gunwales.

A close look at the positions of the four curved thwarts reveals that the builders of the Quebec canoe may have envisioned its crew as having seven (possibly six) paddlers (Fig. 110). The last three places in the stern have curved thwarts behind them, as does the second place from the bow end. Of these four paddling positions, the rear two are wide enough to accommodate only a single paddler. The bow paddler's position, the first two places in front of the center thwart, and the first place in back of this thwart are backed by straight thwarts, implying that these areas were considered as cargo areas by the builders. There may be another logical explanation for the mixture of curved and straight thwarts in this canoe. Some of them may have been replaced during usage, either newly-made or salvaged from worn-out craft.

Sheathing

The sheathing strips or splints are split from northern white cedar, as identified by Nash. They are about 7 to 9 feet long, 3 to 4 inches wide, and 1/16 to 3/32 inch thick. Each splint has generally parallel edges for most of its length; the endmost 4 to 5 inch span at each end is carved so that the edges gradually taper into a point (Fig. 123). The long edges and the tapered ends of the strips show evidence of thinning; these feathered edges and ends are carved down to a sharp edge.

The pattern of overlapping ends indicates that the splints were laid into the canoe in three groups: first at each end, and then a central group in the midsection area. After each end group of splints had been laid in, the following central splints were positioned so that they overlapped well the ends of the previously-laid groups. The two main areas of overlap of the three groups lie at about the midpoint between the first and second pairs of thwarts from the center thwart.

In laying in the sheathing, the first strips were positioned along the midline of the canoe. These strips extend under the heel of the stempiece. Of the eight fur trade canoes in this study, only the Quebec and Bell canoes exhibit such a feature. However, the installation of a split cedar strip beneath the heel of the stempiece has been documented for at least the Ojibwas and the Malecites.[18] In the Quebec canoe, succeeding rows of sheathing splints were then added out to and up the walls. Thus, the overlapping edge of each successive splint faces downward or inward, toward the midline of the canoe. The successive rows of sheathing were laid up the walls to a point about 1-1/2 to 2 inches below the lower edge of the inwale.

The tips of the endmost splints extend well outboard of the headboard; most of them run to or near to the stempiece. No additional short sheathing strips were inserted outboard of the headboard. Nor was any other material, such as wood shavings or moss, stuffed into the ends to support the bark cover.

Ribs

The canoe was built with a total of 68 ribs (34 pairs). Nash identified the wood type as northern white cedar. The area between each thwart contains eight ribs, while two ribs lie outboard of each end thwart. Throughout the length of the canoe, the ribs are spaced at intervals of about 1-3/8 to 1-5/8 inches, measured edge to edge. Figure 124 shows the series of fourteen endmost ribs in the stern of the canoe. These include the endmost two ribs outboard of the end thwart, the eight ribs between the first and second thwarts from the end, and the first four of the eight ribs between the second and third thwarts from the end.

The profile of the midsection ribs is composed of a narrow, very slightly rounded area (nearly flat) in the midsection of the floor, from which the bilge areas curve gradually upward; the upper sections flare slightly outward. The width of the slightly rounded central area gradually reduces toward the ends of the canoe; by the endmost ribs, the profile has become a sharp V form. The curve of the ribs reflects the body plan of the canoe (Fig. 109).

All of the ribs are generally of the same dimensions,

other than varying in length. The width is 2-1/2 to 2-3/4 inches in the area of the floor of the canoe. The tips taper very slightly and gradually as they extend upward, to a width of 2-1/4 inches at a point which is about 2-1/2 inches from the tips (Fig. 125). The thickness of 1/2 inch is maintained over this entire distance. Over the uppermost 2-1/2 inches of each tip, the width tapers quite suddenly, down to about 7/8 to 1 inch at the squared-off tip. Along this same span of 2-1/2 inches, each of the two inboard edges is carved with a broad widening bevel. The flat inboard surface at the end of the tip is carved in a sudden taper into a chisel shape over the uppermost 1/2 to 5/8 inch with a sharp edge at the tip. About 1/2 inch of each tip is hidden from view where it is inserted behind the inwale.

The ribs are carved flat and smooth on much of their flat inboard surface and the edges. The upper two edges of nearly all of the ribs are carved with a bevel running along the full length of the edges.

The sharp V-shaped profile of the endmost two ribs at each end of the canoe involves a very sharp bend at the midpoint (Fig. 124). This rib shape reflects the sharp hull form inboard of the headboards of this rather fast canoe. To achieve the sharp bend without breaking completely through the ribs, a V-shaped groove was cut across the width of the inboard face of each of these ribs at its midpoint. This groove, 1/4 to 3/8 inch deep, allowed the rib to be bent sharply at its midpoint without breaking entirely through. Comparable carved grooves and sharply bent end ribs are found in the Royal and Sault canoes. The endmost rib at each end stands about 8 to 8-1/2 inches inboard of the headboard. The tips of its two upper sections are about 18 inches apart.

In the two bilge areas of each rib, a line was scratched with an awl across the inboard face. These marks appear to have been applied to the ribs by the builders during manufacture. Before the straight ribs were steamed and bent to shape, they were all laid across the gunwales; the positions of the two inwales were marked on each rib with an awl, to indicate the location of the midpoint of the two bends in the rib.[19]

Painted Decoration

All of the painted decoration on the Quebec canoe is found on the bark walls at each end of the craft. The decorations on the right wall at the stern (Fig. 106) in-

Fig. 126. Quebec Canoe: Crowned V.R. painted decoration on each end of both walls.

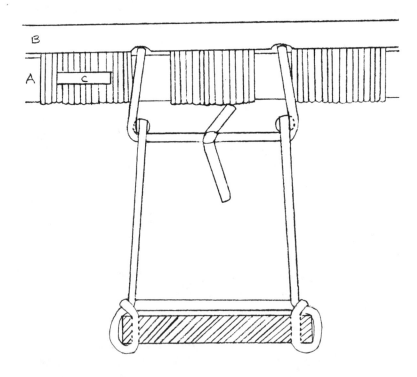

Fig. 127. Quebec Canoe: Suspended board seats. A. inwale, B. gunwale cap, C. thwart.

clude a crown over the letters V. R. (Figs. 126 and C-6) and the words THE QUEBEC in large letters inboard of the crown. The painted elements on the left wall at the bow include an identical crowned V. R. and the inscription LE QUEBEC inboard of the crown. The remaining two end areas of the canoe each bear an identical crowned V. R., without any additional inscription. In each instance, the decorations are applied directly onto the bark surface, without a background of solid color. Each of the painted areas is now moderately faded; there is no evidence of any restoration to the decorations. All of the decorative elements appear to have been applied by a practiced artist, particularly the lettering, which was done in a professional style.

Each crown is located immediately inboard of the headboard, and about 1/2 inch below the reinforcement bark strip. It is positioned between the seam of the end of the main panel of bark and the set of three closely spaced gore slit seams. The upper outboard corner of the crown lies about twelve inches horizontally from the cutwater edge. The crown with its V. R. beneath it fills the upper half of the space between the reinforcement bark strip and the bottom of the canoe.

The crown, angled to match the position of the upward-curved gunwales, measures about nine inches in height and about seven inches in width. It is formed of moderately wide black painted lines, with solid areas of royal blue and yellow added. Differences in the shape of the black outline of the various crowns indicate that they were executed in freehand style rather than by tracing around a pattern. The color scheme of blue and yellow is the same on all four of the crowns.

About 3/8 inch below the crown is found the inscription V. R., in black letters about 2-1/8 inches high, with a period following each letter. This is the abbreviation for the Latin *Victoria Regina*, Queen Victoria. It is this inscription plus the crown which indicates that the canoe was official government property, to be used for official functions involving the British Royal Family. It also places the period of manufacture and usage of the canoe within the years of Victoria's reign, from 1837 to 1901.

The inscriptions THE QUEBEC and LE QUEBEC, at opposite ends and sides of the canoe, apparently indicate the name of this particular craft, as well as representing the bilingual and bicultural nature of the prov-ince of Quebec. The lettering begins about 22 inches inboard of the crown, immediately inboard of the set of three closely spaced gore slit seams. The inscription of black letters lies about two inches below the reinforcement bark strip. The words THE and LE are formed of capital block letters about five inches high. About 1/2 inch above and below the word are two adjacent horizontal lines, each about 3/8 to 1/2 inch wide; the yellow line runs below the black line, in a shadow effect. Identical yellow shadowing of the same 3/8 to 1/2 inch width also appears beneath each letter of the word. The words QUEBEC and QUEBEC are painted in large block capital letters about 7-1/2 inches tall, followed by a large round period. An accent mark is found over the letter E in the French version of the word. These letters are also each shadowed on the lower side with yellow pigment, in the same width as previously described.

At the bow end of the right wall, the outline of another design element is also found (Fig. 115). The outline of a maple leaf, rather deeply scored with wide, dark pencil marks, lies adjacent to the outboard side of the painted crown. The design, which is generally aligned with the top and bottom of the crown, extends to the seam at the end of the main bark panel. It is about 8 inches tall and about 6-3/4 inches wide. The end portion of the right finial of the leaf is covered by the swath of pitch which seals the bark seam. Thus, the leaf outline definitely appears to date from the period when the painted decorations were applied to the canoe and the canoe was used. This is the only unfinished decorative element which is found on the craft.

This unpainted maple leaf design, positioned prominently at the bow of the canoe beside the royal emblems of Queen Victoria, has been considered in the discussion of the history of the Quebec canoe. The unfinished aspect of the leaf design will probably never be explained.

Nails

No nails were utilized in the manufacture of the Quebec canoe. The small nails which were used in the repair of one of the longitudinal side seams are of the machine-cut type, in the style which was available from the 1830s on.[20] The two nails which were installed in the replacement tips of the outwales at the stern end are of the wire nail type, with its round head. This type appeared in widespread use by about 1879. It overtook the cut nail, due to its relatively cheaper price, although some cut nails continued to be produced.[21]

Wood Types

All of the wood and root identifications for the Quebec canoe were done visually by Richard Nash, a highly experienced bark canoe builder. The types of wood used to build this canoe are typical of those used for canoe construction.[22] The inwales, outwales, gunwale caps, stempieces, headboards, sheathing, and ribs are all fashioned from northern white cedar. The thwarts are made of ash, as are also the gunwale pegs. Both white and black ash were used in bark canoes. The lashings are fashioned of the roots of either spruce or eastern larch (tamarack). As previously discussed, if they are of spruce, the most typical type for canoe lashings would be black spruce.

Miscellaneous Features
Seats

The Quebec canoe was at one time fitted with up to seven wooden seats. These were flat boards with holes drilled through their ends (Fig. 127). Adjustable suspension cords encircled the inwales and outwales and passed through the holes in the seat boards. The boards and cords are no longer present, but much evidence of the suspended seats remains.

Pairs of holes for the suspension cords are drilled through the bark wall and the reinforcement bark strip along each wall, slightly forward of all of the thwarts except the endmost one at each end of the canoe. The round holes, 1/2 inch in diameter, lie about 1/2 to 3/4 inch below the outwale, just above the midline of the reinforcement bark strip. They are located in the area on the interior side of the upper walls which is not covered by sheathing strips. The two holes in each pair lie about four inches apart, measured edge to edge. In the Figure 106 photo, three pairs of seat sling holes are visible in the reinforcement bark strip, just forward of each thwart. Light wear is found on the surfaces of the inwale, the outwale, and the bark adjacent to the holes; this wear was caused by the rubbing of the suspension cords.

Before the gunwale caps were installed, shallow grooves were carved into their undersides at the loca-

tions of the seat sling cords. The grooves create sufficient space between the cap and the inwale-outwale unit for the thickness of the cords to pass without raising the level of the cap excessively above the gunwales and the lashing roots.

Wear areas are visible on the upper wall areas of the ribs, about 7 to 8 inches below the pairs of suspension holes; this is about 10 to 11 inches below the top surface of the gunwale caps. These are the locations where the ends of the suspended seat boards bumped and abraded against the ribs. They indicate the height at which the seats were usually hung.

In the Figure 127 drawing, the seat has been reconstructed as if it were made from a board about 6 inches wide and about 3/4 inch thick. It is slung from cordage with a diameter of 1/4 inch, at a height which is about 9 to 10 inches below the top of the gunwale cap.

As mentioned in the thwarts discussion, the positions of the curved thwarts in the canoe imply that the builders envisioned the usual crew of six or seven paddlers sitting in five of the canoe's places (Fig. 110). The pairs of seat sling holes are positioned forward of all but the endmost thwart at each end of the canoe. Thus, four of the five crew positions were accompanied by a suspended seat. The end thwart at the stern is curved; the stern paddler sat on this thwart, requiring no seat. The three places in the midsection which are backed by straight (rather than curved) thwarts were presumably considered as the usual cargo areas, if the canoe were to be used for long voyages. However, seat sling holes are also found in each of these places. When the canoe was used for official ceremonial occasions, seats were probably hung in these usual cargo areas, in the number required for the specific number of passengers.

Provision for Sail and Cordelling Line

No evidence can be observed which would indicate the lashing of either a mast or a cordelling (towing) line to the forward thwarts. The use of the Quebec canoe for ceremonial occasions involving the Royal Family, rather than for long-distance expeditions, probably precluded towing and sailing.

The canoe is not equipped with a permanent perforated thwart or mast step for sailing. Thus, if a sail were sometimes used, the upright mast would have been temporarily lashed to the second or third thwart

Chapter 4—The Quebec Canoe

at the bow end. Or a temporary perforated thwart may have been lashed to one of these thwarts, with the mast then positioned in its hole.

The base of the mast may have been placed into a drilled or carved indentation in a loose board laid down the midline, to step the mast. Sometimes some other object was positioned beneath the base of the mast to protect the canoe.[23] These temporary measures of mast attachment and stepping would leave no permanent evidence that a sail had been used on the canoe. Thus, the lack of such evidence on the Quebec canoe does not rule out the use of sail on this craft.

Flags

No evidence can be found for the attachment of a flag at either the bow or the stern. No space exists outboard of either headboard into which a flag staff could have been inserted. Likewise, there is no space around the head or midsection area of the headboard to permit the lashing of such a staff onto the inboard surface.

Bow/Stern Differences

The builders of the Quebec canoe created a few differences between the bow and the stern ends of the craft, which are listed below. No differences in the form and dimensions of the hull were observed between the forward and rear halves of the canoe, nor in the dimensions of the coating of pitch on the cutwater edge at each end. In addition, all of the seams have their overlapping exterior edge facing toward the midpoint of the canoe (except those of the supplemental pieces of bark which were added to each end of the main bark panel). Thus, there do not appear to be any elements of the canoe which would dictate the proper direction of travel of the canoe for greatest efficiency.

The forward end of the craft is indicated by the position of the seat board holes, which lie forward of each thwart, and by the direction of the concave side of each of the curved thwarts, which faces forward to accommodate the backsides of the paddlers.

A. The supplemental bark pieces which were added to the ends of the main bark panel are about five inches shorter at the bow than at the stern.

B. The name of the canoe is written at the bow in French and at the stern in English.

C. The bow end bears the unfinished maple leaf design, in addition to the emblems of Queen Victoria which are found at both the bow and the stern.

Usage and Wear

The physical evidence indicates that the canoe saw only light usage during the years while it was the property of the British and Canadian governments. (Later, it was not used at all by the Canoe Club.) The bark cover has few scrapes and gouges. The nailed and pitched repair of a section of one of its longitudinal side seams was installed during the period of usage, as were also the pitched repairs of two cracks in the bark cover. Such damage could have occurred during storage or transport of the canoe, or during light usage on ceremonial occasions.

The wooden elements of the canoe show little wear. The replacement of the end tips of the two outwales at the stern was probably necessitated by a single accident, possibly incurred during storage or transport of the canoe.

Construction Tools, Methods, and Materials

The Quebec canoe was manufactured from the traditional forest materials of birchbark, wood, tree roots, and pine or spruce gum mixed with animal fat and pulverized charcoal. It was painted afterward with Euroamerican commercial paints.

The builders of the canoe used the typical array of tools normally employed in canoe manufacture during the nineteenth century. These include an axe, knife, crooked knife, drawknife, awl, rib-setting mallet, pitch melting and applying implements, and paint containers and brushes.

In addition, they utilized a number of techniques that have generally been considered less than traditional in the canoe construction of that era. The installation of support pegs at the tips of the outwales, overlapping bark seams which face the midpoint of the craft, and inwales and outwales fashioned of two sections spliced together at the midpoint have already been discussed. These features are not often encountered in the bark canoe literature. In all other respects, the Quebec canoe was built with methods and materials that have been considered entirely traditional.

The above "nontraditional" features have been observed on a surviving example of a fur trade canoe, a canoe which was chosen for use on extremely high-status occasions. Their presence may reflect more common usage of these manufacturing techniques in the building of such canoes in the mid- nineteenth century than has been previously reported.

Condition

In 1972, Nash and Vaillancourt lowered the canoe from its rope slings in the upper story of the boathouse, where it had been suspended in an upright position since its acquisition by the Canoe Club some time before 1908. They found the bark cover, the sealant pitch, the painted decoration, and virtually all of the wooden elements to be in good, stable condition. A number of the inwale-outwale pegs had become completely displaced due to the upward pressure of the ribs on the inwales. In addition, the endmost thwart at the bow had broken through its carved lashing holes at one end, and the stern tip of the right outwale and gunwale cap had deteriorated. Besides these rather minor areas of damage, the primary element which required restoration was the root lashings: they had become very dry and brittle, and were badly broken in many areas. However, the root lashings were found to be intact in virtually all of the seams, along the gunwales at the bow end (including the filled area between the converging outwales), and the cutwater edges (the entire edge at the stern and the lower half at the bow).

The two restorers inserted a number of new pegs into the original holes through the inwale-outwale unit, carved and installed a new end thwart at the bow, and replaced the deteriorated stern tips of the right outwale and cap. They also removed all of the broken gunwale lashings, and replaced each of them in the span from the stern tip to the second thwart from the stern. In addition, they replaced three outwale-gunwale cap lashings at the bow end, and relashed all of the thwarts to the gunwales. The root stitches were also redone in the upper half of the bow cutwater edge, as well as in the seam in the right wall at the stern which attaches the supplemental piece of bark to the main panel.

An additional restoration procedure involved the removal of a great number of thumb tacks from the canoe. Many years before, the Canoe Club had held a dance in the boathouse; the decorations for the dance had included transforming the suspended voyaging ca-noe into a flying airplane. Wings were laid across its gunwales, and the entire creation was completely covered over with tinfoil, tacked in place. One can only imagine what the nineteenth century builders and paddlers of the Quebec canoe would have thought of such a transformation.

Notes: Quebec Canoe

1. Adney and Chapelle, pp. 114, 116, 123, 124, 125, 127.
2. Ibid., pp. 28-29,102,149.
3. Ibid., pp. 134,136, 139, 140, 143.
4. Christensen, personal communication of December 5, 1994.
5. Guy, p. 23; Gidmark, pp. 43-44.
6. Adney and Chapelle, pp. 138, 141, 147.
7. Ritzenthaler, p. 29.
8. Santucci, p. 11; Hume, pp. 253-54.
9. Adney and Chapelle, p. 17.
10. Hadlock and Dodge, illustrations.
11. Adney and Chapelle, p. 31.
12. Ibid., p. 132.
13. Guy, p. 20.
14. Adney and Chapelle, p. 33 model.
15. Santucci, p. 11; Hume, pp. 253-54 .
16. Morgan; Pope.
17. Adney and Chapelle, p. 118.
18. Ritzenthaler, p. 38; Adney and Chapelle, p. 51.
19. Ritzenthaler, p. 33; Guy, p. 28.
20. Santucci, p. 11; Hume, pp. 253-54 .
21. Ibid.
22. Adney and Chapelle, p. 17.
23. Sha-Ka-Nash, pp. 6-7.

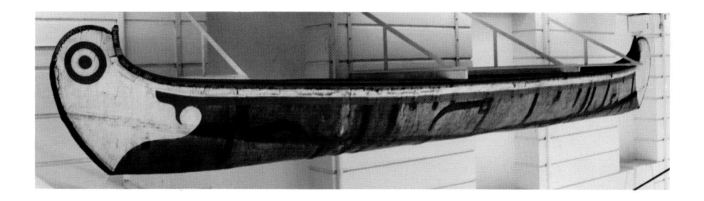

Fig. C-1. Royal Canoe: Painted decorations.

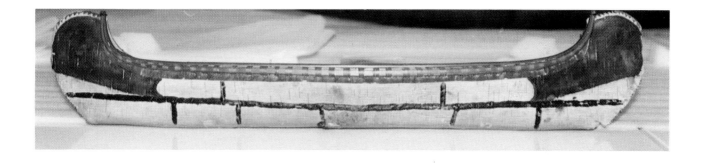

Fig. C-2. Varden Canoe: Painted ornamentation.

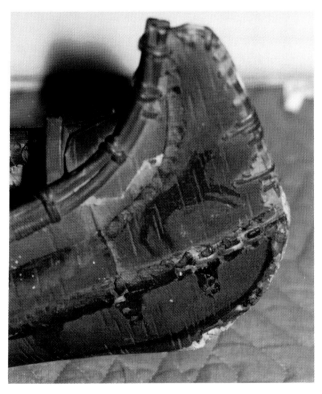

Figs. C-3 (upper), C-4 (left), C-5 (right). Assiginack Canoe and paddling figures.

Fig. C-6. Quebec Canoe: Painted royal symbols at each end of both walls.

Fig. C-7. Catlin Canoe: Painted decorations.

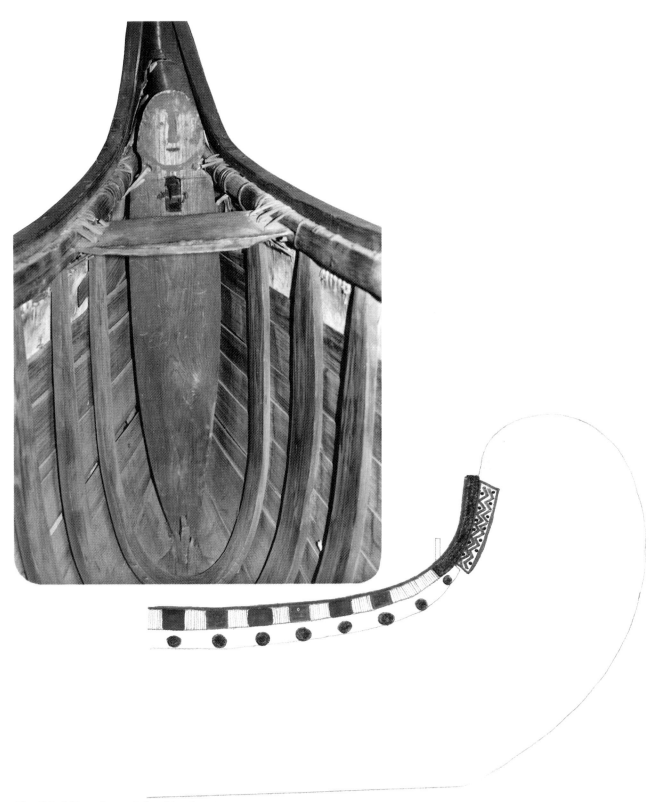

Fig. C-8. Ojibwa Canoe: Painted headboard at bow.
Fig. C-9. Ojibwa Canoe: Painted motifs of gunwales, reinforcement bark strip, and deck piece.

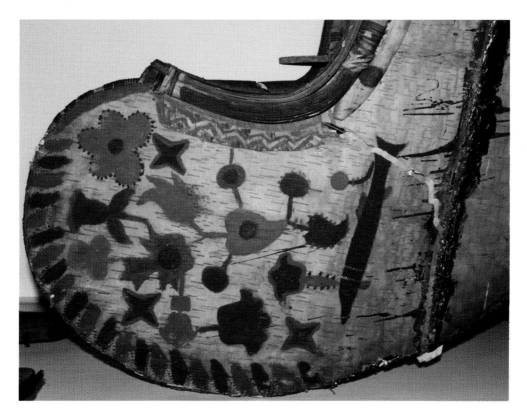

Fig. C-10 (left), C-11 (right). Ojibwa Canoe: Left wall decorations.

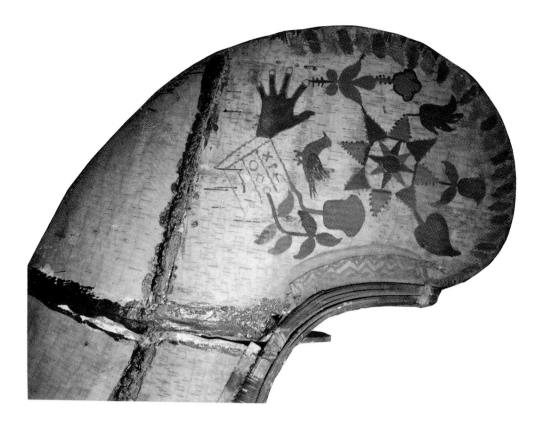

Fig. C-12 (left), C-13 (right). Ojibwa Canoe: Right wall ornamentation.

Models

The period models of voyaging canoes which have survived are of great value as sources of information concerning the full size craft which they were built to represent. Since so very few full size versions now exist, the models are excellent substitutes for study. The early date of manufacture of these models further amplifies their importance.

In many instances, the general form of the various individual parts of the models and the methods of construction are reliable representations of full size canoes. The actual dimensions of the parts of the models are, quite often, less reliable. This is in great part due to the difficulty or even the impossibility of creating and assembling the very small and thin parts of miniature canoes so that they are entirely to the proper scale. Because of this size difficulty, when the dimensions of the individual elements of a model canoe are multiplied by a factor of say eight or twelve, the resultant measurements often do not accurately represent those elements in the full size version which the builder had in mind.

Each of the models presented in this study appears to have been built too short in the midsection, in varying degrees, in relation to the heights of the ends and the midsection walls and/or the width of the beam. Thus, the models often appear to be short, tall, and unusually broad in the midsection beam. Since these canoes were built as detailed miniature likenesses rather than as functioning watercraft, such digressions from the dimensions of full size canoes were apparently of little concern to the model builders.

Besides the importance of the models as sources of information on general forms and building techniques, they are especially valuable when they contain features which are entirely absent on the very few full size craft which have survived. One of the most important of these features is the provision for rigging a sail. None of the four surviving full size fur trade canoes was fitted with a perforated mast thwart or a mast step. Yet three of the four surviving models have such sailing provisions. In this instance, multiplying the dimensions of the sailing elements of the models to full size scale is the best that can be done toward reconstructing these elements as they once existed.

In the construction of full size canoes, the builders took into consideration the strength, flexibility, working characteristics, weight, decay resistance, etc. of the various types of woods and lashing roots which they chose. The miniature canoes were built for display, rather than to be navigated on the water; thus, the choice of woods and roots by the model builders may not have faithfully replicated those which they used when building functional canoes. For this reason, the types of woods and roots which are found in the models were not identified in this study.

The Assiginack Canoe Model

Contents

Assiginack Canoe Model

Numerous features of the Assiginack canoe indicate that it is an Algonkin/Great Lakes Indian style of fur trade canoe, the Type A-1 style of the full size Quebec canoe. These traits include the narrow upswept ends with level horizontal tops, the shortness of the undercut in the profile of the ends, and the form of the stempieces.

The canoe represents the moderately large size of fur trade canoe, the six-place (seven-thwart) version. Based on the sizes of the paddling figures, the model appears to depict a craft which would have been about twenty or more feet long in full size (Fig. 162). The figures were carved so that they sit on top of the thwarts, a practice which was not ordinarily done except when reinforcement bars were lashed on top of the thwarts. Normally, paddlers were positioned lower in the craft, sitting on temporary or permanent seats or kneeling. Their high position makes them appear, at first glance, to be too large in relation to the size of the canoe; but they do match in general the height of the walls and the ends, as well as the beam.

The model was built too short in the midsection, in relation to the height of the walls and the ends (Fig. 128). This makes the beam appear to be much too broad in relation to the overall length. In addition, the ribs and the sheathing strips are much enlarged compared to the rest of the elements. In spite of these inconsistencies of scale, Assiginack went to great lengths to build the individual components of the model in excellent, realistic detail. Therefore, it is an invaluable source of data on full size voyaging canoes.

Overall Dimensions
Length: 36-3/4".
Distance between the outboard sides of the tips of the outwales: 31-1/2" (Fig. 129).
Distance between the inboard faces of the heads of the headboards: 28-1/2".
Depth at the midpoint, from the top of the gunwale caps to the top of the ribs on the floor: 3-5/8".
Height above the baseline: at the midpoint 4", at the bow and the stern 7-5/8".
Beam at the midpoint: 8-3/8" (Fig. 130).
Interior beam, inside the gunwales: 6-7/8".
Total girth around the hull, from gunwale top to gunwale top: 12-3/4".

The Assiginack canoe was built in a large size format but in the standard traditional form and proportions of the small and medium size versions of Algonkin/Great Lakes canoes.[1] In form and proportions, its ends are very similar to certain models of these canoes which were fashioned by Adney (Figs. 18 and 19, Vol. I).

The ends of the canoe rise above the height of the walls at the midpoint by an increase of 91 percent. Of the seven Adney models of Algonkin/Great Lakes canoes which are represented in Chapelle drawings (Fig. 18), six have ends which rise by a factor of 47 to 63 percent, while one rises by 100 percent. Thus, the form of the Assiginack canoe falls within the uppermost range of upsweep of the ends.

Since the craft was built too short in the midsection, it has as a result an excessively wide interior beam, which equals 22.78 percent of the overall length of the craft (Figs. 131 and 132). If the model had been constructed to full length in the midsection area, the beam would compare more closely to the 15.37 percent of the slightly narrow full size Ojibwa canoe, the 16.33 percent of the Quebec canoe, the 17.72 percent of the wide-beamed Sault canoe, and the 18.30 percent of the wide-beamed Royal canoe. The longest standard Algonkin/Great Lakes canoes which Adney reproduced in model form represent canoes 15-1/2 to 19 feet long; these rather wide-beamed craft have interior beams which range from 16.8 to 18.3 percent of the overall length of the canoe. Had the Assiginack canoe been built with a full-length midsection, its beam would probably fall within this range as well.

Hull Form
Profile of the Bottom and Ends
The horizontal span of the bottom extends for 11-1/4

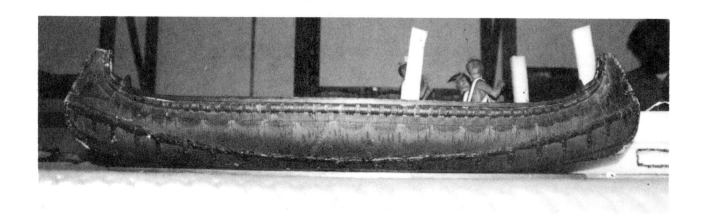

Fig. 128. Assiginack Canoe, with bow to right.

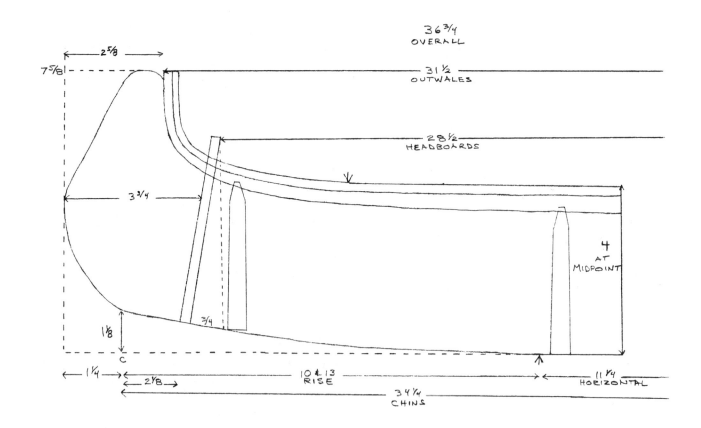

Fig. 129. Assiginack Canoe: Hull profile and dimensions.

- 198 -

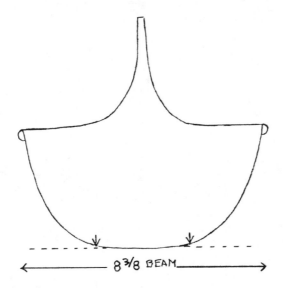

8³/₈ BEAM

Fig. 130. Assiginack Canoe: Body plan. Arrows indicate locations of crease lines.

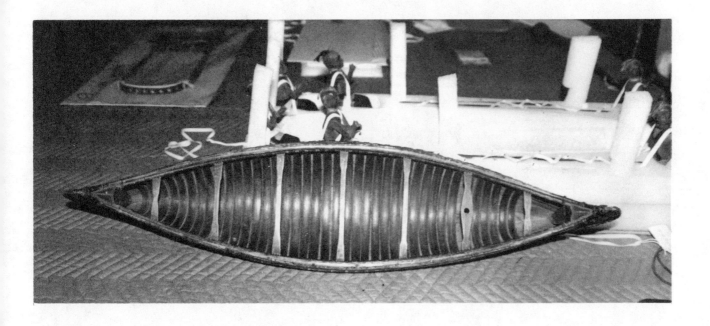

Fig. 131. Assiginack Canoe: Interior view.

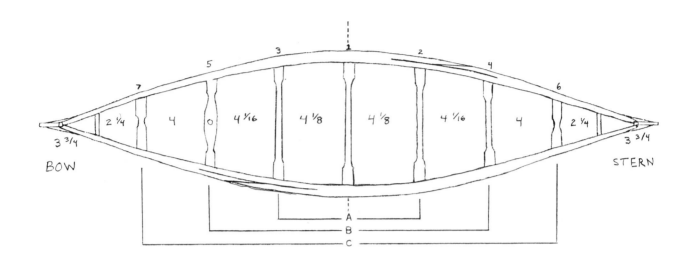

Fig. 132. Assiginack Canoe: Hull form, thwart positions, and locations of outwale splices.

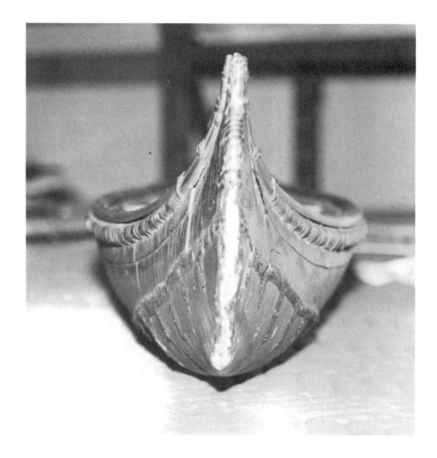

Fig. 133. Assiginack Canoe: End view.

Fig. 134. Assiginack Canoe: Bottom view.

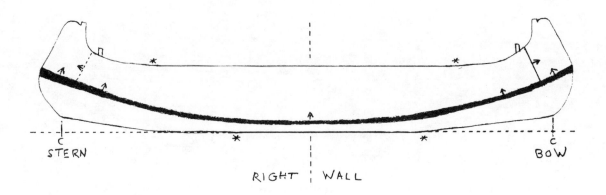

STERN

RIGHT ¦ WALL

BOW

Fig. 135. Assiginack Canoe: Bark panels and supplemental end pieces.

Fig. 136. Assiginack Canoe: Harness stitches of longitudinal side seam and spiral stitches of gore slits, as well as painted decorations.

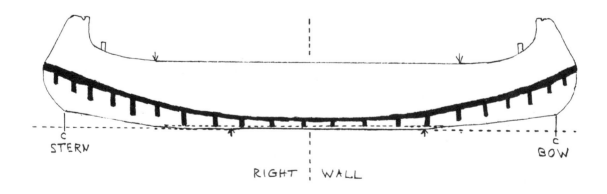

Fig. 137. Assiginack Canoe: Gore slits.

Fig. 138. Assiginack Canoe: Bottom view of gore slits.

Fig. 139. Assiginack Canoe: Side view of gunwale end lashings, bark deck piece, cutwater edge lashings, and painted decorations.

inches, between a point 10 inches inboard of the bow chin and a point 13 inches inboard of the stern chin (Fig. 129). This horizontal span is too short in relation to the overall length of the canoe, since the midsection of the model was built too short. The horizontal span is positioned well forward of a centered location on the craft. From the bow end of the horizontal section, a 10 inch span of considerable rocker (measured on the horizontal base line) gradually rises to a moderately rounded chin (to the point where the stitches of the cutwater edge begin). At the stern, a 13 inch span of considerable rocker gradually rises to the chin. The total length of the bottom between the chins is 34-1/4 inches.

At both ends of the canoe, the chin lies 1-1/8 inches above the horizontal baseline. This height is somewhat higher proportionally than the comparable locations on each of the Algonkin/Great Lakes models made by Adney. The increased height is due to the degree of rocker of the Assiginack model: it is greater than all of Adney's Algonkin/Great Lakes models and his fur trade models, as well as each of the other seven fur trade canoes in this study. Thus, the degree of rocker on the Assiginack canoe appears to be well beyond the norm for these two groups of canoes. The present rocker and chin dimensions on the canoe appear to be original, not altered by warpage.

From the chin, each end of the canoe extends 1-1/4 inches outboard (measured on the baseline) to the outermost point of the end. The cutwater edge at each end curves upward from the moderately rounded chin, beginning 2-1/8 inches outboard of the foot of the headboard. It extends upward and outward in a moderate curve over 3-3/4 inches (measured on the curve) to the point of maximum length of the canoe, creating a rather short undercut profile. Then the virtually straight upper span angles strongly inboard, at about a 25 degree angle from the upright position; it rises for 3-1/2 inches to the highest point of the end. After making a sharp turn inboard, it extends over a short nearly straight span of 7/8 inch to meet the outwales. The total length of the edge, measured on the curve from chin to outwales, is 8-1/8 inches.

Body Plan

The bottom is narrow and very slightly rounded, nearly flat. The bilge is gradually rounded, while the upper walls are straight and flare outward slightly (Figs. 130, 133, and 134). Its bilge area is considerably more undercut than that of the Type A-1 Quebec canoe. The widest area of the bottom lies at the midpoint of the length of the canoe. This width tapers gradually and symmetrically from the midpoint to each end of the canoe.

The Assiginack canoe was built in a form designed for moderately fast paddling with ample cargo capacity. Its features, including a narrow, very slightly rounded (nearly flat) bottom, gradually rounded bilge, rather broad beam, long slender taper to the ends, and a narrow U form inboard of the headboards, contributed to its ease of paddling yet provided generous room for cargo.[2] Various hull forms are depicted in Adney's models of Great Lakes Indian canoes; the Assiginack canoe closely resembles those which are well undercut and gradually curved in the bilge.[3] Its hull form also matches very closely that of the full size Ojibwa fur trade canoe.

Bark Cover
Color and Thickness

All of the panels of bark are light to dark golden tan in color. The thickness of the bark measures 3/32 to 1/8 inch in the bottom panel and 1/16 inch in the side panels. (The thickness profile is visible in several locations.)

Panels

The drawing in Figure 135 shows the seams which join the three panels of bark plus the two supplemental end pieces (one on the right wall at the bow and one on the left wall at the stern). The position of the left wall piece is depicted in the drawing by a broken line on the visible right wall. The arrows indicate the direction of the exposed overlapping edges on the exterior of the canoe.

The bottom of the canoe was made with a single panel of bark, which measures 38-1/4 inches in length and 5-3/4 inches in width. To it was added a long side panel on each wall, 35-1/4 inches long by 3-1/4 inches wide at the midpoint and 3-3/4 inches wide at its one high end. The side panel of the right wall ends 2-7/8 inches short of the bow tip, at a point just outboard of the headboard. A supplemental piece 2-7/8 inches long by 3-3/4 inches high completes the cover of this wall. The side panel on the left wall ends 3 inches short of the stern; its supplemental piece measures 3 inches in length and 3-3/4 inches in height. (Its diagonal seam on the left wall is portrayed in the drawing as a broken line on the visible right wall.) Each of these added pieces extends from the longitudinal side seam up to the top of the high end, and from a point just outboard of the head-board out to the cutwater edge. The lower and inboard edges of the supplemental piece were slid beneath the edges of the adjacent bottom panel and side panel, to be overlapped by those panels. The stated dimensions of each section of bark in the canoe do not include any over-lapped portions which are hidden from view.

If the bark cover were flattened, the maximum width in the midsection would be 12-1/4" (the total girth of the bark of the canoe) in the midsection. Near the ends, the width measures one inch more. The length would be 38-1/4" at the level of the gunwales. This total length of the side panel and the supplemental piece of each wall of the canoe is 1-1/2 inches longer than the length of the assembled canoe, since the side panels follow the curva-ture of the broadening midsection of the canoe, rather than a straight line down the midline.

The canoe builder did not create any weak points in the hull by positioning vertical wall seams directly op-posite each other across the hull of the canoe. The seams which attach the side of each of the supplemental pieces of bark lie at opposite ends of the craft.

Sewn Seams

The original lashing material still survives in all of the sewn seams. No tucked-under ends of seam lash-ing roots are visible for observation and description, all of them having been finished on the hidden interior side. No evidence suggests that a batten strip of wood or root was incorporated into any of the seams for added reinforcement, either on the exterior or the inte-rior side of the bark cover. Since the bottom of the model was constructed of a single panel of bark, the canoe has no bottom seams.

Gore Slits

The long span of bottom bark was laid out on the build-ing bed, and the building frame was placed upon it. As previously discussed, this frame determined the general outline of the bottom of the canoe, particularly the shape of the taper toward the ends. The building frame was usually about as long as the bottom of the canoe, from chin to chin. After the bark was bent upward around the perimeter of the frame, a number of gore slits were sliced at intervals along the sides of the bottom panel. These slices ran from the edges of the bark inboard nearly to the building frame. At each of these slits, a narrow trian-gular slice of bark was removed, to eliminate any over-lapping of the edges of the gore slits.

The slits are stitched closed with split roots in a se-ries of two or three widely spaced spiral stitches, with one stitch per hole (Fig. 136). The portion of each stitch on the exterior side of the canoe is horizontal, while the connector portion running to the next stitch on the interior of the canoe is diagonal. The stitches run through pairs of awl holes which were produced by an awl with a square or triangular cross section. The holes lie about 1/16 inch from the overlapping edge of bark. The visible horizontal portions are 1/8 to 3/16 inch long, and are spaced about 3/16 to 1/4 inch apart.

The lashing roots are 1/16 inch wide (the same as the width of the awl holes) and about 1/32 inch thick, with a half-round cross section. The rounded side, which was scraped somewhat flat, is the side of the root lashing which faces the exterior.

The gore slits in the bottom panel are positioned at quite regular intervals; they extend over virtually the full length of the panel (Figs. 137 and 138). Twenty-one slits are found in each wall; each slit has a mate exactly or nearly exactly opposite it (having been cut on opposite sides of the building frame). The midpoint of the craft falls between two pairs of slits. Eleven pairs lie in the bow half of the canoe, and ten pairs in the stern half. In the midsection area, the slits are posi-tioned at intervals of 2 to 2-1/4 inches. These spans gradually narrow toward the ends of the canoe, reduc-ing to 1-3/8 to 1-5/8 inches.

When the canoe is viewed in side profile, the gore slits extend downward from the longitudinal main seam, which runs the full length of each side of the canoe. In the central, widest area of the canoe, this seam curves down close to the horizontal baseline of the canoe. Here, the gore slits are barely visible in a profile view; they extend down nearly to the slightly rounded bottom of the canoe in this area. Toward the ends of the canoe, where the main seam rises, the full length of the outer six slits at each end is clearly visible, running down the curved bilge area of the lower walls.

The length of each gore slit cannot be measured exactly, since each is covered by a coating of pitch. This pitch extends inboard toward the midline of the canoe beyond the end of each slit. Observation can be made of the length of each pitch strip, which implies the general length and position of the gore slit which it covers. The pitch strips at the midpoint are 1 to 1-1/8 inches long, becoming longer toward the ends of the building frame. Nine pairs of pitch strips run to or nearly to the edges of the frame in the midsection area; the more outboard of these reach 1-1/4 to 1-3/4 inches in length. (The slits beneath the pitch strips all end a little short of the frame, with only the pitch extending to or nearly to the frame.) These nine pairs of midsection slits end well inboard of the ends of the building frame. Outboard from them, six pairs of slits extend out to each end of the canoe. These slits are shorter, from 1 to 1-1/8 inches long. They do not extend down to the bottom of the canoe, but end in the bilge area. At each end of the canoe, one pair of gore slits lies outboard of the chin.

The junction of the slightly rounded bottom with the bilge area on the Assiginack canoe is marked by a slight but clearly defined crease line along most of the span where the bottom panel was folded up around the building frame. Very similar crease lines also occur on the Varden canoe model, on which the lines are more sharply defined. (See pages 248 - 250, and Figs. 172 and 175.) Due to the upward curve of the rounded bottom, the crease line is visible when the canoe is viewed in side profile (Fig. 137). The difference between this crease line and genuine chine lines on bark canoes is discussed in the Varden canoe description.

The outline of the crease lines, at the upward turn of the bilge from the bottom, clearly implies the form and dimensions of the building frame. The length of the frame is usually about the same as the length of the bottom (the distance between the chins). Assiginack positioned the chins very near to the extremities of the canoe; his building frame was much shorter, ending about 2-1/4 to 2-5/8 inches inboard of the chins, at a point four gore slits inboard of each end of the canoe. At the midpoint, the width of the bottom between the crease lines is 3-1/4 inches. This width tapers gradually and evenly toward the ends. At a point about 8-3/4

inches toward each end, the width has reduced to 2 to 2-1/4 inches. This span is the 17-1/2 inch long midsection portion of the canoe which contains the nine pairs of pitched gore slits running to or nearly to the crease lines. Outboard of this area, the building frame tapers to a point at its ends over a distance of about 5-1/4 to 5-1/2 inches. In these end spans, the crease lines become much less sharply defined and more rounded, until they fade out short of the ends of the building frame. In addition, the gore slits in these end areas do not extend to the frame; they end well above the bottom of the canoe.

The above description and measurements indicate rather closely the form and dimensions of the building frame. The maximum width of the building frame that was used to construct slightly rounded and nearly flat-bottomed fur trade canoes was often two-thirds of the interior beam of the gunwales.[4] In the case of the Assiginack canoe, this ratio would produce a measurement of about 4-5/8 inches. The actual width of the building frame of this canoe was much less, 3-1/4 inches at the midpoint, as reflected by the chine lines. But the beam of the Assiginack canoe is excessively broad, invalidating the comparison of this canoe with craft that was built with a conventional beam.

Side Panels to Bottom Panel

After the gore slits were cut and stitched along the side edges of the bottom panel, the side panels were attached to the bottom panel. The seam connecting the side and bottom panels to each other is the prominent longitudinal seam which arcs across the full length of the canoe on each wall.

The lower edges of the side panels are positioned inside the edges of the bottom bark panel. Thus, the edges of the bottom panel are exposed on the exterior of the canoe, facing upward toward the gunwales (Fig. 136). It is not possible to determine on the two longitudinal side seams the amount of overlap of the bottom panel over the side panels, since no interior views are available between displaced sheathing strips to make a determination.

The seams are sewn with split roots in a series of harness stitches, with the two ends of a single root running in opposite directions through the same hole, one stitch per hole. The stitches, 5/16 to 3/8 inch long, are composed of the same awl holes and split roots as those described above for the gore slits, except that these holes and roots are slightly wider, 3/32 to 1/8 inch in width. The horizontal row of stitches lies 1/8 inch below the exposed edge of the bottom bark panel.

Supplemental Pieces

The seams which join the supplemental piece of bark at each end of the canoe to its side and bottom panels are all overlapped seams, with the main panels overlapping the supplemental piece (Fig. 139). On the side panel seam at the stern, the exposed edge which overlaps on the exterior faces toward the stern; on the right wall at the bow, the seam that joins the high end piece to its adjacent side panel overlaps toward the bow. This forward-facing seam at the bow lies generally above the waterline area; thus, it would not often impede the forward movement of the canoe, but it could still receive abrasion during use of the craft. Assiginack chose to install the overlapped edges of the short supplemental piece the same at both ends of the canoe, apparently for solidity of attachment of the piece. He thus disregarded the forward direction of the seam overlap at the bow.

The two supplemental bark pieces are each stitched into the longitudinal side seam and at the cutwater edge. However, the seam which joins each of the supplemental pieces to its side panel was not stitched on the model. Such a lack of stitches in the seam which joins the high end panel to the adjacent wall panel is also found in the Sault canoe.

Seam Sealing

The seams on the canoe were coated with charcoal-blackened melted pitch or gum from spruce or pine trees, of the same description as the gum found on the Royal canoe. The remaining original pitch is now very brittle; it does not indent under thumb pressure.

It is not possible to determine whether a coating of gum was applied to the seams on the interior side of the canoe, as was a typical procedure. The gore slits and the longitudinal side seams were sealed on the exterior of the canoe. There are no runs of melted pitch to indicate the position of the canoe during the pitch application procedure. The swaths of melted gum which cover the seams are 3/8 to 1/2 inch wide. No swath of pitch was applied to seal the vertical seam of

the supplemental bark piece at each end of the canoe. These seams would have been sealed with pitch in a full size craft, as are the comparable unsewn seams of the Sault canoe.

Exterior Hull Surface

The discussion concerning the disruptions in the smooth, even surface of the bark cover of the Royal canoe also applies to the Assiginack canoe as well. Overlapping panel edges and applications of sealant pitch up to 1/16 to 3/32 inch thick have produced seams which stand out from the flat surface of the hull. In addition, the seam of the supplemental piece at the bow end overlaps toward the bow.

Gunwale Elements

All three of the gunwale elements are unusually thick in relation to the overall size of the craft. In addition, the exposed face surface on each is extremely rounded, which is an unusual trait. All of the gunwale elements are angled outward slightly, at the same degree of outward flare as the topsides of the bark walls to which they are attached (Fig. 140).

Inwales

The total length of the inwale on the curve is about 37 inches. This is made up of the span of about 30 inches which is exposed between the headboards plus about 3-1/2 inches at each end which lies outboard of the headboards. The overall length is virtually the same as that of the outwale. In the midsection, the inwale strip is 1/4 inch wide (thick) and 3/8 inch deep (Fig. 140). The lower outboard edge is carved off into a beveled surface about 1/8 inch wide to produce a space into which the tips of the ribs fit. Beginning immediately outboard of the second pair of thwarts from the center thwart, the width and depth of the inwale taper very gradually over a span of about 6-1/2 inches to the headboards. There, the width has tapered down to 1/8 inch, while the depth has reduced to 1/4 inch. The outboard surface and both the top and bottom surfaces of the inwale are carved flat and smooth, while the inboard surface is half-round in cross section; the edges are sharp. The tips, hidden outboard of the headboards, are not visible for observation.

The inwale runs nearly horizontally over much of the length of the canoe, and then rises very gradually

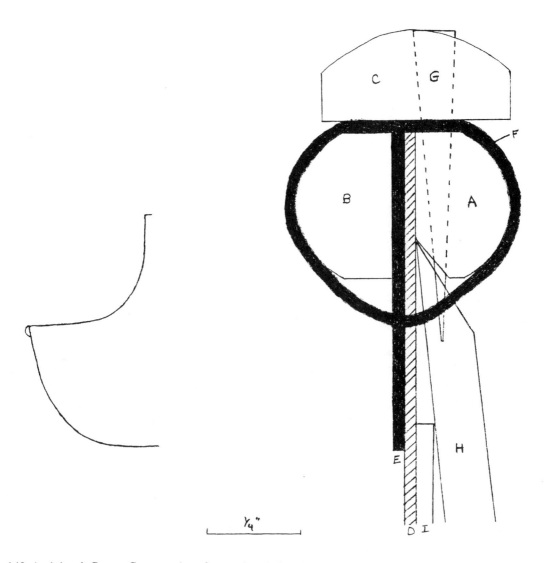

Fig. 140. Assiginack Canoe: Cross section of gunwales. A. inwale, B. outwale, C. gunwale cap, D. bark wall, E. reinforcement bark strip, F. root lashings, G. wooden pegs, H. rib, I. sheathing strip.

- 208 -

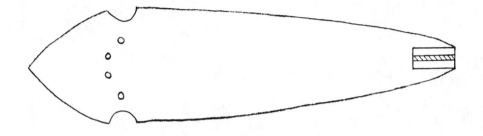

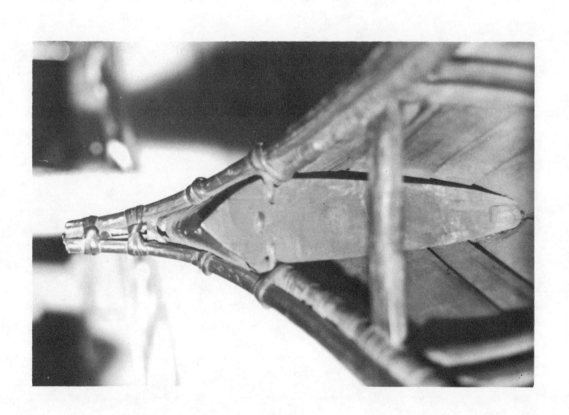

Fig. 141 (left). Assiginack Canoe: Headboard, gunwale ends lashings, bark deck piece.
Fig. 147 (right). Assiginack Canoe: Headboard.

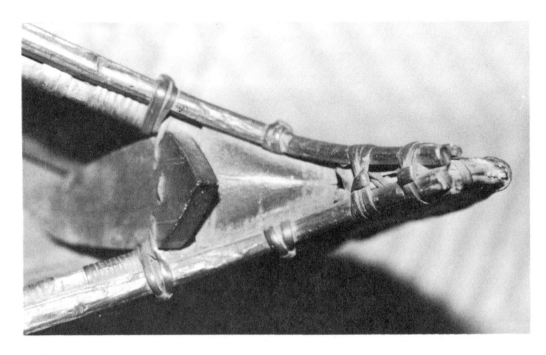

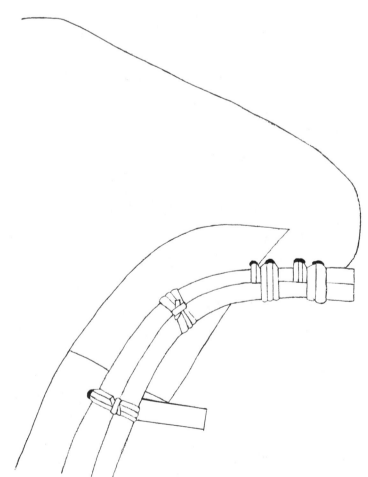

Fig. 142 (left). Assiginack Canoe: Headboard, gunwale ends lashings, bark deck piece.
Fig. 143 (right). Assiginack Canoe: Gunwale ends lashings and bark deck piece.

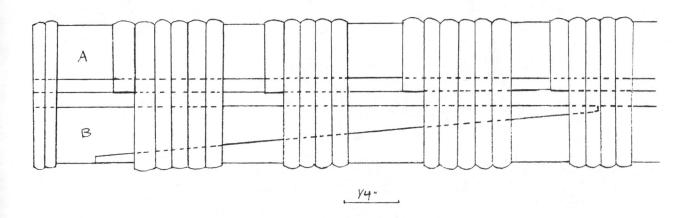

Fig. 144. Assiginack Canoe: Top view of outwale splice. A. inwale, B. outwale.

Fig. 145. Assiginack Canoe: Gunwale lashings and painted decorations.

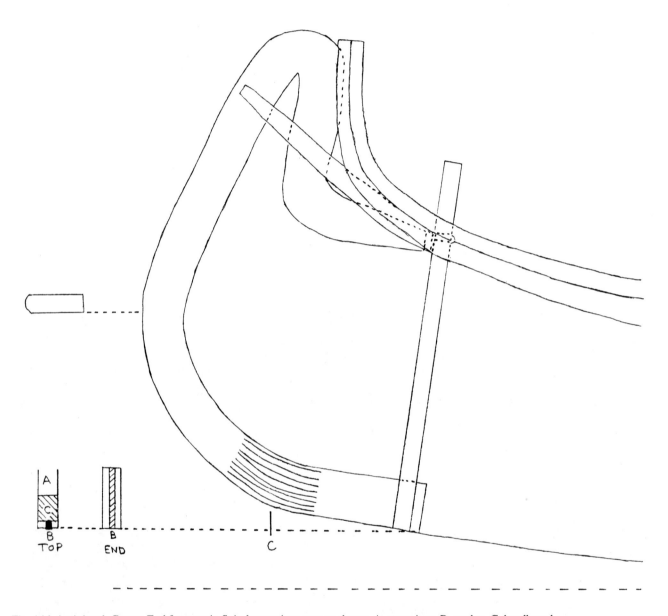

Fig. 146. Assiginack Canoe: End frame unit. Spiral wrappings are not shown. A. stempiece, B. wedge, C. headboard.

toward the ends. At about each end thwart, it begins to curve up moderately toward its ends. At the headboard, the inwale begins to diverge from the outwale; it extends about 3-1/2 inches further, while angling gradually upward to the outer portion of the stempiece (Fig. 146). No split was apparently made in the ends to facilitate the bending of the gradual upward curve of the ends of the inwale.

The inwale fits into a notch which is cut into the side of each headboard (Fig. 141). Two turns of split root bind the inwale to the headboard at the notch. The tips of the inwale are not visible, so it is not possible to determine how they are fastened to the stempiece.

The inwale does not appear to be pegged or nailed to the outwale; this is another trait of this model which is not normally found on full size craft. (There are almost no spaces between wraps in the gunwale lashings, and very few broken and missing root wraps, to afford views of the gunwales beneath the lashings; no pegs or nails are discernible in the few visible areas.) Split root lashings bind the inwale and outwale together, with the top edge of the bark wall and the strip of reinforcement bark sandwiched between them.

Outwales

The total length of the outwale on the curve is 37-7/8 inches, measured on the outside of the curve. In the midsection, it is 1/4 inch wide (thick) and 3/8 inch deep (Fig. 140). In both width and depth, the outwale matches the dimensions of the inwale. Thus, the top and bottom surfaces of the two strips match. Beginning immediately outboard of the second pair of thwarts from the center thwart, the width and depth of the outwale taper very gradually over a span of about 10 inches to their tips. There, the width has tapered down to 1/8 inch, while the depth has also reduced to 1/8 inch. The inboard surface and both the top and bottom surfaces of the outwale are carved flat and smooth, while the outboard surface is half-round in cross section; the edges are sharp. This cross section remains the same for the full length of the outwale. At the tips, the ends are cut off squarely. The description of the painted decoration on the outwales is found on page 227.

The outwales, like those on the Quebec canoe, are each made of two strips of wood spliced together. But unlike the Quebec canoe construction, the splices on the Assiginack canoe do not lie opposite each other across the craft: a span of about 9-3/4 to 10 inches separates them (Fig. 132). Each splice begins about 3/8 to 1/2 inch outboard of the first thwart on each side of the center thwart; it extends diagonally outboard 2-1/4 to 2-3/4 inches. The splice in the right wall, with its exterior end pointing toward the stern, ends 8-1/4 inches forward of the stern headboard. The left wall splice, with its exterior end pointing toward the bow, reaches a point 8-1/4 inches rearward of the bow headboard. Each of the diagonal ends tapers to a thickness of 1/32 to 1/16 inch at the tip (Fig. 144).

The span of the diagonal seam is covered by four spaced groups of gunwale lashings. These lashings, fitting into the overall pattern of the gunwale lashings, bind together the two outwale sections and the single inwale strip into a solid unit. These lashings do not cover the tip of the diagonal seam on the exterior of either of the splices; each tip is visible on the exterior side, and also partially on the upper surface which is not covered by the gunwale cap. No horizontal wooden pegs are visible in the splices, for perhaps the same reason that there appear to be no inwale-outwale pegs in the gunwales. Pegs would normally be present in the outwale splices of a full size craft.

The canoe construction traditions which Assiginack knew apparently indicated that splices in the outwales created weak points in the framing structure of the canoe. Therefore, he positioned the two outwale splices well separated from each other across the hull.

The outwale runs nearly horizontally over much of the length of the canoe, and then rises very gradually toward the ends (Fig. 128). At about each end thwart, it begins to curve up moderately toward its ends. At the headboard, the outwale diverges from the inwale; it sweeps upward in a strong curve to reach a completely vertical position at the tips (Fig. 146). The ends of the outwale sweep outward and upward from the outboard side of the headboards for about 3-1/2 inches on the curve. The tip reaches a point at the same height as the maximum height of the prow of the canoe. No slit was made in the ends to facilitate the bending of the upward curve and the extreme upsweep at the tips.

The tips of the two outwales do not fully converge: they are separated by the 1/8 to 3/16 inch thickness of the combined stempiece and bark walls of the cutwater edge (Fig. 142). The tips are joined to each other by a series of wrapped root lashings (Fig. 143). There is no wooden or bark wedge inserted between the tips of the two strips to assist in making the lashings tight. Nor are the tips pegged or nailed to each other. The split root lashings, 3/32 inch wide, begin 9/16 inch below the tips of the outwales. They wrap in three adjacent spiral turns around the two joined outwales, covering a span of 1/4 inch. The three wraps run through a single hole in the adjacent bark wall, passing through the stempiece inside the bark wall as well.

Below these upper outwale wraps 1/2 inch, an additional two root wraps encircle the outwales, covering a span of 3/16 inch. The root passes through one hole in the wall and the stempiece. In both of these sets of lashings, the end of the root encircles one time the midsection of the two or three spiral wraps, binding them together. Then the tip of the root runs through this central wrapping, to end the lashing. These central wraps lie between the converging tips of the outwales, against the edge of the stempiece.

The triangular area between the two converging outwales is covered by a bark deck (Figs. 139 and 141 to 143). The piece of bark is in a pyramidal form with a 3-1/2 inch straight base and 3 inch convex sides. At the narrower upper end of the deck, a long triangular notch about 1-1/4 inches deep has been cut out. The tip of this notch fits over the inboard curve of the stempiece. This triangular cutout is very similar to that found on the Catlin canoe. The deck piece extends vertically down to the headboard; its ends extend over the edge of the bark walls so that they are visible outboard of the outwales for 3/8 to 1/2 inch. The inboard edge of the deck butts tightly against or overlaps slightly the end of the adjacent gunwale reinforcement bark strips. Each end of the deck is cut in such a manner that it appears to be a continuation of this reinforcement strip. The sharply pointed tips of the deck piece at the bow angle upward and outward from the outwale for about 1/2 inch; in contrast, the comparable ends at the stern are cut off bluntly, with a straight horizontal edge. The area of the deck which lies between the converging outwales bulges roundly upward, rather than presenting a flat surface between the outwales.

The bark deck piece is held in place by the pressure of the outwales, which squeeze the bark down against the bark end panels. In addition, the lower set of root lashings on each gunwale which binds the ends of the outwales to the hull passes through the margin of the bark deck as well. The description of the painted decoration on the ends of the deck is found on page 227.

The bark deck fills all of the gunwale area outboard of each headboard (Fig. 139). Thus, there is no possibility that a flag staff could have been inserted adjacent to the outboard side of the headboard at either the bow or the stern. However, there is enough space between the body of the headboard and the adjacent walls for the wrapping of a cord around the headboard, to bind a flag staff to the inboard face of the headboard, at both the bow and the stern (Fig. 141).

Gunwale Caps

The total length of the gunwale cap is 35-3/4 inches, measured on the inside of the curve. (This is 2-1/8 inches shorter than the outwale, which was measured on the opposite side of the curvature.) In the midsection, the cap is 1/2 to 9/16 inch wide by 1/4 inch deep (thick) (Fig.140). Beginning halfway between the first and second pairs of thwarts from the center thwart, the width and depth of the cap taper very gradually, to a width of 1/8 inch and a depth of 1/8 inch at the tips. The lower surface and both of the sides of the outwale are carved flat and smooth, while the upper surface is half-round in cross section; the edges are sharp. This cross section remains the same for the full length of the outwale. At the tips, the ends are cut off squarely. The description of the painted decoration on the gunwale caps is found on page 227.

The combined width of the inwale (1/4 inch) and the outwale (1/4 inch) is either the same as the width of the gunwale cap or 1/16 inch less than the cap. But the bark wall and the reinforcement bark strip which are sandwiched between the inwale and the outwale add about 1/8 to 3/16 inch more of thickness to the combined gunwales. Also, the degree to which the inwale and outwale were squeezed against the bark and each other when they were all lashed together varies in different areas; probably due to the apparent lack of inwale-outwale pegs, the two elements are not squeezed together tightly. Thus, the gunwale cap is about 3/16 inch narrower than the top of the gunwale unit (inwale, bark layers, and outwale) in most areas of the midsection. The portion not covered by the cap in this area of the canoe is generally the outwale. The width of the cap tapers toward the ends more quickly than the taper of the combined gunwale unit. Since the outboard edge of the cap is aligned generally with the outboard edge of the outwale toward the ends, the area of the inwale that is exposed gradually increases toward the ends. Near the headboards, up to 1/4 inch of the thickness of the inwale is exposed (Figs. 141 and 142). Outboard of the headboard, where the inwale has diverged, the outwale is completely covered by the cap.

The gunwale cap conforms to the curvature of the outwale for its entire length. It runs nearly horizontally over much of the length of the canoe, and then rises very gradually toward the ends. At about each end thwart, the cap begins to curve up moderately toward its ends. At the headboard, it sweeps upward in a strong curve to reach a completely vertical position at the tips (Fig. 143).

The ends sweep upward and outward from the outboard side of the headboards for about 3 inches (measured on the curve), ending exactly at the tips of the outwales. Since the vertical tips of the outwales and caps end at the same height as the tops of the prows, the high bark ends would rest on the ground when the canoe was overturned on its side as a shelter. No horizontal splits were made in the ends of the cap to facilitate the bending of the upward curve and the extreme upsweep of the ends.

From nearly headboard to headboard, the gunwale caps are attached to the inwale by downward-driven wooden pegs. Round holes about 1/8 inch in diameter were drilled downward through the caps and the inwales, between the gunwale lashing groups. The intervals between the holes measure 2-3/4 to 3 inches in the midsection area, reducing to 2 to 2-1/4 inches near the ends. The holes lie along or slightly inboard of the midline of the cap, and angle inboard into the inwale. The endmost holes lie about 1/2 to 3/4 inch inboard of the headboards.

The long slender pegs, about 3/4 to 1 inch long, are about 1/8 inch in diameter at the head (Fig. 140). The four-sided pegs taper to a sharp point at the tip, and fit tightly in the round holes. The pegs were trimmed off so that the surface of the head lies flush with or slightly above the surface of the cap. Most of the tips protrude from the underside of the inwale 1/16 to 1/4 inch, in the area into which the rib tips fit.

From the headboards to the tips of the caps, no pegs fasten the gunwale cap ends; they are attached to the outwales only by four groups of lashings in this area (Figs. 141 to 143). The tips of the two caps are joined to each other and to the tips of the two outwales by lashings of split root about 3/32 to 1/8 inch wide; the two wraps span about 3/16 inch. These two wrappings lie immediately above the upper set of outwale lashings. They completely fill a shallow notch which is carved into the face of each cap, beginning 3/8 inch below the tips. The notch is about 3/16 inch long and about 1/16 inch deep. No wedge is inserted between the tips of the caps to assist in making the lashings tight. Nor are the tips of the converged caps pegged or nailed to each other. To finish, the end of the lashing root encircles the two turns of root on the upper surface of the cap and is locked in place by passing under this central wrap.

About 1/2 inch below the lower edge of the upper set of cap lashings, another set of lashings binds each cap to its respective outwale. This set of lashings, spanning about 1/4 inch, is composed of three turns of root which lie immediately above the lower set of outwale lashings. To finish, the end of the lashing root encircles the three turns of root on the upper surface of the cap; it then ends by passing under the central wrap, effectively locking the end in position. The turns of root in each of these upper two cap lashings pass through a single hole in the bark wall and the stempiece, about 3/16 inch in diameter.

About 3/4 inch below the lower edge of the lower outwale lashings, a third set of lashings binds each cap to its respective outwale. This set of lashings matches the description of the second set in all but two respects. Its final turn around the middle of the lashings lies on the outboard side, and the three turns of root do not pass through a hole in the bark wall; instead, they simply encircle the outwale and the cap. The lowest set of cap lashings lies just inboard of the headboard, about 7/8 inch below the third cap lashings. This set of three wraps, spanning about 1/4 inch, runs through a 3/16 inch hole in the bark wall and wraps around the inwale as well as the cap and outwale. Its ending turn lies on the outboard side of the lashing.

Reinforcement Bark Strips

The reinforcement strip of birchbark increases the thickness of the upper edge of the bark wall where it is attached to the gunwales. Before the inwale and outwale were lashed together onto the upper edge of the bark wall, the reinforcement strip was inserted between the bark wall and the outwale (Fig. 140). Its top edge, like that of the bark wall, was cut off at the level of the top of the inwale and the outwale. When the awl holes were pierced through the wall and the lashings were wrapped around the gunwales, the bark strip was pierced and lashed as well.

The strip extends to a point about 1/4 inch outboard of each headboard (Fig. 139). It extends down 3/8 inch below the lower edge of the outwale along the full length of the strip, without tapering toward the ends. The lower edge of the reinforcement strip generally runs parallel to the lower edge of the outwale for the full length; it was cut slightly irregularly and with a slight degree of undulation. The segments making up the strip were cut to their present width after being installed onto the canoe. There is a knife cut or scratch on the bark wall panel immediately adjacent to the lower edge of the full length of the strip, produced when the strip was trimmed off against the unprotected wall.

Each reinforcement strip is made up of four pieces of bark. The two longer segments in the midsection measure 10-1/4 and 11-3/4 inches. In addition to these long strips, the span beneath the outwale where it curves upward to the headboard is made up of a shorter piece at each end, 4-1/2 to 4-3/4 inches long.

The individual pieces of bark which make up the reinforcement strip overlap each other at their ends, from 1/16 to 3/8 inch. The pieces are not attached at their ends to each other or to the canoe wall in any manner.

The bark deck is bent down on either side between the bark hull and the outwale, and is trimmed to appear as a continuation of the reinforcement bark strip. It is butted against or slightly overlaps each end of the strip outboard of the headboard on each wall (Fig. 139). This deck piece, 3 inches long from headboard to tip, extends beyond the outwale for 3/8 to 1/2 inch. Its edge is cut parallel to the outwale, to match the lower edge of the bark reinforcement strip. The description of the painted decoration on the reinforcement bark strips and the bark deck ends is found on page 227.

Gunwale Lashings

The upper edge of the bark wall is sandwiched between the inwale, the reinforcement bark strip, and the outwale (Fig. 140). It is cut off flush with the top surface of the inwale and the outwale. The four layers of bark and wood are fastened together with spaced groups of root lashings from headboard to headboard (Fig. 145).

Each lashing group normally runs through four or five holes in the bark wall. The holes, generally triangular or square in shape, have widths of 1/16 to 3/32 inch, with rather even edges. The holes were made by an awl with a triangular or square cross section, which was inserted from the exterior side of the wall but not twisted. The holes are spaced about 1/16 inch apart. Each row of holes, spanning 3/8 to 1/2 inch, lies 3/32 to 1/8 inch below the lower edge of the outwale and inwale. The split root lashing material is 1/16 to 1/8 inch wide and 1/32 inch thick, with flat sides and undersurface and a rounded upper surface which was scraped somewhat flat.

To lash the gunwales, a length of split root was drawn nearly to its end through the first hole in the set of four or five holes. The short end of the root was drawn up on the interior side to the top surface of the combined gunwales and inserted down between two of the sandwiched layers of wood and bark. Then, in a simple spiral stitch, the long end of the root passed over the top of the outwale and inwale and through the second hole. The root passed around the combined outwale and inwale a second time, and through the third hole. This pattern was continued through all of the holes; in most cases with one turn per hole. But with narrower roots two turns were run through each hole.

The lashing groups are not connected to each other; each group begins and ends independently. To finish off the root securely before starting a new group of lashings, the end of the root was often inserted into the sandwiched layers atop the gunwale unit. In other cases, the end, when it emerged on the exterior at the final hole, was run horizontally back on the exterior side to and through the second hole from the end. Where it emerged on the interior, the tip was cut off rather short. It was held firmly in place by the turn of root that had previously been run through the hole. Sometimes, rather than running the end of the root on the exterior through one of the holes, it was run horizontally behind the bases of several root wrappings on the exterior, beneath the outwale.

Each typical group of lashings is composed of four to eight turns of root around the gunwale, covering a length of 3/8 to 1/2 inch of the gunwale. When the narrowest roots were utilized, eight turns are sometimes found, and when the widest roots were used, the group usually includes only four turns. An interval of 3/16 to 1/4 inch separates each group of lashings.

The endmost group of lashings at each end of each gunwale is somewhat longer than the majority of the lashings. Extending inboard from the headboards, each of these groups is composed of 7 to 10 turns of split root; they pass through 7 to 9 holes, with usually one turn per hole.

The thwarts are bound into the gunwales with root lashings that fit into the pattern of the gunwale wrappings. The thwart lashing groups are not joined to the adjacent gunwale lashing groups by connector stitches.

Stempieces

The stempiece is visible in several areas of the canoe (Fig. 146). Its heel is visible where it projects into the interior of the canoe at the base of the headboard. The outboard edge is exposed over virtually the entire cutwater edge, where for the most part the sealant pitch is now gone. Its edge is also visible between the converging outwales and gunwale caps, from the point of maximum height down to the bark deck. The upper end, where it meets the headboard, can be seen through a narrow space between the headboard and the bark deck.

The curvature of the stempiece is implied in several areas. The curve of the cutwater edge of the canoe, from chin to outwales, outlines the entire outer curved portion of the stempiece. Also, the stempiece is lashed to the outwales and gunwale caps in four places over a span of about 1-1/2 inches below their tips. The location of the upper end of the stempiece is indicated by its lashing to the headboard.

The total length of the stempiece is about 14 inches, measured on the outboard edge. The heel of the stempiece projects 1/8 inch inboard from the inboard surface of the base of the headboard. At its end, it is 5/8 inch deep (in height) and 3/16 inch thick, with sharp corners and edges. All surfaces of the heel are carved flat and smooth. It does not have notches carved into its sides

for the legs of the headboard to straddle.

On the outboard side of the base of the headboard, the same thickness of 3/16 inch is maintained for the full length of the stempiece. The 5/8 inch depth is maintained until the final bend before it tapers. All surfaces are flat; the two inboard edges are sharp, while the outboard two are moderately rounded.

This is an extremely deep, robust stempiece, compared to the various stempiece models made by Adney, and even the strong ones in the full size Ojibwa canoe. The extreme depth of the laminated stempieces in the Assiginack canoe resembles that of certain types of curved stempieces which were cut from a solid plank and positioned standing on edge. Plank-stem craft include a type of freight canoe made by the Ojibwas (Fig. 26), hunters' canoes of the Algonkins, and canoes built by the Chipewyan, Slave, and Dogrib tribes of northwestern Canada.[5] (These plank stempieces do not extend the full distance from the cutwater edge to the headboard, like those of the Sault and Bell canoes.) The depth of the stempiece in the Assiginack model is virtually identical proportionately to that of the stempiece in the Varden model (Fig. 179). This may suggest that some laminated stempieces were indeed made in this extreme depth in full size fur trade canoes; or it may simply underscore the difficulty of building small model canoes to exact scale.

Beginning outboard of the headboard, the stempiece is divided by a number of splits into lamination layers. The lamination splits extend through the complete upper length of the stempiece to its end. (In the Figure 146 diagram, they are portrayed only in the lowest portion.)

The entire laminated portion of the stempiece is spirally wrapped with cordage at intervals of about 1/8 inch. The two-ply twisted cord, 1/16 inch in diameter, is now dark tan in color. It was not determined whether the string is of native manufacture (of basswood inner bark) or a commercial product. However, all of the other materials which were used by Assiginack in the building of the canoe model are native products; it is therefore quite likely that the cordage he used was also of native manufacture.

From its heel, the stempiece runs about 2-1/16 inches outboard to the chin, which is quite rounded. From the chin, the point at which the stitching of the end begins, the stempiece extends upward and outward in a moderate curve over 3-3/4 inches to the point of maximum length of the canoe. Then the virtually straight upper span angles inboard, at about a 25 degree angle from the upright position; it rises for 3-1/2 inches to its maximum height at the head. There, it makes a sharp, hard downward curve, and extends downward and slightly outboard over about 2-1/2 inches. The degree of sharpness of this bend may have required the breaking of some of the lamination layers on the inside of the curve. The stempiece is lashed to the converged tips of the outwales and gunwale caps on the inboard side of this upper curve. Finally, the stempiece bends sharply inboard, and angles slightly downward as it runs inboard to the headboard. Over this final distance of about 1-1/4 inches, the depth tapers moderately from 5/8 to 3/16 inch. The maximum horizontal distance of the curvature of the stempiece, from the cutwater edge to the outboard side of the headboard, is about 3-3/4 inches. No wooden brace was installed to add stability to the stempiece. The tips of the converged pair of inwales lie adjacent to the stempiece, but they are not visible to observe any fastenings.

Each end of the stempiece is firmly attached to the headboard. At the upper end, a single strand of split root 1/16 inch wide passes through two holes in the headboard and wraps spirally around the end of the stempiece.

(It is not possible to observe the number of spiral wrappings or the length of the span which they cover.)

At the heel of the stempiece, a narrow vertical notch is cut into the flat surface of the end. The notch, about 1/16 inch wide and about 3/32 inch deep, extends over the full 5/8 inch height of the stempiece. A slender wooden wedge tightly fills the entire notch; its surfaces are cut off flush with those of the stempiece. The wedge causes the end of the stempiece to widen, making it fit tightly within the headboard notch.

The stempieces which Assiginack fashioned for the canoe model closely resemble the Great Lakes version Number 1 modeled by Adney (Fig. 19, Vol. I). In the form of its external and internal curvatures, its lashing attachment through the headboard (instead of the stempiece running through the headboard), and its lack of a brace, the Assiginack stempiece parallels the Adney model. It likewise resembles closely the stempiece in the Great Lakes canoe Number 7 modeled by Adney, in Figure 18, Vol. I.

Headboards

The headboard stands with its base about 3-3/8 inches inboard of the outermost point of the cutwater edge (Fig. 129). The outboard side of the base falls 2-1/8 inches inboard of the chin of the canoe. The headboard is angled slightly, so that its head lies 3/4 inch inboard of its base. Of the seven Adney models of Algonkin/Great Lakes canoes which are represented in Chapelle drawings, half of the headboards stand straight upright, while half of them have the head leaning slightly inboard. The side notches beneath the head of the Assiginack canoe fit between the converging inwales. When the canoe is viewed in profile, the low triangular head of the headboard projects about 7/8 inch above the caps.

The overall height of the headboard is 5 inches (Figs. 141 and 147); the height from the shoulders to the base is 3-15/16 inches. Its maximum width is 1-1/8 inches, at the top and the base of the side notches. This maximum width tapers gradually down to the base, where it is 1/4 inch. In all of its areas, the headboard is 1/4 inch thick. The flat inboard surface is carved smooth, all edge surfaces are carved flat, and all corners and edges are sharp.

Below the triangular head, which measures 3/4 inch in height and 1-1/8 inches at its maximum width, a notch is cut out of each side. The inwales fit into these notches, which are 5/16 inch high and 1/8 inch deep. The top and bottom surfaces of each notch angle upward toward the outboard side of the headboard, to accommodate the upward curve of the ends of the inwales.

Inboard 5/32 inch from the middle of each of these inwale notches is a single hole, through which one or two turns of split root lash the inwales to the neck of the headboard. The two irregularly round, tapered holes, about 1/16 inch in diameter, were apparently drilled with an awl with a triangular or square cross section. The split lashing root is 1/16 inch in width.

Just below the upper edges of the inwale notches, 7/8 inch below the pointed tip of the head, are found two small holes. The holes lie 3/16 inch apart, on each side of the vertical midline. Like the other two lashing holes, these irregularly round, tapered holes were apparently drilled with an awl with a triangular or square cross section. A single turn of split root, 1/16 inch wide, runs through the holes; it wraps spirally around the upper end of the stempiece, which butts against the outboard side of the headboard at this position.

The base of the headboard has a rectangular notch cut out, 5/8 inch tall and 3/16 inch wide. The two legs produced by the notch each taper to a sharp point 1/32 inch thick. These legs fit over the heel of the stempiece and are firmly attached to it, due to the wooden wedge which was installed in the end of the heel of the stempiece. The painted decoration of the headboards is described on page 227.

Cutwater Edges

The edges of the bark panels are cut off flush with the rounded edges of the stempiece. Split root battens were installed into the stitched cutwater edge at each end of the canoe, to protect the outboard edges of the bark panels (Figs. 139 and 148). Immediately above the longitudinal side seam, an awl hole was pierced through the cutwater edge, and a split root was drawn to its midpoint through the hole. The root, 3/16 to 1/4 inch wide and 1/16 to 3/32 inch thick, has a half-round cross section. This split root batten extends upward along the full length of both bark sides of the cutwater to the tip of the outwales, in a single piece. The outboard edge of the root is aligned with the bark edge of the cutwater over the entire span of about four inches.

The stitching of the lower cutwater edge begins at the chin, with two end-to-end harness stitches 1/2 to 5/8 inch long. The stitches are made with a single length of root 3/32 to 1/8 inch wide and 1/32 inch thick; it has a half-round cross section, with the round side scraped somewhat flat. These stitches run through three awl holes placed about 3/8 inch from the cutwater edge. Above these two stitches, a series of rather widely spaced spiral stitches extends to the longitudinal side seam. The holes, 1/8 inch in diameter, lie 1/4 to 3/8 inch from the edge, at intervals of about 1/4 inch. One turn of root passes through each hole. One end of the harness stitching root lies beside the cutwater edge, where it is covered by the first three spiral stitches which are made with the opposite end of the same root. The lower portion of the cutwater edge, from the longitudinal seam down to the chin, spans four inches.

The upper portion is also lashed with spiral stitches of the same hole and root dimensions, but the holes lie slightly closer to the edge and to each other. They are positioned 3/16 to 1/4 inch from the edge and lie at intervals of 1/8 to 3/16 inch. Across the top span of the cutwater edge, the stitches are positioned slightly closer together. In two areas, the stitches lie adjacent to each other, rather than separated, and extend much further inboard from the edge. In the lower of these areas, the two lengthened stitches are 3/4 and 5/8 inch long; in the upper area, the lengthened stitch measures 5/8 inch. The longest stitch in each of these sets lies 2-1/2 and 1-7/8 inches below the top, respectively. The entire upper portion of the cutwater edge, which contains the two batten strips along its full length, spans four inches to the tips of the outwales.

The inboard edge of the high end panels and the stempiece are exposed between the converging tips of the outwales and gunwale caps, down to the upper end of the bark deck piece (Figs. 141 and 142). In the upper span of about 1-1/2 inches of this exposed area are found two very widely spaced spiral stitches through the panels and stempiece. They are of the same description as the stitches of the upper cutwater edge. This area between the tips of the outwales is filled with a series of adjacent spiral or figure-eight stitches on each of the other canoes in the study.

In all sewing of the cutwater edge, the stitches pass directly through the stempiece inside the end of the canoe, rather than around it. The root lashings run through awl holes through the stempiece.

The lower portion of the cutwater edge is sealed with blackened pitch in the same manner as the bark seams are sealed (Fig. 148). The swath of pitch begins 1/4 inch inboard of the chin on the bottom of the canoe, and extends upward for four inches on the curve, covering the entire area of stitches up to the split root batten strips. The pitch extends from the outer edge of the prow onto the bark walls for 1/4 to 3/8 inch. The edges of the pitched area are broadly curved, following the contour of the outer edge of the canoe. The upper portion of the cutwater edge is not sealed with pitch. This allowed unobstructed drainage of water out of the canoe when it was overturned on its side on shore.

The total thickness of the cutwater edge is 1/4 to 5/16 inch in the upper area. This thickness includes the stempiece, the two bark panels, the split root battens,

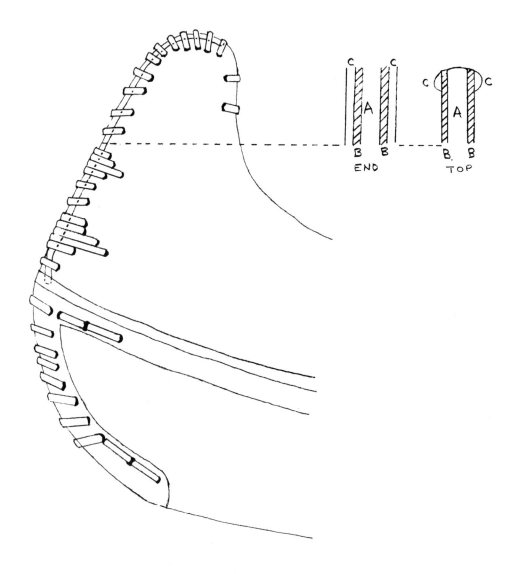

Fig. 148. Assiginack Canoe: Cutwater edge. A. stempiece, B. bark wall panels, C. battens.

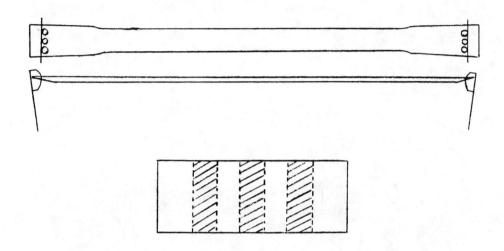

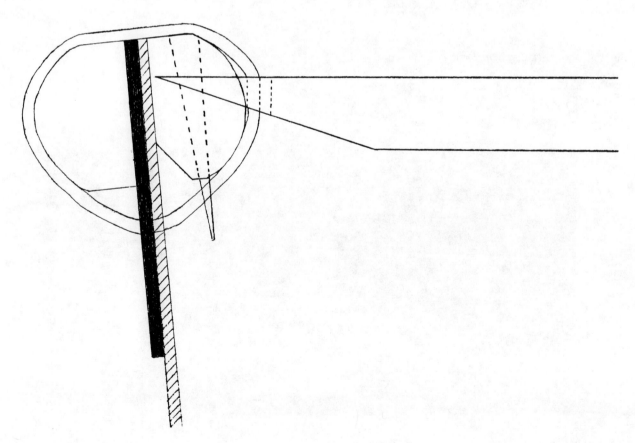

Fig. 149. Assiginack Canoe: Thwarts.

Fig. 150. Assiginack Canoe: Perforated mast thwart.

Fig. 151. Assiginack Canoe: Gunwale and thwart lashings, ribs.

and the stitches. When the pitch in the lower area was intact, the cutwater edge there probably measured about the same thickness as the batten-protected upper area.

Thwarts

The seven thwarts (creating a six-place canoe) are spaced symmetrically, with the center thwart lying exactly at the midpoint of the canoe (Fig. 132). The distances between the thwarts are measured from centerline to centerline. The positions of the thwarts indicate a canoe shape that tapers symmetrically at both ends.

Three pairs of thwarts flank the center thwart. In each of the pairs, the thwart toward the bow is the same length as its sternward counterpart.

Center: Thwart #1: 6-7/8 inches
Pair A: Thwart #2: 6-3/8 inches
        Thwart #3: 6-3/8 inches
Pair B: Thwart #4: 4-7/8 inches
        Thwart #5: 4-7/8 inches
Pair C: Thwart #6: 2 -3/4 inches
        Thwart #7: 2-3/4 inches

The lengths, measured along the longest edge, do not include the hidden portion at each end which fits into the mortise hole in each inwale. The actual length of each thwart is about 3/8 inches longer than each of these measurements, since the additional portion at each end, which extends into but not completely through the inwale, is roughly 3/16 inch long.

The following description applies to six of the seven thwarts (Fig. 149). (The description of the perforated mast thwart follows.) At the center and over most of the length, the thickness is 1/4 inch. The top surface remains level and straight over the entire length of the thwart; the underside remains so for nearly the full length. Over a span of about 9/16 inch at each end of the thwart, the underside angles upward quite suddenly to a sharp tip. At the point where the thwart meets the inwale, the thickness has tapered to 3/32 inch. The thickness continues to taper as the end of the thwart projects about 3/16 inch through the 1/4 inch thickness of each inwale.

The midsection portion of each thwart is 5/16 inch wide. At a point about 1-3/16 inch from each end, the width expands rather suddenly, over a span of 3/16

inch, to 7/16 inch. From the sharp shoulders, the width expands very slightly over a distance of one inch to the junction with the inwale. As the thwart extends through the inwale for about 3/16 inch, it probably continues this very slight broadening. All surfaces of the thwarts are carved flat and smooth, and all edges are sharp.

Each of the six thwarts matches this description (varying only in length), with one minor exception. On the endmost pair of thwarts, the rather sudden widening to the shoulders occurs over a longer span of 3/8 inch, rather than 3/16 inch. Since these two thwarts are very short and the broadening distance is increased, there is no straight-sided portion in the middle; the midsection is made up of a pair of shallow concavities 3/4 inch long.

Another minor difference occurs in the relative position of thwarts # 6 and #7 (the endmost pair). All of the other thwarts are positioned so that their upper and lower surfaces lie in level, horizontal planes. The endmost thwarts are positioned in the gunwales at the point where the gunwales curve upward toward the ends of the canoe. Thus, the planes of the top and bottom surfaces of these two endmost thwarts are also angled upward, with the outboard edge higher than the inboard edge.

Thwart #5, the second thwart from the bow, is perforated as a mast thwart (Fig. 150). Its dimensions of width and its contours are more robust than the other thwarts, due to its heavier usage; but its thickness and end taper are identical to that of the others. At the midpoint, the width of the thwart is 3/4 inch, in the middle of which is carved a 3/8 inch diameter round hole. The width tapers very gradually toward the ends, reaching 3/8 inch at a point 1-3/16 inches inboard of the inwales. There, it broadens over a 3/16 inch span to sharp shoulders 1/2 inch wide. Over the distance of one inch to the inwales, the width increases very slightly, to 9/16 inch at the inwales.

The perforated mast thwart lies 10-5/8 inches from the point of maximum arc of the bow cutwater edge and 6-5/8 inches from the bow headboard. Directly beneath the central hole, a mast step is mounted onto the midline of the floor of the canoe. This feature is described on page 223.

At the point where each of the seven thwarts meets the inwale, a horizontal mortise hole is cut through the midline of the inwale, to receive the end of the thwart (Fig. 151). Each hole is a long slit about 1-1/2 to 1-3/4 inches long by 3/32 inch wide at the midpoint, apparently pierced with the tip of a knife. The mortise hole runs completely through the inwale. The hole is cut at a slight angle, with its inboard end lower than its outboard end. This compensates for the slight outward angle of the inwale, since it angles outward in conjunction with the upper walls of the canoe. The angle of the hole permits the straight horizontal end of the thwart to fit into the hole in the angled inwale. At both ends of all of the mortise holes, a slender crack extends away from the sides of the thwart for 3/4 to 1-1/2 inches; these were apparently produced when the tapered ends of the thwarts were forced into the narrow knife slits.

A vertical wooden peg was driven downward from the upper surface of the inwale through each of the thwarts to hold the end of the thwart firmly in the mortise hole. The pointed tips of the pegs project from the underside of the inwale 1/4 to 3/8 inch. In all respects, these thwart holes and pegs match the description of the gunwale cap pegs, as described on page 215.

Each end of the thwart is lashed with split root to the combined inwale and outwale. The lashings run through three vertical holes in the ends of the long slender thwarts, and two holes in the end thwarts and the mast thwart. The round holes, about 1/16 inch in diameter, are positioned adjacent to the inwales. In the thwarts with three holes, the outer two holes lie about 3/32 inch from the sides of the thwart.

Below the junction of the thwart and the gunwales, there are four awl holes in the bark wall. These lashing holes, spanning about 1/2 inch, extend to about the outer edges of the thwart. All of the previous information describing the lashing of the gunwale elements also applies to the lashing of the thwarts. Of the eight turns of root, one of them lies beside each edge of the thwart and two turns pass through each of the three holes in the thwart. The endmost pair of thwarts and the mast thwart, having only two holes at the end, are lashed with six turns of root in a similar pattern. The thwarts were lashed at the same time as the gunwales. Thus, their lashings fit into the series of lashing groups along the length of the gunwales.

Sheathing

The sheathing strips or splints on the Assiginack canoe model are not fully realistic portrayals of such strips on full size canoes; these are somewhat too long and too wide. The splints are about 15 or 19 inches long, 3/4 to 1-1/2 inches wide, and 3/64 to 1/16 inch thick. On the flat faces, areas of undulating raised grain patterns indicate that the strips were split out rather than carved. Each splint has generally parallel edges for most of its length; the edges are carved rather straight. The endmost 1 to 1-1/4 inches at each end of the strips is carved so that it gradually tapers into a point or a sharply pointed diagonal (Fig. 152). None of the ends or the long edges of the strips are thinned.

The pattern of overlapping ends indicates that the splints were laid into the canoe in two groups: first the 19 inch splints in the bowward half, and then the 15 inch ones in the stern half. The two groups are each made up of 8 or 9 strips. After the bowward group of splints had been laid in, the sternward group was positioned so that the splints overlapped the ends of the previously-laid group for about 1/2 to 3/4 inch. This overlap area occurs about four inches sternward of the midpoint of the canoe.

In laying in the sheathing, the first strip was positioned down the midline of the floor. It extends up to but not underneath the base of the headboard and the stempiece. Successive sheathing splints were then added out to and up the walls, to a point about 1/4 to 3/8 inch below the inwales. The overlapping edge of each successive strip faces downward or inward, toward the midline of the canoe. The overlapping edge extends about 1/16 to 1/8 inch over the previous strip. Toward the inboard ends of the splints, the edges butt against each other, rather than overlapping.

The two strips which were laid in just after the strip down the midline of the floor flank the base of the headboard. The tip of each of these splints at the bow is tapered in a diagonal form. The diagonal side of the tip is further carved into a strongly concave shape, to fit closely around the base of the headboard (Fig. 141).

Toward each end of the canoe at the top of the walls, a gradually widening expanse of the upper bark wall is left exposed, not covered by the straight horizontal strips of sheathing where the gunwales curve upward (Fig. 141). These wider areas of exposed upper wall

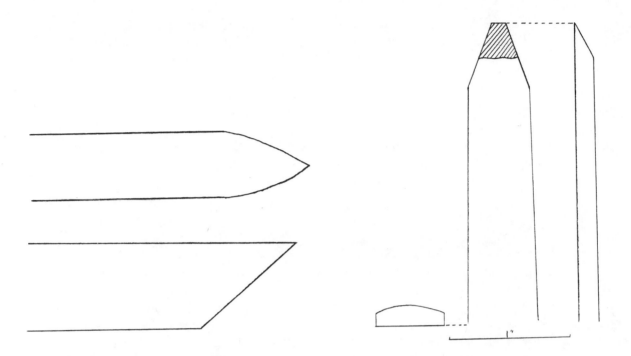

Fig. 152. Assiginack Canoe: Sheathing strips.
Fig. 153. Assiginack Canoe: Ribs and mast step.
Fig. 154. Assiginack Canoe: Ribs.

extend for about 2 inches inboard of the headboards. Beside the headboards, the area of each wall which is not covered by the sheathing splints ranges from 5/8 to 3/4 inches in height.

The tips of the endmost splints extend outboard of the headboard 2 to 3 inches. No additional short sheathing strips were inserted outboard of the headboard to stiffen and support the bark cover at the high ends of the canoe. Nor was any other material, such as wood shavings or moss, stuffed into the ends of the canoe to support the bark cover.

Ribs

There are presently 39 surviving ribs in the canoe. Three ribs appear to be missing outboard of the end thwart at the bow, since there are three ribs in the comparable location at the stern (Fig. 131). The ribs were fashioned extremely wide and thick; but in all other respects, they are very well made. Due to their extreme width, most of the ribs lie adjacent to each other. Since the endmost six to eight ribs at each end of the canoe are slightly narrower, they are separated from each other by up to 1/8 inch.

The profile of the midsection ribs is composed of a slightly rounded area in the midline of the floor, from which the bilge areas curve gradually upward; the upper sections flare slightly outward (Fig. 153). The width of the rounded central area gradually reduces toward each end of the canoe; by the endmost rib, the profile is a narrow U form. The curve of the ribs reflects the body plan of the canoe (Fig. 130).

The midsection ribs in the area of the central thwart are 10-1/4 inches long. This includes the length of about 1/8 inch at each tip which is inserted behind the inwale (Fig. 140). The width of these ribs is 5/8 inch at the midpoint. The width tapers slightly and gradually as the tips extend outward and upward, to 1/2 inch at a point 3/8 to 1/2 inch from the tips. The thickness of 3/32 inch at the edges and 1/8 to 5/32 inch at the domed midpoint is maintained for nearly the full length; it does not taper as the arms rise. Over the uppermost 3/8 to 1/2 inch of each tip, the width tapers rather suddenly, down to about 1/8 inch at the squared-off tip (Fig. 154). The inboard surface at the end of the tip is carved in a sudden taper over the uppermost 1/4 inch span into a chisel shape with a sharp edge at the tip.

The ribs nearer to the ends, besides being shorter, are slightly narrower and thinner than the long midsection ribs. The endmost surviving rib, 7/8 inch from the stern headboard, is 7-1/4 inches long, including the length of about 1/8 inch at each tip which is inserted behind the inwale. The width of 1/2 inch is maintained for nearly the full length, without tapering as the tips extends outward and upward. The thickness of 1/16 inch at the edges and 3/32 inch at the domed midpoint likewise remains the same for nearly the full length. In the uppermost portion of 3/8 to 1/2 inch of each tip, the tapered forms and dimensions are identical to those described above for the midsection ribs.

The ribs are carved very flat and smooth on their side surfaces. The inboard face of each is carved into a very even convex surface, while all edges are sharp. The narrow U-shaped profile of the endmost ribs at the ends of the canoe did not require an extremely square bend at the midpoint. Thus, no groove or scoring was necessary across the midpoint to facilitate the bend.

In the midsection of the canoe, the ribs stand perpendicular to the horizontal plane of the keel line (Fig. 129). Toward the bow and stern headboards, the keel line rises gradually as the rocker of the bottom curves upward. In these rising areas, each rib was installed at a slight angle to the gradually rising keel line. In this manner, the tips of the ribs remain nearly vertically upright, even where the keel line curves upward toward each chin. (If each rib had been installed perpendicular to the keel line, each rib would stand at an angle, with its base well outboard of its tips.) The headboard does stand at an angle, following the curve of the rising floor. Thus, its base lies 3/4 inch outboard of its head. The headboard angles outboard at its base while the ribs stand nearly vertically upright. Due to these differences, the distance between the endmost rib (near its tips) and the upper area of the headboard is 3/8 inch, while the distance between the base of this rib and the base of the headboard measures 7/8 inch.

On the tip area of all of the ribs along one wall, a horizontal line was scratched with an awl across the face surface (Fig. 151). The marks, about 1/4 to 3/8 inch long, lie about 5/16 to 7/16 inch below the beginning of the end taper; this is about 3/4 to 1 inch below the end of each rib. The marks appear to have been applied by Assiginack as he built the canoe. They were probably applied when the ribs were removed from their temporary settings in the canoe, where they had been inserted to dry and set after being bent to shape. The marks would indicate which tip of each rib was to fit against that wall when the ribs were permanently installed.[6] Such a feature is also found on the ribs in the full size Sault canoe.

Painted Decoration

All of the painted decoration on the canoe appears to be original from the period of its construction. The shade of each color and its degree of darkening is consistent throughout the entire canoe, implying that all of the pigments were applied at about the same time. No restoration is discernible on any of the painted surfaces.

The top surface of each end of all of the thwarts is painted brownish red in an area about 1/4 inch wide which lies adjacent to the inwales (Fig. 150). The paint also covers the adjacent root lashings which bind the ends of the thwarts into the inwales. In addition, four slender leaf-shaped forms in brownish red radiate outward from the central hole of the mast thwart; they extend nearly to the edges of the thwart.

Both of the headboards are painted brownish red on the top edge of the head and on the upper 70 percent of the inboard surface (Fig. 141). The painted area ends on the lower portion of the headboard in an irregular oval shape. The pigment also covers the root lashings which bind the headboard to the inwales and to the upper end of the stempiece.

All areas of both of the bark decks are covered with brownish red pigment, including the ends which lie outboard of the outwales (Figs. C-4 and C-5). In addition, the ends of the outwales and the gunwale caps, with their root lashings, are painted the same hue from a point beside the headboard out to their tips.

The entire length of the reinforcement bark strip is painted brownish red. The pigment covers the lower portion of the gunwale lashing roots, but does not extend up into the space 3/32 to 1/8 inch wide between the gunwale lashing holes and the lower edge of the outwale (Figs. 145 and C-3).

Adjacent to the lower edge of the reinforcement bark strip lies a series of 18 scallops on the right wall (Fig. 136) and a series of 16 crescents on the left wall (Fig. 145). The black scallops are 1-1/2 to 1-5/8 inches long in the midsection area of the canoe, reducing slightly toward the ends, to 1 to 1-1/8 inches. Each semicircular scallop measures 1/4 to 7/8 inch in width at its midpoint. An interval of about 1/4 inch separates most of the scallops; a few are more widely spaced, while in several cases they nearly touch each other. The lower side of each black scallop is bordered by a crescent form painted in medium brown paint, which has now faded somewhat. Each crescent measures 3/16 to 1/4 inch in width at its midpoint, tapering to 1/16 to 1/8 inch at its tips. In most cases, the tips of the brown crescents do not extend up into the spaces between the black scallops.

The black crescents which adorn the left wall adjacent to the reinforcement bark strip are 1-7/8 to 2 inches long in the midsection area of the canoe; they reduce slightly in size toward the ends, to 1-3/8 to 1-1/2 inches. Each crescent measures 3/16 to 1/4 inch in width at the midpoint, tapering to sharply pointed tips. The crescents are positioned at intervals of about 1/2 to 5/8 inch, which reduces toward the ends to 3/8 to 1/2 inch. Adjacent to the lower edge of each black crescent is a brownish red crescent, of the same description as the black ones. Each individual set of a black and a red crescent extends about 1/2 to 5/8 inch below the reinforcement bark strip in the midsection of the canoe. Near the ends, this measurement reduces to about 1/2 inch.

In the lower area of the cutwater edge at each end of the canoe, a black stripe curves gradually inboard on each wall from the blackened pitch strip (Fig. 155). The black stripe, 3/16 to 3/8 inch wide, begins at the end of the longitudinal side seam. It curves downward and inboard, separates from the blackened pitch strip, and extends to a point about three inches inboard of the chin. Toward its end it tapers gradually, ending in a sharp point. The span along the bottom and lower bilge areas between the two black painted stripes is filled in with brownish red pigment, from the chin inboard to nearly the ends of the stripes. This red area between the black stripes measures up to 1-3/4 inches in width at its inboard end.

Each of the four high end panels of the canoe is decorated with a series of painted designs. The high end of the right wall at the bow (Figs. 155 and C-5) is painted solidly in brownish red, from its top down to the longitudinal side seam. The red pigment also covers the root lashings of the cutwater edge, and extends

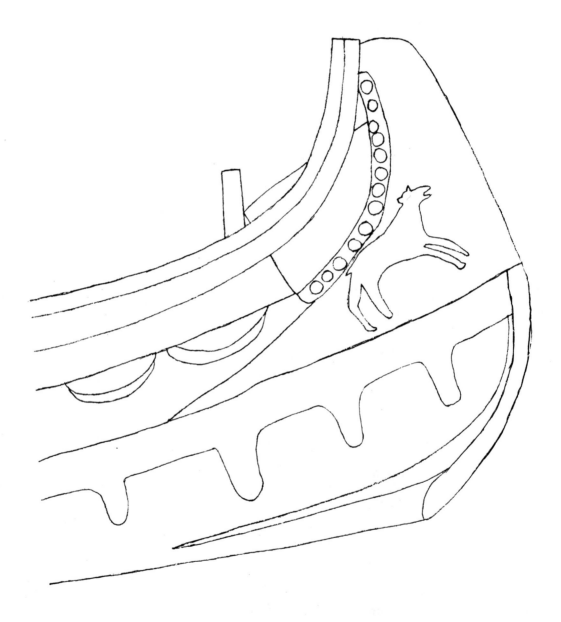

Fig. 155. Assiginack Canoe: Painted decorations on the right wall of the bow.

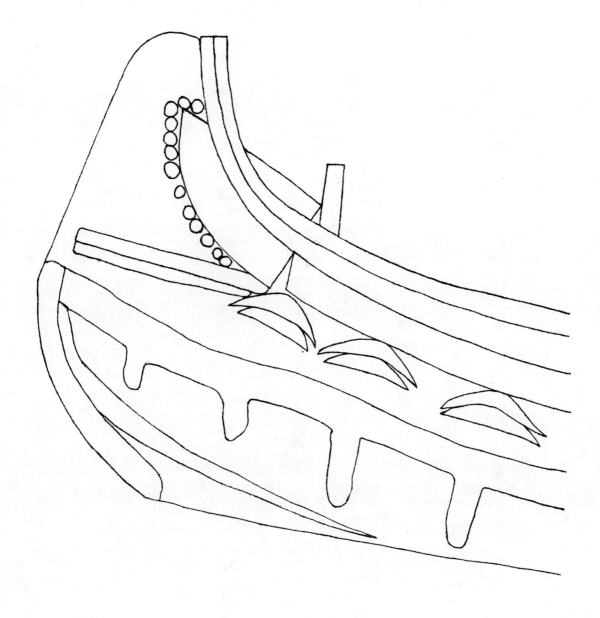

Fig. 156. Assiginack Canoe: Painted designs on the left wall of the bow.

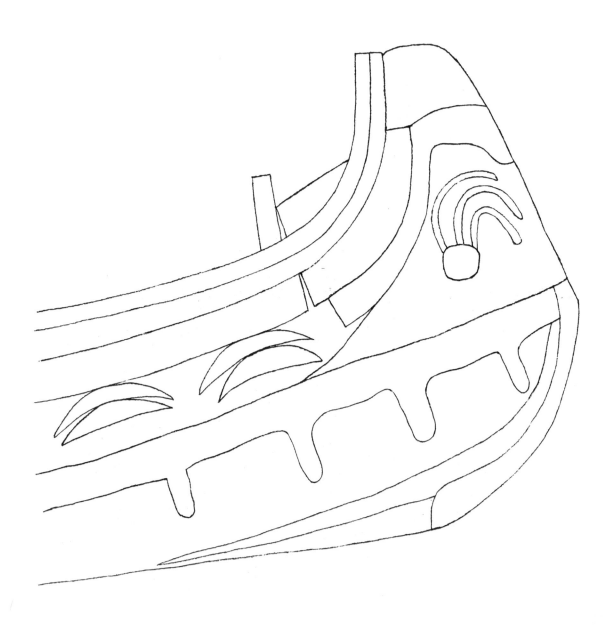

Fig. 157. Assiginack Canoe: Painted decorations on the left wall of the stern.

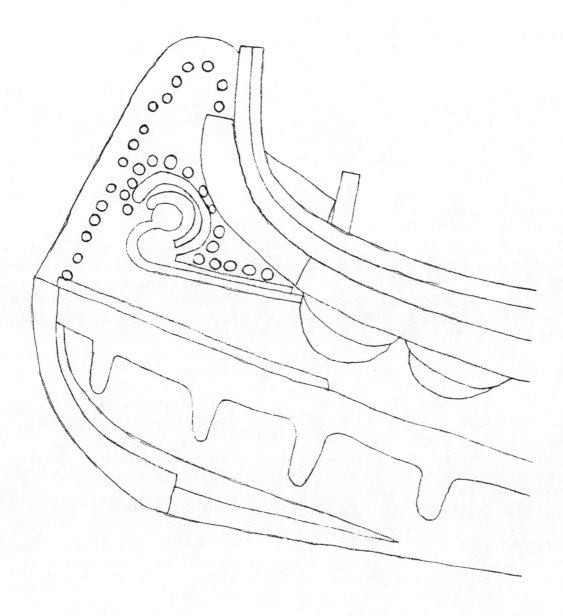

Fig. 158. Assiginack Canoe: Painted designs on the right wall of the stern.

inboard to a curved black stripe which lies beside the end of the bark deck piece. The lower inboard end of the solid red area gradually curves down and back, to meet the longitudinal seam at a point inboard of the headboard. The black stripe runs beside the deck piece from its inboard end up to the highest outwale lashings. Upon the black stripe is painted a series of thirteen dots, about 3/16 inch in diameter. The dots alternate between brownish red and faded medium brown. On the solid red panel, a long-legged black animal with short ears and a short tail faces forward.

On the left wall at the bow (Fig. 156), the entire upper portion of the end panel is painted solidly in black, from the cutwater edge to the end of the bark deck piece and the outwale. The pigment also covers the root lashings of the cutwater edge. On this black background is painted a series of thirteen dots adjacent to all of the perimeter of the bark deck end except its lowest area. The dots, about 3/16 inch in diameter, alternate between brownish red and faded medium brown; they are virtually identical to the series of thirteen dots on the right wall at the bow. Adjacent to the straight lower edge of the solid black panel, two horizontal stripes extend from the inboard ends of the cutwater lashings to the end of the bark deck piece. The upper brownish red stripe measures 3/16 to 1/4 inch in width, while the lower black one is 1/8 to 3/16 inch wide.

The solid area of brownish red on the left wall at the stern (Figs. 157 and C-4) is very similar in form to that which is found on the right wall at the bow, although it does not extend up to the top of the panel. It too covers the cutwater edge lashings, and extends inboard to a curved black stripe which lies beside the end of the bark deck piece. The lower end of the red area, curving downward and forward to the longitudinal seam, ends at a point beside the headboard. The black curved stripe, 3/16 to 3/8 inch wide, begins near the inboard edge of the deck piece; it extends up to the outboard edge of the deck. There, it turns sharply outboard, and curves out to the cutwater edge, while widening moderately. The design elements painted upon the red background include three black stripes, 1/16 to 1/8 inch wide, which curve strongly inboard from the cutwater edge lashing roots. The three stripes terminate at a disc painted in faded medium brown, which measures about 1/2 inch in diameter.

Unlike the other three end panels, the right wall panel at the stern (Figs. 158 and C-3) is not painted with a solid area of brownish red or black. Instead, a brownish red stripe runs adjacent to the longitudinal side seam. The stripe, 1/8 to 3/16 inch wide, extends inboard for four inches from the inboard ends of the cutwater edge stitches to a point beside the headboard. The middle of the high end panel is filled with an elaborate curved design painted in black and brownish red; it measures 2-3/4 inches in length by one inch in height. The lower portion of the device is composed of a horizontal black stripe about 1/4 inch wide, which runs outboard from the edge of the reinforcement bark strip. Near the cutwater stitches, it curves upward and inward, and ends in a round black ball. Adjacent to the upper side of the black stripe runs a brownish red one; this stripe also terminates in a round ball, within the curvature of the black stripe. From this red ball, two red stripes curve strongly upward and outward. A series of sixteen dots runs parallel to the black and red figure. The dots, about 3/16 inch in diameter, alternate between brownish red and black. An identical row of sixteen red and black dots runs parallel to the cutwater edge; it begins at the end of the long red stripe, and extends around the perimeter and down to the outboard edge of the bark deck piece.

All of the painted decoration on the bark cover of the canoe appears to have been applied freehand, rather than by tracing patterns. The occasional repetitions of certain design elements are considerably varied in shape and dimensions; these inconsistencies suggest a freehand application.

Miscellaneous Features
Seats

There is no evidence on the Assiginack canoe which would indicate that it was ever fitted with permanent or temporary wooden seats.

Provisions for Sail and Cordelling Line

Likewise, no evidence can be observed which would indicate the lashing of a cordelling (towing) line to the forward thwarts.

The canoe has been equipped with a permanent perforated thwart and mast step for sailing (Fig. 153). When a sail was used, the upright mast would have been erected through the mast thwart hole, with its base set into the mast step. The perforated thwart has been described on page 223.

The mast step is positioned with its central hole exactly beneath the mast hole of thwart #5, the second thwart from the bow end. The position of this perforated thwart is discussed in its description and is indicated in Figure 132. The mast step, carved from a piece of wood, is positioned atop the sheathing splint which runs down the midline of the floor in the bow half of the canoe.

The mast step piece is 4-7/8 inches long (Fig. 159). It is made up of a raised central pedestal plus a forward and a rearward projection, which fit beneath the ribs. The pedestal is 5/8 inch square at its base. Its walls rise straight up for 1/8 inch, and then angle inward with a bevel which is 1/8 inch wide. The flat top surface of the pedestal measures 1/2 inch square. In its middle lies a carved tapered hole 3/16 inch deep. The diameter of the hole measures 1/4 inch at the top and 1/8 inch at the flat bottom.

The forward projection is 5/8 inch wide at the base of the pedestal. Over its length of 1-1/2 inches, this dimension tapers to about 1/8 inch at the blunt tip. The thickness reduces from 1/8 inch at the pedestal to 1/32 inch at the tip. The rear projection from the pedestal is identical in all respects other than its length, which measures 2-3/4 inches. All surfaces of the mast step are carved flat and smooth, and all edges are sharp. The junctions of the two projections with the raised pedestal are carved sharp and square.

The rib which lies adjacent to the rear edge of the pedestal has a rectangular cutout in its forward edge which fits exactly around the base of the pedestal (Fig. 153). The cutout area, 1/8 inch deep and 5/8 inch long, has flat surfaces and sharp edges. The rib which lies adjacent to the forward edge of the pedestal also has a similar cutout area 1/8 inch deep; but it measures 7/8 inch in length (1/4 inch greater than the pedestal).

Two lines 5/8 inch apart were lightly scored with the sharp tip of an awl across the convex faces of the two ribs which lie immediately sternward of the pedestal. The long rearward projection of the mast step is aligned between these pairs of lines. (The edges of the projection are visible in the spaces between the ribs.)

Assiginack placed the mast step atop the central sheathing strip, and installed these two marked ribs over the rear projection of the mast step; he positioned the cutout area in the edge of the one rib exactly around the base of the pedestal. The two ribs which lie forward of the mast step were then installed. It appears that the cutout area in the one rib did not align with the pedestal; so Assiginack extended the cutout about 1/4 inch toward the left wall to make it fit properly around the pedestal. For the description of another surviving mast step, see the discussion of the carved step which is found on the Catlin canoe.

Flags

No evidence can be found for the attachment of a flag at either the bow or the stern. No space exists outboard of either headboard into which a flag staff could have been inserted. But there is sufficient space around the upper body of each headboard to permit the lashing of such a staff (Fig. 141). A light cord could have encircled the headboard between the edges of the body and the adjacent bark walls or the sheathing strips, to bind a flag staff to the inboard surface of the headboard, at both the bow and the stern.

Bow/Stern Differences

The forward end of the canoe is indicated by the positions of the perforated mast thwart and the mast step, which lie at the bow end of the canoe. Since all of the gore slit seams are butted seams, the only seams which could have a bearing on the efficiency of forward movement are the vertical seams which join the single supplemental piece of bark at each end of the canoe. The exposes edge of this seam at the stern faces sternward, while the one at the bow faces forward. The entire length of this bow seam lies above the general waterline area; thus, its apparently inefficient direction would have little effect on the forward movement of the canoe in most instances, but it could be subject to considerable abrasion from objects.

Assiginack created a number of differences between the bow and the stern ends of the craft, which are listed below. Some of these differences may be only accidental A. The span of rise of the rocker to the chin is 13 inches long at the stern end, compared to 10 inches at the bow. The length of the horizontal span along the bottom is thus placed three inches forward of a central position. The height of the chin is identical at each end of the canoe.

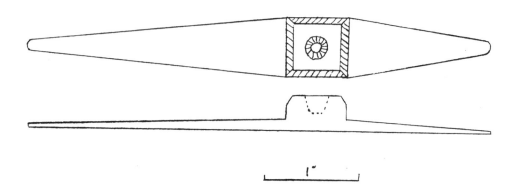

Fig. 159. Assiginack Canoe: Mast step.

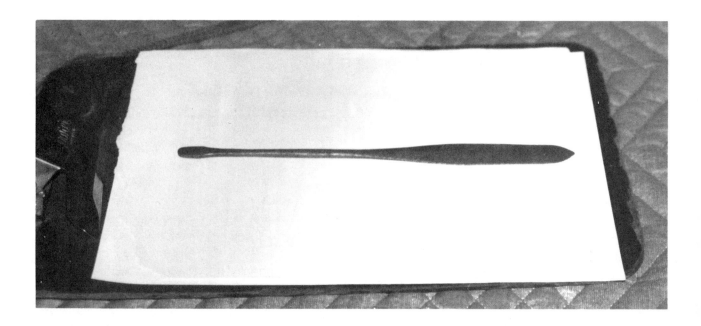

Fig. 160. Assiginack Canoe: Paddle.

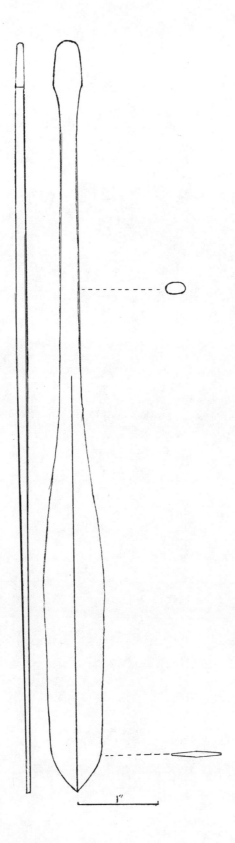

Fig. 161. Assiginack Canoe: Paddles.

Fig. 162. Model canoe and paddlers fashioned by Assiginack in ca. 1815-1827 (photo courtesy of J. Garth Taylor).

B. The outboard ends of the bark deck piece are long and pointed at the bow, and bluntly cut off in a straight edge at the stern.

C. Each of the four high end panels is painted with a different series of design elements. Of these designs, only the one on the right wall at the bow end contains an identifiable creature.

Construction Tools, Methods, and Materials

Assiginack built the canoe from the traditional forest materials of birchbark, wood, tree roots, and pine or spruce gum mixed with animal fat and pulverized charcoal. He painted it afterward with Euroamerican commercial paints.

In the building process, he used the typical array of tools normally employed in canoe manufacture during the nineteenth century. These include a knife or crooked knife, awl, rib-setting mallet, pitch melting and applying implements, and paint containers and brushes. As has been discussed, there is a high probability that he utilized traditional native cordage made from twisted strips of basswood inner bark for the spiral wrapping of the laminations of the stempieces, rather than commercial string. If that is the case, Assiginack used entirely traditional methods and materials when he built the canoe model during the second or third decade of the nineteenth century.

Condition

The bark cover and the wooden elements of the canoe are in excellent condition, although the three endmost ribs at the bow appear to be missing and some damage has occurred to the right end of the deckpiece at the bow. The original root lashings remain intact in all of the seams and in nearly all locations on the gunwales. Only a few of the gunwale lashings are broken; two individual cap lashings have disappeared. Many of the lashings are now missing from both of the cutwater edges.

Most of the original sealant pitch remains on the seams, although it has cracked off in some areas. Nearly all of the pitch has disappeared from the cutwater edge at each end of the canoe. The painted decoration remains nearly intact in all areas of the bark cover. The paint has worn off in some areas of the thwarts, gunwales, headboard top edges, and bark decks. No restoration procedures appear to have ever been carried out on the canoe during its many years of display and storage.

Paddles

Assiginack carved seven paddling figures for the canoe model, each with a paddle (Figs. 162 and C-3). One figure and its paddle are now missing. Each of the surviving six paddles is from 8-7/8 to 9-1/4 inches long (Figs. 160 and 161). All of them are of the same shape and dimensions, with minor variations which are intrinsic to handcrafted items. All surfaces of the paddles are very well smoothed, to eliminate all carving facets.

The grip of the paddle tapers slightly in width over its span of 9/16 inch, from 5/16 inch at the shoulders to 1/4 inch just below its rounded end. In the same span, the thickness also tapers slightly, from 3/32 inch at the shoulders to 1/16 inch at the end. The face and side surfaces are flat, while the edges are slightly rounded.

Below the shoulders, the upper portion of the shaft tapers in width over a span of 5/8 inch, while increasing slightly in thickness. It acquires an oval cross section 1/8 inch thick, which is maintained over the length of the shaft to the throat. Below the shoulders 5/8 inch, the oval shaft is 3/16 inch wide. This dimension increases very gradually and slightly over a span of 2-7/8 inches, to reach 1/4 inch at the throat.

The upper end of the throat is indicated by the upper end of the median ridge, which extends for the full length of the blade to the tip. Over the 2-1/2 inch length of the throat, the width gradually increases, while the cross section thins and flattens. The point of maximum width of the blade lies 2-1/2 inches below the end of the median ridge. Here, the blade is 3/4 inch wide; its thickness is 1/16 inch at the median ridge and 1/32 inch at the edges. The two flat surfaces of the face of the blade each angle slightly upward toward the central midline, creating the low, straight median ridge. These thicknesses and form of the blade are maintained to its tip.

The blade tapers very gradually and slightly over a distance of 2-1/16 inches, from the maximum width of 3/4 inch to 5/8 inch at the beginning of the taper of the tip. The tip, 7/16 inch long, tapers rather suddenly to a sharp point. The edges of the narrow flat sides of the blade are slightly rounded until the beginning of taper of the tip; they are square in the tapered tip area.

These paddles which Assiginack carved are rare surviving examples of a complete set of very well-made early paddles which still accompany a well-documented canoe model and paddling figures. They are an invaluable source of data on the paddles which propelled voyaging canoes of the Great Lakes Indian Type A-1 style during the War of 1812 era.

Paddling Figures

Each of the seven wooden figures which Assiginack carved to man the paddles of the canoe model were made to represent the specific individuals who had been on a specific war party expedition during the War of 1812 (Figs. 162 and C-3). Each is carved from a single piece of wood, with quite realistic proportions, poses, and facial features. Fingers and toes are only partially delineated. Six of the seven figures have survived; four of them paddle on the left and two on the right. The missing figure presumably paddled on the right as well.

All of the men have shaved heads with a strip of hair left running down the midline of the top and back of the head, which is cut short. Each strip of hair is decorated with feathers. Every individual has his ears pierced in the outer rim for jewelry, and each has a distinct set of red and black painted designs on the face, head, and torso.

Only one of the figures now wears hide moccasins; the others are barefooted. The moccasins are of the one-piece style with a puckered center seam. In all other respects, the figures are dressed with the same articles of clothing, with minor variations; each has individual color schemes and decorative elements in his outfit.

Each of the paddlers wears a pair of red or dark blue woolen leggings; two of them have a pair of black cloth garters tied below the knees, to help support the leggings. All six of the men wear a dark blue or red woolen breech clout suspended from a wide cloth waist belt. The unusual aspect of this garment is that the two long ends of the breech clout are raised to the upper chest and shoulder blade level, where they are attached to wide woolen shoulder straps. Five of the men wear a cloth neckerchief knotted beneath the chin or at the back of the neck. The garters, belts, and neckerchiefs are variously made of wool, cotton, or silk.

Notes: Assigniack Canoe
1. Adney and Chapelle, pp.114, 116, 123, 124, 125, 127.
2. Ibid., pp. 28, 29, 102, 149.
3. Ibid., p.123, 124, 125, 127.
4. Ibid., pp. 138, 141, 147.
5. Ibid., pp. 117-18, 124, 155-57.
6. Ritzenthaler, p. 36.

The Varden Canoe Model

Contents

Varden Canoe Model

Several features of the Varden canoe suggest that this model portrays the Type B-1 style of fur trade canoe, the style of the Royal canoe. These traits include the moderate height and breadth of the ends in relation to the height of the walls in the midsection, the moderate degree of undercut in the profile of the ends, and the form of the interior curvature of the stempieces.[1]

The model represents the large size of fur trade canoe, the eight-place (nine-thwart) version. If it portrayed a canoe about thirty feet long, the model would have been built on a scale of about 1 to 15, or 1 inch to 1-1/4 feet. Thus, multiplication of each of the dimensions of the model by a factor of 15 would produce the general dimensions of the full size version which it was built to represent.

However, the model was built too short in the midsection in relation to the heights of the ends and the midsection walls. If the length of the midsection of the canoe is acknowledged to be somewhat short, multiplying the various other dimensions of the model by a factor of about 12 or 13 seems to reproduce more closely the dimensions of the full size version which the model represents.

Overall Dimensions

Length: Presently 25-1/8". About 1/8 inch is now missing from the stern cutwater edge, and about 3/16 to 1/4 inch is missing from the bow cutwater edge. Thus, the original length was about 25-1/2 inches.

Distance between the outboard sides of the tips of the outwales: 20-1/2" (Fig. 164).

Distance between the inboard faces of the heads and bases of the headboards: 20".

Depth at the midpoint, from the top of the gunwale caps to the top of the ribs on the floor: 2-1/4".

Height above the baseline: at the midpoint 2-1/2", at the bow 5-1/8", at the stern 5".

Beam at the midpoint: 4-13/16" (Fig. 165).

Interior beam, inside the gunwales: 4-1/4".

Total girth around the hull, from gunwale top to gunwale top: 7-5/8".

The form of the hull appears a little broad in the beam in relation to the length, since the model was built too short in its midsection length (Figs. 170 and 171). The interior beam is equal to 16.67 percent of the projected original overall length of the canoe. This ratio is greater than the 15.37 percent of the slightly narrow Ojibwa canoe and the 16.33 percent of the Quebec canoe; but it is less than that of the broad-beamed Sault canoe, whose ratio is 17.72 percent, and the broad-beamed Royal canoe, which has a ratio of 18.30 percent. In another comparison, the two Type B-1 ("Tete de Boule/Iroquois") models made by Adney have interior beams which are 15.0 and 16.8 percent of the total length of the canoes.[2] Thus, the beam of the Varden model may be generous, but it is not excessively so.

The bow end rises above the height of the midsection walls by an increase of 105 percent. This is slightly more than the 100 percent increase in the higher-ended one of the two Type B-1 models made by Adney.[3]

Hull Form
Profile of the Bottom and Ends

The horizontal span of the keel line extends for 15-1/4 inches, between a point 2-1/2 inches inboard of the bow chin and a point 3-1/2 inches inboard of the stern chin (Fig. 164). From the bow end of the horizontal section, a 2-1/2 inch span of moderate rocker (measured on the horizontal base line) gradually rises to a definite sharp chin (to the point where the stitches of the cutwater edge begin). At the stern, a 3-1/2 inch span of moderate rocker gradually rises to the chin. The total length of the bottom between the chins is 21-1/4 inches. The present rocker dimensions appear to be original, not altered by any warpage.

At the bow, the chin lies 1/8 inch above the horizontal baseline, while the chin at the stern measures 1/4 inch in height. These chin heights of 1/8 and 1/4 inch would represent on a full size canoe about 1-1/2 to 3 inches, which may be compared to the heights of 2 and 2-1/2 inches of the chins on the Royal canoe.

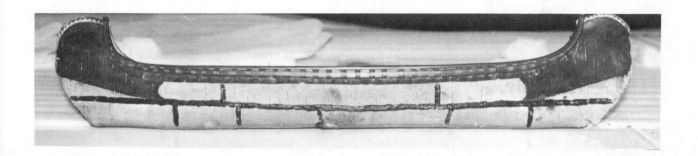

Fig. 163. Varden Canoe, with bow to right.

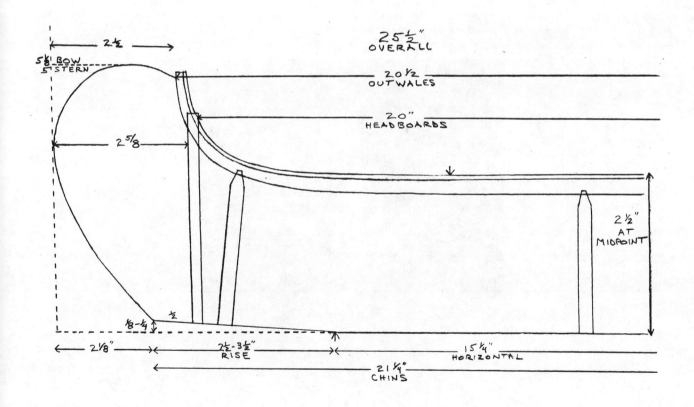

Fig. 164. Varden Canoe: Hull profile and dimensions.

–241–

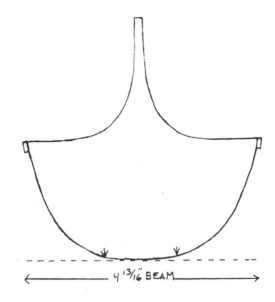

Fig. 165. Varden Canoe: Body plan. The arrows indicate the positions of the crease lines.

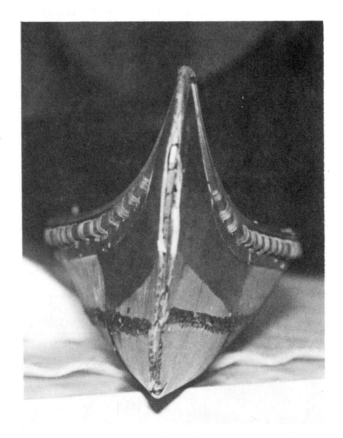

Fig. 166. Varden Canoe: End view of bow.

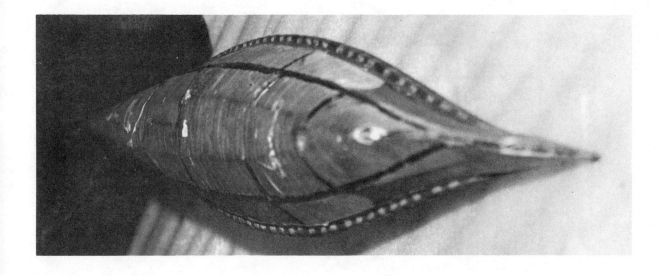

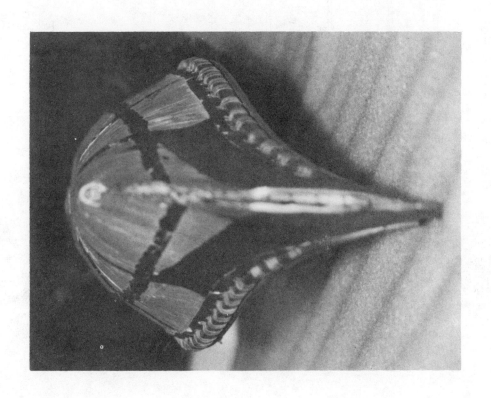

Fig. 167 (left). Varden Canoe: Bottom view of bow.
Fig. 168 (right). Varden Canoe: Bottom view from bow, showing crease lines.

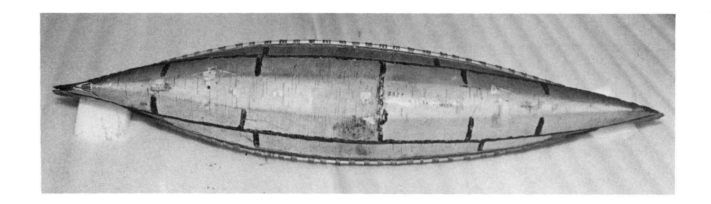

Fig. 169. Varden Canoe: Bottom view showing crease lines and gore slits.

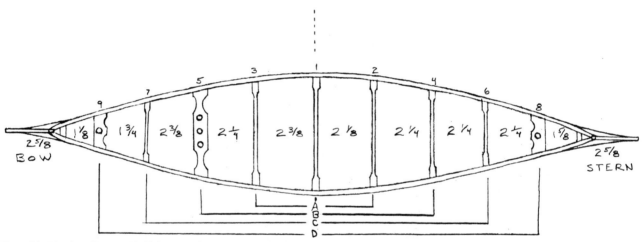

Fig. 170. Varden Canoe: Hull form and thwart positions.

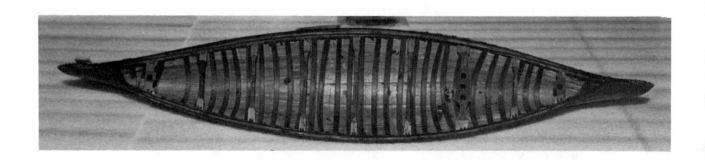

Fig. 171. Varden Canoe: Interior view, with bow to right.

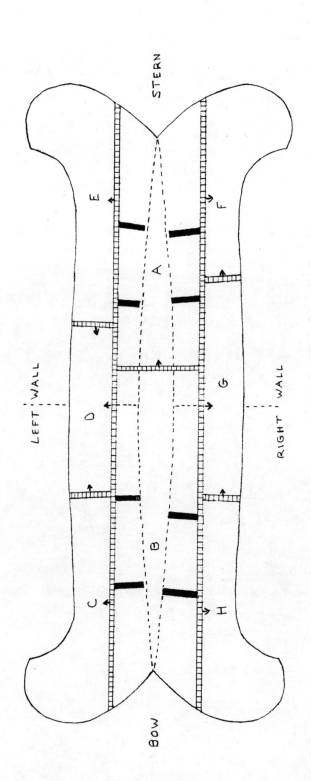

STERN

LEFT WALL

RIGHT WALL

BOW

A

B

C

D

E

F

G

H

PANEL SEAMS

SEWN SLITS

DIRECTION OF OVERLAPPING EDGE ON EXTERIOR

CREASE LINES

Fig. 172. Varden Canoe: Bark cover.

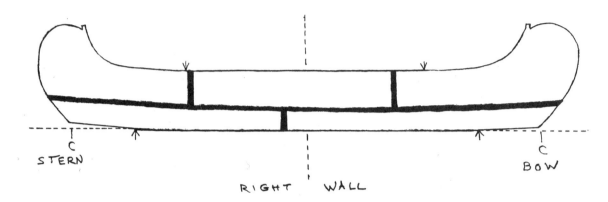

STERN   RIGHT   WALL   BOW

Fig. 173. Varden Canoe: Bark panels.

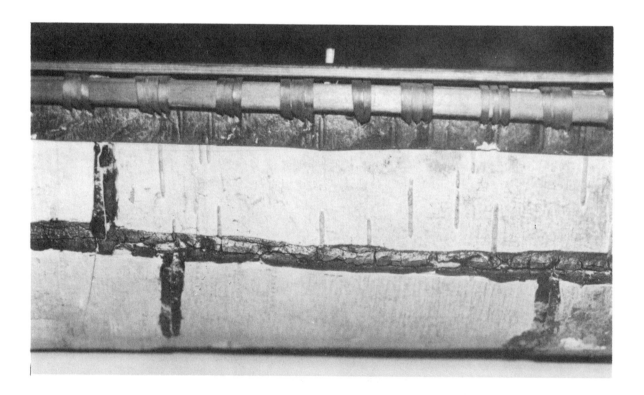

Fig. 174. Varden Canoe: Seams, gunwale lashings, loosened peg in gunwale cap.

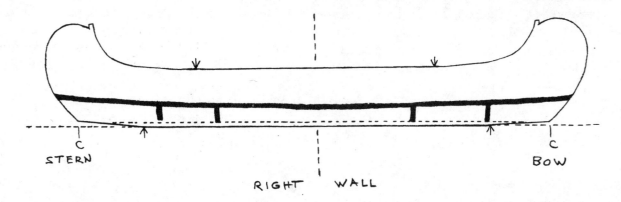

STERN

RIGHT WALL

BOW

C

C

Fig. 175. Varden Canoe: Gore slits.

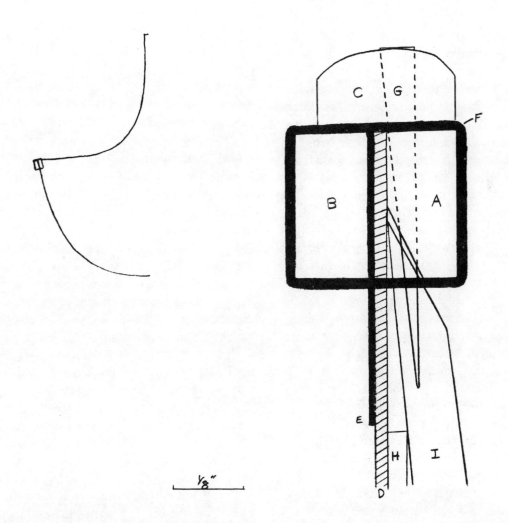

Fig. 176. Varden Canoe: Cross section of gunwales. A. inwale, B. outwale, C. gunwale cap, D. bark wall, E. reinforcement bark strip, F. root lashings, G. wooden peg, H. sheathing, I. rib.

From the chin, each end extends 2-1/8 inches outboard (measured on the baseline) to the outermost point of the end. The cutwater edge at each end curves upward from the sharp chin, beginning 3/8 to 1/2 inch outboard of the foot of the headboard. It arcs upward for 5-3/4 inches (measured on the curve) to the highest point of the end, with a moderately undercut profile. Then it curves downward and inboard over a span of 1 inch to meet the outwales. The total length of the edge, measured on the curve from chin to outwales, is 6-3/4 inches.

Body Plan

Like the Royal canoe, the bottom is narrow and moderately rounded, the bilge is gradually rounded, and the upper walls are straight and flare outward moderately (Figs. 165 to 169). The main difference is that the junction of the rounded bottom and the bilge area on the Varden canoe is marked by a definite crease line. Due to the upward curve of the rounded bottom, this crease line is visible when the canoe is viewed in side profile (Fig. 175). Such crease lines are not to be confused with the genuine chine lines on birchbark canoes that have been reported in Adney and Chapelle for the kayak-form canoes of the Athabascans of northern British Columbia, the Yukon Territory, and the upper Yukon valley, and those of the Alaskan Inuit of the lower Yukon valley and the Alaskan coast.[4] On these flat-bottomed craft, the bark was fitted around a permanent flat bottom frame of poles. The turn of the bilge from the bottom was either a very sudden curve or a sharp angle, which was creased along the longitudinal pole at the outer edge of the bottom frame.

The widest area of the bottom on the Varden canoe lies at the midpoint of the length of the canoe. Its width of 1-1/2 inches is maintained over a span of about 1-1/2 inches at the midpoint. Then this width tapers gradually and symmetrically to each chin of the canoe.

The canoe was built in a form designed for moderately fast paddling with ample cargo capacity. Its features, including a narrow moderately rounded bottom and a gradually rounded bilge, a slightly broad beam, a long slender taper to the ends, and a very narrow U form inboard of the headboards, contributed to its ease of paddling yet provided generous room for cargo.[5] The moderately rounded bottom of the canoe is much narrower and considerably more rounded than the standard cargo canoes of the period as portrayed by Adney, with their slightly rounded or nearly flat bottoms. In addition, the bilge area is considerably undercut and more gradually rounded. These features would reduce the floor space for cargo. The narrow U form which the canoe has inboard of its headboards would increase the roominess somewhat, yet reduce its speed, compared to a sharp V form as found on the Royal canoe. Thus, the Varden model appears to represent a fast-paddling cargo canoe rather than a true express canoe, a version designed to carry a moderate amount of cargo but travel quickly.

Bark Cover

The diagram of the bark cover (Fig. 172) portrays the canoe as if it had been placed in an upside down position and flattened by unsewing the end seams. The drawing is not to exact scale or proportion, and the locations and dimensions of the seams are approximate. All of the seams have been widened for ease of identification.

Color and Thickness

All of the panels of bark are very light golden tan in color. The thickness of the bark ranges from 1/32 to 1/16 inch. (The thickness profile is visible in several locations.)

Panels

On the diagram, the seams joining the eight panels of bark are marked with crosshatching. The arrows indicate the direction of the exposed overlapping edges on the exterior of the canoe.

Exact measurements of the individual panels cannot be taken, since the pitch covering the seams in many cases hides from view the exact positions of the edges of the panels. Only the portions of bark visible on the exterior of the canoe were measured, making no allowance for hidden overlaps. The measurement of the height of the side panels runs to the top of the inwale, where the bark was cut off flush with the top of the inwale. Each side panel was measured at its widest point; the end panels were measured to their present surviving lengths rather than their projected original lengths.

Bottom Panels
A. 11-1/4 inches long x 3-3/4 inches wide
B. 13" L x 3-3/4" W

Left Wall Panels
C. 9" L x 3-3/4" W
D. 6-3/4" L x 1-3/4" W
E. 9-3/4" L x 3-5/8" W

Right Wall Panels
F. 7-3/4" L x 3-5/8" W
G. 8-3/4" L x 1-3/4" W
H. 9" L x 3-3/4" W

If the bark cover were flattened, as in the diagram, the maximum width in the midsection would be 7-1/4 inches (the total girth of the bark of the canoe). The width near the ends measures 4 inches more. The length would be 25-1/2 inches at the level of the gunwales. This total surviving length of the side and end panels of each wall of the canoe is 3/8 inch longer than the surviving length of the assembled canoe, since the side panels follow the curvature of the broadening midsection of the canoe, rather than a straight line down the midline.

The bottom of the canoe was made with two long panels of bark, while each wall was formed by joining two high end panels and one central panel (Fig. 173). In the profile drawing, the panels and seams are positioned exactly as they lie on the canoe.

The canoe builder apparently had no concern about creating weak points in the hull by positioning vertical wall seams directly opposite each other across the hull of the canoe. The seams which attach the side of the two high end panels of the bow (seams C-D and G-H) lie directly opposite each other. (Those attaching the high end panels of the stern are offset from each other by two inches.) The builder positioned all of the seams in the walls well distant from seam A-B in the bottom. No wall seam was placed closer than about two inches from the bottom seam.

Sewn Seams

There are a number of areas on each of the seams where the pitch is now missing; thus, each seam on the canoe can be clearly observed (Fig. 174). Only the two longitudinal side seams and the cutwater edges are stitched on the model; all other seams are only sealed with pitch. The model builder apparently made this decision since the canoe was to be for display only, and its seams would all be hidden beneath the swaths of pitch. This feature would definitely not have been found on full size versions.

No evidence suggests that a batten strip of wood or root was incorporated into the two longitudinal side seams for added reinforcement, either on the exterior or the interior side of the bark cover. None of the edges of overlapping panels appear to have been thinned at the seams. It is not possible to determine on any of the seams the amount of overlap of one side over the other, since no interior views are available.

Bottom Seam

The single seam connecting the two panels of the bottom to each other was the first seam that was made in building the canoe. It is overlapped so that the exposed edge on the exterior faces toward the stern. This seam is not stitched; it is only sealed with pitch. Such a practice is never found on the bottom seams of full size craft.

Gore Slits

After the two bottom panels were joined together, the long span of bottom bark was laid out on the building bed, and the building frame was placed upon it. This frame determined the outline of the bottom of the canoe, particularly the shape of the taper toward the ends. The building frame was about as long as the bottom of the canoe, from chin to chin. When the Varden canoe was built, the bark was bent sharply upward around the perimeter of the frame, creating a definite crease line at the upward turn of the bilge from the bottom. (This unusual feature has been previously discussed.) Then a number of gore slits were sliced at intervals along the sides of the bottom panels. These slices ran from the edges of the bark inboard nearly to the building frame. At each of these slits, a slender wedge of bark was removed, to eliminate any overlapping of the edges of the gore slits; this created seams with butting edges. The slits were not stitched closed; instead, they were only sealed with pitch. Gore slits are nearly always stitched; but instances have been recorded in full size Malecite and Algonkin canoes in which both butted and overlapped styles of gore slit seams were left unsewn, only sealed with pitch. These cases most often involve gore slits which extend up to the gunwales.[6]

The gore slits in the bottom panels are positioned at somewhat irregular intervals well outboard of the mid-section of the canoe and well inboard of the chins (Figs. 172 and 175). They are located on the profile drawing exactly as they lie on the canoe. Four slits are found in each wall, two pairs in each half of the canoe. All of the slits in each wall have a mate located nearly exactly opposite (having been cut on the opposite side of the building frame). None of these pairs are aligned exactly opposite each other: all are offset by 1/8 to 1/4 inch. In traditional building methods, gore slits do not always lie directly opposite one another.[7] The two pairs of slits in the forward half of the canoe are generally placed in about the same positions as the two pairs in the rear half.

When the canoe is viewed in side profile, the gore slits extend downward from the longitudinal main seam, which runs the full length of each side of the canoe. This seam curves down very slightly and gradually toward the horizontal baseline of the canoe in its midsection. The full length of all of the gore slits is visible in the profile view. They run down the curved bilge area of the lower walls, extending down nearly to the crease lines of the bottom of the canoe. The narrow swath of pitch which covers each of the slits extends to the crease lines at four of the slits, and ends about 1/8 to 5/32 inch short of the crease lines at the other four slits, as indicated in the diagrams.

The outline of the crease lines, at the upward turn of the bilge from the bottom, implies the form of the building frame. It was about 21-1/4 inches long, since that is the length of the bottom (the distance between the chins). At the midpoint, the width of the bottom between the chine lines is 1-1/2 inches. Outboard at the first set of gore slits (4 to 4-1/8 inches from the midpoint), the bottom has tapered to 1-1/4 inches. Over the span of 3 to 3-5/8 inches to the second set of gore slits, the bottom reduces to 3/4 inch in width. From this location, the bottom tapers to a point at each chin. These measurements indicate rather closely the dimensions of the building frame. The maximum width of the building frame that was used to construct slightly rounded and nearly flat-bottomed fur trade canoes was often two-thirds of the interior beam of the gunwales.[8]

In the case of the Varden canoe, this ratio would produce a measurement of about 2-7/8 inches. The actual width of the building frame of this narrow round-bottomed canoe was much less, about 1-1/2 inches at the midpoint, as reflected by the chine lines.

Side Panels to Bottom Panels

After the gore slits were cut along the side edges of the bottom panels, the side panels were attached to the bottom panels. The seam connecting the side and bottom panels to each other is the prominent longitudinal seam which arcs across the full length of the canoe on each wall. When the side panels were attached to the bottom panels, a wider panel was installed at each end of both walls, to create the high upswept prows of the canoe.

The lower edges of the side panels are positioned inside the edges of the bottom bark panels. Thus, the edges of the bottom panels are exposed on the exterior of the canoe, facing upward toward the gunwales. The seams were sewn with a needle and dark brown commercial thread 1/32 inch in diameter, to represent split root stitches. The horizontal row of simple in-and-out stitches of doubled thread lies 1/16 to 3/32 inch below the exposed edge of the bottom bark panel. The stitches, 3/16 to 1/4 inch long, are spaced at intervals of 3/16 to 1/4 inch.

Side Panels to Side Panels

The seams which join the side panels to each other are all overlapping seams. In each instance, the exposed edge which overlaps on the exterior faces toward the stern, with one exception. On the left wall toward the stern, the seam that joins the high end panel to the central panel overlaps toward the bow (seam D-E). This forward-facing seam lies generally above the waterline, and thus would not hinder the forward flow of the canoe in most cases; but it could still receive abrasion from objects during use of the canoe. There appears to be no logical explanation for this feature; it probably was an oversight of the builder during construction.

No sewing joins the side panels to each other; they are only sealed with pitch. Such a lack of stitches in seams which join main wall panels to each other is not usually found in full size craft. (The seams which join the end panels in the Sault canoe are not stitched, but they are not main wall panel seams.)

Seam Sealing

All of the seams in the canoe were coated with charcoal-blackened melted pitch or gum from spruce or pine trees, of the same description as the gum found on the Royal canoe. The remaining original pitch is now very brittle; it does not indent under thumb pressure.

A coating of gum may have been applied to all of the seams on the interior side of the canoe, a typical procedure. But no interior views between or beneath the sheathing strips are visible to verify this assumption.

Each of the seams were sealed on the exterior of the canoe. The swaths of melted gum which cover all of the seams are 3/16 to 1/4 inch wide and 1/16 to 3/32 inch thick. The gum sealing the wall panel seams extends up to the lower edge of the reinforcement bark strip.

Exterior Hull Surface

The discussion concerning the disruptions in the smooth, even surface of the bark cover of the Royal canoe also applies to the Varden canoe as well. Overlapping panel edges and applications of sealant pitch up to 3/32 inch thick have produced seams which stand out from the flat surface of the hull. In addition, one end panel seam overlaps toward the bow.

Gunwale Elements

All of the gunwale elements are angled moderately outward, at the same degree of outward flare as the topsides of the bark walls to which they are attached (Fig. 176).

Inwales

The total length of the inwale on the curve is 25-3/4 inches. This is 1-1/2 inches longer than the outwale, since the ends of the inwale extend out to nearly the outboard edge of the stempiece (Fig. 179). (Due to damage of the bark end panel at the stern, the tips of the inwales are clearly visible.) In the midsection, the inwale strip is 1/8 inch wide across the top and 1/4 inch deep (Fig. 176). The bottom surface is only 1/16 inch across, since the lower outboard edge is carved off into a beveled surface to produce a space into which the tips of the ribs fit. Beginning at about the midpoint between the center thwart and the headboards (slightly outboard of the third thwart from each end), the inwale tapers very gradually toward each end. At a point

2-1/4 inches from the tip of the inwale (beside the headboard), the depth has reduced to 3/16 inch, while the width (thickness) has remained the same. Over the final 2-1/4 inches, the depth tapers gradually to 1/8 inch at the tip, while the width reduces to 1/16 inch. All surfaces of the inwale are carved flat and smooth, and all edges are sharp. At the tips, the ends are cut off squarely.

The inwale runs horizontally over much of the length of the canoe, and then rises very gradually toward the ends. By the inboard edge of each end thwart, the height has risen 1/2 inch. From this point, the inwale begins to curve up moderately toward its ends. Inboard of the headboard 1/2 inch, the inwale diverges from the outwale; it extends 2-1/4 inches outboard of the headboard, while angling gradually upward (Fig 179). The tips of the inwales extend to nearly the cutwater edge of the stempiece.

To facilitate the bending of the upward curve of the ends of the inwale, one split was made in the ends, to produce two lamination layers. The very long slit extends inboard from the tip of the inwale for 4-3/4 inches; it ends slightly inboard of the mortise hole of the end thwart at each end of the canoe. The lashings which bind the inwale to the outwale cover the area where the lamination slit ends. These lashings prevent the slit from splitting further inboard.

The inwale fits into a notch which is cut into the side of each headboard (Fig. 178). Two turns of the same brown thread (representing split roots) bind the inwale to the headboard at the notch. The tips of the inwale are also firmly bound in place. At the juncture of the pair of converging inwale tips and the stempiece, two adjacent turns of the same brown thread encircle the pair of inwales 1/4 inch from their tips, passing through the lamination splits in the stempiece.

The inwale is not pegged or nailed to the outwale; this is another trait of this model which is not normally found on full size craft. (Spaces between root wraps in the gunwale lashings afford many views of the gunwales beneath the lashings; no pegs or nails are hidden there.) Split root lashings bind the two gunwale elements together, with the top edge of the bark wall and the strip of reinforcement bark sandwiched between them.

Outwales

The total length of the outwale on the curve is 24-1/4

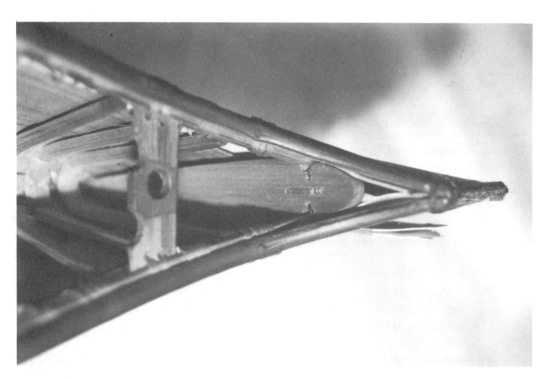

Fig. 177 (left). Varden Canoe: Lashings of gunwale ends and cutwater edge.
Fig. 178 (right). Varden Canoe: Interior view of stern, showing ribs, end thwart, headboard, and gunwale ends.

inches, measured on the outside of the curve. In the mid-section, it is 1/8 inch wide across the top and 1/4 inch deep (Fig. 176). In both width and depth, the outwale has the same dimensions as the inwale. Thus, the bottom surface of the outwale matches that of the inwale. Beginning at about the midpoint between the center thwart and the headboards (slightly inboard of the second thwart from each end of the canoe), the depth of the outwale tapers very gradually, to a depth of 1/8 inch at the tips. The outwale begins this gradual end taper at about the same location as the taper of its parallel inwale. The width (thickness) of 1/8 inch is maintained over the full length of the outwale. All surfaces are carved flat and smooth, and all edges are sharp. At the tips, the ends are rounded off moderately.

The outwale runs horizontally over much of the length of the canoe, and then rises very gradually toward the ends. By the inboard edge of each end thwart, the height has risen 1/2 inch. From this point, the outwale begins to curve up moderately toward its ends. (Fig. 179). Inboard of the headboard 1/2 inch, the outwale diverges from the inwale; it sweeps upward in a strong curve to reach a nearly vertical position at the tips. (The ends are slightly more angled than the virtually vertical outwale ends of the Royal canoe.) The ends of the outwale sweep upward and slightly outboard beyond the inboard face of the headboards for about 7/8 to 1 inch. They rise a total of 2-1/8 inches in height over a span of 1-1/2 inches on the horizontal baseline. The tips reach a point 1/16 inch below the maximum height of the prow of the canoe.

To facilitate the bending of the upward curve and the extreme upsweep at the tips, the same lamination procedure was done as on the inwales: one slit was made, to produce two lamination layers (Fig. 177). The lamination slit extends from the tip inboard for a distance of 3 inches. (It ends about 1-3/4 inches outboard of the point at which the inwale lamination slit ends.) The root lashings which bind the outwale to the inwale cover the area where the lamination slit ends. These lashings prevent the slit from splitting further inboard. The two lamination layers are cut off at the tip of the outwale to form a flat, horizontal end.

The tips of the two converged outwales are joined to each other by wrappings of the same brown thread (representing root lashings). There is no wooden or bark wedge inserted between the tips of the two strips to assist in making the wrappings tight. Nor are the tips pegged or nailed to each other. The thread lashings, beginning 3/32 inch below the tips, wrap in three turns around the two joined outwales. The three wraps do not run through the adjacent bark wall and stempiece, as would be usual in full size canoes; they lie adjacent to the edge of the wall.

The triangular area between the two converging outwales is not covered by a bark deck; it is left open (Figs. 178 and 184). Thus, a flag staff could have been inserted adjacent to the outboard side of the headboard, beside the stempiece, at either the bow or the stern. There is not enough space between the head of the headboard and the gunwale caps for the wrapping of a cord around the headboard, to bind a flag staff to the outboard or inboard face of the headboard; but such a space exists between the midsection of the headboard and the adjacent walls at both the bow and the stern.

Gunwale Caps

The total length of the gunwale cap is 23-1/2 inches, measured on the inside of the curve. (This is 3/4 inch shorter than the outwale, which was measured on the opposite side of the curvature.) In the midsection, the cap is 1/4 inch wide by 1/8 inch deep (thick) (Fig. 176). Beginning at about the midpoint between the center thwart and the headboards, the width of the cap gradually tapers, to a width of 1/8 inch at the tips. The depth of 1/8 inch is maintained over the full length of the cap.

All surfaces are flat and smooth. The lower two edges are sharp, while the upper two are well rounded. At the tips, the ends are carved off somewhat round. The description of the painted decoration on the caps is found on page 267.

The combined width of the inwale (1/8 inch) and the outwale (1/8 inch) is equal to the width of the gunwale cap. But the bark wall and the reinforcement bark strip which are sandwiched between the inwale and the outwale add more thickness to the combined gunwales. Also, the degree to which the inwale and outwale were squeezed against the bark and each other when they were all lashed together varies in different areas. Thus, the gunwale cap is about 1/32 to 3/64 inch narrower than the top of the gunwale unit (inwale, bark layers, and outwale) in most areas of the midsection. In this area of the canoe, the uncovered portion is usually the outwale. The width of the cap tapers more quickly toward the ends than the combined gunwale unit (Fig. 184). Since its outboard edge is aligned with the outboard edge of the outwale toward the ends of the canoe, the area of the inwale that is exposed gradually increases toward the ends. Near the headboards, up to 3/32 inch of the thickness of the inwale is exposed.

The gunwale cap conforms to the curvature of the outwale for its entire length. Thus, it runs horizontally over much of the length of the canoe, and then rises very gradually toward the ends. By the inboard edge of each end thwart, the height has risen 1/2 inch. From this point, the cap begins to curve up moderately toward its ends. Inboard of the headboard about 1-1/2 inches, the cap begins to sweep upward in a strong curve, reaching a nearly vertical position at the tips. The ends of the cap sweep upward and slightly outboard beyond the inboard face of the headboards for about 7/8 to 1 inch. They rise a total of 2-1/8 inches in height over a span of 1-1/2 inches on the horizontal baseline. The tips end exactly at the tips of the outwale, 1/16 inch below the maximum height of each end panel of the canoe (Fig. 177). Since the nearly vertical tips of the outwales and caps end 1/16 inch below the tops of the end panels, the high bark ends would rest on the ground when the canoe was overturned on its side as a shelter. No horizontal splits were made in the ends to facilitate the bending of the upward curve and the extreme upsweep of the ends of the cap.

From headboard to headboard, the gunwale caps are attached to the outwale by downward-driven wooden pegs. At irregular intervals, round holes 1/16 inch in diameter were drilled downward through the caps and the inwales, most of them between the gunwale lashing areas. The holes lie slightly inboard of the midline of the cap, and angle slightly inboard. The intervals between the holes are the greatest in the midsection area, measuring 2-7/8 to 3-3/8 inches. The spans reduce gradually toward the ends, down to 1-1/8 to 1-3/4 inches near the extremities. The endmost holes lie 1-3/4 inches from the tips of the caps, measured on the curve; this is 3/8 to 1/2 inch inboard of the headboards, at about the beginning of the strongest upsweep of the outwales and caps (Fig. 178).

The long slender pegs, 1/2 to 11/16 inch long, taper from about 1/16 inch diameter at the head to a sharp point at the tip (Fig. 176). The sides of the pegs are carved with four to eight bevels, to fit tightly in the round holes. The pegs were driven snug through the cap and the inwale and then trimmed so that the surface of the head lies flush with or barely above the surface of the cap. The pointed tips protrude from the bottom of the inwale, beside the bark wall, up to 1/4 inch.

The tips of the two converged caps are joined to each other and to the tips of the two outwales by wrappings of the same dark brown thread (representing root lashings). No wedge is inserted between the tips of the caps to assist in making the wrappings tight. Nor are the tips of the converged caps pegged or nailed to each other. Beginning 1/8 inch below the tip of each cap, a notch is carved into its upper face, 3/64 inch deep and 1/16 inch long. Four turns of thread fill the notch, encircling both pairs of outwales and caps; the wrappings also cover most of the thread lashings which bind the tips of the outwales together. They do not run through the adjacent bark wall and its stempiece (as is usual in full size craft), but instead lie adjacent to the edge of the bark wall.

Reinforcement Bark Strips

The reinforcement strip of birchbark increases the thickness of the upper edge of the bark wall where it is attached to the gunwales. Before the inwale and outwale were lashed together onto the upper edge of the bark wall, the reinforcement strip was inserted between the bark wall and the outwale (Fig. 176). Its top edge, like that of the bark wall, was cut off at the level of the top of the inwale. When the awl holes were pierced through the wall and the lashings were wrapped around the gunwales, the bark strip was pierced and lashed at the same time.

The strip, running from headboard to headboard (Figs.174 and 177), extends down 1/4 to 5/16 inch below the lower edge of the outwale in the midsection area. This width is maintained toward the ends until the outwale begins its strong upward sweep. There, the strip tapers in a broad curve up to the outwale, ending beside the outboard face of the headboard. The lower edge of the reinforcement strip generally runs parallel to the lower edge of the outwale for the full length; it was cut rather regularly and with little undulation. The strip was trimmed to its present width after being installed on the canoe. There is a knife cut or scratch on the bark wall panel immediately adjacent to the lower edge of the strip along its full length; this was produced when the strip was trimmed off against the unprotected wall.

The majority of the length of the strip is made up of one long piece of bark. In addition to this long strip, the piece beneath the outwale where it curves upward to the headboard is made up of one short piece at each end, 3 to 3-1/2 inches long. The short curved segment at the bow end on each wall overlaps the main strip for about 1/16 inch. The end segment on each wall at the stern butts against the end of the main strip. The pieces are not attached at their ends to each other or to the canoe wall in any manner.

The description of the painted decoration on the reinforcement bark strips is found on page 267. When the canoe is viewed in side profile, there is no additional narrow strip of bark outboard of the headboard, since this canoe has no bark deck piece covering the area where the outwales converge.

Gunwale Lashings

The upper edge of the bark wall is sandwiched between the inwale, the reinforcement bark strip, and the outwale (Fig. 176). It is cut off flush with the top surface of the inwale. The four layers of bark and wood are lashed together with spaced groups of root lashings from headboard to headboard.

Each lashing group normally runs through three holes in the bark wall, occasionally two or four holes (Figs. 174 and 185). The holes, generally triangular in shape, are about 1/16 inch across, with rather even edges. They were made by an awl with a triangular cross section, which was inserted from the exterior side of the wall but was not twisted after piercing the bark.

The holes are spaced 1/16 to 3/32 inch apart. Each row of holes, spanning 1/4 to 5/16 inch, lies immediately below the lower edge of the inwale and outwale. The split root lashing material is 1/16 to 3/32 inch wide and about 1/32 inch thick, with a rectangular cross section. After being split, each side of the root was scraped very flat.

To lash the gunwales, one end of a length of split root was inserted between the lower surface of the inwale and the bark wall on the interior side of the ca-noe. Then, in a simple spiral stitch, the other end of the root passed over the top of the inwale and outwale and through the first hole in the set of three holes. The root passed around the combined inwale and outwale a second time, and through the second hole. This pattern continued through the third hole as well, each hole receiving one turn of root around the gunwales.

Several techniques were used to finish off the root securely before starting a new group of lashings. In most cases, the root was simply cut off rather short after it emerged on the interior side of the third and final hole. Occasionally, a fourth hole was added; then the end of the root ran horizontally on the interior from hole # 3 to hole #4 and through it. On the exterior, the end was either cut off rather short or inserted behind the adjacent lashings beneath the lower surface of the outwale. The techniques which were used to begin and end each of the gunwale lashing groups on the model are not nearly as secure as those utilized on full size canoes; the builder apparently chose these extremely simple techniques for expediency, since the craft was to be used only for display.

Each typical group of lashings is composed of three turns of root around the gunwales, covering a length of 1/4 to 5/16 inch of the gunwales. An interval of 1/4 to 5/16 inch separates each group of lashings. The interval between each group is not spanned by a connector stitch, since each group begins and ends independently. The endmost group of lashings at each end of each gunwale lies about 1/2 inch inboard of the headboard, where the inwale and outwale begin to diverge.

The thwarts are bound into the gunwales with root lashings that fit into the pattern of the gunwale wrappings. The thwart lashing groups are not joined to the gunwale lashings by connector stitches.

Stempieces

The stempiece is visible in several areas of the canoe (Fig. 179). Its heel is visible where it projects through the base of the headboard. Most of the stern stempiece is clearly visible behind the unlashed and broken bark end panel on the left side of the stern; views of the rest of the stempiece are available via this damaged area as well. No bark deck covers the area outboard of the headboard; this affords a view of the stempiece behind the headboard. The laminated upper

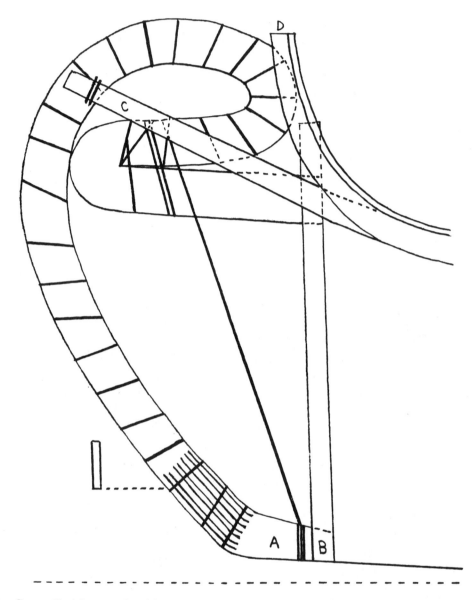

Fig. 179. Varden Canoe: End frame unit, with all string wrappings indicated. A. stempiece, B. headboard, C. inwales, D. outwales.

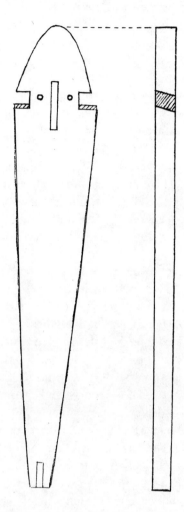

Fig. 180. Varden Canoe: Headboard.

end of the stempiece can be seen where it projects through the headboard. In addition, the curvature of the stempiece is implied by the curve of the cutwater edge of the canoe, from chin to outwales; this outlines the entire outer curved portion of the stempiece.

The total length of the stempiece is about 11-7/8 inches, measured on the outboard edge. The heel of the stempiece ends flush with the inboard surface of the base of the headboard. At its end, it is 1/4 inch deep (in height) by 1/16 inch thick, with sharp corners and edges. All surfaces are flat and smooth. There is no notch in the heel to receive the legs of the headboard where they straddle the heel. The heel area angles upward slightly as it extends 1/2 inch outboard from the headboard to the chin.

From the outboard side of the base of the headboard, the stempiece broadens in depth (height) to 7/16 inch over a span of 1/2 inch. All surfaces are flat and all edges are square. The dimensions of 1/16 by 7/16 inch, with a rectangular cross section, are maintained over the entire upper length of the stempiece, to its junction with the headboard. This is an extremely deep, robust stempiece, compared to the ones in the Royal canoe, the various stempiece models made by Adney, and even the strong ones in the full size Ojibwa canoe. The extreme depth of the laminated stempieces in the Varden canoe resembles that of certain types of curved stempieces which were cut from a solid plank and positioned standing on edge. Plank-stem craft include a type of freight canoe made by the Ojibwas (Fig. 26), hunters' canoes of the Algonkins, and canoes built by the Chipewyan, Slave, and Dogrib tribes of northwestern Canada.[9] (These plank stempieces do not extend the full distance from the cutwater edge to the headboard, like those of the Sault and Bell canoes.) The depth of the stempiece in the Varden model is virtually identical proportionately to that of the stempiece in the Assiginack model (Fig. 146). This may suggest that some laminated stempieces were indeed made in this extreme depth in full size voyaging canoes; or it may simply underscore the difficulty of building small model canoes to exact scale.

Beginning 1/2 inch outboard of the headboard, at a point 5/8 to 11/16 inch from the tip of its heel, the Varden stempiece is divided by seven splits into eight lamination layers 1/16 inch or less thick. The lamina-

tion slits begin at the bend of the chin and extend through the complete upper length of the stempiece to its end. (In the Figure 179 diagram, they are portrayed only in the lowest portion.) The laminated portion of the stempiece (but not its unlaminated heel area) is spirally wrapped at intervals of about 1/4 to 5/16 inch with the same dark brown thread as that which binds the tips of the outwales and caps (representing split roots or strips of basswood inner bark).

The stempiece angles slightly upward from the headboard to the sharp chin, the point at which the stitching of the end begins. From the chin, which lies 1/2 inch outboard of the headboard, the stempiece arcs in a broad curve for 5-3/4 inches to its maximum height at the head. From there, the stempiece curves downward and inboard for 1 inch, to the point where it meets the converged tips of the outwales and gunwale caps. The gunwale lashings which usually bind the stempiece to the gunwales at this location do not pass through the stempiece on the model. At this point, the stempiece curves sharply outboard. Angling slightly downward, it runs out to the inboard side of its outer arc. This curve and span measure 1-3/4 inches. The stempiece then bends very sharply back on itself. Although this bend is extremely sharp, it did not require the breaking of any of the lamination layers on the inside of the curve; since the layers are only about 1/16 inch thick, they could be bent very sharply. Finally, the stempiece extends nearly horizontally inboard to and through the headboard. It ends flush with the inboard surface of the headboard. The sharp bend and final horizontal span measure 2-3/4 inches. The maximum horizontal distance of the curvature of the stempiece, from the cutwater edge to the outboard side of the headboard, is about 2-5/8 inches. No wooden braces were installed to add stability to the stempiece and thus to the high end panel.

The wraps of thread which spiral around the laminated portion of the stempiece end immediately before the stempiece bends very sharply back on itself. Four long wraps of thread then bind the areas on each side of the sharp bend tightly together. The thread finally spans diagonally down to the heel area of the stempiece, where it encircles the heel several times. This final long span may have been added immediately after the steaming and bending procedure, to hold the curved stempiece in its correct form while it dried permanently into that shape.

The tips of the converged pair of inwales extend nearly to the cutwater edge of the stempiece. There, they are bound tightly to the stempiece with the same brown thread, as previously described.

The form of the internal curvature of the stempiece of the Varden canoe, like that of the Royal canoe stempiece, closely resembles the Type B-1 ("Tete de Boule") versions modeled by Adney; these appear on pages 136 and 149 at the far left in Adney and Chapelle. (See page 40 in the Royal canoe discussion.) Although the Varden stempiece lacks horizontal braces, other Type B-1 versions modeled by Adney were also made without braces.

Headboards

The headboard stands 2-5/8 inches inboard of the outermost point of the cutwater edge (Fig. 164). The outboard side of both the head and the base falls 1/2 inch inboard of the chin of the canoe, since the headboard stands exactly upright. The top of the low, rounded head fits between the converging inwales and gunwale caps at or very slightly above the level of the upper surface of the caps. Thus, when the canoe is viewed in profile, the headboard is either not visible or very slightly visible above the caps.

The overall height of the headboard (Figs. 178 to 180) is 3-13/16 inches; the height from the shoulders to the base is 3-3/16 inches. Its maximum width is 3/4 inch at the shoulders, at the base of the side notches. This maximum width tapers gradually over a span of 3-3/16 inches down to the base, where it is 3/16 inch. The sides of this long tapered body are bowed slightly outward from the shoulders to the base. Over its entire length, the headboard is 5/32 inch thick; this dimension is extremely thick, compared proportionately to the headboards in all of the other voyaging canoes in this study, whether full size or model versions. The flat inboard surface is carved smooth, all edge surfaces are flat, and all corners and edges are sharp.

Below the tapered rounded head, which measures 1/2 inch in height and 11/16 inch at its maximum width, a notch is cut out of each side. The inwales fit into these notches, which are 1/8 inch high and 1/8 inch deep. The top and bottom surfaces of each notch angle

upward slightly toward the outboard side of the headboard, to accommodate the upward curve of the ends of the inwales.

Inboard 7/64 inch from the upper portion of each of these inwale notches is a single hole, through which two turns of the same brown thread (representing split roots) lash the inwales to the neck of the headboard. The two round holes, 1/32 inch in diameter, were probably made with a heavy needle or a length of wire.

A rectangular hole lies in the midline of the headboard, at the level of the lower head and upper body. The hole is 7/16 inch high and 1/16 inch wide. The laminated end of the stempiece projects through this hole, ending flush with the surface of the headboard. The end of the stempiece measures 7/16 inch tall by 1/16 inch thick.

The base of the headboard has a rectangular notch cut out, 1/4 inch tall and 1/16 inch wide. The two legs produced by the notch each taper slightly to a sharply cut off end 1/16 inch wide. The legs fit over the heel of the stempiece. The headboard is attached to the stempiece only by the tight fit of these legs over the heel of the stempiece and the upper end of the stempiece through the hole in the headboard. The headboard is not decorated at either end of the canoe.

Cutwater Edges

No wooden batten was built into the stitched cutwater edge to cover and protect the outboard edges of the two bark panels or the stempiece. The edges of the bark panels are cut off flush with the edge of the stempiece.

The cutwater edge was sewed with a needle and the same dark brown commercial thread with a 1/32 inch diameter (representing split root stitches) (Fig. 177). The upper span of 2-1/2 inches around the curve, beginning at the gunwale tips, is sewn in a decorative pattern of stitches composed of twelve tapering wedges. The narrow pointed end of each wedge points upward or inboard, depending on its position on the curve. Each individual wedge is made up of a series of 7 or 8 adjacent stitches. The needle holes, 1/32 inch in diameter, lie at intervals of about 1/32 inch. The first hole in each series is positioned about 3/16 inch inboard from the cutwater edge; the following 6 or 7 holes each lie progressively nearer to the edge, the final hole being 1/16 inch from the edge. The needle and a single strand of thread laid down a continuous spiral stitch, with one turn per hole. Each unit of 7 or 8 adjacent stitches covers a span of about 3/16 to 1/4 inch of the cutwater edge.

On the lower 4-1/4 inch span of the cutwater edge, extending down to the chin, the stitching holes are in a single row, parallel to the edge and 1/16 to 3/32 inch from it. The needle holes, 1/32 inch in diameter, are placed at intervals of 1/8 to 3/16 inch. The needle and a single strand of thread formed a series of individual spiral stitches, with one turn per hole. These stitches are spaced much more widely than those in the upper lashing area of the cutwater edge (where the continuous spiral stitches lie adjacent to each other). Thus, there are intervals of nearly 1/8 to 3/16 inch between each stitch in which the cutwater edge is not covered with stitches.

In all sewing of the cutwater edge, the stitches pass directly through the stempiece inside the end of the canoe, rather than around it. The thread lashings run through needle holes through the stempiece. (Details of the stempiece can be clearly seen behind the broken high end panel at the stern end of the left wall.)

The lower portion of the cutwater edge (the area sewn with widely spaced single spiral stitches) is sealed with blackened pitch in the same manner as the bark panel seams are sealed. (Only traces of the pitch now remain.) The narrow swath of pitch begins at the chin, and extends upward for 4 1/4 inches on the curve; it covers the entire area of spaced spiral stitches up to the wedge pattern stitches. The pitch extends from the outer edge of the prow onto the bark walls for about 3/32 inch. The edges of the pitched area are broadly curved, following the contour of the outer edge of the canoe. The upper portion of the cutwater edge is not sealed with pitch. This allowed unobstructed drainage of water out of the canoe when it was overturned on its side on shore.

The total thickness of the cutwater edge is now about 3/32 inch in all areas, since only traces of pitch now remain in the lower pitched area (the area of the waterline). This thickness includes the stempiece, the two bark panels, and the stitches.

Thwarts

The nine thwarts (creating an eight-place canoe) are not spaced exactly symmetrically (Figs. 170 and 171). The distances between the thwarts are measured from centerline to centerline. Their positioning indicates a canoe shape that tapers slightly asymmetrically toward the two ends at the gunwale level, with the bow half a little wider and more suddenly tapered near the end than the stern.

The center thwart lies at the exact midpoint of the canoe. In comparing the distances to each of the adjacent thwarts (pair A), the span toward the bow is 1/2 inch greater than the sternward span. The distances from the pair A thwarts to pair B are equal, while the span from pair B to pair C is 1/4 inch greater in the bow half than in the stern. The distances from pair C to pair D (the endmost thwarts) reflect the more blunt taper of the bow near its end: the span toward the bow is 1/2 inch shorter than its sternward counterpart. The end thwart at the bow end lies 1/2 inch closer to its headboard than does the stern end thwart to its headboard, another indicator of the blunt bow taper. Both of the headboards are positioned the same distance from the end of the canoe. Thus, the end thwart at the bow lies 1/2 inch closer to its tip of the canoe than the end thwart at the stern. These measurements imply a hull shape in which the bow half has slightly greater width and a more sudden taper near the end compared to the narrower stern half with its longer and more gradual taper.

The lengths of the thwarts also imply the same asymmetry. Four pairs of thwarts flank the center thwart. In the two pairs in the midsection (pairs A and B), the thwart toward the bow is longer than its sternward counterpart.

Center: Thwart #1: 4-1/8 inches
Pair A: Thwart #2: 4 inches
         Thwart #3: 4-1/8 inches
Pair B: Thwart #4: 3-3/8 inches
         Thwart #5: 3-5/8 inches
Pair C: Thwart #6: 2-9/16 inches
         Thwart #7: 2-9/16 inches
Pair D: Thwart #8: 1-1/2 inches
         Thwart #9: 1-1/2 inches

The lengths, measured along the longest edge, do not include the hidden portion at each end which fits into the mortise hole in each inwale. The actual length of each thwart is longer than each of these measurements, since the additional portion at each end extends partially or completely through the inwale.

In comparing pair A, the bow thwart is 1/8 inch

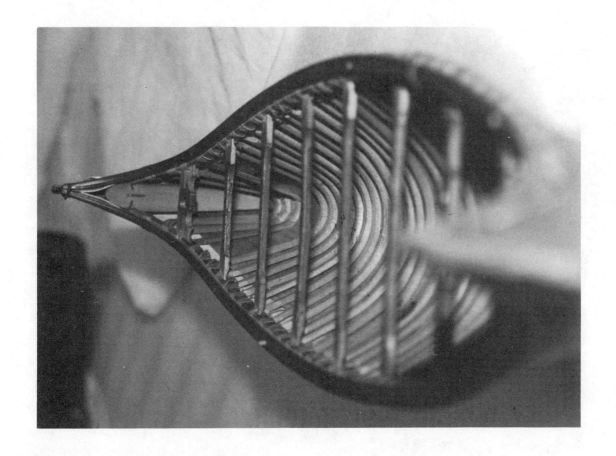

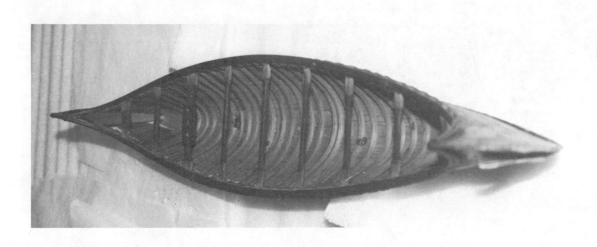

Fig. 181 (left). Varden Canoe: Interior view from the stern.
Fig. 182 (right). Varden Canoe: Interior view from the stern.

Fig. 183. Varden Canoe: Thwart positions, sheathing, and ribs of bow end.

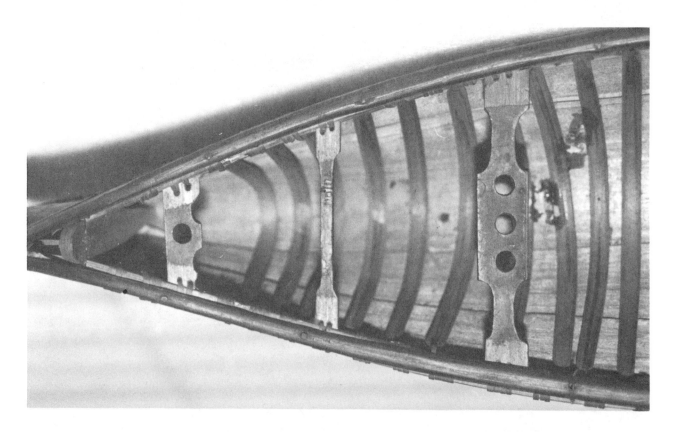

Fig. 184. Varden Canoe: Interior view of bow end, showing thwarts, pegged gunwale caps, headboard, and upper end of stempiece.

-262-

Fig. 185. Varden Canoe: Thwart and gunwale lashings, sheathing, and ribs.

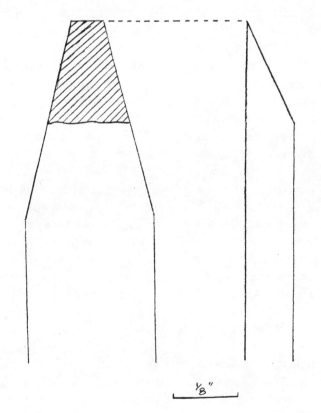

1/8"

Fig. 186. Varden Canoe: Ribs.

longer than its stern counterpart; in the next pair outboard, the bow thwart is 1/4 inch longer. These small differences on the model would represent much larger differences when multiplied to a full size craft. They may be simply variances due to measurement by eye rather than by measuring devices. However, there is a possibility that the builder intentionally made the thwarts slightly longer in the bow half, to create a canoe that is slightly wider in the beam toward the bow than the stern, for greater efficiency of forward movement of the canoe. Considering the positions of the thwarts in the Varden canoe, such asymmetry would have been produced even if the thwarts in the bow half had been exactly the same lengths as their counterparts in the stern (since the bow thwarts are positioned slightly closer to the end of the canoe). This slightly widened bow form is also found in the Royal and Ojibwa canoes, and possibly in the Catlin canoe model. This feature was commonly built into the fur trade canoes that were constructed in the latter nineteenth century at the canoe-building posts of the upper Ottawa River in western Quebec.[10] It was also quite widespread in traditional Indian canoe construction, as has been previously discussed.

The following description applies to six of the nine thwarts (Figs. 181 to 185) (The wide endmost pair of thwarts and the mast thwart are discussed afterward.) The thickness of 1/8 inch remains constant over nearly the entire length of the thwart. About 1/8 to 3/16 inch from each inwale, the underside angles up rather sharply, reducing the thickness to 1/32 to 1/16 inch where the thwart enters the mortise hole. The end probably continues to taper to a sharp edge at its tip; it is not visible in the mortise hole. The top side remains level over the entire length. The width measures 3/16 inch for much of the length of the thwart. At a point 1/2 to 9/16 inch from each inwale, the width suddenly flares to 5/16 inch. This width is maintained from the sharp shoulders to the inwale, and presumably through the entire mortise hole. The length between the shoulders measures 3-3/16 inches on the center thwart; it is shorter on each of the other five standard thwarts. All sides are carved flat and smooth, and all edges are sharp

The endmost thwarts were built much wider, although the thickness and its underside taper near the ends is identical to that of the six standard thwarts described above. All sides are carved flat and smooth, and all edges are sharp. The width of each end thwart measures 1/2 inch over its entire length, except where two semicircular areas are cut out of the inboard edge. These cutout areas, 7/16 to 1/2 inch long and 1/8 inch deep, lie 1/4 inch from each inwale. The distance between the two cutouts measures 5/16 inch. At the midpoint of this distance is a drilled hole 1/4 inch in diameter, on the midline of the thwart. The possible usages of this hole for the attachment of mast guy lines and towing lines, as well as a flag staff receptacle, are discussed later.

These endmost thwarts are positioned in the gunwales at the point where the gunwales curve upward toward the ends of the canoe (Fig. 183). Thus, the planes of the top and bottom surfaces of these two endmost thwarts are also angled upward, with the outboard edge higher than the inboard edge. All of the other thwarts are positioned so that their upper and lower surfaces lie in generally level, horizontal planes.

The perforated mast thwart is positioned 8 inches from the point of maximum outward arc of the bow cutwater edge, and 5-1/4 inches from the bow headboard. The thickness and its underside taper near the ends is identical to that of all of the other thwarts on the canoe. All sides are carved flat and smooth, and all edges are sharp. The width measures 5/8 inch in the perforated midsection and 9/16 inch over the remaining length, except where two semicircular areas are carved out of both edges. These cutout areas, 3/8 inch from each inwale, measure 3/4 inch in length and 3/16 inch in depth. The width between each opposing pair of cutouts is 1/4 inch. The long midsection span between the two cutout areas measures 1-3/16 inches. In this central section, three holes 1/4 inch in diameter are drilled down the midline of the thwart. The holes lie 3/16 to 1/4 inch apart. The possible usages of the two holes which flank the central mast hole, as attachment points for mast guy lines, towing lines, and the halyard, are discussed later.

The mast thwart and the pair of endmost thwarts may have been fashioned with a slightly exaggerated width compared to the other dimensions of the canoe. This may have been done to imply the additional strength which was required for the intended heavy usage of these three thwarts. However, the perforated mast thwart which was installed on some Micmac rough-water sailing canoes, as shown in early photos, was also very substantial: each was fashioned from a carved or sawn plank about 6 inches wide by 2 inches thick.[11] These dimensions were found on mast thwarts of Micmac canoes about 22 feet long. Thwarts designed to support larger sailing rigs on large, heavily loaded fur trade canoes could very well have been more massive in some instances, resembling the mast thwart on the Varden model.

At the point where each thwart meets the inwale, a horizontal mortise slot is cut through the midline of the inwale, to receive the end of the thwart (Fig.185). Each slot is 1/16 inch wide, and 1/16 to 3/32 inch longer than the end of the thwart which was inserted into the slot. The narrow slits were probably pierced in the inwale with the tip of a knife. It is not possible to determine whether each mortise slot runs completely through the inwale, although this was the standard procedure. The slot is cut at a slight angle, with its inboard end lower than its outboard end. This compensates for the moderate outward angle of the inwale, since it angles outward in conjunction with the upper walls of the canoe. The angle of the slot permits the straight horizontal end of the thwart to fit into the slot in the angled inwale.

There is no visible evidence that a vertical wooden peg or nail was driven downward from the upper surface of the inwale through any of the thwarts to hold the end of the thwart firmly in the inwale. If such pegs were installed, they are now hidden from view beneath the gunwale caps and thwart lashings; no peg tips protrude from the bottom of the inwale at the thwart locations.

Each end of the thwart is lashed with split root to the combined inwale and outwale. On both the standard thwarts and the wide ones, the lashings run through two vertical holes in the end of the thwart, about 1/16 inch inboard from the inwale. The holes lie about 3/32 inch apart. On the standard thwarts, the holes are positioned about 1/16 inch from the sides of the thwart, while on the wide thwarts this span measures 1/8 to 3/32 inch. The neatly drilled or punched round holes are 1/16 inch in diameter, with sharp edges.

Below the junction of the thwart and the gunwales, there are three awl holes in the bark wall. These lashing holes, spanning 1/4 to 5/16 inch, extend from 1/32 to 5/32 inch beyond the outer edges of the thwarts. All of the previous information describing the lashing of the gunwale elements also applies to the lashing of the

thwarts. Of the three turns of root in each lashing group, sometimes two turns pass through one of the holes in the thwart and one turn passes through the other hole. In other instances, only one turn passes through each hole. However, three wraps of root usually appear on the exterior of the outwale, to fit into the pattern of the gunwale lashings. No turns of root lie beside the edges of the thwart. The thwarts were lashed at the same time as the gunwales. Their lashings fit into the series of lashing groups along the length of the gunwales.

All of the thwarts, except the endmost one at each end, are painted deep green over the entire span between the shoulders, on the upper surface and both sides. On the endmost thwarts, the green paint ends slightly inboard of the shoulders on the stern thwart and at the midpoint of the semicircular cutouts on the bow thwart (Figs. 184 and 178).

Sheathing

The dimensions of the sheathing strips or splints in the Varden canoe model are definitely not realistic portrayals of such strips on full size canoes; they are much too long, wide, and thick. The splints in the bow half of the canoe are about 15 inches long, while those in the stern half measure about 10 inches. They are 7/8 to 1-1/4 inches wide, and 1/32 to 1/16 inch thick. The surface on the flat faces is very smooth; it does not show the characteristic raised grain pattern which is often created when the strips are split out. Each splint has generally parallel edges for its full length; the edges are carved quite straight. No edges are thinned and feathered. The ends of the strips are not visible for observation of taper and shape.

The pattern of overlapping ends indicates that the splints were laid into the canoe in two groups: first at the bow end, and then at the stern end. The two groups are each made up of 5 strips. After the bow end group of splints had been laid in, the stern group was positioned so that the strips overlapped well the ends of the previously-laid group. Then the inboard ends of all of the stern splints were cut off squarely at the same point; all of these blunt ends are covered by one rib.

In laying in the sheathing, the first strip was positioned down the midline of the floor. It does not extend beneath the base of the headboard. The outboard tip of this central splint has a notch cut out in the midline, 3/16 inch wide by about 1/2 inch deep. The notch fits around the base of the headboard and the heel of the stempiece, with its legs extending past the headboard. After the midline strip was laid in, the successive splints were then added, out to and up the walls to a point 1/4 inch below the inwales. The slightly overlapping edge of each successive strip faces downward or inward, toward the midline of the canoe.

Toward each end of the canoe at the top of the walls, a gradually widening expanse of the upper bark wall is left exposed, not covered by the straight horizontal splints of sheathing where the gunwales curve upward (Fig. 183). These wider areas of exposed upper wall extend for about 2 5/8 inches inboard of the headboards. Beside the headboards, the area of each wall which is not covered by the sheathing strips measures about 7/8 inch in height.

The tips of the splints extend well outboard of the headboard; in some cases, they run to a point beside the cutwater area of the stempiece. No additional short sheathing strips were inserted outboard of the headboard to stiffen and support the bark cover at either of the high ends of the canoe. Nor was any other material, such as wood shavings or moss, stuffed into the ends of the canoe to support the bark cover.

Ribs

The canoe was built with a total of 35 ribs; the fourth one from the stern headboard is now missing. (The two endmost ribs of the bow do not appear in the photos, but they have been preserved.) Throughout much of the length of the canoe, they are spaced at intervals of 1/4 to 5/16 inch, measured edge to edge. Toward the ends of the canoe, the spacing widens slightly, to 5/16 to 3/8 inch.

The profile of the midsection ribs (Figs. 181 and 182) is composed of a narrow moderately rounded area in the midline of the floor, from which the bilge areas curve gradually upward; the upper sections flare moderately outward. The width of the rounded central area gradually reduces toward each end of the canoe; by the endmost ribs, the profile has become a narrow U form with sharp lower corners. The curve of the ribs reflects the body plan of the canoe (Fig. 165). They do not conform to the definite crease lines in the bark cover

which are visible on the exterior of the hull.

All of the ribs have generally the same dimensions, other than varying in length (Figs. 183 to 185). The midsection ribs in the area of the central thwart are 5-7/8 inches long, while those at the ends measure 5 inches. This includes the length of about 3/32 to 1/8 inch at each tip which is inserted behind the inwale (Fig. 176). The width of all of the ribs, about 1/4 inch, is maintained for nearly the full length of each rib; the tops do not taper as they extend outward and upward. The thickness of all of the ribs, about 3/32 inch, is likewise maintained for the full length of each rib to the inwales. Over the uppermost 5/16 to 3/8 inch of each tip, the width tapers quite suddenly, down to 1/16 inch at the squared-off tip (Fig. 186). The inboard surface at the end of the tip is carved in a sudden taper over the uppermost 3/16 inch span into a chisel shape with a sharp edge.

The flat inboard faces of the ribs do not show the characteristic raised grain pattern which is often created when the ribs are split out. The ribs are carved very flat and smooth on virtually all of their flat inboard surfaces as well as the edges. The two outboard edges are sharp, while the two exposed inboard edges are carved very round.

The narrow U-shaped profile of the endmost two or three ribs at each end of the canoe (Fig. 178) was produced by two rather sharp bends, one on either side of the midpoint. No groove or scoring across the ribs was apparently necessary to facilitate these bends.

In the midsection of the canoe, the ribs stand perpendicular to the horizontal plane of the keel line (Fig. 164). Toward the ends of the canoe, the keel line rises gradually, as the rocker of the bottom curves upward. In these end areas, each rib was installed perpendicular to the gradually rising keel line. Therefore, the tops of the ribs angle more and more inboard from their bases. The headboard stands exactly upright, in contrast to the angled ribs. Thus, the distance between the endmost rib at the stern (near its tips) and the upper area of the headboard is 1/2 inch; the distance between the base of this rib and the base of the headboard measures 1/4 inch. At the bow end, the endmost ribs are no longer in their original positions, so no comparable observations can be made concerning the placement of these ribs.

Painted Decoration

All of the painted decoration on the canoe appears to be original from the period of construction. No restoration is discernible on any of the painted surfaces.

The deep green decoration on the thwarts has been previously described. A number of other elements on the canoe are also painted (Fig. C-2). Along the full length of the gunwale caps, the upper surface is painted a dark slightly reddish brown. The reinforcement bark strip is painted a rather bright red.

A large area of solid deep green paint is found on each of the high end panels of both walls. The outer edge of the pigment extends in an even curve to within 3/16 to 1/4 inch of the original cutwater edge. From the edge, the straight bottom of the painted area angles inboard and downward in a gradual diagonal to the longitudinal main seam. This baseline, spanning 4-3/4 to 5 inches, begins 1-1/8 to 1-3/8 inches above the main seam at the cutwater edge. The inboard end of the green painted area has a crescent shape 1/4 inch deep. This concavity is outlined by a parallel stripe, 3/32 to 1/8 inch wide, of the same dark slightly reddish brown paint as that which was applied to the gunwale caps.

Miscellaneous Features
Seats

As in the case of the Royal canoe, there is no evidence on the Varden canoe which would indicate that it was ever fitted with permanent or temporary wooden seats.

Provisions for Sail and Cordelling Line

As has been pointed out in the description of the thwarts, the canoe is fitted with a permanent perforated thwart for sailing (Figs. 183 and 184). The third thwart from the bow has three rather large holes in its midline. When a sail was used, the upright mast would be positioned in the central hole; two guy lines running down from the mast would probably be tied to the two flanking holes. Additional guy lines may have run diagonally from the mast to the hole in the end thwart at the bow. One of the flanking holes in the mast thwart may also have been the lashing location for the end of the halyard, the line which hauled up or let down the sail; or this line may have extended back to one of the rear thwarts or to the hole in the end thwart at the stern (although this thwart was the seat for the stern paddler).

The author has studied in detail an original Alaskan Inuit model of a traditional sailing rig for an umiak (hide-covered boat) which was collected for the Smithsonian Institution in 1879.[12] The rigging for the mast is composed of two guy lines running down from the tip of the mast to positions flanking the base of the mast, as well as two additional guy lines which extend forward diagonally from the mast tip to the prow. The long halyard runs from the top of the mast to a location toward the stern. This surviving native sail rigging may well reflect that which was familiar to the builder of the Varden canoe model.

No mast step was installed on the Varden canoe beneath the perforated mast thwart. Thus, the base of the mast may have been placed into a drilled or carved indentation in a loose board laid down the midline, to step the mast. Or some other object may have been positioned beneath the base of the mast to protect the canoe. These temporary measures of mast stepping would leave no permanent evidence.

As was also mentioned in the thwarts description, there is a distinct possibility that the hole in the center of each end thwart may have served as an attachment point for cordelling (towing) lines. In addition, the two side holes which flank the central mast hole in the third thwart from the bow may also have served the same function, in addition to their role as possible guy line and halyard attachment points. Although the three perforated thwarts may have been made somewhat exaggerated in width, the heaviness of these thwarts implies their rather heavy usage.

Flags

No evidence can be found for the attachment of a flag at either the bow or the stern. But sufficient space exists outboard of both headboards into which a flag staff could have been inserted beside the stempiece (Fig 184). In addition, there is space between the midsection of each headboard and the adjacent walls in which a cord could have encircled the headboard to bind such a flag staff to either the outboard surface or the inboard surface of the headboard. There is also the possibility that the hole in the center of the end thwart at the bow may have served as a flag staff receptacle, as well as for attachment of towing lines and mast guy lines.

Bow/Stern Differences

The builder of the Varden canoe created a number of differences between the bow and the stern ends of the craft, which are listed below. Some of these features were installed for efficient performance of the canoe, while other of the differences between the two ends may be only coincidental.

A. The high end panel at the bow reaches a maximum height of 5-1/8 inches, compared to 5 inches at the stern.

B. The rocker of the bottom rises to the chin over a span of about 2-1/2 inches at the bow compared to about 3-1/2 inches at the stern. The rocker rises to a point 1/8 inch above the horizontal baseline at the bow chin, compared to 1/4 inch at the stern chin. Thus, the sternward rocker rises over a longer span and to a greater height than its bowward counterpart. On the Royal and Sault canoes, the span of the rising rocker is the same length at both ends, while on the Ojibwa canoe the bow span measures four inches longer than the stern span. The measurements of rocker from the full size canoes are to be relied upon much more than those from the models.

C. The positions and lengths of the thwarts create in the bow half a slightly broader beam and a more sudden taper near the end (at the gunwale level) compared to the narrower stern half, with its longer and more gradual taper.

D. All of the overlapping edges of the various bark panels (except one upper wall panel) are lapped so that the edge that is exposed on the exterior side faces sternward. This increases the efficiency and reduces the likelihood of catching on obstructions.

E. The green painted area on the upper surface of the endmost thwart at the bow is considerably shorter than the comparable painted area on its counterpart at the stern. (Neither of the headboards are decorated, and the painted decorations on the exterior are the same at both ends of the canoe.) Thus, the painted end thwart at the bow and the position of the perforated mast thwart well toward the bow end are the only quickly identifiable elements which denote which end of the craft is the forward end.

Construction Tools, Methods, and Materials

The Varden canoe was manufactured from the traditional forest materials of birchbark, wood, tree roots, and pine or spruce gum mixed with animal fat and pulverized charcoal. It was painted afterward with Euroamerican commercial paints.

The builder of the canoe used the typical array of tools normally employed in canoe manufacture during the nineteenth century. These include a knife or crooked knife, awl, pitch melting and applying implements, and paint containers and brushes.

In addition, the builder utilized a tool which has generally been considered less traditional in the canoe construction of that era. A gimlet (a small hand auger) appears to have been used instead of an awl or a knife tip to drill the untapered large holes of 1/4 inch diameter in the three wide thwarts. Due to the small size of the model, the lashing holes in the ends of the thwarts (1/16 inch diameter) and the neck of each headboard (1/32 inch diameter) were probably punched with a needle, a slender metal rod, or a length of heavy wire.

The small size also seems to have instigated the substitution of commercial thread for certain traditional materials on the canoe: dark brown thread with a diameter of 1/32 inch was used to represent split roots in the stitching of the longitudinal side seams and the cutwater edges, as well as in the binding of the tips of the gunwale elements and the necks of the headboards. The same thread used for the spiral wrappings around the laminated stempieces represents split roots or strips of basswood or cedar inner bark. Because of the small size of the model, the use of such thread ought not to be construed as evidence that commercial cordage was sometimes utilized in this period for comparable stitches and lashings on full size voyaging canoes.

If the thread is acknowledged to be representative of split roots and basswood inner bark, the building materials and techniques used in the construction of the Varden canoe model generally represent old traditional procedures, with the addition of a gimlet and commercial paints. Specific omissions and variations from traditional procedures have been mentioned in the course of the description. The traits of this fur trade canoe model, built without nails, appear to reflect the traditional manufacturing techniques which were used to build full size versions in the first third of the nineteenth century.

Condition

The bark cover and the wooden elements of the canoe are in sound, stable condition. However, the bark cover has several areas of breakage. The outermost edge of each cutwater edge is broken off, about 1/4 inch at the bow end and about 1/8 inch at the stern. In addition, a rather deep chip is missing from the edge just above the chin at the bow. At the stern end, the high end panel of the left wall has sustained major damage: a large area of the panel has broken away, extending from the cutwater edge inboard for 1 1/4 inches. The fourth rib from the stern end is now missing. A tiny hole runs through the sheathing strip and the bark bottom on the midline of the canoe just forward of the mast thwart. The hole is presumably related to an implement which was used to hold the canoe in a display at some point.

The original root wrappings remain intact in all of the gunwale and thwart lashings. The thread stitching which represents split root stitches on the cutwater edge is very heavily worn in many areas at both ends of the canoe. Most of the original sealant pitch remains, although it is cracked and missing in some areas; only traces remain on the two cutwater edges. The original painted decoration remains generally intact, although probably slightly faded; a number of areas of paint on the upper surfaces of the thwarts have flaked and worn off.

No repair or restoration procedures appear to have ever been carried out on the Varden canoe.

Notes: Varden Canoe

1. Adney and Chapelle, pp. 134-137, 149.
2. Ibid., pp. 134, 136.
3. Ibid., pp.134, 136.
4. Ibid., pp.158-168.
5. Ibid., pp. 28, 29, 102, 149.
6. Adney 1890, p. 674; Gidmark, p. 44.
7. Adney and Chapelle, p. 57.
8. Ibid., pp. 138, 141, 147.
9. Ibid., pp. 117-118, 124, 155-157.
10. Ibid., p.147.
11. Ibid., pp. 63, 65, 66.
12. Smithsonian, Anthropology Division, Artifact #38882.

The Catlin Canoe Model

Contents

The Catlin Canoe Model

Several features of the Catlin canoe suggest that this is an Ojibwa/Cree style of fur trade canoe, the Type B-2 style of the full size Ojibwa and Sault canoes. These traits include the extended height of the ends in relation to the overall size of the ends, the considerable degree of undercut in the profile of the ends, and the form of the interior curvature of the stempieces.[1]

The model represents the large size of fur trade canoe, the eight-place (nine-thwart) version. It was built much too short and too low in the midsection in relation to the height and breadth of its ends (Fig. 187). Due to this imbalance of proportion within the canoe, no overall scale can be determined. But the builder went to great lengths to build the individual components of the Catlin model in excellent, realistic detail. Therefore, it is an invaluable source of data on full size fur trade canoes, in spite of its inconsistent overall scale.

Overall Dimensions

Length: 48-1/2". (This large format enabled the builder to fashion the components in realistic detail.)

Distance between the outboard sides of the tips of the outwales: 35-1/8" (Fig. 188).

Distance between the inboard faces of the heads of the headboards: 34-1/2".

Depth at the midpoint, from the top of the gunwale caps to the top of the ribs on the floor: presently 4-3/4".

Height above the baseline: at the midpoint presently 5-1/4". Due to many years of storage and display of the canoe without proper support of the ends, the bow end has warped slightly upward and inboard, while the stern end has sagged slightly. The bow is presently 14-3/8 inches high, while the stern measures 13 inches. At the bow, the prow stands 1-1/4 inches above the gunwale tips, compared to 1/2 inch above the tips at the stern. These two heights above the gunwale tips are unchanged from the original construction. They indicate that the bow originally stood 3/4 inch taller than the stern. Based on this fact, the original overall height of the ends is projected to have been about 14 inches at the bow and 13-1/4 inches at the stern. In the

profile drawings in Figures 185, 195 and 197, the projected original form of the ends is portrayed.

Beam at the midpoint: presently 10-5/8" (Fig. 189).

Interior beam, inside the gunwales: presently 9-11/16".

Total girth around the hull, from gunwale top to gunwale top: 17-1/2".

The model was built with a rather low and very short midsection, compared to the size of its ends. The ends are high, like those of the full size Ojibwa canoe. When the ends are considered independently, rather than in conjunction with the stunted midsection, they appear to be generally in proper proportion with themselves, rather than exaggerated. The trait of extremely high ends has been discussed in the Ojibwa canoe description. The form of the high ends of the Catlin canoe is nearly the same as that of the full size Ojibwa canoe, although somewhat lower proportionately.

The beam is very broad in relation to the stunted length (Fig. 190). However, the removal of all of the thwarts from the canoe has allowed the gunwales to splay outward to a certain degree, increasing the beam even more than its original size. This splaying has also reduced the depth of the model. At present, the area of maximum exterior beam, measuring 10-5/8 inches, begins one inch forward of the exact midpoint of the canoe; it is maintained from that point forward for 3/4 inch. The beam tapers gradually to each end of the canoe from the ends of this 3/4 inch-long span. At the exact midpoint of the canoe, the beam is now 10-9/16 inches, 1/16 inch less than the maximum beam. Since all of the thwarts are now missing and some splaying of the gunwales has occurred, these present measurements of the beam do not represent the original form of the model. For illustration purposes, the ends of the canoe have been reduced in size in Figure 190 to match more closely the general scale of the overall length of the canoe.

Hull Form
Profile of the Bottom and Ends

Along the keel line, the horizontal distance of 23

Fig. 187. Catlin Canoe, with bow to right.

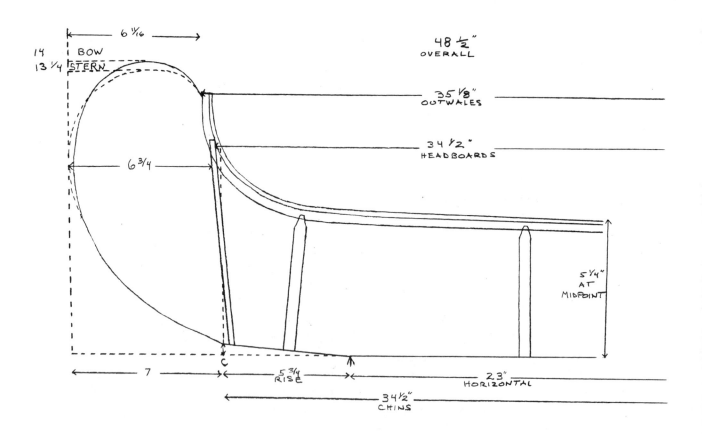

Fig. 188. Catlin Canoe: Hull profile and dimensions.

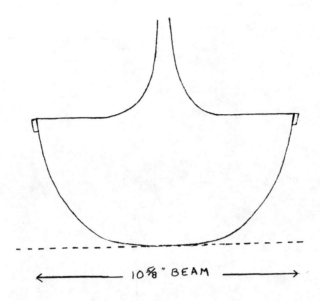

Fig. 189. Catlin Canoe: Body plan. The height of the end is left incomplete, since it was not built to the same scale as the midsection, which is shown.

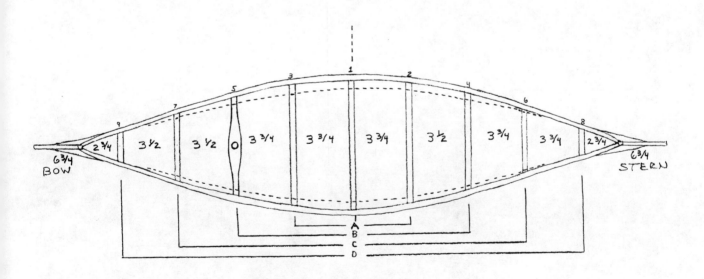

Fig. 190. Catlin Canoe: Hull form and thwart positions. Due to the removal of all of the thwarts, the gunwales have splayed outward to a degree. Broken lines suggest the possible original form of the interior. The shape of each thwart is conjectural.

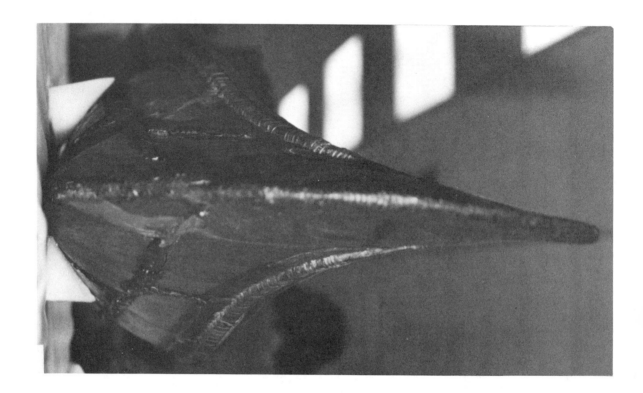

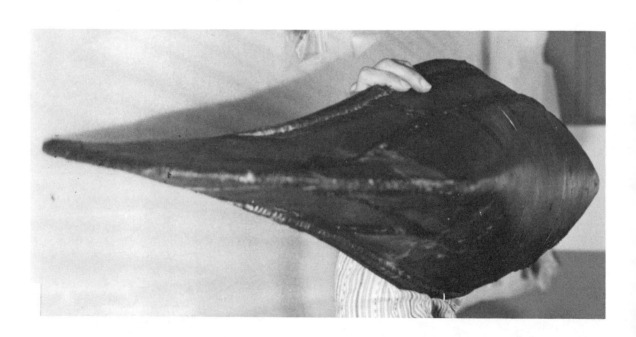

Fig. 191 (left). Catlin Canoe: End view of stern.
Fig. 192 (right). Catlin Canoe: Bottom view from stern.

Fig. 193. Catlin Canoe: Bottom view showing gore slits.

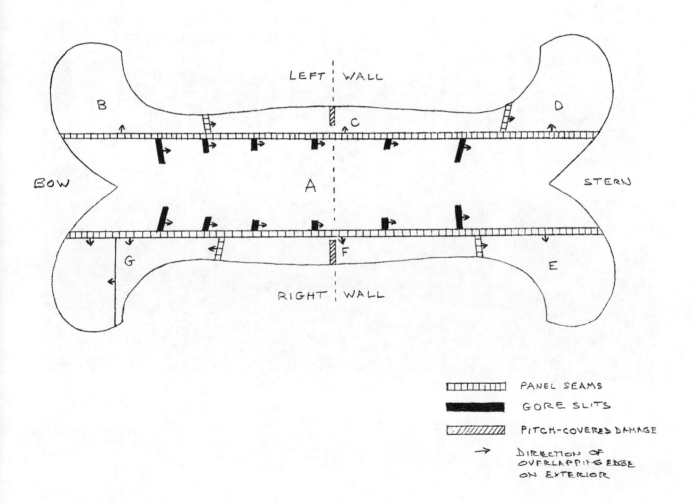

Fig. 194. Catlin Canoe: Bark cover.

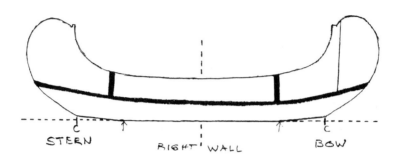

STERN   RIGHT WALL   BOW

Fig. 195. Catlin Canoe: Bark panels.

Fig. 196. Catlin Canoe: Back stitches of longitudinal side seam and spiral stitches of gore slits.

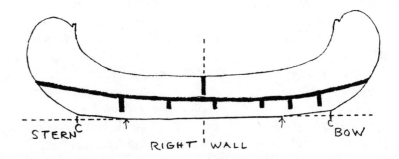

Fig. 197. Catlin Canoe: Gore slits and gunwale area repair.

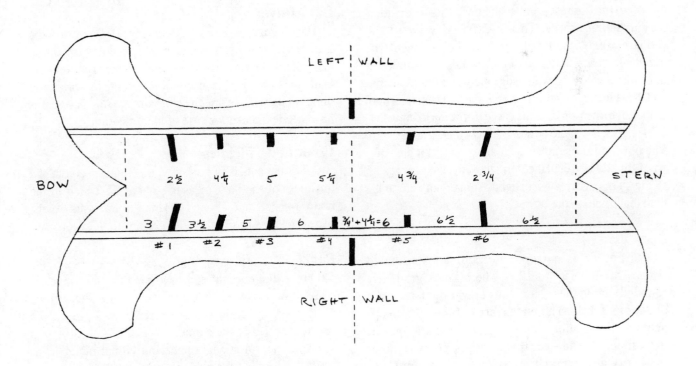

Fig. 198. Catlin Canoe: Gore slits and gunwale area repairs.

inches appears to lie exactly centered within the total length of the canoe (Fig. 188). This is the area which was built proportionately very short on the model. A span of 5-3/4 inches of moderate rocker (measured on the horizontal baseline) gradually rises from each end of the horizontal area, extending to moderately sharp chins. Thus, the total bottom length between the chins is 34-1/2 inches.

The chin at the bow presently stands 3/4 inch above the horizontal baseline, compared to 1/8 inch at the stern. As has been previously mentioned, the bow end of the canoe has warped slightly upward and inboard while the stern end has sagged down slightly. Assuming that both chins were originally built about the same in height, the original rocker at each chin is estimated to have been about 3/8 to 1/2 inch in height.

From the chin, each end extends 7 inches outboard (measured on the baseline) to the outermost point of the end. The cutwater edge at each end curves upward from the moderately sharp chin, beginning about 1/8 inch outboard of the foot of the headboard. At the bow, it arcs upward for 17-1/2 inches (measured on the curve) to the highest point of the end, with a considerably undercut profile. Then it curves downward and inboard over a span of 3-5/8 inches to meet the outwales. At the stern end (which stands 3/4 inch lower than the bow), the cutwater edge measures 18-1/2 inches and 2-3/4 inches in its comparable spans. The total length of the edge, measured on the curve from chin to outwales, is 21-1/8 inches at the bow and 21-1/4 inches at the stern. The bow end rises higher than the stern, but it arcs outward slightly less than the stern; thus, the greater breadth of the stern end creates a slightly longer cutwater edge than that found at the bow.

Body Plan

The bottom is narrow and moderately rounded (Figs. 189 and 191 to 193). The bilge is gradually rounded, while the upper walls are straight and flare outward slightly. The widest area of the bottom appears to lie at about the midpoint of the length of the canoe. To the eye, this width appears to taper gradually and symmetrically from the midpoint to each end of the canoe. The differences in the form of the two halves of the bottom of the canoe, as implied by the gore slits and discussed on page 281,

are not readily apparent to the eye.

The canoe was built in a form designed for moderately fast paddling with ample cargo capacity. Its features, including a narrow moderately rounded bottom and a gradually rounded bilge, a broad beam, a long slender taper to the ends, and a very narrow U form inboard of the headboards, contributed to its ease of paddling yet provided generous room for cargo.[2] The moderately rounded bottom of the canoe is much narrower and considerably more rounded than the standard cargo canoes of the period as portrayed by Adney, with their slightly rounded or nearly flat bottoms. In addition, the bilge area is considerably undercut and more gradually rounded. These features would reduce the floor space for cargo. The narrow U form which the canoe has near its ends would increase the roominess somewhat, yet reduce its speed, compared to a sharp V form as found on the Royal canoe. Thus, the Catlin model may represent a fast-paddling cargo canoe rather than a true express canoe, a version designed to carry a moderate amount of cargo but travel quickly.

Bark Cover

The diagram of the bark cover (Fig. 194) portrays the canoe as if it had been placed in an upside down position and flattened by unsewing the end seams. The drawing is not to exact scale or proportion, and the locations and dimensions of the seams are approximate. All of the seams have been widened for ease of identification.

Color and Thickness

All of the panels of bark are golden tan in color. The thickness of the bark measures about 3/32 inch in the bottom panels and about 1/16 inch in the wall panels. (The thickness profile is visible in several locations.)

Panels

On the diagram, the seams joining the seven panels of bark are marked with crosshatching. The arrows indicate the direction of the exposed overlapping edges on the exterior of the canoe.

Exact measurements of the individual panels cannot be taken, since the pitch covering the seams in many cases hides from view the exact positions of the edges of the panels. Only the portions of bark visible on the exterior of the canoe were measured, making no allowance for hidden overlaps. The measurement of the height of the side panels runs to the top of the outwale, where the bark was cut off flush with the top of the outwale. Each side panel was measured at its widest point.

Bottom Panel
A. 46 inches long x 9-3/4 inches wide

Left Wall Panels
B. 13-1/2" L x 10-1/4" W
C. 26-1/4" L x 3-1/2" W
D. 9-1/2" L x 9-1/2" W

Right Wall Panels
E. 12-1/4" L x 9-1/2" W
F. 22-1/2" L x 3-1/2" W
G. 14-1/2" L x 10-1/4" W

If the bark cover were flattened, as in the diagram, the maximum width in the midsection would be 16-3/4" (the total girth of the bark of the canoe) in the midsection. Near the ends, the width measures 12 inches more at the stern end and 13-1/2 inches more at the bow. The length would be 49-1/4" at the level of the gunwales. This total length of the side and end panels of each wall of the canoe is 3/4 inch longer than the length of the assembled canoe, because the side panels follow the curvature of the broadening midsection of the canoe, rather than a straight line down the midline.

The bottom of the canoe was made of one long panel of bark. Each wall was formed by joining two high end panels and one central panel (Fig. 195). In the profile drawing, the panels and seams are positioned exactly as they lie on the canoe.

The canoe builder did not create any weak points in the hull by positioning vertical wall seams directly opposite each other across the hull of the canoe. The seams which attach the side of the two high end panels at the bow (seams B-C and F-G) are offset from each other by one inch, while those at the stern (seams C-D and E-F) are offset from each other by 2-3/4 inches.

During the manufacture of the model, the forward portion of panel G (the high end panel in the right wall at the bow) was apparently either seriously damaged or found to be defective. Its forwardmost 5-1/2 inches (38 percent of the length of the panel) was replaced

with a supplemental piece. The piece of bark extends from the longitudinal side seam up to the top of the panel for the full height of 10-1/4 inches, and from a point one inch forward of the upswept tip of the outwale out to the cutwater edge. The lower and inboard edges of the replacement piece were slid inside the edges of the adjacent bottom panel and side panel, to be overlapped by those panels. The stitching of the replacement piece is described in the seams discussion .

The 5-1/2 inch-long replacement piece must have been installed in panel G after the panel had already been extensively lashed to the canoe; otherwise, the entire 14-1/2 inch-long panel could have been simply replaced. Apparently, only the minimum amount of damaged area was removed by the builder, to avoid having to relash the gunwales area of panel G and to minimize the amount of the longitudinal side seam which would need to be resewed.

The elaborate porcupine quill stitching of the cutwater edge of the bow matches exactly that of the stern. Therefore, the replacement piece appears to have been installed at the end of the bow during the building procedure, before the bow cutwater edge was stitched. Since the replacement seems to have taken place during manufacture rather than later, it is viewed as a building step rather than as a true repair, although the replacement of the bark piece was executed with typical repair techniques.

Sewn Seams

The original lashing material still survives in all of the sewn seams. No tucked-under ends of seam lashing roots are visible for observation and description, all of them having been finished on the hidden interior side. No evidence suggests that a batten strip of wood or root was incorporated into any of the seams for added reinforcement, either on the exterior or the interior side of the bark cover. Since the bottom of the model was constructed of a single panel of bark, the canoe has no bottom seams.

Gore Slits

The long span of bottom bark was laid out on the building bed, and the building frame was placed upon it. As previously discussed, this frame determined the general outline of the bottom of the canoe, particularly the shape of the taper toward the ends. The building frame was about as long as the bottom of the canoe, from chin to chin. After the bark was bent upward around the perimeter of the frame, a number of gore slits were sliced at intervals along the sides of the bottom panel. These slices ran from the edges of the bark inboard nearly to the building frame. At each of these slits, one edge of the bark was made to overlap the other edge, with the exposed edge on the exterior facing toward the stern. (No slice of bark was removed to create a seam with butting edges). Each overlapping edge was thinned considerably, so that the exposed edges of the gore slits are much lower and less prominent than all of the other overlapping seams on the canoe, which were not thinned.

The slits are stitched closed with split roots in a series of widely spaced spiral stitches, with one stitch per hole (Fig. 196). The portion of each stitch on the exterior side of the canoe is horizontal, while the connector portion running to the next stitch on the interior of the canoe is diagonal. The stitches run through pairs of awl holes which were produced by an awl with a square cross section. The holes lie about 3/16 to 1/4 inch from the overlapping edge of bark. The visible horizontal portions are about 5/16 to 3/8 inch long, and are spaced about 1/4 to 3/8 inch apart.

The lashing roots are 3/32 to 1/8 inch wide (about the same as the width of the awl holes) and about 1/32 to 1/16 inch thick. The sides and undersurface are flat, while the upper surface is rounded. The rounded side is the side of the root lashing which faces the exterior.

The gore slits in the bottom panels are positioned at relatively regular intervals; they extend from the midsection of the canoe out to a point well inboard of the stern chin and to a location relatively near the bow chin (Figs. 197 and 198). They are located on the profile drawing exactly as they lie on the canoe. Six slits are found in each wall; each has a mate exactly opposite it (having been cut on opposite sides of the building frame). Four pairs lie in the bow half of the canoe, and two pairs in the stern half. Whether intentionally or not, the builders installed the majority of the gore slits in the bow half at closer intervals than those in the stern half. In addition, those in the forward half extend considerably closer to the chin of the canoe than those in the rear half.

When the canoe is viewed in side profile, the gore slits extend downward from the longitudinal main seam, which runs the full length of each side of the canoe (Fig. 197). This seam curves upward toward each end moderately and gradually. The full length of all of the gore slits is visible in the profile view, running down the curved bilge area of the lower walls toward the rounded bottom.

The length of each gore slit cannot be measured exactly, since each is covered by a coating of pitch. This pitch extends inboard toward the midline of the canoe beyond the end of each slit. Measurement can be made of the length of each pitch strip, which implies the general length of the gore slit which it covers. The pitch strips in the midsection are shorter, becoming longer toward the ends of the canoe.

The pair of opposing gore slits which lies closest to the midpoint of the canoe (Fig. 198) is pair #4, positioned about 1-3/4 inches forward of the midpoint. The distance between the inboard tips of the two strips measures 5-1/4 inches. At pair #1, the pair of opposing slits closest to the bow end (3 inches from the chin), the distance between the tips measures 2-1/2 inches.

Since the gore slits were sliced from opposite edges of the bottom bark panel inboard nearly to the building frame, the distance between the opposing pairs of slits across the bottom of the canoe ought to reflect the shape and dimensions of the building frame. As previously mentioned, the strip of pitch sealing each gore slit extends further inboard than the actual end of the gore slit itself. Thus, the span measured between the tips of a pair of opposing pitch strips is shorter than the actual distance between the tips of the slits, and likewise shorter than the distance across the building frame. Also, the pitch was not applied to the gore slits in a precise fashion. The gore slits are presented in the diagrams according to the length of their pitch strips.

Some generalities may be deduced concerning the form of the building frame. It was presumably about 34-1/2 inches long, since that is the length of the bottom (the distance between the chins). The two opposing gore slits which were cut in the midsection of the canoe at a position 1-1/2 inches from the midpoint have a 5-1/4 inch span between their pitch strips. Thus, the area of maximum width of the building frame at its midpoint would have been a little wider than this span.

The maximum width of the building frame that was used to construct slightly rounded and nearly flat-bottomed fur trade canoes was often two-thirds of the interior beam of the gunwales.[3] In the case of the Catlin canoe, with its presently widened beam, this ratio would produce a measurement of about 6-1/2 inches. The original beam would probably have produced a figure that was quite close to the two-thirds ratio. The distance between the endmost pair of pitch strips, located 3 inches from the bow chin, measures 2-1/2 inches. This represents in a general manner the degree of taper from the wide midpoint of the building frame to its pointed ends at the chins. However, more detailed information regarding the form of the frame may be gleaned from evidence on the canoe.

At slit pair #6, at a point 6-1/2 inches inboard of the stern chin, the distance between the tips measures 2-3/4 inches. At the comparable point 6-1/2 inches inboard of the bow chin, at slit pair #2, the measurement is 4-1/4 inches. At slit pair #5, which lies 13 inches inboard from the stern chin, the distance between the tips measures 4-3/4 inches. At the comparable position 13 inches inboard from the bow chin (between slit pairs #3 and #4), the measurement is 5 to 5-1/4 inches.

The technique of determining the lengths of the gore slits (and thus the dimensions of the building frame) by examining the lengths of the strips of pitch is slightly imprecise, as has been discussed. But in spite of the necessarily imperfect technique, the above quoted measurements of the pitch strips imply that the bow half of the building frame remained rather broad for much of its length from the midpoint toward the chin, and then tapered rather suddenly to its tip at the chin. In comparison, the stern half of the frame appears to have tapered more gradually and evenly from the midpoint to the chin.

The slits in the bow half are in greater number and generally closer together than those in the stern half. This would seem to imply a greater upward curve of the rocker in the forward half than in the rear half of the canoe. No such difference can now be observed. However, over time the bow has warped upward slightly and the stern has sagged somewhat, so that it is not possible to observe now the exact form of the rocker as it was originally built.

Side Panels to Bottom Panels

After the gore slits were cut and stitched along the side edges of the bottom panel, the side panels were attached to the bottom panel. The seam connecting the side and bottom panels to each other is the prominent longitudinal seam which arcs across the full length of the canoe on each wall. When the side panels were attached to the bottom panel, a wider panel was installed at each end of both walls, to create the high upswept prow of the canoe.

The lower edges of the side panels are installed inside the edges of the bottom bark panel. Thus, the edges of the bottom panel are exposed on the exterior of the canoe, facing upward toward the gunwales (Fig. 196). It is not possible to determine on the two longitudinal side seams the amount of overlap of the bottom panel over the side panels, since the interior views which are available between several displaced sheathing strips do not show enough of these two seam areas to make a determination. Knife cuts in the side panels are found along the full length of the seam just above the exposed edge of bark; they indicate that the exposed edge of the bottom panel was trimmed off after the seam had been stitched.

The seams are sewn with split roots in a series of long back stitches, with one stitch per hole. The stitches, 7/8 to 1-1/8 inches long, are composed of the same awl holes and split roots as those described above for the gore slits, except that these holes and roots are slightly narrower, 1/16 to 3/32 inch in width. Each long main stitch extends forward for 7/8 to 1-1/8 inches on the exterior, and then runs through an awl hole. On the interior side, the root runs backward 1/4 to 3/8 inch, where it returns to the exterior side through an awl hole which lies just below the long span. Then another long main stitch extends forward. Each long span lies in a slightly diagonal position, with its stern end slightly higher than its bow end. The horizontal row of stitches lies with its higher stern stitch holes 1/8 inch below the exposed edge of the bottom bark panel, and its lower bow holes 3/16 to 1/4 inch below the exposed edge.

Side Panels to Side Panels

The seams which join the side panels to each other are all overlapped seams, with the panels overlapping each other about 1 to 1-1/2 inches. (The overlapping area is visible on the interior side above the upper-most sheathing strips, and on the exterior side in the pitched areas, where the overlap is noticeable due to the difference in the levels of the two bark panels.) In each side panel seam, the exposed edge which overlaps on the exterior faces toward the stern, with one exception (Fig. 194). On the right wall at the bow, the seam that joins the high end panel to its adjacent side panel (seam F-G) overlaps toward the bow. This forward-facing seam lies generally above the waterline, and thus would not impede the forward movement of the canoe; but it could still receive abrasion from objects during use of the canoe. There appears to be no logical explanation for this feature; it probably was an oversight of the builder during construction.

The only other overlapping edge which faces toward the bow is found in the seam which joins the replacement piece of bark to panel G at the bow end of the right wall. This seam also lies generally above the waterline.

The seams which join the side panels to each other may not have been stitched on the model. These seams are rather thickly covered with sealant pitch. No raised areas of stitches are reflected in the surface of this pitch, and in places where the pitch has broken away, the exposed bark panel areas contain no stitches. Such a lack of stitches in these wall seams would not have been found in full size craft. But the model was built to serve as only a display; therefore, the builder may have omitted the root stitches from these two panel seams on each wall.

Replacement Section Seams

The replacement section at the forward end of panel G in the right wall at the bow was stitched to both the bottom panel and the main portion of panel G. The stitches which join its bottom edge to the bottom panel, along the longitudinal side seam, presumably match the back stitches of the rest of this main side seam. The seam area was damaged at some point, and was restored with a plaster material which hides these stitches from view.

The spiral stitches which join the replacement section to the rest of panel G are the same in nearly all respects as those which lash the gore slits in the bottom panel. The only difference involves the placement of the awl holes in relation to the overlapping edge of

bark: they do not straddle the seam equally on each side. As the replacement section lies under both the bottom panel and panel G, its awl hole lies immediately adjacent to the overlapping edge of bark, while its neighboring hole lies 5/16 to 3/8 inch inboard of the edge of bark.

Seam Sealing

All of the seams on the canoe were coated with charcoal-blackened melted pitch or gum from spruce or pine trees, of the same description as the gum found on the Royal canoe. The remaining original pitch is now very brittle; it does not indent under thumb pressure.

Apparently no coating of gum was applied to the seams on the interior side of the canoe. The interior areas which are visible between several displaced sheathing strips indicate that the longitudinal side seams and the gore slits were not pitched on the interior side.

All of the seams were sealed with pitch on the exterior of the canoe. The swaths of melted gum which cover the longitudinal main seams are 5/8 to 1 inch wide, while those sealing the gore slits, the wall panel seams, and the gunwale area repairs are 3/4 to 7/8 inch in width. The pitch which seals the wall panel seams and the gunwale area repairs extends up to the lower edge of the reinforcement bark strip. The swath which seals the vertical seam of the replacement bark piece in panel G covers only the lower half of the seam, up to a point well above the waterline. The pitch is thickly applied to all seams, up to 1/8 inch thick in some areas.

Exterior Hull Surface

The discussion concerning the disruptions in the smooth, even surface of the bark cover of the Royal canoe also applies to the Catlin canoe as well. Overlapping panel edges and applications of sealant pitch up to 1/8 inch thick have produced seams which stand out from the flat surface of the hull. In addition, one wall panel seam overlaps toward the bow, as well as the seam of the replacement section.

Damage and Repairs

One vertical crack is found at the midpoint of each wall, extending downward from the gunwales (Figs. 187 and 194). These are locations where the edges of the panels were accidently split during the building of the model. The breaks extend straight downward from the top edge of the bark wall for 2-3/8 or 2-1/2 inches, ending at a point 1/2 or 5/8 inch above the exposed edge of the bottom panel.

The topmost 7/16 inch span of each crack is held firmly in place between the lashed inwale and outwale. The portion that lies behind the reinforcement bark strip below the outwale, about 9/16 to 5/8 inch long, is presumably not sewn. (This area is not visible.)

Beneath the reinforcement strip, the lowest 1-5/16 or 1-7/16 inches of each break is exposed. This span is not stitched closed; it is only sealed with blackened pitch. (The pitch has cracked along the full length of each break, affording a clear view of the breaks and their lack of stitches.) These areas of damage would have always been stitched on a full size canoe; the use of this canoe exclusively for display purposes allowed the builder to omit the root lashings from these two areas of damage.

Gunwale Elements

All of the gunwale elements are angled slightly outward, at the same degree of outward flare as the topsides of the bark walls to which they are attached (Fig. 199).

Inwales

The total length of the inwale on the curve is about 51 inches. This is made up of the 38 inches which is exposed between the headboards plus about 6-1/2 inches at each end which lies outboard of the headboards. The overall length is about 4-1/2 inches longer than the outwale, since the ends of the inwale extend out to nearly the outer edge of the stempiece (Fig. 204). In the midsection, the inwale strip is 3/16 inch wide across the top and 3/8 inch deep (Fig. 199). The bottom surface is only 1/16 to 3/32 inch across, since the lower outboard edge is carved off into a beveled surface to produce a space into which the tips of the ribs fit. All of the midsection dimensions are maintained for the full length of the inwale, without tapering. All surfaces of the inwale are carved flat and smooth, and the edges are sharp. At the tips, the ends are cut off sharply.

In constructing the Catlin model, the builder omitted the midsection span in which the gunwales would

run nearly horizontally over much of the length of the canoe and then begin to rise very gradually toward the ends (Fig. 195). From the midpoint of the canoe, the gunwales curve up moderately toward the ends. Ten inches from the midpoint, at a point 1 inch inboard of the second thwart from each end, the height of the inwale has risen 1/2 inch. Over the following span of 6-1/4 to 6-1/2 inches to the headboard, the inwale curves upward much more strongly, rising another 3 inches in height. About 1 inch inboard of the headboard, the inwale diverges from the outwale; it extends about 7-3/4 inches further, while angling gradually upward (Fig. 204). The tips of the inwales extend to nearly the cutwater edge of the stempiece, ending at the same height as the tips of the outwales. The positions of the inwales outboard of the headboards are clearly indicated on the exterior of the bark end panels by the warpage of the bark around the inwales. In addition, at the bow end the bark deck is now missing and the headboard is very loosely attached, offering a clear view of the inwales to nearly their tips inside the bark walls.

To facilitate the bending of the gradual upward curve of the ends of the inwale, one split was made in the ends, to produce two lamination layers. The slit extends inboard from the tip of the inwale for 6-3/4 to 8-1/4 inches, to a point beside the headboard or up to 1-1/2 inches inboard of the headboard. The lashings which bind the inwale to the outwale cover the area where the lamination slit ends. These lashings prevent the slit from splitting further inboard.

Over the full length of the lamination splits, the ends of the inwale are spirally wrapped with commercial string 1/32 inch in diameter. The string, originally light tan in color, is now a dark golden tan in areas where it was exposed. The original hue has remained in areas which were sheltered within the interior of the ends of the canoe. The spiral wrappings, at intervals of 1/4 to 5/8 inch, extend from the tips of the inwale to a point about 2 inches inboard of the headboards. Two or three rather widely spaced wraps are visible in the area inboard of each headboard.

The inwale fits into a notch which is cut into the side of each headboard (Fig. 200). Two turns of split root bind the inwale to the headboard at the notch. The tips of the inwale are also firmly bound in place. At the junction of the pair of converging inwale tips and the stempiece, two figure-eight wraps of the same com-

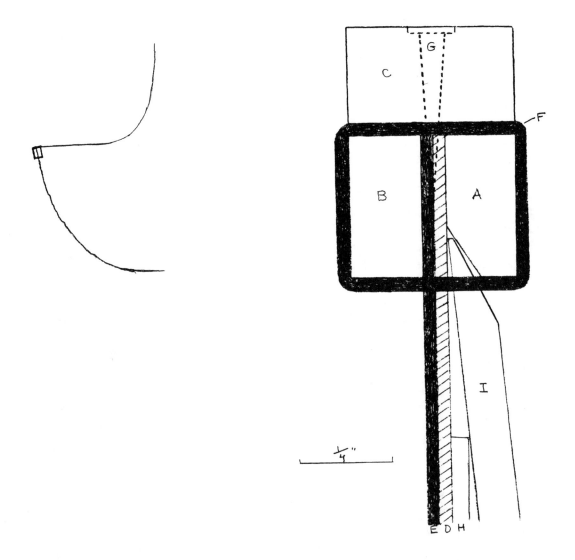

Fig. 199. Catlin Canoe: Cross section of gunwales. A. inwale, B. outwale, C. gunwale cap, D. bark wall, E. reinforcement bark strip, F. root lashings, G. nail, H. sheathing strip, I. rib.

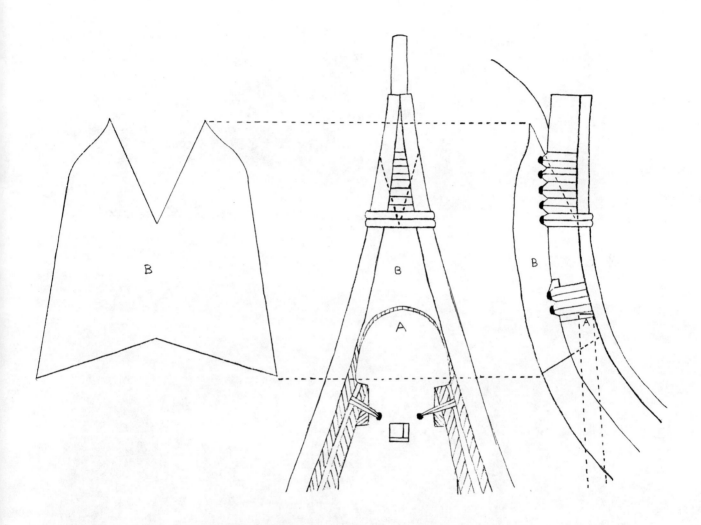

Fig. 200. Catlin Canoe: Bark deck piece and lashings of gunwale ends. A. headboard, B. bark deck piece.

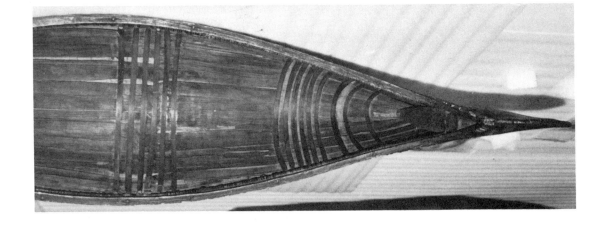

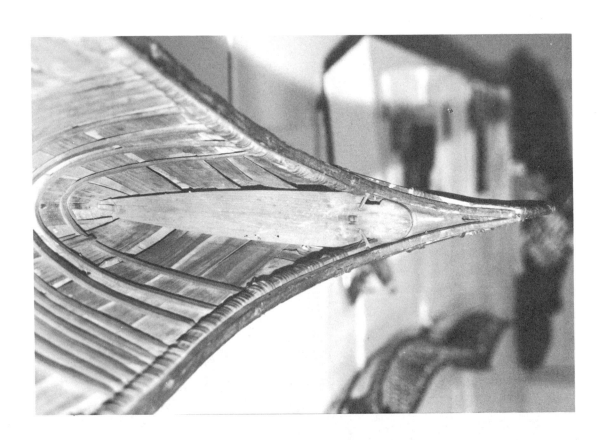

Fig. 201 (left). Catlin Canoe: Interior view of stern half.
Fig. 202 (right). Catlin Canoe: Interior view of stern end, showing sheathing, ribs, headboard, bark deck piece, and gunwale ends.

Fig. 203. Catlin Canoe: Thwart and gunwale lashings, sheathing, and ribs. Arrows indicate former positions of two thwarts. Hand-forged nail of gunwale cap is visible at upper right.

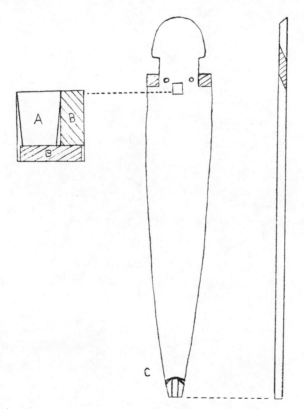

Fig. 205. Catlin Canoe: Headboard. A. stempiece, B. wedges, C. stempiece string lashings.

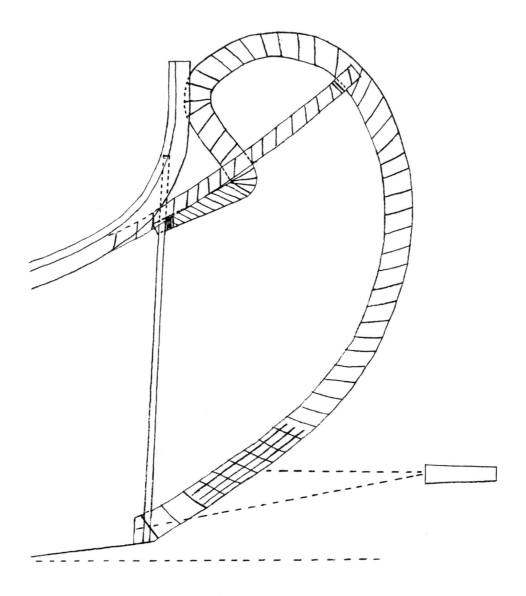

Fig. 204. Catlin Canoe: End frame unit. All wrappings of stempiece and inwales are shown.

mercial string encircle the pair of inwales, squeezing them tightly against the stempiece. The very tips of the inwales are not visible, so it is not possible to determine if they are either pegged to the stempiece or lashed through its lamination layers.

The inwale is not pegged or nailed to the outwale; this is another trait of this model which is not normally found on full size craft. (Spaces between root wraps in the gunwale lashings, as well as a number of broken and missing root wraps, afford many views of the gunwales beneath the lashings; no pegs or nails are hidden there.) Split root lashings bind the two gunwale elements together, with the top edge of the bark wall and the strip of reinforcement bark sandwiched between them.

Outwales

The total length of the outwale on the curve is 46-1/2 inches, measured on the outside of the curve. In the midsection, it is 3/16 inch wide across the top and 3/8 inch deep (Fig. 199). In both width and depth, the outwale matches the dimensions of the inwale. Thus, the top and bottom surfaces of the two strips match. The midsection dimensions are maintained over the full length of the outwale, without tapering. All surfaces of the outwale are carved flat and smooth, and all edges are sharp. At the tips, the ends are cut off sharply. The description of the painted decoration on the outwales is found on page 303.

As noted in the inwale description, the midsection span where the outwale would usually run nearly horizontally over much of the length of the canoe and then begin to rise very gradually toward the ends was omitted. From the midpoint of the canoe, the outwale curves up moderately toward the ends. Ten inches from the midpoint, at a point 1 inch inboard of the second thwart from each end, the height of the outwale has risen 1/2 inch. Over the next span of 6-1/4 to 6-1/2 inches to the headboard, it curves upward much more strongly, rising another 3 inches in height. About 1 inch inboard of the headboard, the outwale diverges from the inwale; it sweeps upward in a strong curve to reach a completely vertical position at the tips (Fig. 204). The ends of the outwale sweep upward above the outboard side of the headboards for 4 inches on the curve. The tip reaches a point 1-1/4 inches below the maximum height of the prow

of the canoe at the bow, and 1/2 inch below the maximum height at the stern. Both of the outwale tips end at the same height above the horizontal baseline; the bark end panel at the bow rises 3/4 inch higher than the panel at the stern.

At the bow end, the ends of the outwales and gunwale caps presently curve inboard well past the vertical position (Fig. 187). (The ends of these two elements are original on the left wall and restoration replacements on the right wall.) It appears that this excessive degree of bend (past the vertical position) is the result of warpage rather than the original form, since the corresponding gunwale elements at the stern end sweep upward to an exactly vertical position. The entire bow end of the craft has warped slightly upward and inboard.

To facilitate the bending of the upward curve and the extreme upsweep at the tips, the same lamination procedure was done on the outwales as on the inwales: three slits were made, to produce four lamination layers, each about 3/32 inch thick. The lamination slits extend from the tips inboard for a distance of about 8-1/2 inches, to a point about 4 inches inboard of the headboards. (This is about 2-1/2 to 4 inches inboard of the point at which the inwale lamination slits end.) The lashings which bind the outwale to the inwale cover the area where the three lamination slits end. These lashings prevent the slits from splitting further inboard. The four lamination layers are cut off at the tip of the outwale to form a generally square, horizontal end.

The tips of the two converged outwales are joined to each other by a series of wrapped root lashings (Fig. 200). There is no wooden or bark wedge inserted between the tips of the two strips to assist in making the lashings tight. Nor are the tips pegged or nailed to each other. The split root lashing material is 1/16 to 3/32 inch wide and 1/32 to 1/16 inch thick, with flat sides and undersurface and a rounded upper surface. The lashings, beginning 3/4 inch below the tips, wrap in eight adjacent spiral turns around the two joined outwales, covering a distance of 3/4 inch. The eight wraps run through four holes in the adjacent bark wall, two turns per hole, passing through the stempiece inside the bark wall as well.

One inch below these upper outwale wraps, at a point immediately above the headboard, an additional four or five root wraps bind the outwale to the bark wall. The root passes through two holes in the wall, two turns per hole. In these latter lashings, the beginning of the root is inserted into the most outboard of the outwale lamination slits, while the other end of the root is inserted between the outwale and the bark wall. This lower set of lashings does not encircle the inwale (which has diverged considerably by this point) nor do they pass through the stempiece. The split root lashing material is 1/16 to 3/32 inch wide and 1/32 to 1/16 inch thick, with flat sides and undersurface and a round upper surface.

The triangular area between the two converging outwales is covered by a bark deck (Figs. 200 and 202). The piece of bark, of the same 1/16 thickness as the bark of the walls, is in a pyramidal form with about a 3 inch base and 3-1/2 inch sides. A broad triangular area has been removed from the base of the deck piece; its upper two sides measure 1-5/8 inches. At the narrower upper end of the deck, a long triangular notch measuring 1-1/2 inches on each long side has also been cut out. The tip of this notch fits over the inboard curve of the stempiece. The gunwale lashings completely covered this upper notch originally. The deck piece extends vertically down to the headboard; its ends extend over the edge of the bark walls so that they are visible outboard of the outwales for 1/2 to 5/8 inch. The inboard edge of the deck butts tightly against the end of the adjacent gunwale reinforcement bark strips. Each end of the deck is cut in such a manner that it appears to be a continuation of this reinforcement strip. The sharply pointed tips of the deck piece angle upward and outward from the outwale for about 5/8 inch, reaching to within 1/8 inch of the stitches of the cutwater edge.

The bark deck piece is held in place by the pressure of the outwales, which squeeze the bark down against the bark end panels. In addition, all of the root lashings which bind the ends of the outwales and the gunwale caps to the hull pass through the perimeter of the bark deck as well. The description of the painted decoration on the edges of the deck is found on page 303.

The bark deck fills all of the gunwale area outboard of each headboard (Fig. 201). Thus, there is no possibility that a flag staff could have been inserted adjacent to the outboard side of the headboard at either the bow or the stern. However, there is enough space between the body of the headboard and the adjacent walls for the wrapping of a cord around the headboard, to bind a flag staff to the inboard face of the headboard, at both the bow and the stern.

Gunwale Caps

The total length of the gunwale cap is 43-3/4 inches, measured on the inside of the curve. (This is 2-3/4 inches shorter than the outwale, which was measured on the opposite side of the curvature.) In the midsection, the cap is 7/16 inch wide by 1/4 inch deep (thick) (Fig. 199). Toward the ends, the width and depth of the cap taper very gradually, to a width of 1/4 inch and a depth of 1/8 inch at the tips. All surfaces are flat and smooth, and all edges are sharp. At the tips, the ends are cut off sharply.

The combined width of the inwale (3/16 inch) and the outwale (3/16 inch) is 1/16 inch less than the width of the gunwale cap. But the bark wall and the reinforcement bark strip which are sandwiched between the inwale and the outwale add about 3/32 to 1/8 inch more of thickness to the combined gunwales. Also, the degree to which the inwale and outwale were squeezed against the bark and each other when they were all lashed together varies in different areas. Thus, the gunwale cap is about 1/16 inch narrower than the top of the gunwale unit (inwale, bark layers, and outwale) in most areas of the midsection. The width of the cap tapers toward the ends, while the width of the combined gunwale unit does not taper. Since the cap is aligned generally down the midline of the gunwale unit for its full length, the area of each edge of the unit that is exposed gradually increases toward the ends. Near the headboards, up to 3/32 inch is exposed on each edge (Figs. 201 and 202). Outboard of the headboard, where the inwale has diverged, the outwale is completely covered by the cap.

The gunwale cap conforms to the curvature of the outwale for its entire length. From the midpoint of the canoe, the cap curves up moderately toward the ends. Ten inches from the midpoint, at a point 1 inch inboard of the second thwart from each end, the height of the cap has risen 1/2 inch. Over the next span of 6-1/4 to 6-1/2 inches to the headboard, it curves upward much more strongly, rising another 3 inches in height. About

1 inch inboard of the headboard, the cap sweeps upward in a strong curve to reach a completely vertical position at the tips. The ends sweep upward above the outboard side of the headboards for 4 inches on the curve, ending exactly at the tips of the outwales. The tip reaches a point 1-1/4 inches below the maximum height of the prow of the canoe at the bow, and 1/2 inch below the maximum height at the stern. Since the vertical tips of the outwales and caps end 1/2 and 1-1/4 inches below the tops of the prows, the high bark ends would rest on the ground rather than on the gunwale tips when the canoe was overturned on its side as a shelter. No splits were made in the ends to facilitate the bending of the upward curve and the extreme upsweep of the ends of the cap.

From headboard to headboard, the gunwale caps are attached to the inwale and outwale by eight downward-driven tacks in each wall (Fig. 203). The hand-forged tacks have irregularly round heads about 1/8 to 5/32 inch in diameter, with irregularities in their shape and indentations in their perimeters. On some of the tacks, the heads are very flat, while others have slightly domed heads. The heads are generally about 1/16 inch thick, but some are thinner and some are up to 3/32 inch thick; each head has irregularities within its thickness. The lengths of the shanks cannot be determined, but they are shorter than the 3/4 inch total thickness of the gunwale unit: no tips protrude through the undersurface of the inwales or outwales. In nearly every instance, the wide shanks have produced a lengthwise crack in the gunwale cap, extending both forward and rearward from the nail hole.

The tacks were driven so that their heads lie nearly flush with the upper surface of the caps. They are positioned generally along the midline of the caps, rather than alternating toward one edge and then the other so that they enter alternately the inwale and then the outwale. The tacks quite often are positioned so that they enter the inwale or outwale by passing through the gunwale root lashings, rather than in the spaces between the lashings.

The spacing of the tacks reflects the areas of each cap which were subjected to the greatest degree of bending. In the midsection, where the cap curves outward considerably, the tacks are positioned at intervals of 3-1/2 to 4-1/2 inches. As the cap straightens

toward each end of the canoe, the intervals widen to 5 to 6-1/4 inches. In the areas where the tips begin their upward sweep toward the headboards, the intervals again reduce to 3 to 3-1/4 inches. The row of tacks along each cap ends 1 to 3 inches inboard of each headboard. Outboard of the headboards, no tacks fasten the upswept caps to their outwales.

The tips of the two converged caps are joined to each other and to the tips of the two outwales by a series of wrapped root lashings (Fig. 200). No wedge is inserted between the tips of the caps to assist in making the lashings tight. Nor are the tips of the converged caps pegged or nailed to each other. Beginning 1-1/2 inches below the tips of the caps (about halfway between the tips and the headboard), two turns of split root lie adjacent to each other immediately below the lashings which bind the tips of the outwales together. They encircle both pairs of outwales and caps, running through one hole in the adjacent bark wall and passing through the stempiece inside the bark wall as well. These cap lashings, spanning about 3/16 inch, are the only lashings which bind the caps to the gunwale unit. The lashing roots are 1/16 to 3/32 inch wide and 1/32 to 1/16 inch thick, with flat sides and undersurface and a rounded upper surface. The description of the painted decoration on the gunwale caps is found on page 303.

Reinforcement Bark Strips

The reinforcement strip of birchbark doubles the thickness of the upper edge of the bark wall where it is attached to the gunwales. Before the inwale and outwale were lashed together onto the upper edge of the bark wall, the reinforcement strip was inserted between the bark wall and the outwale (Fig. 199). Its top edge, like that of the bark wall, was cut off at the level of the top of the inwale and the outwale. When the awl holes were pierced through the wall and the lashings were wrapped around the gunwales, the bark strip was pierced and lashed as well.

The strip, made of bark about 1/16 inch thick, runs from headboard to headboard (Fig. 187). It extends down 9/16 to 5/8 inch below the lower edge of the outwale along the full length of the strip, without tapering toward the ends. The lower edge of the reinforcement strip generally runs parallel to the lower edge of the outwale for the full length; it was cut somewhat irregularly and with a moderate degree of undulation. The segments making up the strip were cut to their present width before being installed onto the canoe. Each of the segments has a slightly different width compared to the adjacent segment; this would not be the case if they had all been trimmed to size after being installed onto the canoe. In addition, there are no knife cuts or scratches on the bark wall panel immediately adjacent to the lower edge of the strip, as would be produced if the strip were trimmed off against the unprotected wall (unless a protective piece of bark were first inserted against the wall to absorb the knife cuts).

Each reinforcement strip is made up of seven pieces of bark. The longer segments in the midsection measure 8-1/2 to 12 inches. In addition to these long strips, the span beneath the outwale where it curves upward to the headboard is made up of shorter pieces at each end, 3-1/2 to 5 inches long.

The individual pieces of bark which make up the reinforcement strip overlap each other at their ends, from 1/4 to 3/4 inch. The exposed overlapping edges face toward the bow on the left wall and toward the stern on the right wall. The pieces are not attached at their ends to each other or to the canoe wall in any manner.

The bark deck piece is bent down on either side between the bark hull and the outwale, and is trimmed to appear to be a continuation of the reinforcement bark strip. It is butted against each end of the strip outboard of the headboard on each wall (Fig. 200). This deck piece, 3-1/2 to 4 inches long, extends beyond the outwale for 9/16 to 5/8 inch. Its edge is cut parallel to the outwale to match the lower edge of the bark reinforcement strip. The description of the painted decoration on the reinforcement bark strips and the bark deck ends is found on page 303.

Gunwale Lashings

The upper edge of the bark wall is sandwiched between the inwale, the reinforcement bark strip, and the outwale (Fig. 199). It is cut off flush with the top surface of the inwale and the outwale. The four layers of bark and wood are lashed together with spaced groups of root lashings from headboard to headboard (Fig. 203).

Each lashing group normally runs through three holes in the bark wall. The holes, generally round in shape, have diameters of 1/16 to 3/32 inch, with irregular edges. The holes were made by an awl with a triangular or square cross section, which was inserted from the exterior side of the wall and twisted.

The holes are spaced 3/32 to 3/16 inch apart. Each row of holes, spanning 5/16 to 3/8 inch, lies immediately below the lower edge of the outwale. The split root lashing material is 1/16 to 3/32 inch wide and 1/32 to 1/16 inch thick, with flat sides and undersurface and a rounded upper surface.

Two basic patterns of root wrappings were utilized to lash the gunwales. The main difference between the two patterns involves the presence or absence of a horizontal connector stitch between the lashing groups. The two patterns are intermingled along both gunwales.

The majority of the lashing groups are not connected to the adjacent groups; in these cases, each group begins and ends independently. To lash the gunwales in this typical pattern, a length of split root was drawn nearly to its end through the first hole in the set of three holes. The short end of the root was drawn up on the exterior side to the top surface of the combined gunwales and inserted down between two of the sandwiched layers of wood and bark. Then, in a simple spiral stitch, the long end of the root passed over the top of the inwale and outwale and through the second hole. The root passed around the combined inwale and outwale a second time, and through the third hole. Then the root encircled the gunwales a final time, and passed once again through the third hole.

To finish off the root securely before starting a new group of lashings, the end of the root was run horizontally back on the interior side to and through hole #2 (Fig. 203). Where it emerged on the exterior, the tip was cut off rather short. It was held firmly in place by the turn of root that had previously been run through the hole. Several such root endings are visible in Figure 203. Sometimes, rather than running the end of the root through hole #2, a new hole was pierced slightly below hole #2 or #1 to receive the end of this horizontal back stitch.

Occasionally, the lashings of this style were begun by passing the short end of the root beside the inwale, rather than the outwale, before insertion into the gunwale sandwich. This procedure caused the horizontal back stitch at the end to lie on the opposite (exterior) side of the canoe, beneath the outwale.

In the second style of gunwale lashings, the groups of root wraps are joined by a horizontal connector stitch 1/8 to 3/16 inch long. This occurs eleven times on the right wall and eight times on the left wall. The pattern begins either the same as the pattern described above, in the sandwiched layers of the top of the gunwales, or via a horizontal connector stitch from the previous group of lashings. In either case, the root makes one turn through each of the holes and around the gunwales, in the same manner as those in the previously described pattern. After the root has wrapped for the fourth time around the gunwales, when it emerges on the exterior side it passes behind the lower portion of the fourth stitch, to maintain its tension. Then the root spans horizontally across to the next set of lashing holes on the exterior side beneath the outwale.

Very occasionally, this horizontal connector stitch spans across between two groups of lashings on the interior side of the canoe, beneath the inwale, in the space in which the tip of a rib is inserted. In these cases, the rib tip usually covers the horizontal stitch; but in a few instances the rib tip was inserted beneath the connector stitch.

Each typical group of lashings is composed of four turns of root around the gunwale, covering a length of 5/16 to 3/8 inch of the gunwale. Where the narrowest roots were utilized, five turns were sometimes found, and where the widest roots were used, the group often includes only three turns. An interval of 1/8 to 3/16 inch separates each group of lashings. The endmost group of lashings at each end of each gunwale lies about one inch inboard of the headboard, where the inwale and outwale begin to diverge from each other.

The thwarts are bound into the gunwales with root lashings that fit into the pattern of the gunwale wrappings. Some of the thwart lashing groups are joined to the adjacent gunwale lashing groups by connector stitches, while others begin and end independently.

Stempieces

The stempiece is visible in several areas of the canoe (Fig. 204). Its heel is visible where it projects into the interior of the canoe at the base of the headboard. Much of the outboard edge is visible in the lower cutwater edge, where for the most part the sealant pitch is now gone. At the bow end, the bark deck outboard of the headboard is missing and the headboard is loosely attached; this affords a clear view of virtually all of the stempiece as well as the ends of the inwales. The laminated upper end of the stempiece can be seen where it projects through the headboard.

The curvature of the stempiece is implied in several areas. The curve of the cutwater edge of the canoe, from chin to outwales, outlines the entire outer curved portion of the stempiece. Also, the stempiece is lashed to the outwales and gunwale caps just below their tips.

The total length of the stempiece is about 27 inches, measured on the outboard edge. The heel of the stempiece projects 3/16 inch inboard from the inboard surface of the base of the headboard. At its end, it is 3/4 inch deep (in height), with sharp corners and edges. The inboard edge is 3/16 inch thick, while the outboard edge is 1/8 inch thick. This produces a tapered cross section which narrows toward the cutwater edge. All surfaces of the heel are carved flat and smooth. The heel angles upward slightly as it extends inboard to the headboard. It does not have carved notches for the legs of the headboard to straddle.

On the outboard side of the base of the headboard, the same tapered cross section, with thicknesses of 1/8 and 3/16, is maintained for the full length of the stempiece. The 3/4 inch depth is maintained until the very sharp bend before it tapers. All surfaces are flat and all edges are sharp.

Beginning about 1-3/4 inches outboard of the headboard, at a point about 2-1/4 inches from the tip of its heel, the stempiece is divided by three splits into four lamination layers, each about 3/16 inch thick. The lamination splits extend through the complete upper length of the stempiece to its end. (In the Figure 204 diagram, they are portrayed only in the lowest portion.)

The entire length of the stempiece, from its heel to the upper end, is spirally wrapped with the same commercial string as that which spirally wraps and binds the laminated tips of the inwales. The string, light tan in color and 1/32 inch in diameter, wraps twice around the heel of the stempiece and the base of the headboard, binding the two elements together. On the unlaminated lower portion of the stempiece, the spiral wraps lie at intervals of 3/4 to 1 inch. Along the arc of the cutwater edge and the curve at the outwales, the string wraps at 1/2 inch intervals. The area of the sharp bend and the span to the headboard has closely placed string spirals, 1/8 to 3/16 inch apart. Finally, four adjacent wraps of string encircle the stempiece just before it passes through the headboard.

From the sharp chin, the point at which the stitching of the end begins, the stempiece arcs in a broad curve upward for 17-5/8 inches to its maximum height at the head. From there, it curves downward and inboard for about 3-5/8 inches, to the point where it is lashed to the converged tips of the outwales and gunwale caps. The stempiece makes a rather hard curve outboard at this point, and extends about one third of the way toward the cutwater edge, to a point just below the inwales. This curve and downward span measure about 2-1/2 to 3 inches. Then the stempiece bends very sharply inboard and downward. The degree of sharpness of this bend required the breaking of the lamination layers on the inside of the curve. During the sharp bend, the depth tapers suddenly from 3/4 to 3/8 inch, while still maintaining all four of the lamination layers. Finally, the stempiece angles inboard to and through the headboard. Over this final span of about 2-1/2 to 3 inches, the depth tapers from 3/8 to 7/32 inch. The maximum horizontal distance of the curvature of the stempiece, from the cutwater edge to the outboard side of the head of the headboard, is about 6-3/4 inches. No wooden braces were installed to add stability to the tall stempiece and thus to the high end panels.

The tips of the converged pair of inwales lie adjacent to the stempiece at a location about 3 inches below the point of greatest height of the stempiece (measured on the curve). The tips of the inwales, as previously described, are bound tightly together with string to squeeze them against the outside surfaces of the stempiece.

The form of the internal curvature of the stempiece of the Type B-2 Catlin canoe, as with the stempiece of the full size Ojibwa canoe, closely resembles the old Algonkin version modeled by Adney; it appears on page 151 at the far left (with a brace) in Adney and Chapelle. (Note that the numerals 1 and 3 beneath the photo have been reversed by Chapelle: the example at the far left matches the early Algonkin form of cutwater edge, while the example at the far right parallels the

Adney Type B-1 "Tete de Boule" model depicted on pages 134-35.)

Headboards

The headboard stands with its base about 7-1/8 inches inboard of the outermost point of the cutwater edge (Fig. 188). The outboard side of the base falls 1/8 inch inboard of the chin of the canoe. The headboard is angled slightly, so that its head lies 1/4 to 3/8 inch outboard of its base. (This is the same direction as the slant of the headboards of the full size Ojibwa canoe.) The top of the low, rounded head fits between the converging inwales and gunwale caps slightly below the level of the upper surface of the caps. Thus, when the canoe is viewed in profile, the headboard is not visible above the caps.

The overall height of the headboard is 9-1/4 inches (Figs. 202 and 205); the height from the shoulders to the base is 7-5/8 inches. Its maximum width is 1-5/8 inches, at the base of the side notches. This maximum width tapers gradually down to the base, where it is 7/16 inch. In all of its areas, the headboard is 3/16 inch thick. The flat inboard surface is planed smooth, all edge surfaces are carved flat, and all corners and edges are sharp. The headboard appears to have been sawn to thickness before it was planed. No plane marks are visible, but hand planing would not necessarily produce visible blade marks. The top edge of the head of the bow headboard angles downward considerably toward the outboard side, while the top edge of its counterpart at the stern is level.

Below the rounded head, which measures 7/8 inch in height and 1-3/8 inches at its maximum width, a tall notch is cut out of each side. The inwales fit into these notches, which are 11/16 inch high and 5/16 inch deep. The top and bottom surfaces of each notch angle steeply upward toward the outboard side of the headboard, to accommodate the upward curve of the ends of the inwales.

Inboard 1/8 inch from the lower area of each of these inwale notches is a single hole, through which two turns of split root lash the inwales to the neck of the headboard. The two irregularly round, tapered holes, about 3/32 inch in diameter, were apparently drilled with an awl with a triangular or square cross section. The split lashing root is very narrow, about 1/32 to 3/64 inch in width.

A square hole lies in the midline of the headboard, with its top 3/32 inch above the bases of the inwale notches. The hole is 9/32 inch high by 9/32 inch wide. The laminated end of the stempiece projects through this hole. Since the stempiece is angled, the upper edge of its end projects inboard about 3/32 inch from the surface of the headboard, while the lower edge ends flush with the headboard surface. The end of the stempiece is 7/32 inch tall, with a tapered thickness of 3/16 to 1/8 inch.

Two wooden wedges are inserted into the hole beside and below the end of the stempiece, to hold the stempiece firmly in the hole. The flat exposed end of the side wedge is 7/32 inch in height by 3/32 inch in width, while the lower wedge measures 1/4 inch by 1/16 inch. The lower wedge ends flush with the surface of the headboard. The upper portion of the side wedge projects about 3/32 inch inboard from the headboard, similar to the angled end of the stempiece. Neither of these two wedges is the end of a horizontal stempiece brace. (No such braces are found on the bow stempiece and headboard, which are clearly visible due to the missing bark deck and the loosely attached headboard.)

The base of the headboard has a rectangular notch cut out, 3/4 inch tall and 3/16 inch wide. The two legs produced by the notch each taper to a sharply cut off base 1/8 inch wide. These legs fit over the heel of the stempiece. The headboard is attached to the stempiece by the tight fit of these legs over the heel of the stempiece, by the string which binds the legs to the heel, and by the tightly wedged upper end of the stempiece through the hole in the headboard. The headboard is not decorated at either end of the canoe.

Cutwater Edges

No wooden batten was built into the stitched cutwater edge to cover and protect the outboard edges of the two bark panels or the stempiece. The edges of the bark panels are cut off flush with the edge of the stempiece.

The upper distance of 13-1/2 inches around the curve, beginning at the gunwale tips, is lashed in a pattern of stitches composed of a series of tapered wedges (Fig. 187). Each individual wedge is made up of a series of 7 to 9 adjacent stitches. The holes, 1/16 inch in diameter, were produced by an awl with a triangular or square cross section. They lie at intervals of 1/32 to 3/64 inch edge to edge. The first hole in each series is positioned 3/8 to 1/2 inch inboard from the cutwater edge; the following 6 to 8 holes each lie progressively nearer to the edge, with the final hole 1/8 to 3/16 inch from the edge. The narrow tip of each wedge-shaped group points upward or inboard in all cases except the lowest three groups at the stern, which point downward. The series of holes is sewn in a simple spiral stitch, with one turn per hole. Each unit of 7 to 9 adjacent stitches covers a span of about 3/4 to 7/8 inch of the cutwater edge.

The unusual aspect of these cutwater stitches is the lashing material itself: the builder used flattened porcupine quills instead of the usual split root material. The flattened quills are 1/16 to 3/32 inch wide and 1/32 inch or less thick. Two colors of quills create an alternating pattern: natural white quills form three wedge-shaped groups, which are followed by three wedge groups of quills dyed greenish blue. This alternating color scheme continues over the entire span that is lashed with wedge-shaped groups of stitches. Greenish blue is a dyed color found rather often in nineteenth century native quill work of the Great Lakes region.

When the painted decoration was applied to the canoe, all of these quill stitches were painted over with black paint. The same paint also forms a series of semi-circular scallops on the end panels adjacent to the quill stitches. (Much of the paint is now worn off from the quills, revealing their original colors.) The evidence seems to indicate that the purchaser of the model (presumably George Catlin) wanted the quill stitches to look like traditional split root stitches; thus, the stitches were painted over. Possibly Catlin himself painted over the quills with black paint.

On the lowest 7-3/4 inch span of the cutwater edge, extending from a point about 2-1/2 inches above the longitudinal side seam down to the chin, the lashings are single spiral stitches of split roots which pass around the cutwater edge at spaced intervals. The holes, at intervals of 3/16 to 1/4 inch edge to edge, lie 1/4 to 5/16 inch inboard from the cutwater edge. Produced by an awl with a triangular or square cross section, the holes are 1/16 to 3/32 inch in diameter. The split lashing roots, 1/16 to 3/32 inch wide and 1/32 to 1/16 inch thick, have flat sides and undersurface and a slightly rounded upper surface. The stitching was done with a single strand of root in a continuous spiral stitch, with one turn per

hole. The stitches are well spaced, so that spans of about 3/16 to 1/4 inch of the cutwater edge are left uncovered between each of the stitches. In one instance where one long length of lashing root ends and another one begins, the end of one of the roots runs along the exposed edge of the stempiece on the cutwater edge for about one inch, beneath the spiral stitches.

In all sewing of the cutwater edge, whether with quills or split roots, the stitches pass directly through the stempiece inside the end of the canoe, rather than around it. The lashings run through awl holes through the stempiece.

The lower portion of the cutwater edge (the area in which spaces occur between the stitches) is sealed with blackened pitch in the same manner as the bark panel seams are sealed. The swath of pitch begins at the chin and extends upward for 7-3/4 inches on the curve, covering the entire area of single spiral stitches up to the wedge pattern stitches. The pitch extends from the outer edge of the prow onto the bark walls for 5/16 to 7/16 inch. The edges of the pitched area are broadly curved, following the contour of the outer edge of the canoe. The upper portion of the cutwater edge is not sealed with pitch. This allowed unobstructed drainage of water out of the canoe when it was overturned on its side on shore.

The total thickness of the cutwater edge is 5/16 to 3/8 inch in the lower pitched area (the area of the waterline), and 3/16 to 1/4 inch thick in the unpitched upper area. This thickness includes the stempiece, the two bark panels, and the stitches, as well as the pitch in the lower area.

Thwarts

None of the nine thwarts which were originally installed in the Catlin canoe have survived. Apparently over time each one was broken; at some point, all of them were removed. The left end of the endmost thwart at the bow broke through the middle of its lashing hole. Half of the hole area as well as the portion which fits into the mortise hole has survived, along with its split root lashings. At the second thwart from the bow, both such end fragments remain, bound into their mortise holes with the original root lashings. At the end positions of the other seven thwarts, the mortise holes and some portions of lashing material remain. Much information can be gleaned from these surviving remnants of the thwarts.

The nine thwarts (creating an eight-place canoe) are spaced in a generally symmetrical pattern (Fig. 190). In the absence of the thwarts themselves, the distances between the thwarts are measured from center to center of the mortise holes. The difference between the 3-1/2 and 3-3/4 inch spans may reflect the inexact nature of this measuring technique rather than the intention of the model builder. The end thwart at the bow end lies the same distance from its headboard as the stern end thwart lies from its headboard. The positioning of all of the thwarts implies a canoe shape that tapers symmetrically toward the two ends at the gunwale level. However, this point deserves closer scrutiny.

The center thwart lies 1/4 inch forward of the exact midpoint of the canoe; in addition, the lengths of the thwarts imply an asymmetrical form. Four pairs of thwarts flank the center thwart. In all four pairs, the bow thwart is longer than its sternward counterpart.

It must be noted that since all of the thwarts are now missing, the gunwales have splayed out somewhat. This warpage appears to have occurred to a slightly greater extent toward the bow end than the stern: space now exists between the sides of the bow headboard and the adjacent widened walls, a detail which is not found at the stern end. Thus, the original lengths of the thwarts are not exactly represented by the present measurements of the distance which they once occupied.

Center: Thwart #1: 9-1/2 inches
Pair A: Thwart #2: 8-7/8 inches
         Thwart #3: 9-3/8 inches
Pair B: Thwart #4: 7-1/2 inches
         Thwart #5: 8-1/8 inches
Pair C: Thwart #6: 5-1/2 inches
         Thwart #7: 5-7/8 inches
Pair D: Thwart #8: 2-7/8 inches
         Thwart #9: 3-5/8 inches

The lengths, measured at the outboard end of each mortise hole, do not include the hidden end portions of each thwart which formerly fit into the mortise hole in each inwale. The actual length of each thwart was about 3/8 inch longer than each of these measurements, since the additional portion at each end, which extended completely through the inwale, was about 3/16 inch long.

In comparing pair A, the bow thwart is 1/2 inch

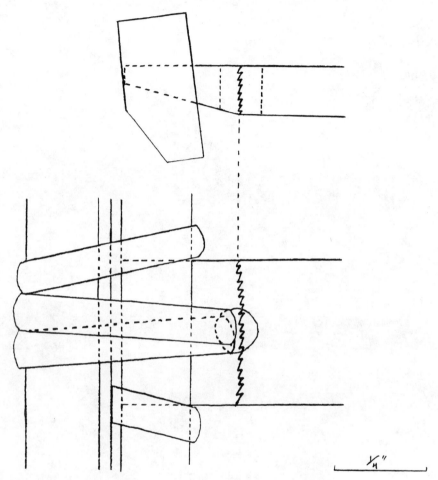

Fig. 206. Catlin Canoe: Thwarts.

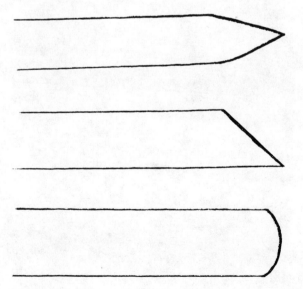

Fig. 207. Catlin Canoe: Sheathing strips.

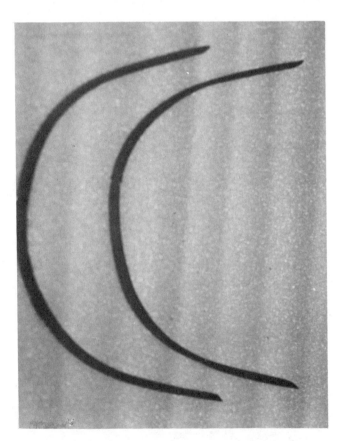

Fig. 208 (left). Catlin Canoe: Interior view from the bow.
Fig. 209 (right). Catlin Canoe: Two ribs.

Fig. 210. Catlin Canoe: Mast step.

longer than its stern counterpart; in the next pair outboard, the bow thwart is 5/8 inch longer. In pair C, the bow thwart is 3/8 inch longer than its stern counterpart; and in the endmost pair, the bow thwart is 3/4 inch longer.

The slightly offset placement of the center thwart as well as the differences in the lengths of the paired thwarts in the two halves of the canoe may or may not be simply variances due to measurement of the builder by eye rather than by measuring devices; the differences are now exaggerated somewhat by warpage. There is a possibility that the builders intentionally made the thwarts slightly longer in the bow half, to create a canoe that is slightly wider in the beam toward the bow than the stern, for greater efficiency of forward movement of the canoe. This possibility is supported by the evidence of the gore slits: they imply that the building frame of the canoe in the bow half remained wider for a longer span and had a more sudden taper near the end than the stern half, with its more gradual and even taper toward the end.

The slightly widened bow form is found in the full size Royal and Ojibwa canoes, as well as in the Varden model. This feature was commonly built into the fur trade canoes that were constructed in the latter nineteenth century at the canoe-building posts of the upper Ottawa River in western Quebec.[4] It was also quite widespread in traditional Indian canoe construction, as has been previously discussed.

The following description applies to each of the surviving remains of the thwarts (Fig. 206). Each thwart remnant is broken through the lashing hole at a point about 1/8 inch from the inwale. At this point, the thwart measures 3/8 inch in width and 1/8 inch in thickness. As the thwart extends to the inwale, the width is maintained, while the thickness tapers to 3/32 inch. It is highly likely that this taper in thickness remains constant to the end of each thwart. The intact portion of the lashing hole, which is 3/32 inch in diameter, lies about 1/16 inch from the inwale and about 1/8 inch from each edge of the thwart. Due to the fragmentary condition of the surviving holes, it is not possible to determine if they were produced with an awl or a gimlet, or whether they may have been burned through with a heated awl. The single lashing hole at the end of each thwart is a feature of this model which does not correctly represent full size

versions, which have two or more such holes at the end of each thwart.

Thwart #5, the third thwart from the bow end, was originally perforated at its midpoint to support a sail mast. The presence of a carved mast step on the midline of the floor immediately beneath the former position of this thwart indicates its use as a mast support. The perforated mast thwart lay 16-3/8 inches from the point of maximum arc of the bow cutwater edge and 9-3/4 inches from the bow headboard. The interior beam between the inwales at this point is presently 8-1/8 inches. Therefore, the mast thwart would have been about 8-1/2 inches in total length (minus the distance that the gunwales have splayed outward at this position).

The mortise holes which formerly held the mast thwart in each inwale have the same dimensions and root lashing pattern as the regular thwarts on the canoe. This indicates that the ends of the mast thwart were of the same measurements as the standard thwarts, as previously described. The width of the thwart must have widened in the midsection area, to accommodate the hole for the mast. The hole in the mast step on the floor, which held the base of the mast, is 1/8 inch square. The hole in the mast thwart would have been at least this size, if not larger, to accommodate the lower mast.

At the point where each of the nine thwarts meets the inwale, a horizontal mortise slot is cut through the midline of the inwale, to receive the end of the thwart (Fig. 203). Each slot is about 5/16 inch long by 3/32 inch wide, apparently pierced with the tip of a knife. In those cases in which the thwart has been missing for a very long time, the slit has nearly closed (such as the two mortise slots in Figure 203). The mortise slot runs completely through the inwale. The slot is cut at a slight angle, with its inboard end lower than its outboard end. This compensates for the slight outward angle of the inwale, since it angles outward in conjunction with the upper walls of the canoe. The angle of the slot permits the straight horizontal end of the thwart to fit into the slot in the angled inwale. At both ends of all of the mortise slots, a slender crack extends away from the opening; these were apparently produced when the tapered ends of the thwarts were forced into the narrow knife slits.

It is not possible to determine whether a vertical tack or wooden peg was driven downward from the upper surface of the inwale through each of the thwarts to hold the end of the thwart firmly in the mortise slot. All views of these thwart end locations are blocked by the close fit of the gunwale caps.

Each end of the thwart is lashed with split root to the combined inwale and outwale (Fig. 206). The lashings run through one vertical hole in the end of the thwart, 1/16 inch inboard from the inwale. The slot, 3/32 inch in diameter, lies about 1/8 inch from the sides of the thwart.

Below the junction of the thwart and the gunwales, there are usually three awl holes in the bark wall. These lashing holes, spanning 5/16 to 3/8 inch, sometimes end slightly short of the outer edges of the thwart, and in other instances extend to the outer edges. All of the previous information describing the lashing of the gunwale elements also applies to the lashing of the thwarts. In the thwart lashings, usually one turn of root lies beside each edge of the thwart, while two turns pass through the single hole in the thwart. The thwarts were lashed at the same time as the gunwales. Thus, their lashings fit into the series of lashing groups along the length of the gunwales.

Sheathing

The sheathing strips or splints on the Catlin canoe model are not fully realistic portrayals of such strips on full size canoes; these are somewhat too long, wide, and thick. The splints are 22 to 26 inches long, 1 to 1-3/8 inches wide, and 3/64 to 1/16 inch thick. On the flat faces, areas of undulating raised grain patterns indicate that the strips were split out rather than carved. A few areas on the flat faces bear long, shallow concave marks left by a crooked knife in the process of thinning the strips (Fig. 203). Each splint has generally parallel edges for most of its length; the edges are carved rather straight. The endmost 1 to 1-1/2 inches at each end of most of the strips is carved so that it gradually tapers into a sharp point (Fig. 207). A few of the splints end in a bluntly rounded tip without any taper. The edge of each of the ends is cut so that it thins down to a sharp edge in a bevel about 1/16 inch wide, which lies sometimes on the inboard side and sometimes on the outboard side facing the bark cover. None of the long edges of the strips are thinned.

The pattern of overlapping ends indicates that the splints were laid into the canoe in two groups: first in the bowward half, and then in the stern half. The two groups are each made up of 11 to 13 strips. After the bowward group of splints had been laid in, the sternward group was positioned so that the splints overlapped the ends of the previously-laid groups for about 1-1/2 to 2 inches. This overlap area occurs at about the midpoint of the canoe.

In laying in the sheathing, two different systems were used. In the bow half, the first strip was positioned down the midline of the floor. It extends up to but not underneath the base of the headboard and the stempiece. Successive sheathing splints were then added out to and up the walls, to a point about 1/4 to 3/8 inch below the inwales. The overlapping edge of each successive strip faces downward or inward, toward the midline of the canoe. The overlapping edge extends 1/8 to 1/4 inch over the previous strip.

When the sheathing splints were subsequently installed in the stern half, the first strips were positioned near the top of each wall. The successive splints were then added, down the walls and across the floor. The overlapping edge of each strip faces upward or outward, away from the midline of the canoe. It is extremely unusual in canoe construction for the builder to use these two different systems of installation of sheathing splints in the two halves of the same canoe.

Toward each end of the canoe at the top of the walls, a gradually widening expanse of the upper bark wall is left exposed, not covered by the straight horizontal strips of sheathing where the gunwales curve upward (Fig. 202). These wider areas of exposed upper wall extend for about 2 inches inboard of the headboards. Beside the headboards, the area of each wall which is not covered by the sheathing splints ranges from 1-5/8 to 1-3/4 inches in height. A short supplemental sheathing strip was added to the right wall beside the stern headboard, to cover an excessive amount of the bark wall which had been thus left exposed (Fig. 202). It extends inboard of the headboard for about 3 inches, angling slightly.

The tips of the endmost splints extend outboard of the headboard up to 6 inches; in some cases, they run to or within 1/4 inch of the stempiece. No additional short sheathing strips were inserted outboard of the headboard to stiffen and support the bark cover at the high ends of the canoe (other than the single strip mentioned above). Nor was any other material, such as wood shavings or moss, stuffed into the ends of the canoe to support the bark cover.

A mast step is carved onto the upper surface of the sheathing splint which runs down the midline of the floor toward the bow end. It is described on page 304.

Ribs

It is not possible to accurately determine the total number of ribs which were originally installed in the Catlin canoe. Presently, twenty ribs survive. Since a number of the gunwale lashings have broken and disappeared, it is no longer possible to count the exact number of spaces between lashing groups which were left open to receive the ribs. There appear to be about 60 to 62 such spaces into which ribs could have been originally installed.

The 20 surviving ribs cover about 13 inches of the 34-1/2 inch span between the headboards. The ribs are spaced at intervals of 1/4 to 3/8 inch, measured edge to edge, in the midsection area. Toward the ends of the canoe, the spacing reduces to 3/16 to 1/4 inch.

The profile of the midsection ribs is composed of a moderately rounded area in the midline of the floor, from which the bilge areas curve gradually upward; the upper sections flare slightly outward (Figs. 208 and 209). The width of the rounded central area gradually reduces toward each end of the canoe; by the endmost rib, the profile is a narrow U form. The curve of the ribs reflects the body plan of the canoe (Fig. 189).

The midsection ribs in the area of the central thwart are 14-1/2 inches long. This includes the length of about 3/32 to 1/8 inch at each tip which is inserted behind the inwale (Fig. 199). The width of these ribs is 5/16 to 3/8 inch for nearly their full length. They do not taper as they extend outward and upward. The thickness of 3/32 to 1/8 inch is likewise maintained for the full length. Over the uppermost 1/2 to 11/16 inch of each tip, the width tapers rather suddenly, down to about 1/8 inch at the squared-off tip (Fig. 203). The inboard surface at the end of the tip is carved in a sudden taper over the uppermost 1/4 inch span into a chisel shape. The tip has a sharp edge about 1/32 inch thick.

The ribs nearer to the ends, besides being shorter, are slightly narrower and thinner than the long mid-section ribs. The endmost surviving rib, 2 inches from the stern headboard, is 12-3/4 inches long, including the length of about 3/32 to 1/8 inch at each tip which is inserted behind the inwale (Fig. 202). The width of 1/4 inch is maintained for nearly the full length, without tapering as the rib extends outward and upward. The thickness of 1/16 inch likewise remains the same for the full length. In the uppermost portion of 1/2 to 11/16 inch of each tip, the tapered forms and dimensions are identical to those described above for the midsection ribs.

Between this endmost surviving rib and the stern headboard, there are three spaces between gunwale lashing groups, into which ribs may have originally fit. No evidence indicates which of these spaces once held the endmost rib, or whether the present surviving endmost rib was originally the endmost one when the model was built.

The ribs are carved very flat and smooth on virtually all of their flat inboard surfaces, as well as the edges, which are sharp. The narrow U-shaped profile of the endmost ribs at the ends of the canoe did not require an extremely sharp bend at the midpoint. Thus, no groove or scoring was necessary across the midpoint to facilitate the bend.

In the midsection of the canoe, the ribs stand perpendicular to the horizontal plane of the keel line (Fig. 188). Toward the ends of the canoe, the keel line rises gradually, as the rocker of the bottom curves upward. In these areas of the rising keel line, each rib was installed perpendicular to the gradually rising plane of the keel line; therefore, the tips of the ribs angle slightly inboard from their bases. The headboard also stands slightly angled, in the opposite direction of the angled adjacent ribs; its base lies 1/4 to 3/8 inch inboard of its head. Thus, the distance between the endmost rib (near its tips) and the upper area of the headboard is greater than the distance between the base of this rib and the base of the headboard.

Painted Decoration

All of the painted decoration on the canoe appears to be original from the period of its construction and its later ownership by Catlin. The shade of each color and its degree of darkening is consistent throughout the entire canoe, implying that all of the pigments were applied at about the same time. No restoration is discernible on any of the painted surfaces.

Along the full length of the gunwale caps, the upper surface and the outer edge is painted deep green (Fig. C-7). At some point, the entire exterior of the canoe was covered with a protective coat of shiny varnish. This varnish layer has darkened extensively over many decades. Due to this darkening, the formerly deep green caps are now greenish black. The thwarts were probably also painted, but they have long since disappeared.

Each of the high bark end panels of both walls is painted solidly in white, from the stitches of the cutwater edge to the longitudinal side seam. The solid white area extends inboard from the cutwater edge for about 6 1/8 inches along the side seam, to end in a straight vertical edge. From this vertical end, a white curled finial extends inboard and upward; it tapers only during its upward rise, and ends in an enlarged, rounded tip. The finial reaches 2-1/4 inches inboard from the vertical edge of the white panel. The coat of white paint also covers the adjacent portion of the reinforcement bark strip and the end of the bark deck as well; it originally also covered the adjacent span of the outwale. Due to the darkening of the varnish layer, the formerly white painted areas are now a very dark tan or light brown color. The original white hue shows through in the extensive network of fine cracks in the varnish layer, as well as in a large area on the left wall panel at the bow, where much of the varnish has worn away.

The outboard perimeter of each solid white panel is surrounded by a black scalloped pattern composed of eight or nine adjacent semicircles. The rounded solid black forms, 1-1/4 to 1-1/2 inches in diameter, completely cover the adjacent wedge patterns of porcupine quill stitches on the cutwater edge. The paint gives the quill stitches the appearance of split root stitches. The painted semicircular forms do not match in any particular manner the wedge patterns of the stitches. Where this perimeter design contains nine semicircles, the black scallops extend over the full span of the cutwater edge down to the main side seam; where eight semicircles have been applied, the sequence ends about one inch above the side seam.

The outwales and their gunwale lashings on both walls were originally painted red on the outboard side and the top surface, over the long span in the midsection between the white end panels. The red pigment, now a slightly brownish red, was probably rather bright red originally, which changed as the coat of aging varnish darkened.

The span of the reinforcement bark strip in the midsection between the white end panels is painted deep green. The paint extends below the bark strip onto the bark wall for 1/4 to 5/8 inch. A narrow stripe of this same green paint, 3/32 to 1/8 inch wide, runs outboard from the green midsection band toward each end of the canoe. This stripe on the bark wall borders the edge of the white-painted portion of the reinforcement bark strip and the end of the bark deck, out to its tip. With the darkening of the overcoating of varnish, these areas of deep green have turned a greenish black color.

A narrow stripe of red, 3/32 to 1/8 inch wide, borders all of the edges of the white finial, the vertical edge of the white panel, and the long green band along the midsection of the canoe. On the right wall of the bow end, this red stripe also borders the green stripe which runs adjacent to the edge of the bark strip and the deck end out to its tip. These red stripes are now slightly brownish red.

After these painted decorations were applied to the model, several of the painted areas on the outwales were covered over with black paint. It is not known whether these black overcoatings were applied to the outwales to cover damaged paint or to simply alter the scheme of the colors. The end portions of both of the outwales were originally painted white (like their adjacent wall panels, reinforcement bark strips, and deck ends). Of the four white ends of the outwales, all but the one on the left wall at the bow were repainted black, along with their gunwale lashings.

In addition, most of the midsection of the outwale on the left wall was repainted with black over its first coat of red. The original red was left visible at each end of the outwale adjacent to the white end panels, for a span of about two inches at the bow end and about 6-1/2 inches at the stern.

In about the middle of each of the four solid white end panels lies a circular rayed device, positioned 2-3/4 inches below and 1-5/8 inches inboard of the cutwater edge. The outer circle, composed of a red stripe 1/4 inch wide, is 4-1/8 inches in maximum diameter. The six bipointed arms or rays within the circle measure 1-7/8 inches in length and 3/8 inch in maximum width at the midpoint. They alternate in the colors of red, deep green, and black (each hue having darkened with the old varnish layer to the same degree as the other pigments on the canoe).

In three of the four devices, the red rays point directly upward and downward; on the right wall at the stern, the red rays extend toward the upper right and lower left positions. The green rays in three of the devices point to the upper right and lower left, and in one case toward the upper left and lower right. The black rays extend three times toward the upper left and lower right, and once directly toward the right and the left. In all of the devices except the one on the right wall at the stern, one set of opposing rays points directly upward and downward.

The extreme degree of regularity and evenness of form and dimensions of the four rayed circular devices and the scallops around the cutwater edge implies the use of traced patterns by the painter. These would probably have been birchbark patterns, as discussed in the description of the painted decorations on the full size Ojibwa canoe. Each element in the circular rayed design of the Catlin canoe was first outlined with a very thin dark outline, in the color of the finished element. Then the outlined interior was filled in, with the same hue as the thin outline, but often less darkly than the outline.

Three distinctions in the various painted decorations on the Catlin canoe indicate which end of the craft was the bow end. The only end area of an outwale which was left in its original coating of white paint (not over-painted in black) is found at the bow, on the left wall. The only instance of a narrow red stripe bordering the white tip of the reinforcement bark strip and the end of the bark deck occurs at the bow, on the right wall. Finally, the only circular rayed device in which the set of red rays do not point directly upward and downward is located at the stern, on the right wall.

Nails

All of the nails used in the manufacture of the Catlin canoe are of the hand-forged type. One size of large-headed tack was utilized, to attach the gunwale caps to the inwales and outwales. These have been described in the gunwale caps discussion.

The nails in this craft are the only examples of hand-forged nails which are found in the eight surviving fur trade canoes included in this study. All of the other nails are of the machine-cut type, except the two wire nails which fasten the replacement tips of the outwales of the Quebec canoe.

Miscellaneous Features
Seats

There is no evidence on the Catlin canoe which would indicate that it was ever fitted with permanent or temporary wooden seats. No areas of wear can be observed on the gunwales or the upper portions of the ribs that can be attributed to the use of such seats.

Provisions for Sail and Cordelling Line

The forward thwarts, to which a cordelling (towing) line would have been tied, were broken and removed at some point. Thus, any evidence concerning this practice has disappeared.

The canoe was equipped with a permanent perforated thwart and mast step for sailing. When a sail was used, the upright mast would have been erected through the thwart mast hole with its base set into the mast step. The data which can be gleaned concerning the missing perforated thwart has been discussed on page 300.

The mast step is positioned with its hole exactly beneath the original location of the midpoint of thwart #5, the third thwart from the bow end. The position of this perforated thwart is discussed in its description and is indicated in Figure 190. The mast step is carved onto the upper flat surface of the sheathing splint which runs down the midline of the floor in the bow half of the canoe (Fig. 210). Measuring 7/16 inch square by 1/4 inch high (thick), the step has flat surfaces, sharp edges, and a sharp and square carved junction with the sheathing strip. The four side walls slant very slightly inward as they rise to the flat top. At the midpoint of the top, a hole is cut to receive the base of a mast. The hole, measuring 1/8 inch square by 1/8 inch deep, does not taper toward its flat bottom. The hole is cleanly cut out, as if it had been produced with a narrow chisel. The square shape and flat bottom of the hole seems to imply that the model builder envisioned the base of a sail mast with a comparable squared form. On the other hand, it is possible that the only chisel that the builder had which was narrow enough to carve out the small mast step hole had a straight bit rather than a curved bit.

The carving of the mast step onto the surface of a full length sheathing splint would probably not have been done on full size canoes. A much shorter length of wood would be more manageable and practical in full size. Note the description on page 233 of the much shorter but comparable carved mast step which is found on the Assiginack canoe.

Flags

No evidence can be found for the attachment of a flag at either the bow or the stern. No space exists outboard of either headboard into which a flag staff could have been inserted. But there is sufficient space around the upper body of each headboard to permit the lashing of such a staff (Fig. 202). A light cord could have encircled the headboard between the edges of the body and the adjacent walls, to bind a flag staff to the inboard surface of the headboard, at both the bow and the stern.

Bow/Stern Differences

The builder of the Catlin canoe created a number of differences between the bow and the stern ends of the craft, which are listed below. Some of these features were installed for efficient performance of the canoe, such as the direction of the overlap of the bark panels. Others may have been added to indicate which end of the craft was the bow, to best utilize the efficiency features. Some of the differences may be only coincidental.

A. The high end panel at the bow is 3/4 inch taller than its mate at the stern. The slightly lower stern end is a little broader in the outward arc of its cutwater edge than the bow end.

B. It is not possible to accurately compare the degree of rise of the rocker at each of the chins, since the bow end of the canoe has warped slightly upward and inboard and the stern end has sagged somewhat. The bow chin presently lies 3/4 inch above the horizontal baseline, while the stern chin presently measures only 1/8 inch in height. The original height of each chin is projected to have been about 3/8 to 1/2 inch.

C. The lengths of the thwarts appear to create in the bow half a slightly broader beam and a more sudden taper near the end (at the gunwale level) compared to the narrower stern half, with its longer and more gradual taper. The same form seems to be also implied

for the lower areas of the hull and the building frame of the canoe, as reflected by the gore slits.

D. All of the overlapping edges of the various bark panels (except the one high end panel at the bow) are lapped so that the edge that is exposed on the exterior side faces sternward. This increased the efficiency and reduced the likelihood of catching on obstructions.

E. The differences in the painted decorations of the two ends of the canoe have been discussed.

F. The top edge is level on the stern headboard, while it angles downward and outboard on the bow headboard.

G. The mast thwart and the mast step lie at the bow end of the canoe.

Construction Tools, Methods, and Materials

The Catlin canoe was manufactured from the traditional forest materials of birchbark, wood, tree roots, and pine or spruce gum mixed with animal fat and pulverized charcoal. It was painted afterward with Euroamerican commercial paints.

The builders of the canoe used the typical array of tools normally employed in canoe manufacture during the nineteenth century. These include an axe, knife, crooked knife, awl, rib-setting mallet, pitch melting and applying implements, and paint containers and brushes.

In addition, they utilized a few tools and techniques that have generally been considered less traditional in the canoe construction of that era. A narrow chisel with a bit 1/8 inch or less in width was used to neatly carve out the 1/8 inch square vertical hole in the mast step. This same chisel may have also been used to cut out the 3/16 inch wide notch in the base and the 9/32 inch wide hole in the body of each headboard. Commercial string was substituted for the traditional strips of basswood or cedar inner bark or split roots for the spiral wrapping of the laminations of the inwales and stempieces and for the binding of the inwale tips.

One of the most visually obvious departures from traditional canoe construction involves the substitution of hand-forged iron tacks for carved wooden pegs, driven with an iron hammer. Tacks fasten the gunwale caps to the inwales and outwales. No pegs or nails were installed to attach the inwales and outwales together. However, the presence of nails in the caps implies that in the full size craft envisioned by the model builders, the inwales and outwales would also have probably been fastened with iron nails; these would have been hidden beneath the gunwale lashings. The use of nails in canoe construction and repair became quite widespread in the early nineteenth century, being used in many areas of North America before 1850.[5] It is of interest to note that a model of a voyaging canoe from the 1830s includes nails in its construction.

Finally, the use of porcupine quills instead of split roots for the stitching of the upper half of each cutwater edge was a decorative substitution which does not reflect traditional canoe construction techniques. The quills were utilized since the builder intended the canoe to be a model for display rather than a functioning watercraft. Ultimately, the quills were painted over, to appear to be standard split root stitches.

Most of the above "nontraditional" features of the Catlin canoe construction (other than the quill stitches) represent practical, labor-saving substitutions and improvements; these elements probably produced a canoe with equal or better performance qualities, with less labor and in less time. Since these traits have been observed on a surviving example of a period fur trade canoe model, they may in fact reflect standard manufacturing techniques used to build such canoes in the first third of the nineteenth century, rather than "nontraditional" variations.

Condition

The bark cover and the surviving wooden elements of the canoe are generally in sound, stable condition, although the bark cover has sustained a number of rather serious breaks. All of the thwarts are now gone, which has allowed the gunwales to splay outward somewhat. More than half of the ribs are now missing, and a few of the surviving ones are cracked and glued. A portion of one side of the hole in the mast step has broken away. The bow headboard is now loosely attached, minus its lashings to the inwale and its wedges which once held the upper end of the stempiece firmly in the headboard hole. The bark deck outboard of the bow headboard is also missing.

The original root lashings remain intact in all of the original bark panel seams and slits and in most locations on the gunwales and cutwater edges. A number of gunwale lashings have broken and disappeared, es-

pecially those at the tips of the outwales and gunwale caps. Much of the original sealant pitch remains, although it has cracked off in many areas. The porcupine quill stitches on the cutwater edges are generally in good condition. The painted decoration remains moderately intact. It has darkened extensively in all areas, due to the darkening of the overcoating of varnish, and has chipped and worn off in many locations on the wooden elements and the cutwater edges.

Several procedures were carried out on the canoe during its many years of display and storage. Thus, the following resultant features do not apply to the original construction of the canoe.

A. A coat of shiny varnish was applied at some point to the entire exterior of the canoe. In the areas of the four white end panels, the varnish now has an extensive network of fine cracks. A large area of the varnish on the white panel on the left wall at the bow has cracked and worn off.

B. At the bow end of the right wall, 8 and 10 inch-long segments of sawn wood have been installed to replace the tip of the outwale and the gunwale cap. These replacement segments are painted grey; they have no gunwale lashings.

C. Tan colored plaster was applied to restore damaged lower areas of the bark cover at each end of both walls.

D. Three or four wraps of commercial string encircle the combined inwale and outwale at the former locations of the ends of a number of the thwarts. At some point after the broken thwarts were removed, these wraps of string were installed in the locations of the former thwart lashings. The string wraps could not have once held the thwarts in place, as replacements for broken root lashings, or they would have been broken when the thwarts were removed. The string wraps on the gunwales may have served as suspension points for the display or storage of the canoe. Strands of string may also have been run across the width of the canoe between these gunwale lashings, in the locations of the former thwarts, in an attempt to prevent the outward splaying of the gunwales; but no such long spans of string across the canoe are now present.

E. Two small holes, about 1-1/2 inches apart, run through the top of each high end of the canoe. These were apparently utilized to suspend the model by strings at some point, either for display or storage.

Notes: Catlin Canoe

1. Adney and Chapelle, pp.136-137, 139, 143, 151.
2. Ibid., pp. 28, 29, 102, 149.
3. Ibid., pp. 138, 141, 147.
4. Ibid., p.147.
5. Ibid., p. 56.

The Bell Canoe Model

Contents

The Bell Canoe Model

Several features of the Bell canoe suggest that this model portrays an Ojibwa/Cree style of fur trade canoe, the Type B-2 style of the full size Ojibwa and Sault canoes. These traits include the extended breadth and moderately tall height of the ends in relation to the height of the walls in the midsection, the moderate degree of undercut in the profile of the ends, and the upright plank stempiece.[1] The model represents the moderately large size of fur trade canoe, the six-place (seven-thwart) version.

The craft was built much too short in the midsection in relation to the height of the ends and the height and breadth of the midsection walls. In addition, the sheathing and ribs are much too large compared to the dimensions of the canoe. Finally, the builder did not bend the ends of the inwales upward and attach them to the canoe. (This latter item would have been invisible when the canoe was in its original undamaged condition.) Due to these deficiencies, the Bell model is not described and illustrated as minutely as the other canoes in the study.

Yet in spite of its deficiencies of scale and its lack of traditional inwale treatment, the Bell model is of considerable value as a source of data. Its ends represent the broad-ended variant of the Ojibwa/Cree (Type B-2) fur trade canoe. In addition, the forms and building techniques of most of the elements of the canoe provide further supporting data to accompany the forms and techniques which are found in the other full size and model canoes in the study.

Overall Dimensions

Length: Presently 44". About 2-1/8 inches is now missing from the damaged end; this projection is based on the premise that the missing stern end had the same dimensions as the intact bow end. (The direction of the exposed overlapping edge on each of the gore slits indicates that the surviving end is the bow of the canoe.) The original length is projected to have been about 46-1/8 inches.

Distance between the outboard sides of the tips of the outwales: 33-3/8" (Fig. 212).

Height above the baseline: at the midpoint 6-7/8", at the surviving bow end 11-9/16".

Beam at the midpoint: 10-7/8" (Fig. 213).

Interior beam, inside the gunwales: 9".

The bow end rises above the height of the midsection walls by an increase of 58 percent. This is considerably more than the 45 and 46 percent respective increases in the Ojibwa and Cree models made by Adney.[2] The end form of the Bell model is broader proportionately than all of the other canoes in the present study. Its breadth, coupled with the moderately undercut profile, closely resembles the Cree version modeled by Adney which appears at the bottom of the photo on page 137 of Adney and Chapelle.

The form of the hull is extremely broad in the beam in relation to the total length, since the model was built very short in its midsection length. The interior beam is equal to 19.51 percent of the projected original overall length of the canoe. This ratio is greater than the 15.37 percent of the slightly narrow full size Ojibwa canoe as well as the broad-beamed Royal and Sault canoes; the latter craft have ratios of 17.72 and 18.30 percent, respectively. In another comparison, the Ojibwa model and Cree model made by Adney have interior beams which are 17.6 and 15.7 percent respectively of the total length of the canoes.[3] Thus, the beam of the Bell model is especially wide.

Hull Form
Profile of the Bottom and Ends

Along the keel line, the horizontal span of about 24 inches appears to lie generally centered within the total length of the canoe. From the end of the horizontal section, a 7-1/2 inch span of moderate rocker (measured on the horizontal baseline) gradually rises to a moderately rounded chin (to the point where the stitches of the cutwater edge begin). The total length of the bottom between the chins is projected to have been 39 inches, based on the assumption that the damaged end had the same dimensions as the surviving end. The present rocker dimensions appear to be original, not altered by any warpage.

Fig. 211. Bell Canoe.

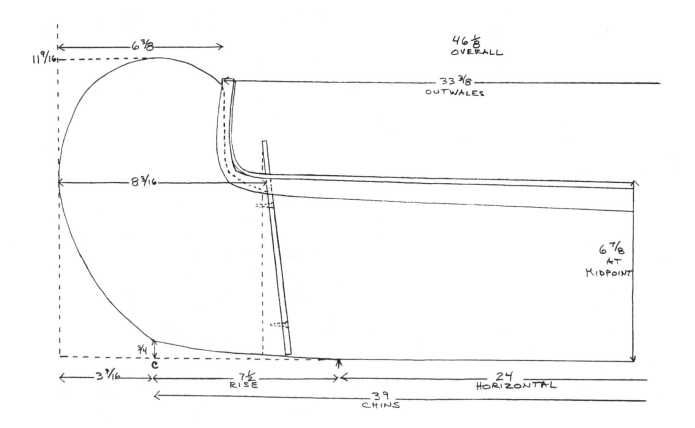

Fig. 212. Bell Canoe: Hull profile and dimensions.

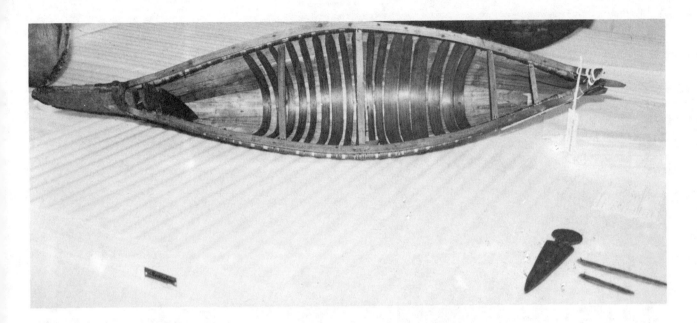

Fig. 213. Bell Canoe: Interior view. Disattached headboard and two thwarts appear at lower right.

Fig. 214. Bell Canoe: End view.

Fig. 215 (left). Bell Canoe: Lower end view.
Fig. 216 (right). Bell Canoe: Bottom view.

At the bow end, the chin lies 3/4 inch above the horizontal baseline. From the chin, the end extends 2-1/8 inches outboard (measured on the baseline) to the outermost point of the end. The cutwater edge arcs upward from the rounded chin for 14 inches (measured on the curve) to the highest point of the end, with a moderately undercut profile. Then it curves downward and inboard over a span of 2-3/4 inches to meet the outwales. The total length of the edge, measured on the curve from chin to outwales, is 16-3/4 inches.

Body Plan

The bottom is narrow and moderately rounded (Figs. 214 to 217). The bilge is gradually rounded, while the upper walls are straight and flare outward slightly. The widest area of the bottom appears to lie at about the midpoint of the length of the canoe. This width tapers gradually and symmetrically to each chin.

The canoe was built in a form designed for moderately fast paddling with ample cargo capacity. Its features, including a narrow moderately rounded bottom and a gradually rounded bilge, a broad beam, a long slender taper to the ends, and a very narrow U form inboard of the headboards, contributed to its ease of paddling yet provided generous room for cargo.[4] The moderately round bottom of the canoe is much narrower and considerably more rounded than the standard cargo canoes of the period as portrayed by Adney, with their slightly rounded or nearly flat bottoms. In addition, the bilge area is considerably undercut and more gradually rounded. These features would reduce the floor space for cargo. But the narrow U form which the canoe has near its ends would increase the roominess somewhat, yet reduce its speed, compared to a sharp V form as found on the Royal canoe. Thus, the Bell model may represent a fast-paddling cargo canoe rather than a true express canoe, a version designed to carry a moderate amount of cargo but travel quickly. However, since this is a model not to scale, one must not read too much into the interpretation of its features.

Bark Cover
Color

All of the panels of bark are golden tan in color.

Panels

The bottom of the canoe was made with one long panel of bark, while each wall was formed by joining two high end panels and one central panel (Fig. 211). During the construction process, a small supplemental piece of bark was added to the top of both end panels at the bow end, which did not have sufficient height. (Fig. 218). The two pieces were inserted behind the top edges of the two end panels. The upper edge of the extra pieces is cut in a broad semicircular form which blends into the broad curve of the cutwater edge. At the point of maximum height of the end of the canoe, the supplemental pieces project 1/2 inch above the main panels. The stitching of these pieces is described in the seams discussion. The question arises as to why the builder added the two pieces to the bow rather than simply cutting the stern 1/2" lower.

Sewn Seams

The original lashing material still survives in all of the seams. No tucked-under ends of seam lashing roots are visible for observation and description, all of them having been finished on the hidden interior side. No evidence suggests that a batten strip of wood or root was incorporated into any of the seams for added reinforcement, either on the exterior or the interior side of the bark cover. Since the bottom of the model was constructed of a single panel of bark, the canoe has no bottom seams.

Gore Slits

After the long span of bottom bark was laid out on the building bed and the building frame was placed upon it, the bark was bent upward around the perimeter of the frame. Then a number of gore slits were sliced at intervals along the sides of the bottom panel. These slices ran from the edges of the bark inboard nearly to the building frame. At each of these slits, one edge of the bark was made to overlap the other edge for about 1/4 inch, with the exposed edge on the exterior facing toward the stern. (No slice of bark was removed to create a seam with butting edges). Each overlapping edge was thinned somewhat, so that the exposed edges of the gore slits are lower and less prominent than the other overlapping seams on the canoe, which were not thinned.

Each of the slits is stitched closed with split roots in a series of three rather widely spaced spiral stitches, with one stitch per hole (Fig. 220). The portion of each stitch on the exterior side of the canoe is horizontal, while the connector portion running to the next stitch on the interior of the canoe is diagonal. The stitches run through pairs of awl holes which lie about 3/16 to 5/16 inch from the overlapping edge of bark. The visible horizontal portions are about 1/2 to 5/8 inch long, and are spaced about 1/2 to 7/8 inch apart.

The split lashing roots are about 3/32 to 5/32 inch wide, about the same width as the awl holes. The sides and undersurface of the roots are flat, while the upper surface is rounded. The rounded side is the side of the root lashing which faces the exterior.

The gore slits in the bottom panel are positioned at regular intervals; they extend from a point outboard of the midsection of the canoe out to a location well inboard of the chins (Fig. 211). Four slits are found in each wall; each has a mate generally opposite it (having been cut on opposite sides of the building frame). Two pairs lie in the bow half of the canoe, and two pairs in the stern half. The two pairs of slits in the forward half are generally placed in about the same positions as the two pairs in the rear half. A span of about 12 inches in the midsection contains no slits. Outboard 8 to 8-3/8 inches from the first pair of slits in each half of the canoe lies the second pair. The end most pair of slits at the intact bow end is positioned about 4 inches from the chin.

When the canoe is viewed in side profile, the gore slits extend downward from the longitudinal main seam, which runs the full length of each side of the canoe. This seam curves upward moderately and gradually toward each end of the canoe. The full length of all of the gore slits is visible in the profile view, running down the curved bilge area of the lower walls toward the rounded bottom. All of the slits are generally the same in length.

Side Panels to Bottom Panels

After the gore slits were cut and stitched along the side edges of the bottom panel, the side panels were attached to the bottom panel. The seam connecting the side and bottom panels to each other is the prominent longitudinal seam which arcs across the full length of the canoe on each wall. When the side panels were attached to the bottom panels, a wider panel was installed at each end of both walls, to create the high upswept prows of the canoe.

The lower edges of the side panels are positioned inside the bottom bark panel (Fig. 220). Thus, the edges of the bottom panel are exposed on the exterior of the canoe, facing upward toward the gunwales. The side panel extends below the edge of the bottom panel for approximately 1-3/4 to 2 inches.

The side seams are sewn with split roots about 3/32 to 5/32 inch wide, with flat sides and undersurface and a rounded upper surface. The simple in-and-out stitches, about 1/2 to 3/4 inch long, lie in a horizontal row. They follow a line which was scored with the tip of an awl on the bottom bark panel about 3/8 to 1/2 inch below the exposed edge of the panel. The exposed edge of the bottom panel was cut off after the longitudinal seams had been sewed, as evidenced by a row of knife cuts in the side panels just above the edge along its full length.

Side Panels to Side Panels

The seams which join the side panels to each other are overlapping seams (Fig. 219). The previous description and illustration of the three spiral stitches which seal each gore slit also apply to these side panel seams.

Supplemental Pieces

The two supplemental pieces of bark which were added to the highest tip of the bow end are stitched to the top of the end panels with a row of simple in-and-out root stitches (Figs. 218 and 219). The stitches, about 3/16 to 3/8 inch long, run in a horizontal row about 3/8 inch below the exposed overlapping edge of the main panel of bark. Many of these stitches are covered by the stitches of the cutwater edge; this indicates that the extra pieces were added to the end during construction, before the cutwater edge was lashed, rather than later as a repair procedure.

Seam Sealing

All of the seams in the canoe were coated with charcoal-blackened melted pitch or gum from spruce or pine trees, of the same description as the gum found on the Royal canoe. The remaining original pitch is now very brittle; it does not indent under thumb pressure.

No coating of gum was applied to the seams on the interior side of the canoe. (The broken stern end affords interior views of the main side seams and two gore slit seams.)

Each of the seams was sealed on the exterior of the canoe. The swaths of melted gum which cover all of the seams are quite wide. The gum sealing the wall panel seams extends up to a point just below the lower edge of the reinforcement bark strip.

Exterior Hull Surface

The discussion concerning the disruptions in the smooth, even surface of the bark cover of the Royal canoe also applies to the Bell canoe as well. Overlapping panel edges and applications of sealant pitch have produced seams which stand out from the flat surface of the hull.

Gunwale Elements

All of the gunwale elements are angled slightly outward, at the same degree of outward flare as the topsides of the bark walls to which they are attached.

Inwales

The length of the visible portion of the inwale on the curve is about 30-1/2 inches. This is the span between the two end decks. An additional 3/4 to 1 inch of length extends beneath the bark deck at each end. In the midsection, the inwale strip is about 3/8 to 7/16 inch wide across the top and about 3/4 to 13/16 inch deep (Fig. 221). The bottom surface is narrower than the top, since the lower outboard edge is carved off into a beveled surface to produce a space into which the tips of the ribs fit. From the midpoint of the canoe, the depth of the inwale tapers very gradually toward each end. At the point where the inwale disappears beneath the end deck, the depth has reduced to about 1/2 to 9/16 inch, while the width (thickness) has remained about the same. All surfaces of the inwale are carved relatively flat and smooth. The outboard edges are sharp, while the two inboard edges are carved with a moderately wide bevel along the edge.

In constructing the Bell model, the builder omitted the midsection span in which the gunwales would run nearly horizontally over much of the length of the canoe. From the midpoint of the canoe, the inwale rises very slightly and gradually toward the ends (Fig. 219). At a point about 1 inch outboard of the headboard, the height has risen 5/8 inch. Here the inwale diverges from the outwale, just outboard of the lower edge of the bark deck. While the outwale sweeps upward in a very sharp curve, the inwale does not curve upward at all. Instead, it continues straight for a short distance, 3/4 to 1 inch, to converge with the upright plank stempiece. The tips of the two converged inwales are not attached in any manner to the stempiece or to each other. When the canoe was in its original intact condition, the ends of the inwales would not have been visible, hidden beneath the deck and behind the walls. However, with the entire bark cover broken off from the stern end, the tips of the two inwales are completely exposed (Figs. 212 and 213).

The inwale fits into a notch which is cut into the side of each headboard (Fig. 222). Two turns of split roots bind the inwale to the headboard at the notch.

The inwale does not appear to be pegged or nailed to the outwale; this is another trait of this model which is not normally found on full size craft. (Spaces between root wraps in the gunwale lashings afford many views of the gunwales beneath the lashings; no pegs or nails are visible there.) Split root lashings bind the two gunwale elements together, with the top edge of the bark wall and the strip of reinforcement bark sandwiched between them.

Outwales

The total length of the outwale on the curve is about 41 inches, measured on the outside of the curve. In the midsection, it is about 3/8 to 7/16 inch wide across the top and about 3/4 to 13/16 inch deep (Fig. 221). In both width and depth, the outwale has the same dimensions as the inwale. Thus, the bottom surface of the outwale matches that of the inwale. From the midpoint of the canoe, the depth of the outwale tapers very gradually, to a depth of about 3/8 inch at the tips. The width (thickness) of about 3/8 inch is maintained over the full length of the outwale. All surfaces are carved relatively flat and smooth. The inboard edges are sharp, while the outboard edges are carved with a moderately wide bevel. At the tips, the ends are cut off square.

As noted above, the model builder omitted the midsection span in which the gunwales would run nearly

Fig. 217. Bell Canoe: Interior view showing ribs and thwarts profile, sheathing, headboard, bark deck piece, and gunwales.

Fig. 218. Bell Canoe: Lashings of gunwales, thwarts, gunwale ends, bark deck piece, and supplemental bark pieces at top of end panel.

Fig. 219. Bell Canoe: Profile view. Wooden pegs of warped gunwale cap are clearly visible.

Fig. 220 (left). Bell Canoe: In-and-out stitches of side seam and spiral stitches of gore slits. Knife marks parallel to the exposed edge of the bottom panel and the lower edge of the reinforcement bark strip indicate trimming after assembly.

Fig. 221 (right). Bell Canoe: Cross section of gunwales. A. inwale, B. outwale, C. gunwale cap, D. bark wall, E. reinforcement bark strip, F. root lashings, G. wooden peg, H. rib, I. sheathing strip.

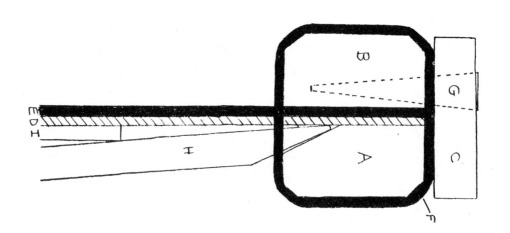

Fig. 222. Bell Canoe: Headboard and lashings of gunwale ends.

Fig. 223. Bell Canoe: Gunwale and thwart lashings, sheathing, and ribs. Mortise hole is visible at center due to disattached thwart.

horizontally over much of the length of the canoe. From the midpoint of the canoe, the outwale rises very slightly and gradually toward the ends (Fig. 219). At a point about 1 inch outboard of the headboard, the height has risen 5/8 inch. Here the outwale diverges from the inwale; it sweeps upward in a very hard curve of virtually 90 degrees, and extends in a vertical position up to its tip. The upswept end of the outwale extends straight upward above the sharp curve for about 3-1/2 inches. The tip reaches a point 1/2 inch below the maximum height of the prow of the canoe.

To facilitate the bending of the extreme upward curve near the tip, three slits were made in the end, to produce four lamination layers. The lamination slits extends from the tip inboard for a distance of about 7 inches; they end just inboard of the headboard. The root lashings which bind the outwale to the inwale cover the area where the lamination slits ends. These lashings prevent the slits from splitting further inboard. The four lamination layers are cut off at the tip of the outwale to form a square end.

The tips of the two converged outwales are joined to each other by a series of wrapped root lashings (Fig. 218). There is no wooden or bark wedge inserted between the tips of the two strips to assist in making the wrappings tight. Nor are the tips pegged or nailed to each other. The lashings, beginning 1/2 inch below the tips, wrap in seven adjacent turns around the two joined outwales, covering a distance of 7/8 inch. These seven wraps run through four holes in the adjacent bark wall. Below these upper outwale wraps 1-1/4 inches, an additional five wraps bind the outwale to the gunwale cap. This lower set of lashings does not run through holes in the bark wall.

The triangular area between the two converging outwales is covered by a bark deck (Fig. 218). The piece of bark is in a triangular form. The builder made a decorative cut in the form of a shallow V across the bottom of the deck piece in a shape virtually identical to that of the deck on the Catlin canoe (Fig. 200). The deck piece extends vertically down to a point about 7/8 inch from the headboard; its sides extend over the edge of the bark walls so that they are visible beyond the outwales for 1 to 1-1/8 inches. The inboard edge of the deck overlaps at an angle the end of the adjacent gunwale reinforcement bark strip. Each edge of the deckpiece is trimmed in such a manner that it appears to be a con-

tinuation of the reinforcement strip. The upper end of the deck piece extends up to the cutwater edge. The area of the deck which lies between the converging outwales bulges roundly inboard, rather than presenting a flat surface between the outwales.

The bark deck is held in place between the outwales and the bark end panels by friction. In addition, the first wedge-shaped group of stitches of the cutwater edge and all of the root lashings which bind the ends of the outwales and the gunwale caps to the hull pass through the bark deck as well.

Although the triangular area between the two converging outwales is covered by a bark deck, there is an undecked area of about 7/8 inch adjacent to the headboard (Fig. 218). Thus, a flag staff could have been inserted on the outboard side of the headboard at the bow. (The stern end is now missing.) In addition, there is enough space between the head of the headboard and the gunwales for the wrapping of a cord around the headboard, to bind a flag staff to the outboard or inboard face of the headboard.

Gunwale Caps

The total length of the gunwale cap is about 38-1/4 inches, measured on the inside of the curve. (This is about 2-3/4 inch shorter than the outwale, which was measured on the opposite side of the curvature.) In the midsection, the cap is about 13/16 to 7/8 inch wide by about 3/16 inch deep (thick) (Fig. 221). Beginning a little inboard of the headboard, the width and depth of the cap gradually taper toward the ends, to about 3/8 inch in width and about 3/16 inch in depth (thickness) at the tips. All surfaces are carved moderately flat and smooth, and all edges are sharp. At the tips, the ends are cut off square.

The combined width of the inwale (3/8 inch) and the outwale (3/8 inch) is slightly less than the width of the gunwale cap. But the bark wall and the reinforcement bark strip which are sandwiched between the inwale and the outwale add more thickness to the combined gunwales. Also, the degree to which the inwale and outwale were squeezed against the bark and each other when they were all lashed together varies in different areas. Thus, the gunwale cap is equal to or slightly narrower than the top of the gunwale unit (inwale, bark layers, and outwale) in most areas of the midsection. The uncovered portion is sometimes the outwale and sometimes the inwale. The width of the cap tapers toward the ends, while the combined gunwale unit does not taper (Fig. 217). Since the outboard edge of the cap is generally aligned with the outboard edge of the outwale near the end of the canoe, the area of the inwale that is exposed gradually increases toward the ends. Outboard of the headboards, up to 3/8 inch of the width of the inwale is exposed.

The gunwale cap conforms to the curvature of the outwale for its entire length. Thus, it rises very slightly and gradually from the midpoint of the canoe (Fig. 219). At a point about 1/2 inch outboard of the headboard, the height has risen 5/8 inch. Here the cap sweeps upward in a very hard curve of virtually 90 degrees, and extends in a vertical position up to its tip. The upswept end of the cap extends straight upward above the sharp curve for about 3-1/2 inches. The tip ends about 1/4 inch below the tip of the outwale, about 3/4 inch below the maximum height of the prow of the canoe. Since the nearly vertical tips of the outwales and caps end 1/2 and 3/4 inch below the tops of the end panels, the high bark ends would rest on the ground rather than on the gunwale tips when the canoe was overturned on its side as a shelter. No lamination split was required in the end to facilitate the bending of the extreme upward curve of the end of the cap, since it is very thin.

From headboard to headboard, the gunwale caps are attached to the outwale by downward-driven wooden pegs. At irregular intervals, round holes about 3/16 to 1/4 inch in diameter were drilled downward through the caps and the gunwales, many of them through the gunwale lashings. The holes lie both inboard and outboard of the midline of the cap, in no particular pattern. The intervals between the holes are the shortest in the curved midsection area; these spans increase gradually toward the ends. The endmost holes lie 3/4 to 1-1/2 inches inboard of the headboards.

The long slender pegs were driven through the cap and into the inwale or outwale and trimmed so that the surface of the head lies flush with or barely above the surface of the cap. The tips do not protrude from the bottom of the gunwales.

The tips of the two converged caps are joined to each other and to the tips of the two outwales by wrappings of root lashings (Fig. 218). No wedge is inserted between the tips of the caps to assist in making the wrappings tight. Nor are the tips of the converged caps pegged or nailed to each other. Beginning 1/2 inch below the tip of each cap, one turn of root encircles both pairs of outwales and caps, running through one of the outwale lashing holes in the adjacent bark wall. Immediately below this single wrap, two more root wraps encircle the two gunwale caps (but not the outwales), binding the tips of the caps together.

Reinforcement Bark Strips

The reinforcement strip of birchbark increases the thickness of the upper edge of the bark wall where it is attached to the gunwales. Before the inwale and outwale were lashed together onto the upper edge of the bark wall, the reinforcement strip was inserted between the bark wall and the outwale (Fig. 221). Its top edge, like that of the bark wall, was cut off at the level of the top of the inwale. When the awl holes were pierced through the wall and the lashings were wrapped around the gunwales, the bark strip was pierced and lashed as well.

The very wide strip runs to a point well outboard of each headboard (Figs. 218 and 219). It extends down 1 to 1-1/4 inches below the lower edge of the outwale in the midsection area. This width is maintained to the ends of the strip, without tapering. The lower edge of the reinforcement strip generally runs parallel to the lower edge of the outwale for the full length; it was cut quite irregularly and with much undulation. The strip was trimmed to its present width after being installed on the canoe. There is a knife cut or scratch on the bark wall panel immediately adjacent to the lower edge of the strip along its full length; this was produced when the strip was trimmed off against the unprotected wall. Another row of knife cuts below the edge of the bark strip reveals that the strip was previously cut off at this lower position (Fig. 220).

The entire length of the strip is made up of one long piece of bark. Beneath the sharp upward curve of the outwale, the strip abruptly ends in a straight vertical edge. When the canoe is viewed in side profile, there is an additional piece of bark continuing past the end of the reinforcement strip. This is the end of the bark deck piece which covers the area where the outwales converge. The inboard end of this deck overlaps at an angle the straight vertical end of the reinforcement strip.

Gunwale Lashings

The upper edge of the bark wall is sandwiched between the inwale, the reinforcement bark strip, and the outwale (Fig. 221). It is cut off flush with the top surface of the inwale. The four layers of bark and wood are lashed together with spaced groups of root lashings from headboard to headboard.

Each lashing group runs through from 5 to 9 holes in the bark wall (Figs. 219 and 223). The holes were made by an awl with a triangular or square cross section, which was inserted and then twisted after piercing the bark. Each row of holes, spanning about 5/8 to 1-1/4 inches, lies immediately below the lower edge of the inwale and outwale. The split root lashing material is 3/32 to 5/32 inch wide, with flat sides and undersurface and a rounded upper surface.

To lash the gunwales, one end of a length of split root was inserted down between the sandwiched layers at the top of the gunwale unit. Then, in a simple spiral stitch, the other end of the root passed around the outwale on the exterior and through the first hole in the set of holes. The root passed around the combined inwale and outwale, and through the second hole. This pattern continued through each hole, with each hole receiving usually one turn of root. Occasionally, when a root narrowed toward its end, two turns were passed through a single hole. To finish off the root securely before starting a new group of lashings, the root was simply cut off rather short after it emerged on the interior side of the final hole.

Each group of lashings is composed 5 to 9 turns of root around the gunwales, covering a length of about 5/8 to 1-1/4 inches of the gunwales. An interval of about 3/16 to 1/2 inch separates each group of lashings. The interval between each group is not spanned by a connector stitch, since each group begins and ends independently. The endmost group of lashings at the end of each gunwale lies about 1/2 to 5/8 inch outboard of the headboard, where the inwale and outwale begin to diverge; this is just inboard of the sharp bend of the outwale.

The thwarts are bound into the gunwales with root lashings that do not fit into the pattern of the gunwale wrappings. The thwart lashings fit between the gunwale lashings.

Stempieces

The upright plank stempiece is visible in the undecked space between the headboard and the lower edge of the bark deck, as it was visible when the canoe was originally constructed (Figs. 212 and 218). In this space of about 7/8 inch, the upper inboard edge of the plank and a portion of its side surfaces can be seen.

The form of the stempiece is implied in two areas (Fig. 212). The curve of the cutwater edge of the canoe, from the base of the headboard to the outwales, outlines the outer curved portion of the stempiece. Also, the stempiece is fitted along its entire straight inboard edge to the straight outboard surface of the headboard.

The plank extends the full distance from the cutwater edge to the headboard. To form the end frame unit, the headboard was nailed to the vertical edge of the stempiece with two horizontal machine-cut nails. The form of the stempiece of the Bell canoe and its nail attachments to the headboard are very similar to those of the full size Sault canoe.

Headboards

The headboard stands about 8-3/16 inches inboard of the outermost point of the cutwater edge, well inboard from the end of the canoe (Fig. 212). The outboard side of the base falls about 5-3/8 inches inboard of the chin. The headboard is moderately angled, so that its head lies about 1 inch outboard of its base. (This is the same direction as the slant of the headboards in the full size Sault and Ojibwa canoes.) The side notches beneath the head fit between the converging inwales and gunwale caps. When the canoe is viewed in profile, the headboard projects about 1-3/8 inches above the caps.

The maximum width of the headboard occurs at the shoulders, at the base of the side notches (Fig. 222). This maximum width tapers gradually down to the base, which ends in a bluntly cut off point. The sides of this long tapered body are bowed slightly outward from the shoulders to the base. Over its entire length, the headboard is about 1/4 inch thick, having been carved from a sawn board. The flat inboard surface is planed smooth, all edge surfaces are carved flat, and all corners and edges are square.

Below the rounded head, a tall curved notch is cut out of each side. The inwales fit into these notches. A single black pencil line runs completely across the neck of the headboard exactly at the base of the two notches. The line was presumably drawn across the headboard during the building process to indicate the location of the bottom surface of the inwales, and thus the location of the notches that were to be cut to receive the inwales. The bottom surface of each notch is level horizontally; it does not angle upward, since the ends of the inwales do not curve upward. Inboard from the lower portion of each of these inwale notches is a single hole, through which two turns of split roots lash the inwales to the neck of the headboard.

The headboard is attached to the stempiece by two widely spaced horizontal nails driven along the midline. The two original machine-cut nails were replaced at some point with two round-headed wire nails, in different locations than the two original nails. The headboard is not decorated at either end of the canoe.

Cutwater Edges

No wooden batten was built into the stitched cutwater edge to cover and protect the outboard edges of the two bark panels or the stempiece. The edges of the bark panels are cut off flush with the edge of the stempiece.

The cutwater edge is sewed with stitches of the same split roots, 3/32 to 5/32 inch wide, as those used on the other seams (Figs. 218 and 219). The upper distance of about 3-1/8 inches around the curve, beginning at the gunwale tips, is sewn in a pattern of stitches composed of three triangles. The narrow end of each triangle points inboard. Each individual triangle is made up of a series of 7 to 11 adjacent stitches. The first awl hole in each series is positioned about 11/16 to 3/4 inch inboard from the cutwater edge; the following holes each lie progressively nearer to the edge, the final hole being about 3/16 inch from the edge. The split roots form a continuous spiral stitch, with one turn per hole. Each unit of 7 to 11 adjacent stitches covers a distance of about 7/8 to 1-1/2 inches of cutwater edge, forming a triangular pattern.

On the middle distance of the cutwater edge, extending down to a point about 2-1/2 inches above the main side seam, the stitching holes are in a single row,

parallel to the edge and 3/8 to 1/2 inch from it. These spiral stitches lie adjacent to each other, with one turn per hole.

The lowest portion of the cutwater edge is sealed with a row of simple in-and-out stitches which lies parallel to the edge and about 3/8 to 1/2 inch from it. The stitches are about 1/2 to 5/8 inch long. To finish off the end of the root at the chin, the tip runs back underneath the previous stitch and then through an additional hole into the interior of the canoe.

The lower portion of the cutwater edge (the area sewn with in-and-out stitches plus about one inch of the edge sewn with spiral stitches) is sealed with blackened pitch in the same manner as the bark panel seams are sealed. (Only traces of the pitch now remain in some areas.) The narrow swath of pitch begins at the chin, and extends upward for about 9-1/2 inches on the curve. The pitch extends from the outer edge of the prow onto the bark walls for about 1/2 to 5/8 inch. The edges of the pitched area are broadly curved, following the contour of the outer edge of the canoe. The upper portion of the cutwater edge is not sealed with pitch. This allowed unobstructed drainage of water out of the canoe when it was overturned on its side on shore.

Thwarts

The endmost two thwarts at the bow end are no longer lashed in place, and the third thwart from the stern end is now missing. However, their mortise holes indicate the exact original positions of each of these thwarts. The seven thwarts (creating a six-place canoe) are spaced symmetrically. Their positioning indicates a canoe shape that tapers symmetrically toward the two ends at the gunwale level. The lengths of the thwarts also imply the same symmetry.

The following description applies to each of the seven thwarts (Figs. 213 and 217). The thickness remains constant over nearly the entire length of the thwart. Near each inwale, the underside angles moderately upward, reducing the thickness where the thwart enters the mortise hole. The end continues to taper to its tip within the mortise hole. The top side of the thwart remains level over the entire length of the thwart; the width remains the same over the full length as well. All surfaces are planed flat and smooth, and all edges are sharp.

At the point where each thwart meets the inwale, a

horizontal mortise hole is cut through the midline of the inwale, to receive the end of the thwart (Fig. 218). Each hole matches closely the dimensions of the end of the thwart which is inserted into the hole. The mortise holes do not run completely through the inwale. (The interior of several of the holes is visible, where the thwarts are out of place or missing.) The hole is cut at a slight angle, with its inboard end lower than its outboard end. This compensates for the slight outward angle of the inwale, since it angles outward in conjunction with the upper walls of the canoe. The angle of the hole permits the straight horizontal end of the thwart to fit into the hole in the angled inwale.

No vertical wooden peg or nail was driven downward from the upper surface of the inwale through any of the thwarts to hold the end of the thwart firmly in the mortise hole. (The ends of several of the thwarts are visible to indicate this.)

Each end of the thwart is lashed with split root to the combined inwale and outwale. The lashings run through two vertical holes in the end of the thwart, positioned slightly inboard from the inwale. The previous information describing the lashing of the gunwale elements also applies to the lashing of the thwarts. Four turns of root lash each thwart end: two turns pass through each of the holes in the thwart, with no turns of root placed beside the edges of the thwart. The thwarts were not lashed at the same time as the gunwales; they were lashed later. Their lashings do not fit into the series of lashing groups along the length of the gunwales, but instead fit between the gunwale lashing groups.

Sheathing

The dimensions of the sheathing strips or splints in the Bell canoe model are not realistic portrayals of such strips on full size canoes; they are somewhat too long, wide, and thick. The surface on the flat faces is rather smooth, although there are a number of areas of raised grain pattern to indicate that the strips were split out rather than carved. Each splint has generally parallel edges for its full length; the edges are carved quite straight. The ends of the strips taper to a bluntly cut off tip. These ends are clearly visible at the stern end, where the bark cover is now missing (Fig. 211)

The pattern of overlapping ends indicates that the splints were laid into the canoe in two groups: first at the bow end, and then at the stern end. The two groups are each made up of 9 to 11 strips. After the bow end group of splints had been laid in, the stern group was positioned so that the strips overlapped well the ends of the previously-laid group.

In laying in the sheathing, the first strip was positioned down the midline of the floor. It extends about 1/2 inch beneath the base of the headboard and the plank stempiece. The Quebec canoe is the only other craft of the eight included in this study which has its midline sheathing strip extending beneath the base of the headboard and the stempiece. Successive splints were then added, out to and up the walls to a point about 3/4 to 7/8 inch below the inwales. The slightly overlapping edge of each successive strip faces downward or inward, toward the midline of the canoe.

Toward each end of the canoe at the top of the walls, a slightly widening expanse of the upper bark wall is left exposed, not covered by the straight horizontal splints of sheathing where the gunwales curve upward (Fig. 222). These areas of exposed upper wall widen only slightly, since the gunwales curve upward only slightly before reaching the headboard.

The tips of the splints extend well outboard of the headboard; in some cases, they run to a point about 3 inches outboard of the upswept outwales. No additional short sheathing strips were inserted outboard of the headboard to stiffen and support the bark cover at the end of the canoe. Nor was any other material, such as wood shavings or moss, stuffed into the end of the canoe to support the bark cover.

Ribs

Seventeen of the original ribs have survived (Fig. 213). Of these, seven are massive in width, some of them up to twice the width of the ribs which have conventional dimensions. All but one of these unusually wide ribs are found in the stern half of the canoe.

The shape of the midsection ribs (Fig. 217) is composed of a narrow moderately rounded area in the midline of the floor, from which the bilge areas curve gradually upward; the upper sections flare slightly outward. The width of the rounded central area gradually reduces toward each end of the canoe. By the endmost ribs, the shape had probably become a narrow U form. (No end ribs have survived to verify this supposition)

The curve of the ribs reflects the body plan of the canoe.

The width of all of the ribs is maintained for nearly the full length of each rib; the tips do not taper as they extend outward and upward. The thickness of all of the ribs is likewise maintained for the full length of each rib. Over the uppermost section of each tip, the width tapers quite suddenly, to a squared-off tip (Fig. 223). The inboard surface at the end of the tip is carved in a sudden taper into a chisel shape (Fig. 221).

The flat inboard faces of the ribs show in some areas the characteristic raised grain pattern which is created when the ribs are split out. The ribs are carved quite flat and smooth on their flat inboard surfaces as well as the edges. All of the edges are sharp.

Miscellaneous Features
Seats

There is no evidence on the Bell canoe which would indicate that it was ever fitted with permanent or temporary wooden seats.

Provisions for Sail and Cordelling Line

No evidence can be observed which would indicate the lashing of either a mast or a towing line to the forward thwarts.

Flags

No evidence can be found for the attachment of a flag at either the bow or the stern. However, sufficient space exists between the headboard and the bark deck into which a flag staff could have been inserted (Fig. 218). In addition, there is space between the head of the headboard and the gunwales in which a cord could have encircled the headboard to bind such a flag staff to either the outboard surface or the inboard surface of the headboard.

Bow/Stern Differences

Since the entire bark cover is now missing from the stern of the canoe, there is very little data available with which comparisons of the two ends of the canoe can be made. The only obvious indicator of which end of the canoe is the bow is offered by the gore slits in the bottom panel. All of the overlapping edges of the gore slits are lapped so that the edge that is exposed on the exterior side faces sternward. This increases the efficiency and reduces the likelihood of catching on obstructions.

Construction Tools, Methods, and Materials

The Bell canoe was manufactured from the traditional forest materials of birchbark, wood, tree roots, and pine or spruce gum mixed with animal fat and pulverized charcoal. No paints were applied to the model.

The builder of the canoe used the typical array of tools normally employed in canoe manufacture during the nineteenth century. These include an axe, knife or crooked knife, awl, and pitch melting and applying implements.

Most of the building materials and techniques that were used in the construction of the Bell canoe model generally represent old traditional procedures. Some of the omissions and variations from traditional methods have been mentioned in the course of the description. The installation of a plank stempiece which extends the full distance from the cutwater edge to the headboard and the nailing of the headboard to the edge of this plank have also been discussed. The majority of the traits of this fur trade canoe model appear to reflect the traditional manufacturing techniques which were used to build full size versions in the mid-to-latter nineteenth century.

Condition

The surviving bark cover and the wooden elements of the canoe are in generally sound, stable condition. But the entire stern end of the bark cover is now missing, from a point inboard of the upswept ends of the outwales. In addition, one thwart and a number of ribs at each end are missing.

The original root lashings remain intact in virtually all of the sewn seams, in nearly all of the gunwale lashings, and in many of the thwart and headboard lashings. The split root stitches on the cutwater edges are broken and missing in numerous areas. Much of the original sealant pitch remains, although it is cracked and missing in a number of areas.

No repair or restoration procedures appear to have ever been carried out on the Bell canoe, other than the replacement with round-headed wire nails of the two original machine-cut nails in each headboard which attach the headboard to the plank stempiece.

Notes: Bell Canoe

1. Adney and Chapelle, pp. 136-137, 139, 143.
2. Ibid., pp. 139, 143.
3. Ibid., pp. 139, 143.
4. Ibid., pp. 28, 29, 102, 149.